A PLAIN ACCOUNT OF CHRISTIAN SPIRITUALITY

In Honor of Floyd T. Cunningham

Edited by
David A. Ackerman

A PLAIN ACCOUNT OF CHRISTIAN SPIRITUALITY
In Honor of Floyd T. Cunningham

Edited by David A. Ackerman

Copyright © 2023 Asia-Pacific Nazarene Theological Seminary
Ortigas Avenue Extension Kaytikling, Taytay, 1920
Rizal, Philippines
(632) 8658-5872 | (632) 8658-7632
info@apnts.edu.ph www.apnts.edu.ph

ISBN: 978-1-56344-115-8 (paperback) / 978-1-56344-133-2 (hardback)

Cover design by Ervz and Grace Tia

Page composition by Scott Stargel

All Scripture quotations, unless otherwise indicated, are taken from the Holy Bible, New International Version®, NIV®. Copyright ©1973, 1978, 1984, 2011 by Biblica, Inc.™ Used by permission of Zondervan. All rights reserved worldwide. www.zondervan.comThe "NIV" and "New International Version" are trademarks registered in the United States Patent and Trademark Office by Biblica, Inc.™

Scripture quotations marked (ESV) are from The ESV® Bible (The Holy Bible, English Standard Version®), copyright © 2001 by Crossway, a publishing ministry of Good News Publishers. Used by permission. All rights reserved.

Scripture quotations marked (NLT) are taken from the Holy Bible, New Living Translation, copyright ©1996, 2004, 2015 by Tyndale House Foundation. Used by permission of Tyndale House Publishers, Carol Stream, Illinois 60188. All rights reserved.

Scripture quotations marked (NRSV) are from the New Revised Standard Version Bible, copyright © 1989 National Council of the Churches of Christ in the United States of America. Used by permission. All rights reserved worldwide.

Images in Chapter 4 provided by unsplash.com (https://unsplash.com/license). Used by permission.

TABLE OF CONTENTS

List of Contributors 5
Introduction 9
    David A. Ackerman

Part I: Spirituality in the Bible

1. Walking with God in the Old Testament 29
    Oh, Won Keun
2. Were the "False Prophets" Intentionally Deceptive and/or Spiritually Inferior? 55
    Mitchel Modine
3. Catholicity in the Four Canonical Gospels: Discipleship, the Gospel, and the Church 71
    Jason V. Hallig
4. *Pneumatikos* in Pauline Perspective 95
    Darin H. Land
5. Jesus, the Founder and Perfecter of Faith: Spirituality in Hebrews 117
    David A. Ackerman

Part II: Theological Foundations

6. Christlikeness and Spirituality 143
    Diane Cunningham Leclerc
7. Nazarene and Wesleyan Spirituality: The Interplay of Spirit and Structure 165
    David McEwan

PART III: Spirituality of the People

8. Practical Ways of Nurturing Children's Spirituality 189
    Nativity A. Petallar
9. Spirituality of Adults 213
    Clark G. Armstrong

10 Towards Coherence: Exploring Spirituality as
a Unifying Link in Theological Education 241
Bruce G. Allder

11 Spirituality in Leaders 267
Edward LeBron Fairbanks

12 Advocacy as a Spiritual Discipline: To Listen and
to Speak, to Struggle and to Rest, to Lament and
to Hope 287
Marie Joy D. Pring-Faraz

Part IV: Situated Spirituality

13 Unique Challenges Christians Face in India 305
Stella Bokare

14 Christian Spirituality in Animistic Contexts 321
Neville Bartle

15 Spirituality in the Workplace 339
Fletcher Tink

16 Christianity in a Post-Christian World 361
Elisa Bernal Corley

Part V: Spirituality in Dialogue

17 Corporate Worship and Spiritual Transformation 385
Becky Davis

18 Ethics and Spirituality 405
Phillip Davis

19 Critical Pedagogy in Theological Education
and Spirituality 425
Ernesto Lozano

20 On Spirituality as Embodied Holiness:
A Wesleyan Perspective 449
Charlie M. Cubalit

LIST OF CONTRIBUTORS

Dr. David A. Ackerman is Professor of New Testament and Academic Dean at APNTS.

Dr. Bruce G. Allder is Senior Lecturer in Liturgy, Pastoral Theology and Practice at Nazarene Theological College (Australia) and Regional Education Coordinator for the Church of the Nazarene Asia-Pacific.

Dr. Clark G. Armstrong is pastoring Marshall Church of the Nazarene in Missouri and also teaches Pastoral Theology and Christian Education courses at APNTS.

Dr. Neville Bartle is a retired missionary and educator residing in New Zealand.

Dr. Stella Bokare is the Global Program Director for International Child Care Ministries.

Dr. Elisa Bernal Corley received her PhD in Religion and Society from Princeton Theological Seminary.

Rev. Charlie M. Cubalit is Pastor of Pinget Community Bible Church, adjunct professor at Philippine Nazarene College and Philippine Baptist Theological Seminary, and a PhD candidate at Saint Louis University, Baguio, Philippines.

Rev. Becky Davis is a PhD student at the University of Aberdeen and Chaplain at APNTS.

Dr. Phillip Davis is Associate Professor of Theology at APNTS.

Dr. Edward Lebron Fairbanks is retired and was former President of Mount Vernon Nazarene University in the USA and Global Educational Commissioner for the Church of the Nazarene.

Dr. Jason V. Hallig is pastoring International Christian Fellowship in the Philippines and is also Adjunct Professor of New Testament at APNTS.

Dr. Darin H. Land is Assistant Area Director of Asia for the Free Methodist Church and is also Adjunct Professor of New Testament at APNTS.

Dr. Ernesto Lozano earned his PhD in Transformation Learning from APNTS and is an independent scholar in Peru involved in district Nazarene Discipleship International ministry.

Dr. Diane Cunningham Leclerc is Professor of Historical Theology at Northwest Nazarene University in the USA.

Dr. David McEwan is Associate Professor of Theology and Pastoral Theology of Nazarene Theological College (Australia).

Dr. Mitchel Modine is Professor of Old Testament at APNTS.

Dr. Nativity A. Petallar is Associate Professor of Holistic Child Development at APNTS.

Dr. Marie Joy D. Pring-Faraz is a pastor and Assistant Professor of Research and Urban Ministry at APNTS.

Dr. Oh, Won Keun is the pastor of the DaeKwang Church of the Nazarene in South Korea and is also Adjunct Professor of the Old Testament at APNTS.

Dr. Fletcher Tink is the program director of the PhD in Transformational Development program at APNTS.

Rev. Dr. Floyd Timothy Cunningham

INTRODUCTION

The highest call for every human being is to become like our Lord Jesus Christ. This book has been written in honor of one who has exemplified this journey throughout his distinguished 40-year career at Asia-Pacific Nazarene Theological Seminary: Rev. Dr. Floyd Timothy Cunningham. He is known both for his scholarship and spirituality, which exude gentleness, generosity, and Christlikeness. His enduring concern as a minister of the gospel and professor of church history has been to see those who come to the seminary grow in the grace and knowledge of the Lord Jesus Christ. He has exemplified and shown others the balance articulated long ago by Charles Wesley: "Unite the two so long disjoined, knowledge and vital piety: learning and holiness combined, and all truth and love, let all men see."[1]

The theme of this book is spirituality in its many facets. The term "spirituality" often brings confusion and debate. It is often used in combination with another word in the formula "spirituality of . . . ." Many books have been written and studies conducted over the centuries on spirituality. Spiritual Theology emerged as a well-defined branch of theology in the seventeenth century through Giovanni Scaramelli, S. J. (1687–1752), who sought to form an "ascetical and

---

1   Charles Wesley, "A Collection of Hymns for the use of the People called Methodists, 1780," Hymn 461, 1.5, in *The Works of John Wesley*, Oxford Edition (Oxford: Clarendon, 1983), vol. 7, 644.

mystical theology as a science of the spiritual life."[2] In the last few decades, the number of studies on this topic has exploded.

Thomas R. Albin provides a broad and helpful starting definition of spirituality as "a holistic involvement of the person in a spiritual quest that involves the body as well as the spirit, gender and social location as well as human nature, emotion as well as mind and will, relationships with others as well as with God, socio-political commitment as well as prayer and spiritual practices."[3] This definition "involves self-transcendence, an openness to the infinite that does not deny the particularity of the individual, but subverts any tendency to reduce spirituality to a purely private or narcissistic quest for one's own self-realization."[4]

As a unique field of study in theology, spirituality deals with neither abstract statements of faith (or doctrine) nor principles of conduct (morality or ethics) but with the disciplined life in Christ. Our understanding of spirituality has changed since the modern era, but the basic principles remain. Christian spirituality is about our journey on earth as disciples of Jesus Christ, with all its challenges and victories, simplicity and complexity, and ups and downs. Spirituality, from a Christian perspective, always revolves around Jesus.

This book explores Christian spirituality from the many perspectives represented by those who have taught, studied, or been involved in the administration at APNTS. The life of Dr. Cunningham has impacted each contributor. The book begins with an exploration of spirituality in the Scriptures, followed by chapters that deal with theological foundations. Then discussions that deal with various sets of people follow, emerging from the acknowledgment that Christian spirituality

---

2 Jordan Aumann, O. P., *Christian Spirituality* (San Francisco: Ignatius Press, 1985), 10.

3 Thomas R. Albin, "Spirituality in the Methodist Tradition," in *T&T Clark Companion to Methodism* (ed. Charles Yrigoyen, Jr.; London: Bloomsbury, 2014), 276.

4 Albin, "Spirituality in the Methodist Tradition," 276.

is a dynamic reality that invites sensitivity to the diversity of spiritual experiences. The next section deals with Christian spirituality in various contexts, aiming to educate readers about the unique challenges, opportunities, and expressions of Christian discipleship in the world. Finally, a set of chapters explore the relationship between spirituality and other fields of study. Overall, the chapters engage current issues in the light of biblical witness and contemporary research and reflection.

Dr. Cunningham has been on the front lines of developing spirituality in the next generation of church leaders. His influence has gone around the world, represented in the many alumni of APNTS serving in ministry today. The focus of his teaching ministry has always been to encourage people to bridge cultures for Christ by being like Christ. Christian spirituality and theological education are inseparable. Without vital spirituality, all our efforts in theological education are for naught.

Floyd Timothy Cunningham was born in Washington, DC, in 1954. He is the oldest of three children born to Floyd Enus Cunningham (1921–1992) and Eleanor Wagner Leighton Cunningham (1923–2019). In the early years of Floyd's life, the family lived in Rockville, Maryland, and attended the local Church of God (Anderson). In 1964, the Cunningham family moved to Gaithersburg, Maryland, and began attending the local Church of the Nazarene. Floyd gave his life to Christ in the summer of 1965 at a Nazarene camp meeting and soon after became a member of the Church of the Nazarene. These deep holiness roots would continue to grow in the young Floyd's life.

At the age of 16, Floyd felt God calling him into ministry. This path led him to attend Eastern Nazarene College, from which he graduated in 1976 *cum laude* with a Bachelor of Arts in Religion and History. He next continued his studies at Nazarene Theological Seminary, where he served as the student assistant for Dr. J. Kenneth Grider. He graduated from NTS in 1979 with a Master of Divinity *cum laude*. He continued his studies at Johns Hopkins University under Timothy L. Smith, receiving his Master of Arts degree in history in 1981 and his Doctor of Philosophy in history in 1984. His dissertation was entitled, *The Christian Faith Personally Given: Divergent Trends in Twentieth-Century American Methodist Thought*.

God opened the next door for Floyd in the Philippines when he was recruited in 1982 by the founding president of APNTS, Dr. Donald Owens. After defending his doctoral thesis, Floyd moved to the Philippines in November 1983 to begin teaching at the seminary. Since then, he has served as an associate professor (1983-1991), professor (1991-2004), and distinguished professor of Church History (since 2004). Administratively, he has been dean of students and chaplain (1983-1987), academic dean (June 1989-2008), officer-in-charge (2001-2003), the fifth president (2008-2013), and most recently, interim academic dean (2021-2022). Under his presidential leadership, the Holistic Child Development program was started, extension centers in Fiji and Papua New Guinea were begun, the New Life Mission Center was constructed, and the Bresee Institute East was established. His tenure is known for seeking to build bridges with the local community and churches around the seminary. When people think of APNTS, what often comes to their minds first is Dr. Floyd Cunningham.

Rev. Cunningham has carried out his call to ministry also through pastoral service. He was ordained an elder in 1988 through the Mid-Atlantic District Church of the Nazarene. He served as a pastor in the Philippines for six years. He helped plant a church in Teresa, Rizal, in 1985. He pastored the Diliman Church of the Nazarene, Quezon City, from 1989 to 1991 and the Central Church of the Nazarene, Cubao, from 1991 to 1992. He has spoken at many churches throughout the Philippines and USA. His sermons are always witty, simple to understand, and applicable to those listening.

Dr. Cunningham has brought his pastoral heart to his teaching and mentoring ministry. He always gathers a cohort of men around him to disciple in his covenant group. In his capacities as a professor, dean, and president, he has always left his door open for students and is approachable in his gentle way. The list of courses he has taught at the seminary is long, focusing especially on history, theology, and culture. He has also expanded his expertise in holistic child development and related topics. Every course he has taught has been well prepared, organized, and presented, but also rigorous. He has upheld the highest standards for his students, which, although students may complain, has also challenged them to reach their highest potential. But more than simply being the teaching of academic data, his courses have striven for spiritual transformation. His teaching ministry has been extensive throughout the Asia-Pacific Region, with courses at most of the Nazarene educational institutions in the region. He also served as the Asia-Pacific Regional Education Coordinator from 2002–2008. In this position, he furthered the cooperative development of education in the many institutions serving this diverse part of the world.

Dr. Cunningham's research and writing have been significant and extensive. He is considered by many the foremost church historian in the Church of the Nazarene. He was the general editor of the most recent denominational history, *Our Watchword and Song*. He has spent significant time researching Nazarene missions in Asia, and in particular, the Philippines. His book *Holiness Abroad* won the Smith-Wynkoop Award from the Wesleyan Theological Society in March 2004. He is currently writing a book on the history of Philippine Protestantism. His other writings (see Published Works below) have supported the expansion of the church and mission by inviting people to remember from where we have come and like Whom we are to become.

If this book included all the tributes to Dr. Cunningham that have been offered, it would become encyclopedic in length. Much appreciation goes to each of the authors of these chapters who took the time and effort to prepare their special contributions in honor of Dr. Cunningham. A special thanks also goes to Marie Osborne who helped proofread the book before publication.

The following are historical and current tributes written by the various presidents of APNTS.

Tributes

From E. LeBron Fairbanks (1984–1989)

> One of the earliest persons I met on the Asia Pacific Nazarene Theological Seminary (APNTS) campus in June 1984 was the newly minted Johns Hopkins University Ph.D., Floyd Cunningham. He arrived on campus the previous fall to join other founding faculty members in launching APNTS in November 1983. In addition to his teaching responsibilities, Dr. Cunningham was appointed by President Don Owens as the Seminary's first Dean of Students.
>
> Dr. Floyd worked closely with the Seminary Leadership Team as we applied for "Recognition" status for our academic programs, a necessary step for International students to enter the country on a student visa. Although this process began in December 1984, the Seminary did not receive the special status from the Philippine Department of Education, Culture, and Sports (now CHED) until August 1988. APNTS was the first graduate level Seminary not associated with a university to receive the "Recognition" status.
>
> The scholarly Cunningham was impressive during this period, and I appointed him in 1989 as the academic dean of the Seminary. I reflect on this action as perhaps my most significant decision at APNTS!

My family and I returned to the Manila campus for the spring semester of 2008 to teach and speak. It was also my privilege to serve the APNTS Board in June 2008 as a consultant as the Board worked through the process of selecting a new Seminary president. Dr. Cunningham, who had served the previous two years as interim president, was elected. I was asked to join several Board leaders to communicate this news to Dr. Floyd. As I recall, he took several weeks to accept his election.

During these years since his arrival on campus in late 1983, Dr. Cunningham has been described as the **anchor** of the Seminary, holding it steady during various "rocky" times; the **glue** ensuring the various academic, administrative, and constituency components communicated with and understood each other, especially during transitions in presidential leadership; and the steady **"listening ear"** and **institutional resource** who had quality time for students, pastors, community residents, and denominational leaders. And yet, he was consistently reading and writing. I believe his goal was to read 50 books a year!

The Seminary campus community, as well as the Asia Pacific Region Church of the Nazarene, will miss our friend greatly! My hunch is, however, we will stay in touch with him through his continued writings of books and journal articles! We hope so because we still need him!

On November 28, 2000, at APNTS's Heritage Day celebration, Dr. John M. Nielson[5] (1989–2001) announced Floyd Cunningham as the first recipient of the Bridge Builder Award, which is "an elite award . . . occasionally given in the history of APNTS in honor of long years of service and significant contributions to the mission of the seminary." He wrote:

---

5 During the editing of this book, Dr. Neilson went to be with the Lord on April 28, 2023.

> He is the repository of our history, of precedent, and of the rationale behind carefully developed policy. He has been our primary liaison with the agencies of the Philippine Government, with accrediting agencies, and has played a significant role in our search for needed faculty. Dr. Cunningham takes on the tedious task of arranging class and teaching schedules so that the needs of students and of faculty are woven into a manageable whole. He is being relied on increasingly as a resource person by the General Church. He has been my strong right arm throughout my years here at APNTS. . . . Dr. Cunningham has devoted his entire professional life to Asia-Pacific Nazarene Theological Seminary making invaluable contributions to the lives of generations of students and leaving an indelible mark upon the identity of the institution. His shadow is long. His service has been exemplary. His faithfulness has been enduring. His commitment has been firm.[6]

Dr. Hitoshi "Paul" Fukue (2003–2007) recently wrote:

> How blessed is APNTS to have had Dr. Floyd T. Cunningham over these many decades as a professor, Academic Dean, and President! He is no doubt a special gift from God to APNTS. Many teachers, staff, and students have come to and gone from APNTS, but Dr. Floyd (as I would like to call him) has been always there as a steady pillar anyone could rely on, ask advice from, and work joyfully together with. It is hard for me to picture APNTS without Dr. Floyd, but it is my earnest prayer that God will grant a second and a third Dr. Floyd to the future of this great institution. The Apostle Paul said to the Colossian Christian by the name of Archippus, "See to it that you complete the work you have received in the Lord" (4:17). Dr. Floyd has

---

6 John M. Nielson, "News Briefs," *The Mediator* 2:2 (April 2001): 120.

certainly done the work well he received in the Lord through APNTS. Dr. Floyd, we pray that you will continue to be active in your service to the Church even after you retire from APNTS in your unique way, which I am sure you will. Thank you for all your prayers, kindness, thoughtfulness, and warm friendship. God bless you, Dr. Floyd!

Seung-An Im (2014–2016)

As I heard the news that Dr. Floyd T. Cunningham will retire from Asia Pacific Nazarene Theological Seminary, two Korean popular proverbs appear in my mind. "Time flies like arrows," and "No giants can stop the flying years." Dr. Cunningham, who was born in 1954, by the year 2024 will have been with APNTS for 40 years. These four decades at APNTS have flown like arrows, and no one, including himself and his close friends, can stop these years, as the Korean proverbs say.

I met him twice in Korea before starting my ministry at APNTS with him. My first meeting with him was at the Nam Seoul Church of the Nazarene in 2000 and the second at KNU in 2001. A memory from these two occasions reminds me that he is a man with a smile without many words. It was the same while he and I served at APNTS with our sincere colleagues from 2014-16. As I arrived at and left APNTS, he smiled at me with warm kindness but few words. His bright smile, I think, could have many meanings, conveying both a mind of sound rationale and a heart of matured passion. I trust him to have a good balance of right reason and good emotion in any circumstance.

He is a man of righteousness and mercy. As a professor, he seems to be both a strictly disciplined "Vater" and a very warm "Mutterliebe." Sometimes he looks very authoritative but paradoxically persuasive. These two are made possible because he is a man of simplicity and honesty grounded in love. Yes, he is a man of love! His roles for 40 years at APNTS have been multiple: professor and scholar, administrator and minister, operator and manager, etc. Yet, most of all, he has been a faithful and simple man of love! Like Jesus who "loved them [his disciples] to the end," Dr. Cunningham has loved his students always.

Who is Dr. Cunningham? He is a man of love like St. Paul describes in 1 Corinthians 13:4-8a: Dr. Cunningham does not envy, parade himself, behave rudely, seek his own, rejoice in iniquity. He is kind and not puffed up or provoked. He suffers long and rejoices in the truth. He bears all things, believes all things, and endures all things. He thinks no evil. He never fails. He is certainly a person of love towards his students and friends, including me who is so little not only in my height but also in all ways. To me, at least, all of these are true. No one can stop his 40 years at APNTS in the Philippines, and also no one can stop his love for God in heaven. I pray for him to stay healthy in his spirit (*pneuma*), mind and heart (*psyche*), and body (*soma*) until the Day of Coming Back of the Lord of Love, Jesus Christ!

Bruce Oldham (2016–2019)

What a gift Dr. Floyd Cunningham has been to the global Church of the Nazarene! Over his forty years of service as a professor, academic dean, and president at Asia-Pacific Nazarene Theology Seminary, Dr. Cunningham helped shape scores of pastors, ministry leaders, and faculty members who sat under his excellent teaching and personal care. They, in turn, multiplied the church's impact across the myriad of nations and people groups of Asia-Pacific, from Mongolia to New Zealand and from Myanmar to the Pacific Islands, along with churches in every region whose students made their way to Manila to study and depart empowered to make disciples of all nations. Dr. Cunningham's authorship of scores of scholarly and practical resources, his travels to teach and preach, and his supportive relationships have played a major role in the success of the Church of the Nazarene and sister denominations with whom he participated in ministry. What I treasured personally as I served alongside him while at APNTS was his example as a humble servant-leader and a cherished friend. He made us all better!

Larry Bollinger (2020–present)

Historian David McCullough said, "History is who we are and why we are the way we are." This truth applies to our very own historian, Dr. Floyd Cunningham. Floyd represents the best of who we are, and no one person has had more influence over why we are the way we are. Asia Pacific Nazarene Theological Seminary is, in part, a product of this man's vision, faithfulness, dedication, and service. His fingerprints are not only on our systems, facilities, and curriculum. More importantly, they are impressed upon the students he has impacted through incarnational ministry both in and out of the classroom. Whether teaching, mentoring, or just having fun, he has been a favorite amongst our students for 40 years. This collection of writings, done in honor of Dr. Floyd, is a small expression of the gratitude felt by the APNTS family. May this work be as fruitful for the Kingdom as the one whom it honors.

Published Works

BOOKS

Expressing a Nazarene Identity. Lenexa, KS: Global Nazarene Publications, 2018.

Horinesu wo ikiru kami no tami. [God's People Living in Holiness]. Translated by Toshio Izuka and Hiromichi Izuka. Tokyo: Japan Holiness Association, 2014.

Our Watchword and Song: A Centennial History of the Church of the Nazarene. Kansas City: Nazarene Publishing House, 2009. General editor and co-author. Translated into Korean.

Examining Our Christian Heritage II. Kansas City: Clergy Services, 2004.

Examining Our Christian Heritage I. Kansas City: Clergy Services, 2003. Trans. into Spanish. Revised edition, 2017.

Holiness Abroad: Nazarene Missions in Asia. Lanham, MD: Scarecrow, 2003.

The Christian Faith Personally Given: Divergent Trends in Twentieth-Century American Methodist Thought. Ph.D. Dissertation, The Johns Hopkins University, 1983. Ann Arbor: University Microfilms International, 1984.

MAJOR ARTICLES AND CHAPTERS

"Wandering in the Wilderness: Black Baptist Thought after Emancipation." *American Baptist Quarterly* 4 (September 1985): 268–281. Reprinted in *Church and Community among Black Southerners, 1865-1900.* Edited by Donald G. Nieman. Hamden: Garland, 1994.

"Lynn Harold Hough and Evangelical Humanism." *The Drew Gateway* 56 (Fall 1985): 16–30.

"Harold Sloan and Methodist Essentialism." *The Asbury Theological Journal* 42 (Spring 1987): 65–76.

"Christ, the Word, the Light and the Message: A Wesleyan Reflection on the World Mission." *Asia Journal of Theology* 5 (April 1991): 104–118. Reprinted in *Evangelical Review of Theology* 16 (January 1992): 10–27.

"Mission Policy and National Leadership in the Church of the Nazarene in India, 1898-1960." *Indian Church History Review* 25 (June 1991): 17-48.

"Pacifism and Perfectionism in the Preaching of Ernest F. Tittle." *Methodist History* 31 (October 1992): 26-37.

"The Beginnings of the Church of the Nazarene in Korea (1932-1966)." *Bokyum Gwa Shinhak* [Gospel and Culture] 4 (1992): 145-170.

"The Early History of the Church of the Nazarene in the Philippines." *Philippine Studies* 40 (First Quarter 1993): 51-76.

"Mission Policy and National Leadership in the Church of the Nazarene in Japan, 1905-1965." *Wesleyan Theological Journal* 28 (Spring-Fall 1993): 128-164.

"Reflections on Wesley's Understanding of Social Holiness." *Taiwan Wesleyan Theological Journal* 1 (1997): 87-101.

"Inter-religious Dialogue: A Wesleyan Holiness Perspective." In *Grounds for Understanding: Ecumenical Resources for Responses to Religious Pluralism*, 188-207. Edited by S. Mark Heim. Grand Rapids: Eerdmans, 1998.

"Faithful: The Church of the Nazarene in North China." *The Mediator* 3 (October 2001): 15-62.

"Telling the Story of the Church of the Nazarene: A Wesleyan Reflection on Church History." *The Mediator* 4 (2002): 1-14.

"Diversities within Post-War Philippine Protestantism." *The Mediator* 5 (October 2003): 42-144.

"Asia-Pacific Nazarene Theological Seminary: The First Twenty Years." *The Mediator* 5 (April 2004): 36-59.

"Holiness Embodied in the Asia-Pacific Context." *Didache: Faithful Teaching* 4 (January 2005).

"The Wesleyan Middle Way in Asian Context." In *International Nazarene Festschrift in Commemoration of Dr. Kim, Young Baik*, 308-326. Edited by Park Cheol-Woo. Seoul: Korea Nazarene Publishing House, 2007.

"A Historical Overview of Fundamentalism." In *Square Peg: Why Wesleyans Aren't Fundamentalists*, 11-26. Edited by Al Truesdale. Kansas City: Beacon Hill, 2012.

"Common Ground: The Perspectives of Timothy L. Smith on American Religious History." *Fides et Historia* 44 (Summer/Fall 2012): 21-55.

"A Wesleyan Historian's Response to Post-Modernism." *The Mediator* 12 (April 2017): 53-79.

"Evangelicals and the Next Christendom." In *Whatever Happened to Evangelicalism?* 125-149. Edited by Al Truesdale. Kansas City: Foundry, 2017.

"The Church of the Nazarene." In *Encyclopaedia of the Bible and Its Reception*. Edited by Christine Helmer et al. Berlin: De Gruyter, forthcoming.

OTHER PUBLICATIONS

"A Charge to Become." *Conquest* (February 1973): 15.

"The Church is Not the Buildings, but the People." *World Mission* (November 1989): 12-13.

"Missionaries: Mortal Men and Women." *The Preacher's Magazine* (June/July/August 1990): 31-32, 74.

"The Changing Missionary Role." *World Mission* (October 1992): 17.

"Early Japanese Missions in Asia." *World Mission* (February 1994): 14-16; and *World Mission*, (March 1994): 4-5.

"Holiness: The Name of God Glorified in Us." *Word and Ministry* (January/February/March 1996): 36-38.

"Education for the Preparation of Ministers in Asia." *The Mediator* 1 (January 1996): 17–21. Reprinted in Japan. Reprinted, *The Mediator* 5 (April 2004): 66–72.

"Are We Ready for His Delay?" *Word and Ministry* (July–September 1996): 34–36.

"Thomas and Beginnings in India." *Word and Ministry* (October–December 1996): 59–61.

"Aloben and Beginnings in China." *Word and Ministry* (January–March 1997): 15–17.

"Christianity in the Mongol Empire." *Word and Ministry* (July–December 1997): 16–19.

"Celebrating One Hundred Years of Nazarene Missions, 1898–1998." *The Preacher's Magazine* (December/January/February 1997–1998): 38–39.

"Messages for the Month of June." *Worship and Preaching: The Annual Sermon Guidebook*, 66–80. Edited by Kim Kwang Ki. Manila: The Mission Information Institute, 1998.

"Asia-Pacific Nazarene Theological Seminary Heritage Day." *The Preacher's Magazine* (September/October/November 1998): 7–9.

"A Christian Mind." *Theological Education Today* (July–December 1999): 1, 4. Contributor, *Dictionary of Asian Christianity*. Grand Rapids: Eerdmans, 2000.

"Who are Nazarenes? Part 1." *Philippine Field Newsletter* (August 2000): 1–2. Part 2, *Philippine Field Newsletter* (November–December 2000): 3, 5. Part 3, "Phineas Bresee and the Church of the Nazarene in California." *Philippine Nazarenes Today* (2001): 3, 7. Part 4, "Nazarenes are Evangelistic." *Philippine Nazarenes Today* (October 2002): 3. Part 5, "Nazarenes Believe in Education." *Philippine Nazarenes Today* (February 2004). Part 6, "Nazarenes, Social Issues, and Politics." *Philippine Nazarenes Today* (June 2004).

"A Word to the Wise." *The Mediator* 2 (October 2000): 79–85.

Following Jesus Discipleship Program. With Al Truesdale, Hal Cauthron, Linda Alexander and Wes Eby. Olathe: Jesus Film Harvest Partners, 2001. Translated into Spanish: *Lecciones de Discipulado Siguiendo a Jesus,* 2002. Published on-line: http://www.jfhp.org/resources/discipleship_materials/following-jesus.cfm "Response" to "Characteristics of the Early Church of the Nazarene"; and "Endnote: Memory." Global Theology Conference, Church of the Nazarene, Guatemala City, April 4–7, 2002, published on-line (http://Wesley.nnu.edu/2002-GNTC).

"Answer" [on Daoism]. *Holiness Today* (June 2002): 4.

"Ministering Grace." *The Mediator* 4 (October 2002): 104–105.

"Footprints: Samuel Bhujbal." *Holiness Today* (April 2003): 10–11.

"Footprints: Chung Nam Soo." *Holiness Today* (May 2003): 42–43.

"Footprints: Hsu Kwei Pin." *Holiness Today* (September 2003): 8–9.

"Footprints: Nobumi Isayama." *Holiness Today* (December 2003): 8–9.

"Tribute to the Manaoises." *The Mediator* 5 (April 2004): 60–62.

"Francis Asbury," and "Phineas Bresee." In *All Out for Jesus.* Edited by Everett Leadingham, 81–90, 101–108. Kansas City: Nazarene Publishing House, 2007.

"Discussing Together as We Walk Along: Endnote to Global Theology Conference 2007." *Didache: Faithful Teaching* 7 (June 2007). Presented at the Global Theology Conference, Netherlands, April 3, 2007.

"The Name of God Glorified in Us." In *Holiness Sermons and Commentaries.* Edited by Viollydia C. Lartec. La Trinidad, Benguet: Luzon Nazarene Bible College, 2007.

Book review, *A Century of Holiness Theology,* by Mark Quanstrom. *Wesleyan Theological Journal* (Fall 2008): 230–34.

"Building New Bridges." [Inauguration Address]. *The Mediator* 7 (October 2009): 1-11. Reprint, *Didache: Faithful Teaching* 8 (Winter 2009).

"Christ is Victor." *Holiness Today* (March/April 2011): 23.

"Leadership in the Church of the Nazarene in Korea and Other Countries in Asia" [in Korean]. *Intelligence and Creation* 13 (2010): 7-39. Reprinted, *The History and Faith of Korea Nazarene University, Supplement of the Intelligence and Creation*. Choenan City: Korea Nazarene University, 2010, 61-93; and *Nazarene Progress: The History and Faith of Korea Nazarene University*, 111-143. Chonan City: Korea Nazarene University, 2011.

"Church of the Nazarene," "Reformation," and "Revivalism." In *Global Wesleyan Dictionary of Theology*. Edited by Al Truesdale. Kansas City: Beacon Hill, 2013.

Book review, *Mission History of Asian Churches*, edited by Timothy K. Park. *Journal of Asian Mission* 14 (2013): 125-27.

Daily devotions, in *Reflecting God: Devotions for Holy Living* 74 (September, October, November 2013): 33-39.

"What Then Shall We Be: The Past, Present, and Future of the Church of the Nazarene." *Didache* 13 (March 2014), 7 pp., presented at Global Theology Conference III, Church of the Nazarene, Johannesburg, South Africa, March 25, 2014.

Book review, *Conflict, Conquest and Conversion* by Eleanor Tejiran and Reeva Spector Simon. *Journal of Asian Mission* 15 (2014): 119-21.

Book review, *Introducing World Christianity*, edited by Charles E. Farhadian. *Journal of Asian Mission* 16 (2015): 69-72.

Book review, *Christians in South Indian Villages* by John B. Carman and Chlkuri Vasantha Rao. *Journal of Asian Mission* 16 (2015): 77-80.

"Response to 'A God of Immeasurably More.'" *The Mediator* 13 (2017): 77–79.

Book review, *Explorations in Asian Christianity*," by Scott Sunquist. *Journal of Asian Mission* 18 (November 2017): 119–123.

Book review. *Shaping Christianity in Greater China*," edited by Paul Woods. *Journal of Asian Mission* 19 (November 2018): 79–82.

"Hiram F. Reynolds and the Shape of Nazarene Missions." *Holiness Today*, September/October 2019.

"The Church in Global Perspective: Reflections on the Past, Challenges for the Future." Workshop, Asia-Pacific Church of the Nazarene Regional Conference, October 19 and 21, 2019.

Book review, *Protestantism in Xiamen: Then and Now*, edited by Chris White. *Journal of Asian Mission* 20 (November 2019): 119–23.

— David A. Ackerman, editor

PART I

SPIRITUALITY IN THE BIBLE

1

WALKING WITH GOD IN THE OLD TESTAMENT

Oh, Won Keun

Introduction

The picture and function of Abraham within early Jewish and Christian traditions have received sufficient attention among scholars so that we have a fair understanding of Abraham's significant role in these circles. Nevertheless, two kinds of problems arise from our survey of the scholarly investigations of the place of Abraham in both early Jewish and Christian traditions.

First, despite a wide variety of different interpretations around the figure of Abraham in the reception history of the Bible, the scholarly tendency is mostly geared to view early biblical traditions through the lens of later materials to understand the appropriation of Abraham within the context of the later communities, instead of viewing it in its immediate literary context of Genesis. Consequently, a proper examination of the nature of the Abrahamic covenant as presented by Genesis in its own canonical setting has not been fully carried out.

Second, aside from the motifs with which New Testament writers are primarily concerned in relation to Judaism, such as the elements of God's covenant promise, what it means to be heirs of this promise, the meaning of law and circumcision in the realization of the covenant promise, God's relation to the Gentiles, and the character of faith and righteousness, no extensive investigations of Abraham has been made on the specific question about "holiness," a fundamental biblical motif structurally developed in the Genesis account of Abraham.

I propose that, instead of looking retrospectively at the Abraham narrative through the lenses of later communities, it should be better to start with the Abraham narrative itself, to which all the later traditions make efforts to relate, viewing it on its own terms within a broader literary context of the Pentateuch. In this way, the Abraham narrative develops and portrays the concept of holiness as the essential nature of the covenant promise given to Abraham.

I. Contextual Clues

Genesis gives a unique view of holiness compared to other books in the Pentateuch.[1] Few studies have specifically examined the theme of holiness in Genesis. Perhaps a reason for this is that this topic has been pre-empted by other biblical motifs, such as promise (mainly that of the individual elements of the promise like descendants and land) and righteousness. Another reason for this lack of scholarly interest in searching for holiness in Genesis results from the apparent paucity of holiness language in Genesis compared to the other books of the Pentateuch.[2] Nevertheless, a close examination of clues about holiness from the larger context of the Pentateuch shows that Genesis also has a distinctive concern with holiness, which in turn plays a key role in the meaning and purpose of the covenant promise given to Abraham.

---

1 Wright, "Holiness (OT)"; Muilenburg, "Holiness."
2 Moberly, *Genesis 12-50*, 85.

The formative impact of the Abraham narrative can be viewed from a canonical perspective. The successive stories of Isaac, Jacob, and Joseph are linked to the Abraham tradition with how they succeed to the covenant promise initially given to Abraham. What is particularly noticeable about the way in which the Pentateuch is put together is the constant attempt to make Abraham a point of departure. In the Pentateuch, Abraham is remembered not only as an ancestor of the people but more so as an initial recipient of the covenant promise upon which the identity of the Israelites, a people of the covenant, firmly stands.

Outside Genesis, the references to Abraham in the Pentateuchal material are, without exception, references to God's covenant promise to the patriarchs and his remembrance of the oath to them.[3] Abraham appears in Exodus–Deuteronomy in connection with the names Isaac and Jacob, usually as the leading name, and always in passages that trace back to what has been told in Genesis, particularly the promise sworn to them by the Lord (Exod 2:24; 3:6, 15, 16; 4:5; 6:3, 8; 32:13; 33:1; Lev 26:42; Num 32:11; Deut 1:8; 6:10; 9:5, 27; 29:13; 30:20; 34:4). What is of interest in all these references to Abraham is that he is a reminder of God's covenant promise, the dominant motif in the Pentateuch.[4]

In Exodus, the promise of God's covenant relationship with the descendants of Abraham is most clearly expressed by two main figures, God and Moses. The Exodus event is introduced with reference to God's remembrance of his covenant with the fathers: "God heard their groaning and he remembered his covenant with Abraham, with Isaac and with Jacob" (2:24). In a similar fashion, the deliverance from Egypt becomes an expression of divine promise to the fathers: "I appeared to

---

3 Houtman, *Exodus*, 330–31.
4 Clines, *Theme of the Pentateuch*, 32–47; Noth, *A History of Pentateuchal Traditions*, 54–8; Von Rad, *Old Testament Theology*, 1:167; and Zimmerli, "Promise and Fulfillment," 89–122.

Abraham, to Isaac and to Jacob. . . . I also established my covenant with them to give them the land of Canaan, where they resided as foreigners. Moreover, I have heard the groaning of the Israelites, whom the Egyptians are enslaving, and I have remembered my covenant" (6:3–5).

At Sinai, this covenant promise reached its fulfillment when the Lord revealed his purpose for the people whom he rescued from Egypt in remembrance of the covenant promise with Abraham in Exodus 19:6, "You will be for me a kingdom of priests and a holy nation." The Lord reaffirms this grand purpose for the people in Leviticus 19:2, "Be holy [*tmîm*] because I, the LORD your God, am holy," and Deuteronomy 18:13, "You must be blameless [*qdôš*] before the LORD your God." D. Swanson comments,

> These key texts [Exod 19:5; Lev 19:2] for understanding the purpose of the people of God, which suddenly introduce the demand of holiness, cause us to cast our eyes back to what precedes them to look for clues as to what it means to be holy, and to be a holy nation. The starting place for looking for the clues of Exodus 3 and 19, and Leviticus 19, is to ask in what ways Genesis prepares us for the comments of God from the Mountain.[5]

II. Structural Overview of the Main Abraham Narrative

From a literary perspective, the whole Abraham narrative unit in Genesis can be arranged as follows:

11:27b–32	Transition from the foregoing generation with genealogy
12:1—22:19	Main body
22:20—25:11	Transition to the following generation with genealogy

---

5 Swanson, "Holiness in Genesis 12—50," 1.

The main Abraham narrative (12:1—22:19) is bracketed by a widely recognized *inclusio* structure. Cassuto argues that with this *inclusio* structure, the Abraham narrative is set out with numerical symmetry, and the theme develops progressively stage by stage. Abraham is put to repeated tests, which amount to ten in all. The first ordeal is preceded by a divine promise to Abraham of a general nature, and after each trial, he receives consolation in the form of a renewed assurance by God or of a specific act for his benefit. Cassuto states, "Thus there is fashioned a chain of alternating light and shade, in continuing succession, until the last and most sublime promise, which is given to Abraham at the end of the final and severest ordeal—that of the offering of Isaac."[6] Cassuto points out the ten trials as follows:

1. The first ordeal: 12:1-7 (command to "go"-promise)
2. The second ordeal: 12:10—13:4 (famine and Sarah in danger)
3. The third ordeal: 13:5-18 (family strife with Lot-promise)
4. The fourth ordeal: 14—15 (rescue of Lot-promise)
5. The fifth ordeal: 16—17 (family strife-promise)
6. The sixth ordeal: 17—18:15 (circumcision-promise)
7. The seventh ordeal: 18:17—19:28 (Lot in jeopardy)
8. The eighth ordeal: 20:1—21:7 (Sarah in danger)
9. The ninth ordeal: 21:8-34 (departure of Ishmael)
10. The tenth ordeal: 22:1-19 (offering of Isaac-promise).

The last trial corresponds to the first: "go from your country"; and "go to the land of Moriah." In the former passage, there is the command to leave his father; in the latter, to bid farewell to his son. In both episodes, the blessings and promises are similar in content and in phrasing.[7]

---

6 Cassuto, *Genesis*, 294–6.
7 Cassuto, *Genesis*, 296.

Allied to Cassuto's analysis and pertaining to the parallel structure between Genesis 12:1-9 and 22:1-19, Rendsburg arranges the main Abraham narrative as follows:

  A Genealogy of Terah (11:26-32)

    B Promise of a son and the start of Abraham's spiritual odyssey (12:1-9)

      C Abraham lies about Sarah; the Lord protects her in a foreign palace (12:10-20)

        D Lot settles in Sodom (13:1-18)

          E Abraham intercedes for Sodom and Lot militarily (14:1-24)

            F Covenant with Abraham; annunciation of Ishmael (15:1—16:16)

            F' Covenant with Abraham; annunciation of Isaac (17:1—18:15)

          E' Abraham intercedes for Sodom and Lot in prayer (18:16-33)

        D' Lot flees doomed Sodom and settles in Moab (19:1-38)

      C' Abraham lies about Sarah; God protects her in a foreign palace (20:1-19)

    B' Birth of son and climax of Abraham's spiritual odyssey (21:1—22:19)

  A' Genealogy of Nahor (22:20-24).[8]

Indicating a similar concentric arrangement of the Abraham narrative, Wenham also asserts that "this overall structure reinforces the sense of parallel between Gen 12:1-9, Abraham's call, and 22:1-19, his testing. The first tells of Abraham's first encounter with God, the

---

8 Rendsburg, *The Redaction of Genesis*, 28–29.

second of his final encounter."⁹ In any case, Williamson is correct to conclude that the literary structure pairs 12:1-9 with 22:1-19, which in turn suggests that they function as an *inclusio* in the Abraham narrative.¹⁰

As well as these literary structural indications, the remarkable similarities in content between 12:1-9 and 22:1-19 constitute a basic framework for the major part of the Abraham narrative, namely, 1) both episodes start with the phrase *lk lk*, which does not occur again in the Old Testament; 2) in both cases the divine instructions carry an element of promise; 3) they are met with Abraham's immediate obedience; and 4) just as the account of the initial call is preceded by genealogical information that introduces the main character of the next episode, so the story of the final call is followed by a genealogical note having the same function (cf. 11:26-32; 22:20-24).

The substantive elements of both passages are the divine command and promise and Abraham's response in obedience. On each occasion, Abraham is given specific instructions to follow (cf. 12:2; 22:2). Then, in both passages, a series of divine promises (cf. 12:2-3; 22:15-18) are matched with Abraham's compliance (cf. 12:4a; 22:3). What is noticeable in a comparison of the two passages is, however, the inverted order of these elements: in ch. 12, the order is command, promise, and obedience, whereas in ch. 22, it is command, obedience, and promise.

Williamson concludes that such an inversion of order is surely significant and instructive and that it puts more emphasis on Abraham's obedience than on the divine oath in the case of ch. 22.¹¹ Moberly also points out the importance of Abraham's obedience in ch. 22, saying, "A promise which was previously grounded solely in the will and purpose of Yahweh is transformed so that it is now grounded *both* in the will

---

9 Wenham, "Akedah," 98.
10 Williamson, *Abraham*, 219 n. 5.
11 Williamson, *Abraham*, 218.

of Yahweh *and* in the obedience of Abraham."[12] Thus the whole story, beginning in 12:1-9 and concluding in 22:1-19, could be seen as a test of Abraham's response to the divine command.

However, it should also be noted that Abraham's obedient response to the divine command is further challenged by a solemn divine imperative *hthlk* when the covenant promise is reaffirmed in ch. 17. Chapter 17 is placed at the center of the concentric structure shown above (F') in parallel with ch. 15 (F), where Abraham is considered righteous on account of his faith. This would suggest that the meaning of the command (*hlk*) that starts both the beginning and the end of the *inclusio* (cf. 12:2; 22:2) is contemplatively recapitulated at the heart of the narrative as a timeless command for a righteous man before God in association with the word *tmm* in 17:1. This interesting association between *hlk* and *tmm* will offer a decisive clue as to how to present the underlying principle for Abraham's obedience, which is set out in 12:1-9 and made evident in 22:1-19. A careful study of this subtle literary structure leads to the conclusion that holiness in the present narrative context is the rationale for Abraham's unfailing obedience to God Almighty and a necessary character of the faithful in the realization of the covenant promise.

III. The Idea of Holiness in Genesis 12:1–9

There can be little doubt that the central theme of this section, let alone the Abraham narrative as a whole, is that of covenant promise.[13] However, when it comes to the implication derived from this passage, scholarly opinions differ from each other. The first opinion attempts to stress the force of the so-called "unconditional" nature of the promise. Wenham comments that "the divine speech consists of *a command* . . . followed by *a series of promises* (vv. 2-3) that heavily outweigh the

---

12 Moberly, "Akedah," 320.
13 See Abela, *The Themes of the Abraham Narrative*. Cf. Clines, *Theme of the Pentateuch*.

command, showing where the chief interest of the passage lies."[14] In a similar way, Moberly avers, "One of the most notable features about the divine promises elsewhere in Genesis is that they always constitute a *unilateral* and *unconditional* offer on God's part."[15] On the covenant promise given to Abraham, Moberly points out that unlike the covenant at Sinai, where great emphasis is laid upon Israel's responsibilities within the covenant along with severe warnings of judgment for disobedience (Deut 28), the covenant with Abraham puts its emphasis upon what God promises to do for Abraham, to give him both descendants and land.[16]

However, such an understanding of 12:1–3 as a purely gracious pronouncement raises a question.[17] It is noteworthy that the divine call and announcement of the promise in 12:1–3 are set in motion by Abraham's obedient response to the challenge delivered to him (12:4). From the very beginning, the divine imperative "go" directs attention to some extent on the condition upon which the fulfillment of the covenant promise depends. As Hamilton comments, "the promise to give the land to Abram (v. 7) follows the promise to show the land to Abram (v.1), and 'show' becomes 'give' only when Abram makes his move."[18] Although he puts much emphasis on the unconditional nature of the covenant promise, Wenham also highlights Abraham's obedience, noting that each part begins with the keyword "go" (*hlk*; vv. 1, 4), and this is also almost the final word of the section (v. 9).[19]

The second opinion attempts to stress the inevitability or passiveness on the part of Abraham to follow a divine command in the realization of the covenant promise. Westermann suggests that the divine

---

14 Wenham, *Genesis 1–15*, 274. Emphasis is mine.
15 Moberly, "Akedah," 318. Emphasis is mine.
16 Moberly, "Akedah," 318.
17 Turner, *Announcements*, 55 n. 2; Williamson, *Abraham*, 230.
18 Hamilton, *Genesis 1–17*, 371.
19 Wenham, *Genesis 1–15*, 269.

command "go" and Abraham's response "went" together do not illustrate the significance of Abraham's obedience. Westermann maintains that to consider the command to "go" as a difficult command is a misunderstanding of what is meant here. He further argues that it is also a mistake to see the command as a "test" of Abram to cut himself off from his country, his kindred, and his father's house.[20] Westermann says, "It was aimed solely at rescuing the group from or preserving it in the crisis."[21] In so doing, Westermann insists that Abraham's response is natural and not obedient. Thus, the intention of 12:4a is not obedience. Rather, it is a normal and natural thing that Abraham should go as God commands him.[22]

Nonetheless, Westermann is less than convincing. First of all, he does not take account of the overall structure of Genesis. In 12:1–9, what is in contrast to the preceding narrative units (2:4–11:26) is not the blessing on God's part (that is constant throughout) but the obedient response on the human part. As Sarna rightly maintains, "In silent, unwavering obedience to the divine will, 'as the Lord had commanded him,' the patriarch picks himself up and goes forth, accepting his new destiny in perfect faith."[23] So Hamilton is correct in saying that "it is clear that Abram is presented to the reader as a paragon of faith and obedience."[24]

Abraham's response to God's command was an essential prerequisite on Abraham's part for the fulfillment of the covenant promise. As the following story reveals, the fulfillment of the covenant promise is beyond the confines of Abraham's lifetime, even beyond that of

---

20 Contra. Von Rad, who says, "Apparently the narrator intends to represent Abraham's departure as a paradigmatic test of faith" (*Genesis*, 166); see also Waltke, *Genesis*, 209; Turner, *Genesis*, 64.
21 Westermann, *Genesis 12–36*, 148.
22 Westermann, *Genesis 12–36*, 152.
23 Sarna, *Genesis*, 90.
24 Hamilton, *Genesis 1–17*, 376.

Genesis.[25] Thus, what is stressed at the outset is the "command-response" pair rather than the "promise" itself because, from a literary perspective, the fulfillment of the covenant promise is contingent upon Abraham's response to the command. As the text says: "So Abram went, as the Lord had told him" (v. 4a), Abraham's response meets the necessary prerequisite, at least on his part, for the fulfillment of God's promise just given to him. And he continues to go on his journey (v. 9).

By drawing our attention to Abraham's obedience, 12:1–9 presents a dramatic reversal of the narrative. In contrast to the ever-increasing failure of human beings as mainly depicted in the preceding narrative units, this pericope shows the possibility that there is a right way of life for humans and prepares for the elucidation of the idea of holiness as the underlying principle of Abraham's response to the divine command in the context of the covenant promise.

IV. The Idea of Holiness in Genesis 17:1–2

Alexander contends that it is Abraham's "blameless walk" that has to be ascertained prior to the fulfillment of the covenant promise in the Abraham narrative.[26] Turner argues that what is put to the test is Abraham's blameless behavior, saying, "It began with a promise contingent simply on obeying the command to 'go,' but developed into an arrangement dependent on Abraham's blameless behavior" (that is, in Turner's words "rigorous ethical requirements").[27] In so doing, Turner concludes (relating ch. 17 to ch. 22) that the Abraham narrative is designed to show whether Abraham is prepared to present himself ethically "blameless."[28] However, the evidence from the narrative itself is to the contrary and hardly presents Abraham as ethically blameless.

---

25 Turner, *Genesis*, 62–3.
26 Alexander, "Abraham Reassessed," 16. Cf. Wenham, *Genesis 16-50*, 15 n. 2a.
27 Turner, *Announcements*, 94; Turner, *Genesis*, 81. Cf. Williamson, *Abraham*, 242; Driver, *Genesis*, 185.
28 Turner, *Announcements*, 92.

In 17:1, *being* blameless is a natural consequence that the observance of the first imperative, *walk*, will unreservedly involve. The construction of the commands in 17:1 means that the first imperative, *walk*, is related as effect to cause to this second imperative, *be*. Abraham cannot be blameless if he does not walk. But if he walks, then blameless he will be. In the overall context of the Abraham narrative, the emphasis of 12:1-9 is upon the divine command and Abraham's compliance. Just as the covenant promise is contingent on Abraham's response to the command, *go*, in 12:1-9, so the same covenant is still contingent upon Abraham's response to the divine command, *walk*, in ch. 17, which in turn anticipates its ratification with the final command, *go*, in 22:1-19. Genesis 17:1b-2 can be read as follows: "Walk before me and *you will be blameless*. And I will make my covenant between me and you. . . ."

Genesis 12:1-9 demonstrates that a certain obligation is placed upon Abraham. From the outset, this obligation is the divine command that is reflected in the imperative, *go*, and the fulfillment of the promise is contingent upon whether or not Abraham would comply with this command. Although basically consistent with this thrust of the initial divine speech (12:1b-3), 17:1-2 nevertheless adds new elements.

First is the addition of the significant holiness word *tmîm* (usually rendered "whole," "perfect," or "blameless")[29] in the section where the divine command is uttered as a condition prior to the establishment of the covenant promise (17:1b; cf. 12:1). Applied to human beings, the word *tmîm* usually denotes an ethical value (cf. 6:9; Prov 2:21).[30] Accordingly, Driver argues (commenting on Gen 17:1) that to be "blameless" signifies "simply the duty of leading generally a righteous

---

29 *Theological Dictionary of the Old Testament* 3:307; Cf. Turner, *Genesis*, 81; von Rad, *Genesis*, 197-8; Hamilton, *Genesis 1-17*, 458; Wenham, *Genesis 16-50*, 20; Speiser, *Genesis*, 122; Sarna, *Genesis*, 123; Vawter, *Genesis*, 218.

30 *Theological Dictionary of the Old Testament* 3:307; Cf. Driver, *Genesis*, 185; Turner, *Announcements*, 76.

and holy life."³¹ In a similar way, Turner avers that "be blameless" indicates "rigorous ethical requirements," and he concludes that the promise is now "dependent on Abraham's blameless behavior."³²

If we accept this view, however, the fulfillment of the promise is rather up in the air, in that the internal evidence from the following narrative is to the contrary, which hardly presents Abraham as ethically blameless.³³ Thus, it must not be correct to say that Abraham's *tmîm* refers to general ethical behavior in the present narrative context. In the present context, the narrative does not explicitly show the quality of holiness reflected in the word *tmîm*. No matter how significant semantic value it may have pertaining to the idea of holiness, the emphasis of the narrative is not upon the meaning of the word *tmîm*. If there is any, the meaning of *tmîm* should be illuminated in association with and/or on the basis of the command "walk" (a condition that has an immediate effect to cause "be blameless") in the present syntactical arrangement.

The condition with which Abraham is called upon to comply in 17:1 is not what he can do on his own ("walking blamelessly all by himself") but what he must do in relationship with or in solidarity with God ("walk before me"). And this is certainly the kind of holiness that the present narrative makes every effort to highlight in the life of Abraham, which is further supported by the covenant formula in 17:7. As Williamson maintains, the notion that the command referred to in 17:1 explicitly involves a special relationship with God is well reflected later in the covenant formula: "to be your God and the God of your

---

31 Driver, *Genesis*, 185.
32 Turner, *Announcements*, 94; Turner, *Genesis*, 81. Cf. Williamson, *Abraham*, 242.
33 Abraham's subsequent behavior, let alone his lie to Pharaoh about the identity of his wife (12:10–20), is anything but blameless, with a laugh of derision at Yahweh's promise (17:17), his bias toward Ishmael (17:18), his refusal to acknowledge Sarah's place in the plan (ch. 21). Cf. 12:10–20; 20:1–18.

descendants after you" (17:7).³⁴ In this regard, Westermann rightly says, "By the *hthlk lpnî* God orders Abraham . . . to live his life before God in such a way that every single step is made with reference to God and every day experiences him close at hand."³⁵

This humble walking before God, nevertheless, does not express something passive or natural, as Westermann mistakenly stipulates.³⁶ Rather it denotes a conscious, faithful, obedient, and communal relationship,³⁷ as the phrase "walk before me" usually "expresses the service or devotion of a faithful servant to his king, be the latter human (1 Kgs 1:2; 10:8; Jer 52:12) or divine (prediluvians: Gen 5:22, 24; 6:9; the patriarchs: here [17:1]; 24:40; 48:15; priests and Levites: Deut 10:8; 18:7; Judg 20:28; Ezek 44:15)."³⁸

In the light of this stipulation, it is more than convincing that the idea of the holy in the command "be blameless" has to do with the constant relationship with God, which is reflected in the first command, "walk before me." In walking before God, therefore, Abraham will be blameless. In this respect, von Rad is surely correct in suggesting that "blameless" should be understood in relationship to God rather than in the sense of moral perfection, with the basic meaning "whole" that refers to solidarity in this human-divine relationship.³⁹

Furthermore, the parallelism between 12:1-3 and 17:1-2 suggests to us that the meaning of the second imperative, "be a blessing," in 12:2 may be identified with the second imperative "be blameless" in 17:1 since both are understood as the immediate consequence of

---

34 Williamson, *Abraham*, 107.
35 Westermann, *Genesis 12-36*, 259.
36 Westermann says that the phrase "walk before me" does not express some sort of high demand but something natural (*Genesis 12-36*, 259). Cf. Turner, *Announcements*, 178.
37 Contra Westermann, Wenham, *Genesis 16-50*, 20. Cf. von Rad, *Genesis*, 198-9.
38 Hamilton, *Genesis 1-17*, 461.
39 Von Rad, *Genesis*, 198. Cf. Tigay, "Psalm 7:5," 184-5.

the implementation of the command "go" in the context of the covenant promise. That is, "being holy" in solidarity with the Holy One is a blessing that God wants to bring upon all the families of the earth through Abraham.

On the basis of our analysis, therefore, we can reasonably conclude that the imperative "walk before me" is the holiness command in which Abraham is called upon to live an ongoing life of obedience in the presence of the God Almighty, which will eventually involve his *tmîm* (holiness in solidarity with God) as well as the fulfillment of the covenant promise in due course. So, in the realization of the covenant promise, the only condition that is placed upon Abraham is his humble walking before God, regardless of lapses due to his weakness that are evident in the following narrative.

V. The Idea of Holiness in Genesis 22:1–19

The idea of holiness elucidated in the command in 12:1-3 and 17:1-2 awaits its full illumination in the climax of the Abraham narrative in 22:1-19. Alexander contends that ch. 22 must be interpreted in the light of ch. 17, in that the account of the testing of Abraham in ch. 22 is concerned primarily with the ratification of an eternal covenant between God and Abraham, which is first mentioned in ch.17.[40] Thus 22:15-18 records a divine oath given to Abraham as a consequence of his obedient response to the command that he should sacrifice his only son Isaac.[41] As Alexander puts it, "Abraham is tested by God in order to ascertain whether or not he truly fulfills the conditions laid upon him in 17:1. . . . Clearly, the events of ch. 22 show beyond doubt the deep loyalty of Abraham to God."[42]

---

40 Alexander, "Genesis 22," 17–22. On this point, both Turner and Williamson agree with Alexander. See Turner, *Announcement*, 92; Williamson, *Abraham*, 245.
41 Alexander, "Genesis 22," 17, 19.
42 Alexander, "Genesis 22," 21.

Genesis 22:1–19 thoughtfully restates the conditional aspect of the divine promise and clearly reinforces the fact that Abraham has obediently fulfilled the divine holiness command upon the implementation of which the fulfillment of the divine promise is resolutely assured. The remarkable similarities in content between 12:1–9 and 22:1–19 have suggested that they function as an *inclusio*, which constitutes a basic framework for the Abraham narrative. In view of this overall structure, most noticeable in ch. 22 is the fact that both episodes start with the divine imperative "go," which was already announced twice in chs. 12 and 17, imposing the notion of obligation with it in the context of the covenant promise. Therefore, its repetition here recalls that the former announcements invite us to contemplate the relationship of the command in ch. 22 to those in the previous chapters. From the very beginning, the divine imperative "go" in 12:2 has directed our attention to some extent to the condition upon which the whole covenant promise depends.

The narrative in ch. 22 repeats the holiness command of 17:1–2, adding as an important element the word *yr'*, which has a certain semantic value with respect to the idea of holy. Even though ch. 22 is the only episode so designated as a test that invites us to discern it with a specific focus,[43] the whole story, in fact, beginning in 12:1–3, could be seen as a test of Abraham's faithfulness, obedience, and perseverance.[44] Stressed at the outset is the *command-response* in which fulfillment of the covenant promise is contingent upon Abraham's response to the divine command. As the text shows (12:4a), Abraham's

---

43 Turner, *Announcements*, 90.

44 At the outset we should note that although this is the only divine command in the story designated as a "test," it is not unique; other incidents in the Abraham narrative also have the quality of a test. Turner, *Announcements*, 90. Cf. Cassuto, *Genesis*, 2:294–6; Skinner, *Genesis*, 327; Von Rad, *Genesis*, 239.

immediate response meets the only condition on his part for the fulfilment of God's promise just given to him, and he goes on his journey (v. 9).[45]

The faithful obedience of Abraham becomes critical to the narrative in ch. 22. Genesis 22:1-2 reads: "Some time later God tested Abraham. He said to him, 'Abraham!' 'Here I am,' he replied. Then God said, 'Take your son, your only son, whom you love—Isaac—and go to the region of Moriah. Sacrifice him there as a burnt offering on a mountain I will show you.'" These opening words point back to the fact that, after the expulsion of Hagar and Ishmael in ch. 21, there could be no uncertainty as to the significance of Isaac for the realization of the divine promise: it is on Isaac alone that Abraham's future hope rested.[46] Therefore, God's demand "sacrifice him there as a burnt offering" is a command at the climax of the Abraham narrative designed to show whether Abraham will fulfill the sole condition that has been placed upon him, regardless of the consequences he can imagine.[47]

As we investigate the divine command in ch. 22, we notice that from the outset, it is God who "tested" (22:1) Abraham. Some scholars see this admission as divesting the story of any tension.[48] Thus it is commonly argued that, as it is only a test, we know in advance that God has no intention of going through with it. However, White has correctly seen that "the reader has no reason to think that because this is a test, God does not intend for Abraham to actually go through with it to the bitter end. . . . The category of the 'test' serves not to lessen the

---

45 Infinitive absolute of the verb *hlk* often has an idiomatic use, stressing "continually" (Ross, *Biblical Hebrew*, 168, 319).
46 Turner, *Announcements*, 87. Cf. Yarchin, "Imperative and Promise," 173.
47 Cf. Sarna, *Understanding Genesis*, 160; Speiser, *Genesis*, 164; Lawlor, "The Test of Abraham," 22; Westermann, *Genesis 12-36*, 357; Wenham, *Genesis 16-50*, 99; Turner, *Announcements*, 87; Williamson, *Abraham*, 237.
48 Skinner, *Genesis*, 328; Von Rad, *Genesis*, 239; Sarna, *Genesis*, 151; Speiser, *Genesis*, 164; Coats, *Genesis*, 158; Westermann, *Genesis 12-36*, 361.

suspense for the reader, but to provide an explanation for the command of God without which it would be totally dissociated from the narrative context."[49]

As Sailhamer points out, nothing in the preceding chapters would have hinted at this sort of request.[50] The reader is as surprised and shocked by the Lord's request as Abraham himself would have been. In the narrative context, as Turner says, "Abraham is not privy to the information given to the reader; he simply receives the divine command, without any explanatory glosses, and the tension is not relieved for him until the angel of Yahweh calls from heaven (22:11)."[51] In this regard, Wenham is surely correct in arguing that though the comment "God tested Abraham" does slightly alter our view of what follows, it must not obscure the awful situation in which Abraham found himself confronted with a choice between his affection for his son and his trust in God.[52] Simply but seriously, the narrative keeps "the reader's attention focused on the inward struggle of Abraham as he carried out the Lord's request."[53]

In this suspicious context, God's command is immediately followed by Abraham's action, "Early the next morning Abraham got up . . . set out for the place God had told him about" (v. 3). There is no puzzlement seen this time, no matter how often he may have been puzzled thus far. As Och rightly put it, "In contrast to previous situations where Abraham either questioned Divine intentions or expressed dismay at the abandonment of a son, here there is only the silence of acceptance.

---

49 White, "The Initiation Legend of Isaac," 13.
50 Sailhamer, *The Pentateuch*, 177.
51 Turner, *Announcements*, 90.
52 Wenham says that "your son, your only son Isaac, whom you love" acknowledges Abraham's paternal devotion to his son, which reminds us of the costliness of the command (Wenham, *Genesis 16-50*, 113).
53 Sailhamer, *The Pentateuch*, 177.

... This is the moment that both Abraham and God have been waiting and preparing for since they set out together from Haran."[54]

Of special interest here is that the narrative provides us with the rationale for this uncompromising obedience, illustrating that Abraham has fulfilled the condition repeatedly announced in chs. 12 and 17 and here in ch. 22. In the immediate context, the key to the rationale of the divine command is found in 22:12: "Now I know that you fear God, because you have not withheld from me your son, your only son." By itself, this verse would indicate that before the test, God did not know whether Abraham was willing to accept his plans without question or not.[55] Through a comparison with other passages in which God is said to be "tester," Lawlor demonstrates that the point has been reached where "the reason Yahweh deemed it necessary to test Abraham was to know what was in his heart, to test his obedience to, and fear of, Yahweh when his promised and beloved son was at stake."[56] In the same way, Williamson contends, "As the text explicitly states, the purpose of the test was to ascertain whether or not Abraham 'feared God' (Gen 22.12)."[57]

Sarna is opposed to this view and, when commenting on the phrase "for now I know" (v. 12), says, "It is not that God's foreknowledge is wanting but that, for Abraham's sake, the quality of character that now exists only potentially must be actualized."[58] This rather theological assertion is corroborated by Hamilton's observation that the text articulates God's knowledge of what Abraham has in his heart. The use of the word *yr'h* (with God as subject) with the word *yr'* (with

---

54 Och, "Abraham and Moriah," 305.
55 Turner insists that the narrative of Genesis 22 gives no grounds for assuming that Yahweh has foreknowledge of Abraham's intention (*Announcements*, 91 n. 1). Cf. Driver, *Genesis*, 216; Speiser, *Genesis*, 166; Brueggemann, *Genesis*, 187.
56 Lawlor, "Test of Abraham," 28.
57 Williamson, *Abraham*, 242.
58 Sarna, *Genesis*, 153.

Abraham as subject) may suggest that God, who sees the end from the beginning, has already seen that Abraham fears him (cf. 22:8, 14).[59] The implication given by this view is that 22:12 is God's concluding remark on Abraham's "fear of God" that has always been the rationale for Abraham's obedient responses from the very beginning of the narrative.

In fact, this view is preferable to that which divests God of knowledge of Abraham's intention from both the overall and immediate narrative context. First, we should remember the fact that this is not the first time Abraham obeys God in the context of the covenant promise. Abraham's usual response to God was that of obedience, despite several disgraceful incidents at times when he was puzzled. Moreover, from a rigidly literary standpoint, the actual command remains unfulfilled (that is, Isaac remains intact), which implies that God had known Abraham's intention even before the test was exacted and prepared a ram on behalf of Isaac. Sarna avers, "It is not important that the act was unfulfilled, for the value of the act may lie as much in the inward intention of the doer as in the final execution."[60] In any case, it can be reasonably held that what is ascertained in ch. 22 is more than a single act of obedience in offering of Isaac; rather, it is Abraham's "fear of God" coupled with the command "go" (chs. 12, 17, 22) which works as the underlying principle for all of his obedience.

In the light of this analysis, we can reasonably hold that, coupled with the timeless command "walk before God," the phrase "fear God" recapitulates the nature of the holiness of Abraham, which is the sole condition placed upon him for the fulfilment of the covenant promise. That is, in the present narrative context, the meaning of the command in the phrase "walk before God" is made clear by the addition of the phrase "fear God," conveying "walk in fear of God." In this fashion, the

---

59 Hamilton, *Genesis 18–50*, 112–3. Cf. *Theological Dictionary of the Old Testament* 6:310.
60 Sarna, *Genesis*, 153.

divine test in ch. 22 serves in the Abraham narrative as a conclusive demonstration of Abraham's willingness to comply with the divine initiative, showing that in fear of God, Abraham has fulfilled the sole condition—"walk before God"—that will effectively bring about the fulfilment of the covenant promise. Thus, the kind of holiness that the Abraham narrative as a whole has attempted to portray is not what Abraham can earn as a reward but what he can experience by faithfully living in relationship or in solidarity with God. By constantly walking in fear of the Holy One, Abraham will be holy (despite some lapses from human weakness and puzzlement), which, coupled with the faithfulness of God, will fulfill God's ultimate desire to bring blessing upon all the families of the earth.

Conclusion

Our reading of Genesis 12:1—22:19 illustrates that the main Abraham narrative is much more concerned with holiness than is normally realized. From our analysis, the idea of holiness in the Abraham narrative can be summarized as follows.

First, holiness in the Abraham narrative is a life-long command in the covenant relationship with God. In the literary context of Genesis as a whole, it is with Abraham that God restores the divine-human relationship which had been lost by people turning away from God in 2:4—11:26. This restored relationship begins with the initial divine command "go" that places a condition upon Abraham for the covenant relationship (12:1-3). From this initial announcement onwards, the Abraham narrative structurally develops the idea of holiness in a repeated form of a "command-compliance" pair until it is told that Abraham is finally ascertained to meet the holiness command laid on him, "walk in fear of God," and thus ascertained to be "blameless" in relationship with his God. In this respect, the Abraham narrative views holiness as a life-long response of the faithful to the divine command in the context of the covenant promise.

Second, Abrahamic holiness is the underlying principle of the obedient life of the faithful. The Abraham narrative represents holiness in the form of an "unspecified" underlying principle for Abraham's constant walking in fear of God, no matter how puzzled he may be in complex life situations. Holiness in the Abraham narrative is not presented in the form of rules and regulations nor in the form of different levels or grades, as is the case with the rest of the Pentateuch. Although sharing some common language of holiness (e.g., *tmîm* and *yr'*), the elusive presentation of holiness in the Abraham narrative lacks cultic or moral emphasis, which is in contrast to the Priestly and Deuteronomic holiness. Rather, the kind of holiness that the Abraham narrative as a whole has attempted to portray is not what Abraham can earn as a reward but what he can experience in solidarity with God. So, the holiness of Abraham is relational. As the narrative structurally presents, in his lifetime Abraham did just as the Lord had told him (12:4); Abraham faithfully believed the Lord (15:6), and finally, he went to offer Isaac and thus approved his fear of the Lord (22:12). His lifelong obedience becomes even more evident as Genesis expresses it in the form of personal testimonies: once by Abraham, "The LORD, before whom I walk" (24:40); and by Jacob, "The God before whom my ancestors Abraham and Isaac walked" (48:15; cf. 17:1).

Third, Abraham's holiness in the Abraham narrative is the sole condition on his part upon which the fulfilment of the covenant promise is contingent. As noted above, the realization of the promise is dependent upon whether or not Abraham meets this condition, granted that God's faithfulness toward His covenant promise is always the same (cf. 24:27). Therefore, the Abraham narrative presents that both Abraham's holiness in his faithful walking before God and God's steadfast faithfulness toward the covenant promise, as two sides of a coin, are the essential attributes of the respective parties in the covenant relationship.

Lastly and most importantly, Abrahamic holiness that is to be realized by God-fearing walking in the divine-human relationship is the nature of blessing that God wants to bring upon all the families of the earth, which forms the theme of the Pentateuch as a whole. This theme is further elaborated when the God of Abraham commands Israel to be holy as he is holy (Lev 19:2) so that the people of Israel function as a kingdom of priests and a holy nation among all nations (Exod 19:6). Therefore, other elements of the covenant promise, no matter how significant they may look, should be interpreted in the context of this overarching theme of the Pentateuch.

In relation to the Pentateuch, holiness in the Abraham narrative shares something in common with the other books of the Pentateuch in view of the fact that holiness is the necessary condition for the fulfilment of the already-stated covenant promise. However, Abrahamic holiness is distinguished from that in the rest of the Pentateuch because, while the covenant promise is an established fact as a consequence of Abraham's holiness "approved" in Genesis (22:12; cf. 24:1, 40), it is only a future possibility dependent on Israel's holiness "commanded" in the other books of the Pentateuch (cf. Exod 20; Deut 28). In this respect, it can be held that Abrahamic holiness puts forward a model of the divine-human relationship for the following generations in the covenant promise.

Bibliography

Abela, A. *The Themes of the Abraham Narrative: Thematic Coherence within the Abraham Literary Unit of Genesis 11:27–25:18*. Malta: Studia Editions, 1989.

Alexander, T. Desmond. "Abraham Re-assessed Theologically: The Abraham Narrative and the New Testament Understanding of Justification by Faith." In *He Swore an Oath: Biblical Themes from Genesis 12-50*, edited by R. S. Hess, G. J. Wenham, and P. E. Satterthwaite, 7–28. Carlisle: Paternoster, 1994.

———. "Genesis 22 and the Covenant of Circumcision." *Journal for the Study of the Old Testament* 8, no. 25 (February 1983): 17–22.

Botterweck, G. Johannes, and Helmer Ringgren. *Theological Dictionary of the Old Testament*. Vol. 3. Grand Rapids: Eerdmans, 1978.

Brueggemann, Walter. *Genesis*. Atlanta: John Knox, 1982.

Cassuto, Umberto. *Genesis: From Noah to Abraham*. Jerusalem: Magnes, Hebrew University, 1964.

Clines, David J. A. *The Theme of the Pentateuch*. Sheffield: JSOT, 2001.

———. "The Ancestor in Danger: But Not the Same Danger." In *What Does Eve Do to Help? And Other Readerly Questions to the Old Testament*, JSOTSup 94, 67–84. Sheffield: JSOT Press, 1990.

Coats, George W. *Genesis*. Grand Rapids: Eerdmans, 1983.

Driver, S. R. *Genesis*. London: Methuen, 1907.

Hamilton, Victor P. *Genesis 1–17*. Grand Rapids: Eerdmans, 1990.

Houtman, C. *Exodus Vol. 1*. Historical Commentary on the Old Testament. Kampen: KOK, 1993.

Lawlor, John I. "The Test of Abraham: Genesis 22:1–19." *Grace Theological Journal* 1, no. 1 (1980): 19–35.

Moberly, R. W. L. "Abraham's Righteousness (Genesis xv 6)." In *Studies in the Pentateuch*, edited by J. A. Emerton. VTSup 41, 103–30. Leiden: Brill, 1990.

———. *Genesis 12–50*. Sheffield: Sheffield Academic, 1992.

———. "The Earliest Commentary on the Akedah." *Vetus Testamentum* 38 (1988): 302–23.

Muilenburg, J. "Holiness." *The Interpreter's Dictionary of the Bible*, vol. 2, edited by G. A. Buttrick. Nashville: Abingdon, 1962.

Muraoka, Takamitsu. "On the So-Called Dativus Ethicus in Hebrew." *The Journal of Theological Studies* 29, 2 (1978): 495–98.

Noth, Martin. *A History of Pentateuchal Traditions*, translated by B. W. Anderson. Englewood Cliffs: Prentice-Hall, 1972.

Och, Bernard. "Abraham and Moriah: A Journey to Fulfillment." *Judaism* 38, 3 (1989): 292–309.

Rendsburg, G. A. *The Redaction of Genesis.* Winona Lake: Eisenbrauns, 1986.

Ross, Allen P. *Introducing Biblical Hebrew.* Grand Rapids: Baker, 2001.

Sailhamer, John H. *The Meaning of the Pentateuch: Revelation, Composition, and Interpretation.* Downers Grove: InterVarsity, 2009.

Sarna, Nahum M. *Genesis.* Philadelphia: Jewish Publication Society, 1989.

———. *Understanding Genesis.* New York: Schocken, 1966.

Skinner, John. *A Critical and Exegetical Commentary on Genesis.* New York: Scribner, 1910.

Speiser, E. A. *Genesis.* Garden City: Doubleday, 1964.

Swanson, Dwight. "Re-Minting Christian Holiness: Holiness in Genesis 12–50." *The Flame* 65, 3 (1999): 4–6.

Tigay, J. H. "Psalm 7:5 and Ancient Near Eastern Treaties." *Journal of Biblical Literature* 89 (1970): 178–86.

Turner, Laurence A. *Announcements of Plot in Genesis.* Sheffield: JSOT, 1990.

———. *Genesis.* Sheffield: Sheffield Phoenix, 2009.

Vawter, Bruce. *On Genesis: A New Reading.* Garden City: Doubleday, 1977.

von Rad, Gerhard. *Genesis.* Philadelphia: Westminster, 1972.

———. *Old Testament Theology*, vol. 1. New York: Harper, 1962.

Waltke, Bruce K. *Genesis*. Grand Rapids: Zondervan, 2001.

Wenham, Gordon J. 1995. "The Akedah: A Paradigm of Sacrifice." In *Pomegranates and Golden Bells: Studies in Biblical, Jewish, and Near Eastern Ritual, Law, and Literature in Honor of Jacob Milgrom*, 93–102. Winona Lake: Eisenbrauns, 1995.

———. *Genesis 1-15*. Waco: Word, 1987.

Westermann, Claus. *Genesis 12-36*. Richmond: John Knox, 1963.

White, Hugh C. "The Initiation Legend of Isaac." *Zeitschrift Für Die Alttestamentliche Wissenschaft* 91, 1 (1979): 1–30.

Williamson, Paul R. *Abraham, Israel and the Nations: The Patriarchal Promise and Its Covenantal Development in Genesis*. Sheffield: Sheffield Academic, 2000.

Wright, D. P. "Holiness (OT)." *Anchor Bible Dictionary*, vol. 3. New York: Doubleday, 1992.

Yarchin, William. "Imperative and Promise in Genesis 12:1-3." *Studia Biblica et Theologica* 19 (1980): 164–78.

Zimmerli, Walter. "Promise and Fulfillment." In *Essays on Old Testament Hermeneutics*, ed. C. Westermann, 89–122. London: SCM, 1963.

2

WERE THE "FALSE PROPHETS" INTENTIONALLY DECEPTIVE AND/OR SPIRITUALLY INFERIOR?

Mitchel Modine

Introduction

The book of Jeremiah pays a great deal of attention to the phenomenon of false prophecy. Other books in the Hebrew Bible, both inside and outside the "prophets,"[1] contribute to the question to a smaller degree. For a prophetic example, Micah 3:5[2] complains of "the prophets who lead [God's] people astray." In the Pentateuch, the programmatic statement comes from Deuteronomy 18:15–22, which first promises that new prophets "like" Moses will arise, and second answers a reasonable question, namely how the Israelites should be able to discern

---

[1] In the Hebrew division of the Bible, the prophets include Joshua—2 Kings (except for Ruth), Isaiah–Ezekiel (except for Lamentations), and the twelve "Minor Prophets."

[2] Throughout the remainder of this article, if a biblical citation appears without the book title, Jeremiah is intended.

whether a prophet or someone who claims to be a prophet was genuinely sent by God. Two criteria are at issue. First, if the prophet speaks in the name of a different deity, he or she is automatically excluded. Second, if the prophet speaks in the name of Yhwh,[3] then the matter hinges on whether the prophecy comes true. Determining what is true and false prophecy is a difficult matter and one that has occupied the attention of a long list of scholars of prophetic literature in general and Jeremiah in particular.

In this article, I will discuss the issue of false prophecy along the lines of the spirituality of the so-called "false prophets." That is, I will ask whether and to what extent the prophets whose prophecy is judged to be false are intentional enemies of God. By way of analogy, the early centuries of the Christian Church may be characterized as a long attempt to define orthodoxy over against various positions judged heretical. To take just one example, in the fifth century AD, a British monk named Pelagius argued that human will was sufficient for salvation unaided by God's grace. Augustine successfully argued against this position. However, he did not accuse his opponent of wrongdoing apart from his false teaching. In fact, he praised him for his exhortations toward morality. As Benjamin Warfield notes: "although [Augustine] was rejoiced when he heard . . . of the zealous labors of this pious monk in Rome towards stemming the tide of luxury and sin, and esteemed him for his devout life, and loved him for his Christian activity, he yet was deeply troubled when subsequent rumors [sic] reached him that he was 'disputing against the grace of God.'"[4] In other words, though Pelagianism was judged heretical, it does not follow that Pelagius was a bad person or that he set out deliberately to destroy Christianity.

---

3   A long-standing practice avoids pronouncing the Holy Name of God. Many translations use "LORD," reflecting the translation of the Greek Septuagint. Recently, Gafney has called this translation into question. See Appendix B to *Womanist Midrash*, 281–92.

4   Warfield, "Introductory Essay," xxii.

In fact, from his own perspective, Pelagius sought rather to *improve* Christianity by purging it of elements he found erroneous. Pelagius, therefore, was not a deliberate enemy of God. I will demonstrate in this essay that one could say the same thing about the "false prophets" in the book of Jeremiah.

The thesis of this article is that, within the bounds of a religious belief community, there are usually no grounds to assume that people whose statements run counter to orthodoxy are necessarily out to destroy the belief community.[5] I will explain this in two sections. First, I will summarize Francisco Arena's 2020 article[6] dealing with the issue of Jeremiah's purportedly prophetic opponents. These opponents share the feature of never being directly quoted making prophetic statements. Second, I will closely examine the story of the dispute between Jeremiah and the prophet Hananiah. Arena does not deal much with Hananiah precisely because he is the only one of five prophetic opponents actually called a prophet. Finally, I will conclude with some remarks on a thickened interpretation of opposition in the Bible, expressed as a hermeneutic of generosity.

Francisco Arena: Did the False Prophets Prophesy Falsely?

Francesco Arena works through the several stories in the book of Jeremiah of conflict between the prophet and variously named opponents: Passhur (19:14—20:6), Hananiah (ch. 28), Ahab and Zedekiah (29:20-23), and Shemaiah (29:24-32).[7] Arena correctly notes that

---

5 It is important to note that I limit this analysis to *religious* belief communities, thus excluding other kinds of persuasive speech and the intrusion into religious belief communities of debates and methods of argumentation more at home within other types of belief communities, such as political parties.

6 Arena, "False Prophets in the Book of Jeremiah," 187-200.

7 The book of Jeremiah is well-known for having quite different chapter-and-verse designations in the Hebrew and Greek (Septuagint) texts, which would affect all of the stories of conflict here except that involving Passhur. As this is not crucial for my argument, I will follow the chapter and verse numbers given in the Masoretic Text.

Hananiah is the only one who is explicitly referred to with the term נביא (*nabi'*) "prophet." The others are merely said to have prophesied. Arena's main contention is that "the accusation of prophesying falsehood at the expense of some of [Jeremiah's] adversaries is ideological and represents the product of later redactional intervention intended to emphasize the role of Jeremiah as the only true prophet of Yahweh in the book."[8] Arena thus correctly identifies a potentially circular argument in this material, viz., identifying a false prophet as one who prophesies falsely and a true prophet as one who prophesies truthfully.

There seems good reason to accept the heavily redactional and ideological nature of the prophetic conflict stories in Jeremiah.[9] However, it does not follow from this that Jeremiah did not face substantial opposition to his preaching.[10] Arena works through the presentation of the various named opponents in the book, concluding, except in the case of Hananiah (ch. 28), that they are not prophets at all. First, Passhur is some kind of official "in charge of the maintenance of public order in the Temple."[11] Whatever this function precisely meant, it is interesting that another named opponent, Shemaiah the Nehelamite, accuses a different high priest of not dealing properly with the "mad" prophet Jeremiah. In furtherance of his task to keep order, Passhur "punishes Jeremiah because he uttered an oracle of judgment against Jerusalem."[12] Jeremiah apparently interprets this opposition as false prophecy. This is a curious charge, however, for opposition to a prophetic word and offering an alternative one are entirely different

---

8   Arena, "False Prophets in the Book of Jeremiah," 189.

9   Throughout the remainder of this essay, any references to persons (i.e., Jeremiah or one of his named opponents) should be understood as: "X the ideological creation," not necessarily reflecting any historical person.

10 To be fair, Arena does not address this question, staying within the book itself. He thus aligns himself with now well-established tradition of Jeremiah scholarship that expresses doubt as to the book's apparent biographical information for the prophet.

11 Arena, "False Prophets in the Book of Jeremiah," 192.

12 Arena, "False Prophets in the Book of Jeremiah," 192.

matters. Moreover, while it is certainly possible for one person to combine the functions of temple official and prophet (or priest and prophet, like Jeremiah and Ezekiel),[13] the text in no way explicitly states that Passhur was a prophet.

Jeremiah's conflict with Ahab and Zedekiah appears in 29:20–23. These opponents may or may not be in mind in the quotation in Jeremiah's letter of the people suggesting that God has raised prophets for them in Babylon (29:15). Like Passhur, their words are never quoted. Unlike Passhur, they are not described as having any direct contact with Jeremiah. Verse 21 merely describes them as "prophesying a lie in [God's] name." The book assigns this perception to Jeremiah, as noted. However, the "letter" (29:1, so called because it was "sent from Jerusalem . . . to Babylon") contains a dramatic change in tone just a few verses before the passage in question. Verses 1–14 are hopeful for a long and relatively comfortable life, even though the people are still in exile. Verse 15, however, starts with a diatribe against various opponents. This invites speculation as to whether this was a redactional insertion.

Moreover, Ahab and Zedekiah are accused of "commit[ing] adultery with their friends' wives" (29:23).[14] This charge accompanies the decidedly less specific "they have done a disgraceful thing in Israel [נבה לב בישראל]." While adultery is a grave sin, and while it was probably bad to do a "disgraceful thing," whatever that is supposed to mean, one cannot help but wonder if Jeremiah (or the editors) may be committing the *ad hominem* fallacy by bringing them up now. Notwithstanding the facts that first, both adultery and false prophecy are sins; and

---

13 Neither Jeremiah nor Ezekiel is described in their respective books performing priestly duties. In addition, the identification of Jeremiah as a priest is less certain, as the superscription (1:1) merely indicates that he came from a priestly family. That the high priest in 2 Kgs 22 (2 Chr 34) has the same name as Jeremiah's father is immaterial, as the genealogies in 1 Chr 6 suggest that the name was somewhat common.

14 All translations of the biblical text in this chapter are author's own.

second, that these men may very well have done these things, it is not credible to link these allegations.

As it turns out, the only one of the four accused false not-really-prophets Arena discusses whose speech the book reports at all is Shemaiah. Shemaiah had written to the high priest Zephaniah son of Maaseiah, that Jeremiah should have himself been punished as a false prophet. Arena points out that this was a true statement. The question, of course, remains whether Shemaiah was right in saying that Jeremiah was a madman. In fact, this is related to the central question within the dispute between Hananiah and Jeremiah, to which I now turn.

Will the Real Prophet of Yhwh Please Stand Up?

Hananiah, appearing in Jeremiah 28, is unique amongst the five named "prophetic" opponents of Jeremiah. First, he is the only one called a נביא (*nabi'*) "prophet." The story begins in a straightforward manner, setting the time frame as the beginning/fourth year of the reign of King Zedekiah (r. 597–586 BC). The story starts out as a first-person narrative, assumedly starring Jeremiah, but the redactional layers again show themselves when the perspective abruptly shifts to third-person in v. 5. Hananiah is introduced, also in a straightforward manner, as "the prophet Hananiah son of Azzur, who was from Gibeon." The text does not give any further information as to the call of Hananiah. This is not surprising, as many of the named prophets in the Bible, especially among the Twelve, lack this detail. Nevertheless, that the text introduces Hananiah as a prophet sets up the conflict rather well. That is, the reader may assume that the rather different prophecies attributed to the two prophets caused some confusion among the populace, who may have listened to them, and perhaps even among their circles of disciples. Assuming the possibility that this debate could have taken place, the argument has the "powerful effect of presenting all the available options for understanding and responding to the disasters of the exile and the destruction of Jerusalem."[15]

The most important among the unique features of Hananiah is that his speech is not directly described as false, nor is he called a false prophet, at least not in the Hebrew text. Verse 15 does accuse Hananiah of having "made this people trust in a lie," which may suggest that Hananiah convinced at least some who knew about the debate. Interestingly, the Septuagint gives the game away by introducing Hananiah as ὁ ψευδοπροφήτης *(ho pseudoprophētēs)* "the false prophet." In fact, the Septuagint makes this translation decision throughout Jeremiah and once in Zechariah. In each case, the Hebrew does not include an equivalent word like שקר *(shqr)*, "false," though many people are said, as noted above, to have prophesied falsely. Robert Carroll notes that the Septuagint's "use of [this term] to qualify Hananiah may be an idiosyncrasy of that edition, but it does expose the ideology of the redactors."[16] The Septuagint apparently believed that this town (Jerusalem) was not big enough for the both of them, whereas the Hebrew text seemed not to have any problem leaving the tension in place, only to resolve it at the right time (see below). Carroll again: "The redaction is committed to Jeremiah, *therefore Hananiah is false.*"[17]

Second, a lengthy line of prophecy attributed to Hananiah in 28:2 includes the characteristic prophetic formula, "Thus says Yhwh." Indeed, Hananiah uses the lengthy formula found only in Jeremiah: "Thus says Yhwh of Hosts, God of Israel."[18] Furthermore, Hananiah is reported as performing a prophetic sign-act of breaking the ox yoke that Jeremiah was wearing while he walked around Jerusalem (see 27:2). Jeremiah had done this to proclaim that Judah, and all the other

---

15 Modine, *The Dialogues of Jeremiah*, 159.
16 Carroll, *Jeremiah*, 542.
17 Carroll, *Jeremiah*, 550 (emphasis original).
18 The title "Yhwh of Hosts, God of Israel" occurs only five times outside Jeremiah.

nations besides, would come under the yoke of King Nebuchadnezzar of Babylon because this is how Yhwh wanted it. Hananiah, in breaking the yoke, declared, "Thus says Yhwh of Hosts, God of Israel: I have broken the yoke of the King of Babylon! Within two years' time, I will return to this place all the holy items belonging to the Temple of Yhwh that King Nebuchadnezzar of Babylon took from here and brought to Babylon. I will also bring back King Jeconiah, son of Jehoiakim of Judah and all the exiles who went to Babylon, says Yhwh, for I will break the yoke of the king of Babylon" (28:2–4).

Before jumping to the end of the story and condemning Hananiah, the reader should note this prophet's faith. This is a bold statement of faith indeed! In other words, like Pelagius, who sought to improve Christianity, Hananiah sought to improve the faith of his fellow Judeans. It seems, moreover, that Hananiah demonstrated his superiority over Jeremiah, at least for a time: "By taking the yoke off Jeremiah's neck and breaking it, Hananiah conveys . . . that he has the authority to nullify Jeremiah's actions and words."[19] This is not merely a nationalistic statement, however, for Hananiah is from the provincial town of Gibeon, and, generally speaking, in the ancient world as today, provincial towns are not often keen to support the interests of the ruling elite, whether that be in Manila or Washington or Jerusalem. In the same vein, Carroll writes that Hananiah's statement "is both radical and revolutionary in its political context and cannot be construed as support for the ruling classes."[20]

As noted in the introduction, condemning the statements of a "false prophet" does not necessarily impugn the faith of the individual. Recalling the case of Ahab and Zedekiah, they may have been adulterous and shameful, but it is fallacious to link these things with whatever prophecy they may have uttered. Nevertheless, this point is even

---

19 Varughese and Modine, *Jeremiah 26–52*, 78.
20 Carroll, *Jeremiah*, 549.

more forceful in the case of Hananiah. This is so because nowhere is Hananiah accused of anything other than the theological/ideological sins of "making this people trust in a lie" and "rebellion against Yhwh" (vv. 15–16), as serious as these things are. Given that the letter of Jeremiah accused Ahab and Zedekiah of adultery and other shameful acts—even disconnecting these charges from the charge of false prophecy—it strains credibility to suppose that the opportunity to impugn Hananiah similarly would have been missed. In other words, the "opposition research" against Hananiah must have failed to turn up anything rather than the editors having declined to use it. This would be consistent with the moral uprightness generally associated with God's called prophets, which is why it is so devastating when accusations of immoral behavior by God's prophets are so devastating and so resisted, even in the face of overwhelming evidence.

Chapter 28 is finally unclear as to whether Hananiah's death was a judgment on his prophecy. The Hebrew text does show Jeremiah's claim that Hananiah will die: "Look, I am sending you off the face of the land.[21] This year you will die because you have spoken rebellion against Yhwh." The Septuagint does not include the statement about rebellion against Yhwh. In any event, Hananiah likely did not think that he had done anything of the sort.

The judgment that Hananiah was a false prophet and that this is the reason he was killed, presumably by God, is thus seen to be foundering without a foundation. Furthermore, the apparent extension of the test for Deuteronomy 18 for prophecy apparently voiced by Jeremiah (vv. 7–9) does not help clear the ground. It is unclear from ch. 28 whether this was meant to say that only positive prophets were to be judged by whether their prophecies came true. Anyway, this runs up against a problem in that Hananiah is never given the chance to see whether

---

21 The modern translations' rendering "off the face of the earth" (NRSV, NIV2011, NASB1995) assumes too much.

his prophecy would have come true since he dies in that very year, in the seventh month (28:17). The Septuagint does not include the note that Hananiah's death occurred in the same year, further problematizing the relationship between his prophecy and his death. Carroll ultimately concludes: "So it is futile to seek to demonstrate the falseness of Hananiah's position or to justify his condemnation. . . . Nor is it necessary for the modern exegete to join in the editorial excoriation of Hananiah with further denunciations of lying prophets who manipulate divine words for their own ends."[22] In other words, interpreters simply have no ground to impugn Hananiah's motives.

Thickened Interpretation: Developing a Hermeneutic of Generosity

Through a close analysis of the conflict between two prophets of Yhwh, Hananiah and Jeremiah, I have demonstrated that judging a prophet's statements to be false in no way calls for impugning the prophet's spiritual condition. Notwithstanding that sixth century BC Hebrew thought may not have been concerned about spirituality in the same way as some parts of twenty-first AD Christianity may be, the book of Jeremiah simply does not provide enough information to make settled judgments. I also compared the story of Hananiah to the disputes with Passhur, Ahab and Zedekiah, and Shemaiah. I also compared these with the dispute between Augustine and Pelagius in the fifth century AD. In the case of Ahab and Zedekiah, Jeremiah seems to have accused them of adultery and other shameful behavior along with false prophecy. Though they may have done these things—and they are unquestionably bad—it is inappropriate to link the alleged false prophecy with the alleged adultery. In the case of Pelagius, Augustine praised him for his moral behavior and exhortation yet still condemned him for false teaching. This analysis certainly also has implications for how one views the opponents of Jesus in the Gospels.

---

22 Carroll, *Jeremiah*, 550.

Rather than being cartoonishly wicked, they were faithful to God as they understood faithfulness. The realization that they were not trying to undermine God's will in any way—even if, from a Christian standpoint, they were incorrect (see Acts 5:38–39)—has fueled a groundswell of efforts to eliminate the application to one's opponents of pejorative/anti-Semitic epithets like "Pharisaical."

In the case of Hananiah, Jeremiah neither alleges him to have been morally wicked nor praises him. I suggested that a lack of allegation does not imply hesitancy to accuse but rather a lack of immoral behavior. Therefore, I argue that Hananiah in particular, and other opponents named and unnamed in general, should be given the benefit of the doubt. In other words, neither any of Jeremiah's prophetic or quasi-prophetic opponents nor Pelagius may be reasonably said to have intentionally set out to destroy true faith in Yhwh or Christian belief, respectively. Neither can their morality be impugned in the absence of credible evidence of wrongdoing.

In the context of a debate, to accuse someone of a deliberate falsehood is an *ad hominem* attack. Thus, the rules of the British House of Commons include the following: "Any abusive or insulting language used in debate will be required to be withdrawn immediately. Accusations of deliberate falsehood may only be made on a substantive motion. No such accusations should be made in the course of other proceedings: if they are, they must be withdrawn immediately."[23] The penalty for refusing to retract such an accusation is generally expulsion from the chamber for the remainder of the day. Several YouTube videos of the enforcement of such a penalty are available.[24]

I contend this assumption is valid for all manner of similar debates, particularly within the realm of religion. That is, it stands to reason

---

23 House of Commons, *Rules of Behavior and Courtesies in the House of Commons*, 8.
24 For a recent example, see The Independent, *SNP's Ian Blackford Ejected from Parliament for Saying Boris Johnson Misled MPs*.

that those judged as "heretics" or "false prophets" do not set out deliberately to deceive, especially when such deception might be catastrophic for the faith-tradition that they support.[25] Arguments may still be wrong, and their implications may still pose a genuine threat, even if their proponents fail to see those threats when they make the argument.

The thickened interpretation invited by this study seems similar to what YouTuber John Green recently called "a hermeneutic of generosity," helpfully shortened to "an H of G."[26] In the video description, he writes: "To me, seeing others in the most generous possible light does not mean accepting injustice or oppression. It means believing that oppression and injustice are addressable, because these things aren't happening because people are inherently evil or systems are inherently corrupt." Quoting a recently deceased colleague, Green says that an H of G means "I know you're a good guy. Therefore, I will interpret the things you say and do in a favorable light." Green goes on to say that he assumes a given person is good unless there is strong evidence to the contrary. Amongst Jeremiah's opponents, Ahab and Zedekiah give some of the strongest evidence to the contrary, but, as I have noted, this evidence is flimsy because it is only alleged and because the accusation gives off a strong vibe of *ad hominem*.

Green continues: "Almost everyone is trying their best and almost everyone sees their own actions in a generous light." This suggestion is also borne out by my analysis of Jeremiah's opponents in the previous pages. Green further notes that "the H of G is hard to do in practice," and he gives several examples of situations that may try one's

---

25 I exclude from this statement those engaged in deliberately misleading propaganda. Furthermore, a biblical counterexample to this is the intentionally deceptive spirit apparently sent by Yhwh against King Ahab (1 Kgs 22:19–23). In this case, the prophets in question are not deliberate in their deception of Ahab. The anthropological questions raised by this account are outside the scope of the present chapter.

26 The following paragraph is a distillation of Green, *An H of G*.

patience. Similarly, it is remarkably easy merely to accept the judgment that Jeremiah's prophetic opponents are horrible people because they were teaching something that the editors of the book thought to be false or that turned out in the light of subsequent history to be false. Moreover, one could write off Pelagius or Marcion or Arius or any of the great cloud of (false) witnesses as irredeemably horrible people. Yet, is this not to call into question the radical love of God? The prophet Jonah, in the story named for him, apparently desired to see the Ninevites destroyed for their wickedness, and he was unhappy when Yhwh turned toward them in love instead (see Jer 18). In fact, the narrator of Jonah tells us that the prophet was so unhappy he expressed his desire for God to kill him, much like Jeremiah would say to Hananiah that Yhwh would send him off the pitch for doing what he, Jeremiah, thought was incorrect. This does not mean, again, that all statements, beliefs, teachings, prophecies, etc., are equally admissible. The spirits still ought to be tested to see whether they are from God (see 1 John 4:1–6). Some ought to be rejected outright, some ought to be rejected after exploration, some ought to be accepted after exploration, and some ought to be accepted outright. But in no case should a person be rejected unless that person gives reason for rejection and remains unrepentant of that reason.

Green further notes that an individual gains benefit from being generous toward the other: "I have found that when I can employ an H of G . . . I am on average more empathetic, more curious, more engaged, and less judgmental, angry, and miserable." I have long maintained—and often, like Green, struggled to maintain—in my personal life the idea that loving your neighbor as yourself (Lev 19:18; Mark 12:31 and parallels) means understanding that your neighbor is a self, or perhaps even imagining that the neighbor is yourself. This idea frees one from silly notions such as limiting one's obligation to love others by refusing to love oneself, for example. Green concludes: "The H of G is hard work precisely because it asks us to believe that together we can address our shared problems: the failures of empathy and resource allocation that lead to marginalization and impoverishment." While the stories of Jeremiah's prophetic opponents may not find purchase in this idea, it is clearly significant for the prophetic movement in general, what Gustavo Gutiérrez called "God's preferential option for the poor."

Conclusion

In this essay, I have endeavored to show that "false prophets" and "heretics" must not be seen as intentionally antagonistic toward their respective faith-traditions. While their prophecies or teachings may, in the light of history or conciliar opinion, be judged false, this does not mean that they themselves are inherently wicked. Certainly, it does not mean that they are beyond the reach of the redemptive grace of God. To do this, I have explored, in particular, the debate between two prophets of Yhwh, Hananiah of Gibeon and Jeremiah of Anathoth. Though Hananiah presumably persisted in his false teaching until his death just a few months after his confrontation with Jeremiah, he is still presented as a morally upright person. At the very least, neither informal rumors nor formal allegations of immoral behavior may be attached to him. As this is not the case with other prophetic opponents of Jeremiah, Hananiah must therefore be seen in a different light than they are. Though false prophets and heretics say things that must not be believed, to say that they are wicked simply on that basis is unwarranted. Rather, a hermeneutic of generosity is called for in nearly every situation. This hermeneutic of generosity not only views one's or one's group's opponents in a more favorable light but also has salutary benefits for the individual or group that adopts it.

Bibliography

Arena, Francesco. "False Prophets in the Book of Jeremiah: Did They All Prophesy and Speak Falsehood?" *Scandinavian Journal of the Old Testament* 34.2 (2020): 187–200. https://doi.org/10.1080/09018328.2020.1807104.

Carroll, Robert R. *Jeremiah*. Old Testament Library. Louisville: Westminster John Knox, 1986.

Gafney, Wilda. *Womanist Midrash: A Reintroduction to the Women of the Torah and the Throne*. First edition. Louisville: Westminster John Knox, 2017.

Green, John. *An H of G*. YouTube Video. Vlogbrothers, 2022. https://www.youtube.com/watch?v=ovrzKCQ2JTM.

House of Commons. *Rules of Behavior and Courtesies in the House of Commons*. London: House of Commons, 2021. https://www.parliament.uk/globalassets/documents/rules-of-behaviour.pdf.

Modine, Mitchel. *The Dialogues of Jeremiah: Toward a Phenomenology of Exile*. Gorgias Dissertations in Biblical Studies. Piscataway: Gorgias, 2009.

The Independent. *SNP's Ian Blackford Ejected from Parliament for Saying Boris Johnson Misled MPs*. YouTube Video, 2022. https://www.youtube.com/watch?v=GUC9Pa7uti4.

Varughese, Alex, and Mitchel Modine. *Jeremiah 26–52: A Commentary in the Wesleyan Tradition*. New Beacon Bible Commentary. Kansas City: Beacon Hill, 2010.

Warfield, Benjamin B. "Introductory Essay on Augustin and the Pelagian Controversy." In *Nicene and Post-Nicene Fathers: First Series*, Vol. 5, edited by Alexander Roberts, xiii–lxxi. Reprint. Peabody: Hendrickson, 1996.

3

CATHOLICITY IN THE FOUR CANONICAL GOSPELS: DISCIPLESHIP, THE GOSPEL, AND THE CHURCH

Jason Valeriano Hallig

Introduction

The Christian faith affirms through its theological confession and tradition the catholicity of the church: "We believe in the holy *catholic* church." Ignatius was the first to use the word "catholic" in reference to the church and its inherent relationship with Jesus Christ: "Where Jesus Christ is, there is the Catholic Church."[1] Catholicity is a mark of the church that defines its life and mission as the community of disciples of Jesus Christ.[2] With the other three marks of the church—one,

---

1   Ignatius, *Epistle to the Smyrnaeans*, viii. 2.
2   For more information on the church as a community of disciples, see Dulles, *Models of the Church,* 204-226.

holy, and apostolic, catholicity has functioned as the canon for the true church.³ Though the word "catholic" is neither rejected nor denied, the tacit spirit among evangelical churches on the word is one of suspicion. Understandably, evangelicals do not want to be associated or mistakenly identified with a church that bears the word "catholic." Hence, the catholicity of the church is meagerly given attention among evangelical scholars.

Moreover, the evangelical discussion on the catholicity of the church is one that is often seen as belonging to the intellectual auspices of church historians and systematic theologians. Rarely does this "mark" become a subject of discussion in biblical studies or even part of the church's spiritual formation. And so, we must ask, can we find support from the Scripture for the catholicity of the church? Boldly we must confess our answer in the affirmative. I strongly believe that the catholicity of the church is firmly rooted in the four canonical Gospels in particular and the Bible in general.⁴ Both the gospel and the Gospels are inconceivable apart from the truth of the catholicity of the church—an identity that defines not only the nature of the church but also the mission of the church. The catholicity of the church is anchored in its relationship with Christ as the Lord or Head of the church. Avery Dulles rightly calls it the "catholicity of Christ." He finds three aspects in this: first, the incarnation as "a mystery of divine plenitude"—God's fullness in and through him; second, Christ's fullness as the head of creations; and third, Christ's headship over the church.⁵

A careful study of the four canonical Gospels reveals that catholicity is central to the evangelists' narrative presentations of the life of

---

3 The Roman Catholic uses the word "notes" to distinguish the true Church from false ones or apostates of the Church.

4 Torrance believes that "the church had its earthly beginning in Adam" ("The Foundation of the Church," 201).

5 Dulles, *The Catholicity of the Church*, 34-47.

Christ in and through their triadic literary themes—discipleship, the gospel, and the church—in relation to the "witness" of Christ's community of disciples.[6] From a narrative perspective, the catholicity of the church serves as the tacit narrative causality of the triadic literary themes that define the movement of the narrative plot of each of the Gospels.

Catholicity and Discipleship

New Testament scholars have long recognized the importance of the motif of discipleship in the four canonical Gospels. Dulles sees discipleship as the very life of the church of Jesus Christ in his proposal that another appropriate model of the church is that of a "community of disciples."[7] In the four Gospels, discipleship is the causal factor of the sub-story of Jesus and his disciples from the call to the commission. For example, J. D. Kingsbury notes that in the Gospel of Matthew, the story of the disciples follows the contours of the story of Jesus in terms of discipleship and is driven by the plot of conflict:

> In the second part (4:17—16:20), Matthew tells of the ministry of Jesus to Israel (4:17—11:1). Parallel to this, he tells of the call of the disciples and their mission to Israel (4:17—11:1). Also in the second part, Matthew tells of Israel's response to Jesus, which is one of repudiation (11:2—16:20). Parallel but contrasting to this, he tells of the disciples as being the recipients of divine revelation (11:2—16:20). In the third part (16:21—28:20), Matthew tells of Jesus' journey to Jerusalem and his suffering, death, and resurrection. Parallel to this, he shows how the disciples are led to

---

6   I adopt Hur's witness plot of Luke-Acts as applicable to the four Gospels in his book *A Dynamic Reading of the Holy Spirit in Luke-Acts*, 185-191. See also Kingsbury, *Conflict in Luke*; Matera, "The Plot of Matthew's Gospel," 233-253; Powell, *What is Narrative Criticism?*; and Smith, *A Lion with Wings*. Each of these authors posits a plot that centers on God's redemptive plan in Christ.

7   Dulles, *Models of the Church*, 204-226.

appropriate Jesus' evaluative point of view according to which suffering sonship is a summons to suffering discipleship, or to servanthood.[8]

Discipleship is that all-inclusive call for intimacy and commitment to knowing Christ and making him known to all the nations:[9] "As Jesus was walking beside the Sea of Galilee, he saw two brothers, Simon called Peter and his brother Andrew. They were casting a net into the lake, for they were fishermen. 'Come, follow me,' Jesus said, 'and I will send you out to fish for people.' At once they left their nets and followed him" (Matt 4:18-20; see also Mark 1:16-18; Luke 5:1-11; John 1:35-51). Right at the outset of his ministry, Jesus began working on his mission by calling his disciples. This calling foreshadows the church and indicates the necessity of the mission because the disciples formed an essential element in many aspects of Jesus' ministry as described in the following chapters of the book of Matthew,[10] and also because of the role the disciples would later have in proclaiming the kingdom of God, which Jesus inaugurated in and through his life and ministry. By calling the disciples, Jesus demonstrated what they would later be and do in their own ministries and mission to the world of calling and making more disciples. Brunner points this when he writes,

> Jesus did not just come, teach here and there, work miracles, die, and then rise. He came and *made disciples*. Jesus' discipling work is important to Matthew's understanding of the gospel *and the church*. Consequently, right after focusing on Jesus' own

---

8 Kingsbury, *Matthew as Story*, 129. Also see Lincoln, *The Gospel According to Saint John*, 13.

9 The goal of "knowing Christ" is to become Christ-like, which involves sharing in the suffering of Christ.

10 France, *The Gospel According to Matthew*, 103. The same applies to the other three Gospels.

presence in his Word, Matthew turns our attention to Jesus' use of his Word in calling the disciples to share his ministry.[11]

He adds,

> In Matthew's Gospel one of Jesus' important services is to create a ministry of workers by which to shape his church to engage the world. Through Jesus' way of making ministers and Christian workers *then* we can learn how to make ministers and Christian workers *now*.[12]

The story of the disciples was the beginning of the story of the church. The community of disciples foreshadowed the church. In his mission, Christ already had the church in sight. It was the call of the disciples that gave impetus to the life and mission of the church as catholic. On the one hand, this call depicts the nature of the relationship between Christ and his church. It is this relationship with Christ indeed that makes the call to discipleship communicative of the catholicity of the church. Catholicity is first and foremost *Christocentric*, for where Christ is, there is the catholic church indeed. The catholicity of the community of disciples is anchored in how the disciples embraced the lordship of Jesus:[13] "Come, follow me." The lordship of Jesus is essentially one of grace. The call offered the disciples the "divine plenitude" in Christ—a gift of the fullness of God to the church through the call. Moreover, the disciples' response to the lordship of Jesus was an expression of faith. There is no discipleship without faith in Christ, not only as the bearer of the fullness of God, but as the redeemer of the people of God. The call looked forward to the cross of redemption and Christ's resurrection and exaltation—the objective content of the

---

11 Bruner, *Matthew*, 142.
12 Bruner, *Matthew*, 142.
13 For a discussion on *kyrios* (Lord) in the four Gospels, see Ladd, *A Theology of the New Testament*, 169; Guthrie, *New Testament Theology*, 291-94; Marshall, *The Origins of New Testament Theology*, 99-108.

faith of the disciples. In relation to the life of the disciples, the goal of the call to discipleship was one of intimacy.[14]

On the other hand, the call to discipleship was not only relational but also missional.[15] The disciples were called not only to follow Jesus by being his disciples, but also to make disciples, which involved their commitment to the proclamation of the kingdom of God to all nations. As such, the mission of the disciples would not only be about their own personal salvation or their own walk with Jesus, but it would involve the redemption of the world, a whole course of humanity for whom Jesus would give himself as a ransom. Missional catholicity is another aspect of the catholicity of the church. By calling the disciples and giving them the responsibility of making disciples, Jesus literally gave the world into the hands of the disciples, who were a handful of unlearned individuals whom he had chosen and yet placed on their shoulders the most holy and heavy task of making disciples of all nations. As disciples of Jesus Christ, they carried the weight of calling the world to submit to his universal lordship. They also had the mission of establishing the universal kingdom of God here on earth as it is heaven. What a privilege and task—a call to discipleship!

In summary, the nature of the call to discipleship in the four Gospels reveals both the catholic life of the church—Christ to the church, and the catholic mission of the church—Christ to the world. Discipleship embodies the catholicity of the church—who we are and what we are in Christ—we are catholic, called to be disciples and make disciples.

Catholicity and the Gospel

Discipleship focuses on the call; the gospel provides the content, the message in which the call is anchored—Jesus Christ. Again, the

---

14 Dulles notes, "Even within the community of disciples there were degrees of intimacy" (*Models of the Church*, 208).

15 See Dulles excellent discussion on the relationship between discipleship and mission in *Models of the Church*, 220-22.

catholicity of the gospel is centered on the "person of Christ," or more aptly, on the "proclaimed person of Christ." The gospel in the Gospels is presented as one that is catholic—Christ to the world. And with that, catholicity is also *cosmocentric*.[16] This *cosmocentricity* is noticeable in the evangelists' presentation of their gospel. The life, death, and resurrection of Jesus were not intended to present salvation exclusively for the Jews. The evangelists accented this truth in their Gospel accounts. For example, "For Luke Christ is not confined to Israel and its people. He portrays the gospel as truly catholic. The life and ministry of Jesus, though particular, was retold in such a way that the unique challenges and needs of the readers' faith community were addressed."[17] Similarly, Matthew testifies to the inclusivity of the gospel. The life and ministry of Jesus are not exclusively Jewish. Kingsbury writes, "Matthew's narrative therefore revolves around the theme of salvation not only for the Jews but also the inclusion of the Gentiles in the future of the kingdom. Such a twofold theme is what is developed in the conflict of Matthew's narrative plot."[18] With such inclusivity, no culture or nation has a monopoly on the good news of salvation. The Christian gospel is a gospel for all nations.

The story of Jesus—his life (birth and ministries), death, and resurrection—is the story the Gospels intended not only for Israel but for all nations. Using narrative criticism, I will examine how each of the Gospel narratives points to this catholic truth of the gospel, that is, how the evangelists presented the story of Jesus as centering on the universal redemptive plan of God—a plan given in and through the life and ministry of Jesus for all nations. As such, the life and mission of the church are defined as catholic.

---

16 Here, the word "universal" comes to play and one that communicates the inclusivity of the church both in its life and its mission.
17 Hallig, "Contextualization of the Life and Ministry of Jesus," 136.
18 Kingsbury, *Matthew As Story*, 43.

Matthew: The Fulfillment of the Promise

Each of the evangelists portrayed the life and ministry of Jesus as the fulfillment of the promise God gave to Abraham, Isaac, and Jacob.[19] Matthew puts more emphasis on this fulfillment motif. France writes,

> The essential key to all Matthew's theology is that in Jesus all God's purposes have come to fulfillment. This is, of course, true of all New Testament theology, but it is emphasized in a remarkable way in Matthew. Everything is related to Jesus. The Old Testament points forward to him; its law is "fulfilled" in his teaching; he is the true Israel through whom God's plans for his people now go forward; the future no less than the present is to be understood as the working out of the ministry of Jesus. . . . Matthew leaves no room for any idea of the fulfillment of God's purposes, whether for Israel or in any other respect, which is not focused in this theme of *fulfillment in Jesus*. In his coming a new age has dawned; nothing will ever be quite the same again.[20]

Matthew, in fact, begins his Gospel presentation with the genealogy of Jesus, the Christ (Matt 1:1-17). The point of the genealogy was to show to Matthew's community that the universal promise of God to Abraham, Isaac, and Jacob as it ran in and through the story of Israel has come to its fulfillment in Jesus as the one who would save the people from their sins (Matt 1:21). The salvation of people is the ultimate goal of God's redemptive activity by which all nations would come to share in the blessing of Abraham. Quoting Donald Senior, Flemming also emphasizes how Matthew presents the story of Jesus as the turning point of God's redemptive history:

---

19 This is a direct literary connection with the Old Testament. The New Testament cannot be taken out of its relationship with the Old Testament, for the story of the New Testament is part and parcel of the story found in the Old Testament. Hence, the New Testament cannot be studied only as a literature, but also as a Scripture.

20 France, *The Gospel According to Matthew*, 38.

Matthew reassures his audience on the one hand that in following Jesus the promised Messiah, "they were being completely faithful to their Jewish heritage and would find in Jesus' teaching and example the embodiment of all that God had promised Israel." On the other hand, Matthew's story proclaims that in the life, death and resurrection of Jesus, God has brought about a turning point in the history of salvation. Israel's rejection of its King and the church's mission to the Gentiles (Mt. 24:14; 28:18-20) mean that God is calling non-Jews to be a part of a new people of the kingdom; the future of Matthew's Jewish Christian readers is with the Gentiles.[21]

Matthew's narrative indeed revolves around the theme of the universal salvation inclusive of both Jews and Gentiles, which is the overall plot of the Gospel of Matthew.

For Matthew, therefore, Jesus was the king not only of the Jews but also of the Gentiles. Christ indeed is the messiah-king of all nations. The title "King of the Jews" is an all-inclusive messianic title that embraces all peoples of the earth—an irony indeed. The irony is revealed in how the Jews rejected Christ as their king and savior, leading to the preaching of the gospel to all the nations, affirming the kingship of Jesus as universal and the fulfillment of the promise given to Abraham and his offspring. Consequently, the subjects of the kingdom are no longer limited to the people of Israel. The kingship of Jesus now includes the nations of the earth. Hence, the title "King of the Jews" could aptly be interpreted as "King of the Nations," or put another way, "King of the Faithful" inclusive of both Jews and Gentiles. The Great Commission highlights this truth in terms of the inclusiveness of the gospel and its calling: "All authority in heaven and on earth has been given to me. Therefore *go and make disciples of all nations*, baptizing

---

[21] Flemming, *Contextualization in the New Testament*, 245. See also Senior, *The Gospel of Matthew*, 84.

them in the name of the Father and of the Son and of the Holy Spirit, 20 and teaching them to obey everything I have commanded you. And surely I am with you always, to the very end of the age" (Matt 28:18-20). In Jesus, the kingdom is now made available to all the nations of the earth. France notes that the kingship of Jesus is a declaration of his universal sovereignty—the climax of the very gospel itself.[22] With the gospel, the promised blessing now comes to reality. Indeed, Christ is the offspring of Abraham and the one through whom all nations would come to be blessed.

In Jesus Christ, the purposes of God for Israel and the nations come together. That Jesus is the offspring of Abraham is an important theological sign that points to the reality of the universal, promised blessing given to Abraham. This reality comes into fullness in the life and ministry of the new community of faith—the church, whose membership is catholic and whose mission is to *make disciples of all nations.*

Mark: The Dawn of the New Age

The Gospel of Mark points readers to the beginning of the gospel of Jesus Christ as the dawn of the new age. Mark was the first of the four evangelists to have given attention to the non-exclusivity of the fulfillment of the promise of God by announcing the good news primarily to a Gentile community. Such a radical beginning, in and through which the universal promise of God breaks in, ushers the covenant to its new people inclusive of both Jews and Gentiles. As such, the gospel is also the beginning of the new people of God—the church whose membership is no longer ethnocentric but catholic and whose mission now includes all nations—a catholic mission.

Contrary to popular Jewish messianic expectations, Mark presented Jesus as the suffering Messiah in and through whom all nations would come to faith and share in the blessing of the covenant. Mark does this

---

22 France, *The Gospel According to Matthew*, 45

to encourage his community to endure their own experience of suffering. William Lane notes this beautifully:

> When Roman believers received the Gospel of Mark they found that it spoke to the situation of the Christian community in Nero's Rome. . . . They found that nothing they could suffer from Nero was alien to the experience of Jesus. Like them, he [Jesus] had been misrepresented to the people and falsely labeled (Ch. 3:2f., 30).[23]

Mark anchored the theme of suffering in Isaiah's presentation of the Christ, who would come to save the many from sin (Isa 53). Thus, it is right to say that Mark's emphasis on the suffering of Jesus is a commentary on the messianic prophecy of Isaiah intended for all nations (Isa 40-66). The gospel then for Mark is, at the outset, a catholic gospel intended for all nations (Mark 13:10) rather than for the ethnic Israel. With the gospel of Jesus Christ, the dawn of the new age has indeed come. The covenant reached a new historical fulfillment with the inclusion of the Gentiles into the people of God. The identity of the people of God is expanded but not in terms of an ethnic expansion of the people of Israel.[24] The new messianic community, though commenced with Israel, is not ethnically Israel but a new people—the church whose membership and mission are not in terms of the Abrahamic line and Israel's ethnic identity as a nation but in terms of Abrahamic faith and his offspring in and through Jesus Christ.

Mark further highlights the dawn of the new age as related to the new community—the church—with his interest in the Gentile mission. The story of Jesus in Mark revolves around Jesus' ministry in Galilee and its surrounding areas. Scholars believe that the Galilean ministry

---

23 Lane, *The Gospel According to Mark*, 15.
24 See Vanlaningham, "An Evaluation of N. T. Wright's View of Israel in Romans 11," 179-93, where the author argues contra Wright's position that Israel is the church.

in Mark is highly symbolic of Mark's interest in the Gentile mission. R. Allan Cole notes,

Marxsen and those who follow see a highly symbolic use of the word "Galilee" in Mark. To them, "Galilee" stands as a symbol for the wider Gentile Christian world, just as "Judea" or "Jerusalem" stand for the Jewish world. . . . Galilee therefore stands for Gentile mission, and what we have here is an encouragement of the largely Gentile church of Rome to engage in it.[25]

Mark's Gospel is a catholic Gospel indeed. The preaching of the gospel to all the nations makes this emphatic: "And the gospel must first be preached to all nations" (Mark 13:10). That the gospel had reached Rome (the center of human civilization at that time) and that Christ was proclaimed to the people of Rome already indicate the new age in God's redemptive history—from Jerusalem to Rome, and from Israel to all the nations.

Luke: The Good News for the Poor

Of the Synoptic Gospels, Luke is the most catholic. In his book *A Dynamic Reading of the Holy Spirit in Luke-Acts*, Ju Hur points to how the plot of Luke-Acts depicts a geographical expansion that shows the witness of the church not only to Jews but also to Gentiles:

> The plot depicts a geographical expansion, which is carried out by leading Spirit-inspired characters. Thus, the narrator highlights the geographical setting in developing the plot, e.g. Jesus' witness from Galilee to Jerusalem in the Gospel and his disciples' witness from Jerusalem, through Judea and Samaria, and to Rome in Acts. Jerusalem thus seems to be the geographical center of Luke-Acts (or at least of the Gospel). Nevertheless, from the beginning, the gospel of or the witness to Jesus is to be delivered beyond the territory of Israel (Lk. 2:32; Acts 1:8;

---

25 Cole, *The Gospel According to Mark*, 95.

2:5-11): the salvific witness is directed not only to Jews, but also to Gentiles (Lk. 2:32; 24:47; Acts 1:8), first through Jesus who is depicted as chosen, baptized/anointed and commissioned by God (Lk. 4:18, 43; 9:48; 10:16; Acts 3:20, 26), and then through Jesus' followers who are similarly chosen, baptized (metaphorically and literally) and commissioned through the risen Jesus by God (Lk. 9:2; 10:1, 3; 22:35; 24:49; Acts 1:5, 8; 2:4; 9:17; 26:17). Most importantly, readers can see at almost every critical plot-stage of the mission in Acts (8:29, 39, 10:19; 11:12; 13:2, 4; 16:6, 7; 19:21; 20:22) that the Holy Spirit appears as a reliable mission supporter and/or director who, on the one hand, empowers and guides the witnesses and, on the other, verifies certain groups as God's people. In this regard, the plot is developed through a geographical expansion caused by God's divine agent, that is, the Spirit (including an angel of the Lord), and by God's human agents, that is, Spirit-inspired witnesses, in order to fulfill the plan of God.[26]

Indeed, the concept of salvation in Luke's narrative is not exclusive but inclusive. Jesus is the Savior of not only the people of Israel, though in particular he came for them, but also of the whole world (Luke 3:21). Moreover, the meaning of the saving acts of Christ is not limited to Jewish traditional understanding of repentance, forgiveness, and faith. Flemming writes, "Jesus offers liberation from whatever forces create brokenness and exclusion in the human situation, and whatever tries to frustrate God's redemptive purpose."[27] The presentation of Luke's expanded meaning of salvation includes Jesus' healing ministry and compassion for the outcast of the society—the poor, the oppressed, the sick, the lepers, the "sinners," the tax collectors, women, children,

---

26 Hur, *A Dynamic Reading*, 190-91
27 Flemming, *Contextualization in the New Testament*, 254.

Samaritans, and Gentiles. Luke's inclusive salvation is the movement of his narrative plot and characterization in the third Gospel.

The life and ministry of Jesus centered on his saving activities for the poor. At his inaugural address to his hometown people in Nazareth, Jesus announced before them his mission to proclaim the very gospel to the poor: "The Spirit of the Lord is on me, because he has anointed me to proclaim good news to the poor. He has sent me to proclaim freedom for the prisoners and recovery of sight for the blind, to set the oppressed free, to proclaim the year of the Lord's favor" (Luke 4:18-19). Luke's gospel was inseparable from Jesus' activities and associations with the poor. Luke's portrayal of Jesus emphasized how Jesus literally ministered to and identified himself with the poor. Luke further presented Jesus as faithful to God and his given mission, which Jesus clearly said, "The Son of Man came to seek and save the lost" (Luke 19:10).

Jesus knew his mission and was faithful to it by his association with the lowly ones of society by eating and drinking with them. When asked by the Pharisees and the teachers of the law as to why he ate and drank with tax collectors and sinners, Jesus answered, "It is not the healthy who need a doctor, but the sick. I have not come to call the righteous, but sinners to repentance" (Luke 5:31-32). The first-person pronoun "I" echoed in their ears as the "Son of Man," telling them why he came and for whom he came. Eating with sinners was, for Jesus, an act that fulfilled his mission of bringing salvation to sinners. To do otherwise would be to deny the one who sent him.

Jesus' faithfulness is highlighted further by Luke's characterization of him as a friend of sinners. Jesus' association with sinners and tax collectors was seen and criticized by the Pharisees and other religious leaders in terms of friendship (though in a negative sense, Luke 7:34), enriched and enlivened by eating and drinking with them. Such criticism is ironic. Green notes, "This is the irony of the criticism both John and Jesus received: They are rejected for behaviors that are actually symptomatic of their faithfulness to the work for which God set them apart."[28] Such presentation of Jesus in and through the words of the Pharisees and religious leaders, with Jesus' confirmatory response, qualifies Luke's characterization of the Son of Man as a faithful Savior who was a faithful friend to sinners and other outcasts.

The poor in Luke take the central stage in Jesus' public ministry.[29] Apparently, the poor in Luke do not refer only to the poor of Israel but also the poor of all nations. These "poor" include anyone who sees himself or herself under the mercy and grace of God—the poor, the prisoners, the blind, and the oppressed. The poor are those who are completely dependent on God for life and sustenance. Indeed, in and through Jesus, the gospel was preached to the poor; hence, Luke's Gospel is the good news for the poor.

John: The Word for the World

The Gospel of John is unique among the four Gospels. The evangelist's presentation of the life and ministry of Jesus is more theological than historical. John not only presents the words and deeds of Jesus but also interprets them in the context of proclaiming Christ by calling people to believe as did the other evangelists: "But these are written that you may believe that Jesus is the Messiah, the Son of God, and that by believing you may have life in his name" (John 20:31). To John, however, it is more explicit than implicit, as in the Synoptics, that the gospel of Jesus Christ is not exclusively for the Jews but also inclusive of the Gentiles. It is a gospel for the world (John 3:16). With Israel's rejection of Jesus as the Messiah, the message is made available to anyone who would believe in him, whether Jews or Gentiles: "Yet

---

28 Green, *The Gospel of Luke*, 203. See Hallig, "The Eating Motif in the Third Gospel," 206-22.

29 See David, "Rich and Poor," 701-10.

to all who did receive him, to those who believed in his name, he gave the right to become children of God" (John 1:12). The concept of the "children of God" now extends clearly and theologically to non-Jews who believe in the gospel. Such an extension is in accord with God's redemptive history—the saving of all mankind: "Look, the Lamb of God, who takes away the sin of the world" (John 1:29b).

Hence, John presents Jesus as the Word for the world: "In the beginning was the Word . . . in him was life, and that life was the light of all mankind . . . the true light that gives light to everyone was coming into the world" (John 1:1-9). This is supported by what Jesus said about himself, "I am the light of the world. Whoever follows me will never walk in darkness, but will have the light of life" (John 8:12). The other "I Am" sayings of John present Christ as inclusively inviting men and women to faith so they might have life in him. The personal claims Jesus makes about himself and his mission present him as the Messiah of the world—the Word for the world. This is most clearly seen in his dialogue with the Pharisee named Nicodemus: "For God so loved the world that he gave his one and only Son, that whoever believes in him shall not perish but have eternal life" (John 3:16). The reference to the *world* is clearly directed to all the nations—all people who would come to believe regardless of their ethnic identity. This reference supports the biblical idea of redemptive history as directed toward all nations. The call of Abraham has the world as its very goal—for God so loved the world. And so, in Christ, the promise given to Abraham and his children now comes to its fullness in the life and ministry of Jesus.

To John, the story of the life and ministry of Jesus is more than a story of the Jewish carpenter or the king of the Jews. Focusing on the life and ministry of Jesus as a story accentuates the Jewish characteristics of the gospel. To get out of this mold, John opted to offer a more interpreted story of the life and ministry of Jesus, and by doing so, effectively communicated a gospel for the world. John's goal for writing was more than the retelling of the life and ministry of Jesus in the fashion of the writers of the Synoptic Gospels. He wrote with a theological purpose that uncovers the identity of Jesus as the Messiah, the Son of God, in and through whom people have *life* (John 20:31). John's characterization of Jesus supports his narrative intent of faith and life. John presented Jesus as the Son of God—a more theological characterization of Jesus. Ladd highlights the centrality of this title when he writes,

> One of the most distinct differences between the Synoptics and John is the different role Jesus' sonship to God plays. In the synoptic tradition, Jesus is reticent to speak of his sonship and God's Fatherhood. . . . However, Jesus speaks of God as Father 106 times in John, and the usage is not restricted to any period of his ministry or to any group of hearers. He speaks of "my Father" twenty-four times in John, eighteen in Matthew, six in Mark, three in Luke. It is obvious that Jesus' sonship is the central Christological idea in John, and that he writes his Gospel to make explicit what was implicit in the Synoptics. The Gospel is written that people may believe that Jesus is the Messiah, but more than Messiah, he is the Son of God (20:31).[30]

Such theological characterization supports the plot of John as revolving around the sovereign identity of Jesus as the Son of God. Culpepper believes that the character of Jesus in the Gospel of John is static and does not change.[31] Right at the beginning in the prologue, Jesus is presented with an intimate relationship with the Father—as the pre-incarnate Word who was with God and was God himself (John 1:1-18). This is described in the middle of the narrative both in words and events and is sustained towards the end of the narrative by informing believers that Jesus is the Son of God. Such theological characterization of Jesus

---

30 Ladd, *A Theology of the New Testament*, 283-84.
31 Culpepper, *Anatomy of the Fourth Gospel*, 103-4.

presents him as the Word for the world whose identity and mission are revelatory of his intimate relationship with God as co-equal and the world as God's co-creator.

Catholicity and the Church

All four evangelists understood that the call to discipleship and the preaching of the gospel give birth to the life and mission of the church. The Gospels were written in the context of the life and mission of the church. The church is the community of the gospel of Christ—a community of disciples and a community of faith. Hence, catholicity is also church-centered or *ecclesiocentric*. But this, of course, is inseparable from the first two—Christ (*Christocentric*) and the world (*cosmocentric*). The disciples themselves knew that it was Christ himself who built the church: "And I tell you that you are Peter, and on this rock I will build my church, and the gates of Hades will not overcome it" (Matt 16:18). The above study on the gospel in the Gospels points to the characteristic of the church as catholic. This is what Ignatius recognized in his statement, "Where Christ is, there is the catholic church." The catholicity of the church is first and foremost expressed in its relationship with Christ, whom the evangelists announced as the King not only of the Jews but also the Gentiles. Jesus is not only the Jewish Messiah (of which each of the evangelists was fully convinced) but also the Lord of all nations. Jesus is Lord, which all the evangelists announced to both Jews and Gentiles. The portrayal of Jesus as Lord is a portrayal of his universal kingship—as such, Jesus is the King of kings and the Lord of lords.

The church is the community of disciples from all nations (Matt 28:18-19). Israel, as an ethnocentric community, had come to its end; a new and *renewed* Israel has come—a community out of the nations of the earth. Was the creation of the church a rejection of Israel? God forbid! The church was the fulfillment of what Israel was really called to become since the call of Abraham: "Go from your country, your people and your father's household to the land I will show you. I will make you into a great nation, and I will bless you; I will make your name great, and you will be a blessing. I will bless those who bless you, and whoever curses you I will curse; and all peoples on earth will be blessed through you" (Gen 12:1-3). Abraham was called neither for his own sake nor the sake of a nation after him—Israel, but for the sake of a universal community of the earth as the ultimate goal of Abraham's election and God's covenant with him and his offspring. Old Testament scholars affirm this truth:

> The choice and blessing of Abraham and the unconditional promises of land and nationhood have as their ultimate goal the blessing of all earth's communities. The beginning of redemptive history offers a word about its end. The salvation promised Abraham will ultimately embrace all humankind.[32]

Christ came in the spirit of the Abrahamic covenant and for its fulfillment. Christ is Abraham's offspring who opened up the promised blessings to all nations in and through the church. In Christ and through his church, all nations shall come to be blessed. Indeed, God's saving acts in Israel's history were the beginning of the long process and the bigger picture of redemptive history that would find its completion in the blessing of all nations through Jesus Christ and his church. Israel's story is an open-ended story pointing to its greater fulfillment in the Son of Abraham (Matt 1:1), who would draw all people to him (John 12:32), ending the alienation of humanity from God and from one another and thereby creating a people out of many nations—a catholic people, the church. And by this, the evangelists were aware that, though the church is the renewed community of Israel—a community of Jesus' disciples, the church remained as the covenant

---

32 LaSor, Hubbard, and Bush, *Old Testament Survey*, 112.

people of God but *now* as the new covenant people who had their roots and foundation in the old Israel. Therefore, the church as a catholic community is both in continuity and discontinuity with the old Israel. It is in continuity because the promised blessing given to Abraham and his offspring was meant for all nations, and the church in Christ fulfills that. It is in discontinuity because the church is no longer associated with ethnocentric Israel. Hence, the church is no longer Israel but has taken a new identity, one that is more inclusive as a catholic identity.

The catholicity of the church in the four Gospels is demonstrated further in the relationship of the church with the kingdom of God. This relationship protects the church from becoming ethnocentric. The evangelists, one way or another, all shared in the proclamation of the kingdom of God in and through the life and ministry of Jesus. They did not disassociate the kingdom of God from the gospel they preached. For them, the content of the gospel is the kingdom of God. There is no gospel without the kingdom of God. At the heart of the kingdom of God, however, is the person of Jesus Christ. David Wenham demonstrates this in his presentation of God's mission in the world in relation to the kingdom:

> 1. The *context*: The one creator God, the God of Israel, in his love and in fulfillment of the Scriptures, intervened through Jesus to complete his saving purposes through his people Israel and thus to bring a broken and hostile world back under his rule and to restore it to the love and perfection that God intended.
>
> 2. The *center*: Jesus was the Spirit-filled Messiah of Israel and the Son of God. Through his life, teaching, and supremely through his death and resurrection he announced and inaugurated the saving rule of God, inviting others to receive the divine gift.
>
> 3. The *community*: Those who receive Jesus and his salvation by faith—baptism and eucharist are expression of such faith—are through and with him the true Israel—children of God, having

the Holy Spirit of sonship. They are called to live as a restored community in loving fellowship with God and with each other and to proclaim and live the good news of restoration in the world.

4. The *climax*: The mission of restoration will be complete at the Lord's return to judge the world, when evil will finally be overcome, God's people will be raised and perfected, and the whole of creation will be restored to its intended glory.[33]

In summary, the life and ministry of Jesus demonstrated and delivered to the community of disciples the reality and totality of the kingdom of God with them. Jesus handed over the kingship of God from the Father to the church in and through his redemptive work: "Repent for the kingdom of God is near" (Matt 4:17, 23; Mark 1:14-15; Luke 4:21). The Kingdom was demonstrated by words and deeds in both the life and ministry of Jesus: from his conception and birth, through his public ministries of teaching, preaching, and healing, and finally by his death, resurrection, and ascension. These are the objective contents of the gospel in the accounts of the four canonical Gospels that represent the authoritative interpretations of the events of the life and ministry of Jesus centered on the kingdom of God.[34] The kingdom of God is an inclusive invitation from God to all nations in Christ through the church. This inclusivity of the kingdom defines the catholicity of the church both in terms of membership and mission.

Conclusion

The catholicity of the church in the four canonical Gospels is one that is embedded in the evangelists' narrative accounts of the life and ministry of Jesus through their triadic literary themes—discipleship,

---

33 Wenham, "Unity and Diversity in the New Testament," 712-13.

34 The emergence of the Gospel traditions occurred in response to the various needs of the early church and the challenges of the heretics particularly the Gnostics.

the gospel, and the church—vis-à-vis the plot of witness. Each of the evangelists affirmed the fact that the community of disciples was the incipient church whose life and mission were defined in terms of "catholic," derived primarily from its relationship with Jesus Christ (*christocentric*) and its mission to proclaim the gospel to all the nations (*cosmocentric*).

Hence, the catholicity of the church is a biblical concept that the church fathers later developed and reconstructed into a theological mark of the church enshrined in the catholic creeds: "We believe in the one, holy, *catholic*, and apostolic church." The word "catholic" apparently does not refer to a particular denominational church but to the Church of Jesus Christ inclusive of all disciples of Christ from all nations. It is an affirmation of the historical, theological, and biblical concept of the church embedded in the very gospel that all four canonical Gospels present in their narrative accounts of the life and ministry of Jesus.

Bibliography

Bruner, Frederick Dale. *Matthew: A Commentary, vol. 1, The Christ-book, Matthew 1–12*. Grand Rapids: Eerdmans, 2007.

Cole, R. Alan. *The Gospel According to Mark*. Grand Rapids: Eerdmans, 1989.

David, P. H. "Rich and Poor." In *Dictionary of Jesus and the Gospels*, edited by Joel B. Green, Scot McKnight, and I. Howard Marshall, 701–10. Downers Grove: InterVarsity, 1992.

Culpepper, R. Alan. *Anatomy of the Fourth Gospel: A Study in Literary Design*. Philadelphia: Fortress, 1987.

Dulles, Avery. *Models of the Church*. New York: Double Day, 1987.

———. *The Catholicity of the Church*. Oxford: Clarendon, 1985.

Flemming, Dean. *Contextualization in the New Testament: Patterns for Theology and Mission.* Downers Grove: InterVarsity, 2005.

France, R. T. *The Gospel According to Matthew: An Introduction and Commentary.* Grand Rapids: Eerdmans, 1985.

Green, Joel B. *The Gospel of Luke.* Grand Rapids: Eerdmans, 1997.

Guthrie, Donald. *New Testament Theology.* England: InterVarsity, 1981.

Hallig, Jason V. "Contextualization of the Life and Ministry of Jesus in the Four Gospels and Its Significance in Proclaiming the Gospel to Asian Cultures in the 21st Century." In *Jesus Among the Nations: Christology in Asian Perspective.* Manila: Asia Theological Association, 2017.

———. "The Eating Motif in the Third Gospel and Luke's Characterization of Jesus as the Son of Man." *Bibliotheca Sacra* (2016): 206–22.

Hur, Ju. *A Dynamic Reading of the Holy Spirit in Luke-Acts.* London/New York: T & T Clark, 2001.

Ignatius, *Epistle to the Smyrnaeans.* http://www.earlychristianwritings.com/text/ignatius-smyrnaeans-hoole.html.

Kingsbury, J. D. *Conflict in Luke: Jesus, Authorities, Disciples.* Minneapolis: Fortress, 1991.

Kingsbury, J. D. *Matthew As Story.* Philadelphia: Fortress, 1988.

Ladd, George Eldon. *A Theology of the New Testament.* Grand Rapids: Eerdmans, 1993.

Lane, William L. *The Gospel According to Mark.* Grand Rapids: Eerdmans, 1974.

LaSor, William Sanford, David Allan Hubbard, and Frederic William Bush. *Old Testament Survey: the Message, Form, and Background of the Old Testament.* Grand Rapids: Eerdmans, 1982.

Lincoln, Andrew T. *The Gospel According to Saint John.* Peabody: Henrickson, 2006.

Marshall, I. Howard. *The Origins of New Testament Theology*. Downers Grove: InterVarsity, 1976.

Matera, F. J. "The Plot of Matthew's Gospel." *Catholic Biblical Quarterly* 49 (1987): 233–253.

Powell, M. A. *What is Narrative Criticism? A New Approach to the Bible*. London: SPCK; Minneapolis: Augsburg, 1990.

Senior, Donald. *The Gospel of Matthew*. Nashville: Abingdon, 1997.

Smith, S. H. *A Lion with Wings: A Narrative-Critical Approach to Mark's Gospel*. Sheffield: Sheffield Academic, 1996.

Torrance, Thomas F. "The Foundation of the Church." In *Theological Foundations for Ministry: Selected Readings for a Theology of the Church in Ministry*, edited by Ray S. Anderson, 199–215. Edinburg: T. & T. Clark, 1979.

Vanlaningham, Michael G. "An Evaluation of N. T. Wright's View of Israel in Romans 11." *Bibliotheca Sacra* 170 (April–June 2013): 179–93.

Wenham, David. "Unity and Diversity in the New Testament." In Ladd, George Eldon, *A Theology of the New Testament*, by George Eldon Ladd, 684–719.

4

PNEUMATIKOS IN PAULINE PERSPECTIVE

Darin H. Land

There is a robust interest in spirituality in the present world, as even a cursory investigation reveals. A Google search for the word "spirituality" returns about 1.34 billion results. Similarly, there were at least 10,000 posts on Twitter during the week of June 23–30, 2022 using the hashtag #spirituality.[1] Though not conveying the content or perspective of the contributors, these statistics nevertheless reveal widespread attentiveness to spiritual concerns.

Paul also displayed a keen interest in spirituality. Among all the New Testament writers, he used the term "spiritual" (Greek πνευματικός, *pneumatikos*) by far the most. This essay begins by examining Paul's use of this word, moves deeper by considering the realm of the Spirit in Paul's understanding, then explores spiritual gifts and their function in the church today. The essay closes with the relationship between

---

1 "Hashtag Tracking Tool for Twitter and Instagram. Try It Now!," accessed June 30, 2022, https://www.tweetbinder.com/.

spiritual gifts and honor. As we shall see, in Pauline perspective, the adjective *pneumatikos* describes the new world of the Spirit inhabited by Spirit-gifted individuals who honor one another for their generous use of spiritual gifts for building the body of Christ.

Paul's Use of *Pneumatikos*

Pneumatikos occurs 24 times in the Pauline Epistles—25 if you include the adverbial form, *pneumatikōs* (Table 1). The word occurs elsewhere in the New Testament only two times (again, three, if counting the adverbial form), strongly indicating it is a favorite term for Paul.[2] According to Stephan P. Pretorius, "The adjective spiritual is a Christian neologism and is used by Paul to describe that which pertains to the Holy Spirit."[3]

Fifteen of the 24 Pauline occurrences (plus the adverbial use) are found in 1 Corinthians, likely reflecting Paul's response to a specific problem in the Corinthian church. Commentators widely agree that a core issue in Corinth was division related to whose spiritual gift was best.

Ref	Modified Word	Gender	Personal?	Holy Spirit?
Rom 1:11	gift	N	No	Yes?
Rom 7:14	law	M	No	No
Rom 15:27	(blessings)	Ambiguous	No	Yes?
1 Cor 2:13	(people/words)	M/N	Yes/No	Yes
1 Cor 2:13	(truths)	N	No	Yes

---

2 Some scholars regard Colossians and Ephesians as pseudonymous. But even if one were to concede this point, their use of *pneumatikos* would have been influenced by Paul's affinity for the term.

3 Pretorius, "Understanding Spiritual Experience," 158.

Reference	Modified word			
1 Cor 2:14*	[adverb]			Yes
1 Cor 2:15	(person)	M	Yes	Yes
1 Cor 3:1	(people)	M	Yes	Yes?
1 Cor 9:11	(something sown, i.e., seed)	N	No	Yes?
1 Cor 10:3	food	N	No	No
1 Cor 10:4	drink	N	No	No
1 Cor 10:4	rock/Christ	F	No/Yes	No
1 Cor 12:1	(gifts or people)[4]	Ambiguous	No/Yes	Yes
1 Cor 14:1	(gifts)	N	No	Yes
1 Cor 14:37	(person)	M	Yes	Yes?
1 Cor 15:44 (2x)	body	N	No	Yes?
1 Cor 15:46 (2x)	(body)	N	No	No?
Gal 6:1	(people)	M	Yes	Yes?
Eph 1:3	blessing	F	No	Yes?
Eph 5:19	songs	F	No	Yes?
Eph 6:12	(forces)	N	No?	No
Col 1:9	wisdom and understanding	F	No	Yes?
Col 3:16	songs	F	No	Yes?

Table 1: Uses of *pneumatikos* in Paul. Words in parentheses indicate the modified word is not explicitly stated but inferred from the context.

---

4   Surprisingly, the NET editors—normally so prolific in explaining translational challenges—do not mention the possibility of translating as "spiritual people" rather than "spiritual gifts" or "things." Ekem argues strongly for the former translation ("Spiritual Gifts," 54-74). Kuwornu-Adjaottor suggests combining the two options as "spiritually-gifted persons" ("Spiritual Gifts," 260-73).

As indicated in Table 1, *pneumatikos* in the Pauline Epistles can refer to spiritual people (four–six times; seven if we include Christ), spiritual body (four times), spiritual gifts (three times), spiritual blessings (twice), spiritual songs (twice), spiritual concepts (words or truth, once or twice; wisdom and understanding, once), and spiritual food and drink (two times). It can be used to describe the Mosaic law (once), spiritual seed (once), and dark spiritual forces (once). Interestingly, spiritual food and drink are explicitly connected to the spiritual rock, whom Paul says is Christ (1 Cor 10:3–4). Still referring to Table 1, *pneumatikos* can modify masculine nouns (at least five times), feminine nouns (five times), and neuter nouns (at least 11 times).[5]

Pneumatikos is used in a personal way at least four and possibly as many as seven times, and it is clearly related to the Holy Spirit at least six times. However, it is clearly *unrelated* to the Holy Spirit only five times, while 11 of the remaining 12 instances still seem to point to the Holy Spirit. In other words, the weight of evidence seems to suggest that when Paul describes something as spiritual, he is drawing attention to its relation to the Holy Spirit.

Paul's diverse usage of the word *pneumatikos* illustrates his broad understanding of the term. He normally uses the term in a positive sense, the sole exception in Ephesians 6:12 when it refers to forces of evil. For Paul, *pneumatikos* is a descriptor for all that pertains to the Holy Spirit and the realm the Holy Spirit creates.

---

5 The statistics include those circumstances where the modified word is merely understood but clear from the context. The uncertainty in the statistics reflects three points of grammatical ambiguity: 1 Cor 2:13, where the referent could either be people (*pneumatikos* as masculine) or words (*pneumatikos* as neuter); 1 Cor 12:1, where the gender ambiguity could indicate either spiritual gifts or spiritual people; and Rom 15:27, with ambiguous gender but clear referent.

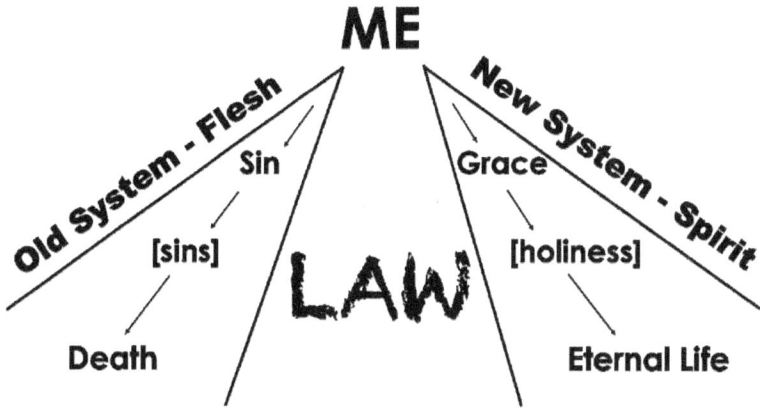

Figure 1: The new way of holiness in Romans 6—8

Spirit Versus Flesh in Paul

To understand Paul's meaning for *pneumatikos* more deeply, consider his use of the phrases "realm of the flesh" (Rom 7:5) and "the new way of the Spirit" (Rom 7:6). Paul regards these two constructs as competing systems under which people might live. As Philip F. Sheldrake correctly notes, "The concept of spirituality stems from the Greek words *pneuma* and *pneumatikos* as employed in the Pauline letters. Spirituality here fundamentally means a way of life, or life in the Spirit, in contrast to living in ways opposed to the Spirit of God."[6]

Paul explains the two systems in Romans 6:19–22. Both are characterized by an initial truth, a logical sequence, and a final consequence.

---

6 Sheldrake, "Christian Spirituality," 20. Cf. Jones, "Paul Confronts Paganism in the Church," 716. Speaking about 1 Cor 15:45, Jones says, "In Paul, ψυχή [psychē] generally means physical life. Paul is not referring to 'a living person' as such but is describing two orders of existence, determined by two principles, ψυχή and πνεῦμα [pneuma] They presuppose two stages in God's creative, redemptive plan. Ψυχή is the mode of creational life; πνεῦμα that of future, new-creational life." But also note that in 1 Cor 15, Paul is comparing soul (psychē) and spirit rather than contrasting flesh (sarx) and spirit.

As illustrated in Figure 1[7], the initial truth for the realm of the flesh is that sin reigns in the life of everyone who lives there. Because sin reigns in those who live in the old system, the logical sequence—the inevitable result—is the commission of sins. The sin problem leads to sinful acts. From time to time people living in the old system might act righteously, but almost accidentally, so to speak. The final consequence of this terrible system is death for all who dwell there.

The new system of the Spirit begins with grace, God's grace mediated through Jesus' sacrifice. Just as those under sin inevitably commit sins, so also those under grace act according to holiness. Yes, those living in the Spirit may, from time to time, act sinfully. But such sinful acts are rightly regarded as anomalous to the new normal. As Stanley E. Porter states, "In [Galatians], Paul speaks of life in the Spirit as antithetical to living according to human sinful nature. Life in the Spirit is not under the obligations of the law and produces spiritual fruit. To live in the Spirit is to behave according to the Spirit (5:16–25)."[8] Sinful acts are the consequence of the intrusion of the old system and are not part of the logical progression within the Spirit's realm. They must be put to death, as Paul says (Col 3:5), because they do not belong; but they do not disqualify the Spirit-realm resident from the characteristic sequence of the new system. The glorious consequence of this new, marvelous system is eternal life for all who dwell there.

As Jerry L. Sumney rightly observes,

> One of the distinctions between previous times and the end times is that in the eschatological time the Spirit empowers believers to live for God. Paul recognizes that in previous times people were unable to live for God. They were unable because they lived in a realm ruled by sin and were unable to escape. He

---

7 In Rom 6–8 the Law is not part of either system but is useful because it reveals which system one is following.

8 Porter, "The Holy Spirit in the New Testament," 49.

speaks of this as living "according to the flesh" (Rom 8:1–8). But the coming of the Spirit signals that God has now strengthened believers with the Spirit; God has transferred them into the realm of the Spirit where they can live for God (Rom 8:12–17). This great blessing demands that recipients of the Spirit live in a way that reflects the presence of the Spirit.[9]

Spiritual Gifts

In my experience, there is pressure in today's church to distinguish spiritual gifts from natural gifts, reflecting a desire to identify one's unique gift given upon Spirit baptism.[10] But this thinking fails to recognize every gift as a spiritual gift. Even gifts like intellect, personality, and aptitude, are given by God. Since God is spirit, these gifts are rightly described as spiritual gifts.

We may be misled by Paul's use of the word "manifestation" in 1 Corinthians 12:7. A manifestation is a visible demonstration of an unseen reality, so we expect manifestations to be spectacular, unmistakable, and even miraculous. Manifestations of the Spirit can be spectacular (e.g., Acts 2). Yet this is not a necessary criterion for the Spirit's work. Recall Elijah's experience in 1 Kings 19:11–14, where the Lord was revealed in the still, small voice instead of the mighty wind or powerful earthquake. Similarly, the Spirit's gifts are sometimes manifested in seemingly ordinary ways if only we have eyes to see the Spirit's empowering activity.

We are especially at risk of overlooking the subtler manifestations of the Spirit when we insist on dissociating spiritual gifts from natural gifts. Therefore, we should consider the function of the spiritual gifts in addition to their source. Their source is the Holy Spirit, regardless of whether given at birth or rebirth.

---

9   Sumney, "The Holy Spirit in Paul," 68.
10 On Spirit baptism, see my article, "Just as He Determines," 115–19.

Focusing on the function of spiritual gifts reminds us that all gifts are useful for the Lord's work. When we classify gifts as either spiritual or natural, we naturally reserve the former for sacred work and relegate the latter to secular work. But God can use all kinds of gifts. In 1 Corinthians 12, Paul insists that every spiritual gift is equally valuable within the body of Christ because each gifted person offers an indispensable service to the body.[11]

Therefore, we should pay attention to what the gifts accomplish in the community of believers. Paul offers a (partial) list of spiritual gifts in 1 Corinthians 12:8-10. When we examine the meaning of the terms he uses, we begin to see that the gifts are fully operational in today's church.

Word of wisdom and word of knowledge.[12] These gifts are commonly understood to be insights that could not have been known without divine revelation. But when we focus on wisdom, a different picture emerges. Consider the wisdom of Solomon. The story illustrating Solomon's surpassing wisdom has nothing to do with secret knowledge. Rather, it pertains to discernment and creative engagement with people. From this perspective, wisdom enables an ability to work well with people. A wise person perceives how others think and feel, and use these perceptions to help others interact well with each other, maximize their potential, and thrive in the abundant life that Jesus promises.

When we limit our understanding of a word of wisdom to secret knowledge miraculously revealed, we miss those whom the Spirit has

---

11 Paul does seem to concede in 1 Cor 14:1 that there are greater gifts when he urges the Corinthian believers to pursue the gift of prophecy over other gifts. However, what makes one gift greater is not the prestige that it offers to the recipient. Rather, a gift is greater because it has a greater impact on the vitality of the body of Christ.

12 According to Soards, "The way Paul clusters wisdom, knowledge, revelation, and teaching suggests some relationship and similarity among these phenomena, although the exact nuance that Paul intends to impart by the use of these different words is not recoverable from his letters," *1 Corinthians*, 258. Cf. Conzelmann, *1 Corinthians*, 209.

gifted with a special ability to work well with people. These gifted people may use their God-given gift—their spiritual gift—in secular settings where it is valued instead of in the church, where it is viewed as unspiritual.

People who may unknowingly have the gift of wisdom include counselors, public relations (PR) professionals, and teachers. Counselors guide people to health and wholeness. Trained counselors can maximize their spiritual gift. Rather than seeing training as a substitute for the spiritual gift of wisdom, we should understand it as a way to sharpen one's God-given ability.

Similarly, PR professionals use their understanding of people (i.e., their wisdom) to shape a message to motivate people to action. Church people may view PR professionals as manipulators. But when this gift is turned to godly purposes, God can use it to draw people to himself and promote holiness of thought and deed.

Teachers, too, use their spiritual gift of wisdom to motivate people to learn, grow, and thrive. Teaching can be a distinct spiritual gift (Rom 12:7). But when teachers use their understanding of people as part of the teaching process, they may be exhibiting the gift of wisdom.

Faith. Commentators dispute whether faith in this list of spiritual gifts means faith common to all believers or special faith the Holy Spirit gives to selected believers.[13] This lack of consensus suggests Paul might have been intentionally ambiguous. This ambiguity suggests the presence of a both/and scenario at work here: Paul may have intended *both* the ordinary faith that all believers share *and* the additional faith unique to certain believers. The extra faith may be the ability to see a God-created future that others cannot yet see. Thus, visionary leaders who communicate a vision of what God is doing in the world and motivate others to join God in this work may be exhibiting the spiritual gift of faith.

---

13 Soards, *1 Corinthians*, 258–259.

Interestingly, the Greek word for "faith" can also be translated as "faithfulness." Thus, the ability to remain faithful to the Lord despite humanly insurmountable difficulties can be a spiritual gift. Those who walk humbly with the Lord through all the ups and downs of life reveal the Spirit's activity through the gift of faith.[14]

Healing. It is widely agreed that God works through the skills of medical professionals to bring healing to sick people, whether believers or unbelievers. It is less widely acknowledged that God has gifted those same medical professionals with the knowledge and skills needed to practice their healing skills. And it is still less recognized that this gifting is a spiritual gift. Ultimately, God is the healer, and the Spirit is the one who provides doctors, nurses, and other medical personnel with their healing gift.

But there are other sources of God's healing whose human agents may have the spiritual gift of healing. Music can bring both physical and emotional healing. And there is some truth in the saying that laughter is the best medicine. Thus, musicians and comedians may have gifts of healing from the Holy Spirit. Rather than dismissing such people as frivolous to the church's work, we should celebrate their Spirit-giftedness and empower them to minister through these gifts.

Miraculous powers. If we really believe that God answers prayer, it follows that God works miracles in response to our prayers. Therefore, those known for their powerful and effective prayers (sometimes called prayer warriors) may have miraculous ability. We can be distracted by looking for miracles as spectacles and miss the everyday miracles that result from the prayers of everyday saints. Yet prayer warriors have the gift of miraculous powers.

---

14 In this book of honor for Dr. Floyd T. Cunningham, I think it is appropriate to suggest that his faithfulness in service to the Lord throughout his career at Asia-Pacific Nazarene Theological Seminary has been a manifestation of the Spirit's gift of faith/faithfulness that has edified the body of Christ in immeasurable ways.

As noted above, spiritual gifts are evidence of the Spirit's activity. These gifts are far more prevalent than we often recognize. And since the gifts are more prevalent, so also is the Spirit's presence. The Spirit's activity is visible, not only in the spectacular but also in the mundane, not only among those deemed super spiritual but even in those who have yet to receive Christ. For Wesleyans, this is not a new teaching. This is prevenient grace. Those spiritual gifts denigrated as one's natural gifts are the working of the Holy Spirit to draw people to God. I am not denying the spectacular manifestation of spiritual gifts any more than insisting that prevenient grace denies the importance of a conversion experience. I am only inviting us to recognize the Spirit's gifts in both spectacular and ordinary ways—and to impress upon us the importance of using all gifts for God's glory.

Prophecy. People often understand prophecy to mean telling what will happen in the future. The biblical concept of prophecy certainly allows for this idea (e.g., Acts 11:28), but the core of biblical prophecy is somewhat different. Prophecy in the Bible is speaking the truth to change present behavior.

The paradigmatic account of biblical prophecy is Nathan's confrontation of David's sinful behavior in the matter of Uriah and Bathsheba. Recall how Nathan the prophet entered David's presence and told the story of a rich man stealing a poor person's beloved sheep. When David ruled that the rich man deserved death, Nathan said to him, "You are the man" (2 Sam 12:7). This episode reveals the central purpose of biblical prophecy: to expose sinful behavior, defend the powerless, and lead people toward repentance, restitution, and restoration.

Though we may not see people predicting the future today in a stereotypical way, we surely see believers confronting evil, pointing out hypocrisy, challenging those who abuse their power, and advocating for the powerless. Christian lawyers, justice advocates, and those who confront others' errors are examples of modern-day, Spirit-gifted prophets.

The Bible is clear that the prophetic vocation is a lonely, dangerous one. Few people enjoy being told their behavior is sinful and needs to change. The life of prophets can be difficult and even desperate. The church, though, must celebrate the prophets in our midst who have the courage to confront our blindness and self-centeredness. Rather than shunning them, we must respond with repentant joy for the Spirit's gift that leads us to be more aligned with God's will.

Discernment of Spirits. Discernment of spirits means the ability to distinguish between good and evil forces at work in the spirit world. It might also mean the ability to sense hierarchies in the spiritual realm or even an awareness of the work of evil through the actions and intentions of humans.

What we call intuition may, in fact, be the gift of spiritual discernment. Rather than dismiss people, who, without solid evidence, warn of hidden agendas and wrong motives, we would do well to weigh whether the Holy Spirit might have enabled them to discern spirits for our benefit. Of course, we should avoid ungrounded accusations, but we must evaluate warning signs.

Tongues. The New Testament describes the gift of tongues in two distinct ways. Acts portrays people speaking in foreign languages that they apparently had not previously known. But Paul depicts speaking in tongues as utterances unintelligible to people. However, when Paul mentions speaking in human or angelic tongues in 1 Corinthians 13:1, he seems to embrace both aspects of the one spiritual gift.

The spiritual gift of speaking in human tongues has the clear purpose of communicating the good news in a clear and powerful way that points people to Christ, as on the day of Pentecost. While not all evangelists speak in foreign languages, they do exude the more salient part of the gift, namely, proclaiming the gospel with clarity and power so that people respond to God's gracious gift.

Still focusing on clear gospel communication, it is possible for the Holy Spirit to distribute this gift to individuals in ways other than the ecstatic utterance of previously unknown human words. Media producers and communications experts are especially talented (i.e., gifted) in presenting the gospel in compelling ways. Though they may not recognize their talent as the gift of tongues, when they use their skills for the sake of God's kingdom, surely, they are accomplishing the congruent purpose.

Regarding what he terms tongues of angels, Paul describes the purpose of this spiritual gift in 1 Corinthians 14:2-4: "For anyone who speaks in a tongue does not speak to people but to God. Indeed, no one understands them; they utter mysteries by the Spirit. . . . Anyone who speaks in a tongue edifies themselves."

The Holy Spirit has other ways of effecting this self-edification other than speaking in tongues. In my own experience, I can point to times when music was used by the Spirit for my personal edification. Whether through tongues, music, or other means, the Holy Spirit builds up the believer's faith through a deep experience of God. The individual is edified directly, but the congregation is strengthened indirectly. As the congregation witnesses the confidence of the one whom the Spirit has edified through this gift, the members draw strength from that person's assurance.

The point Paul is making in 1 Corinthians 14, however, is that the gift of tongues is a lesser gift because it directly affects the recipient alone, while the other gifts—especially prophecy—edify the whole body of Christ. For Paul, the gift of tongues is indispensably valuable, but the gift of prophecy is even more so.

Interpretation of tongues. In Paul's thinking, the gift of interpretation is more valuable than the gift of tongues for the same reason that prophecy is greater, namely, that it edifies the whole body. Interpretation of tongues takes mysteries and sentiments expressed in unintelligible, heavenly language and makes them understandable to others. The interpreter makes hidden spiritual truths clear to the listeners.

A similar function occurs any time one believer makes complex biblical, spiritual, or theological truths easy for others to grasp. Those who excel in public speaking, writing, or leading small group Bible studies share this gift with the church.

Spiritual Gifts Today

In the Pauline conception, *pneumatikos* has to do with the Holy Spirit. Those whom Paul describes as *pneumatikoi* exhibit the gifts of the Spirit, that is, special abilities from the Holy Spirit. But Paul also says that every believer has received manifestations of the Spirit for the common good (1 Cor 12:7). When we draw a hard line between spiritual gifts and natural gifts, we easily miss a significant part of what God is doing in our midst.

A closer look at the spiritual gifts Paul mentions in 1 Corinthians 12:8–10 reveals the function of the gifts as fully operational in the church today, even if we normally overlook them. Counselors, PR professionals, and teachers exhibit the gifts of wisdom and knowledge. Visionaries and motivational speakers demonstrate the gift of faith. Medical professionals, musicians, comedians, lawyers, intuiters, language experts, and writers all exhibit the gifts of the Spirit in various ways.

The spiritual gifts are given to individual believers for the benefit of all. Paul sees those gifts that have a deeper impact on the body as the greater gifts. He encourages believers to seek the greater gifts, not because they impress others but because they help others.

Spiritual Gifts and Honor

In Romans 12:10, Paul tells his readers to outdo each other by aiming to be better than their peers ("Outdo one another," ESV). This sounds very much like the quest for honor characteristic of the New Testament's cultural context—but with a twist. Rather than trying to outdo each other by *gaining* honor, Paul tells his Roman audience to outdo each other by *giving* honor.

Giving honor to those who use their spiritual gifts for the benefit of the community is one way to fulfill Paul's Romans 12:10 admonition. In 2 Corinthians 9:15, Paul references God's indescribable gift. Many readers wrongly assume he is talking about the gift of salvation in Christ. But instead, he is talking about interdependency between Jewish believers (who benefit the whole church through their theological resources) and Gentile believers (who bolster Jewish believers with their monetary resources). The whole complex is God's gift because God is the source of both theological and monetary resources.

This same dynamic is visible in the distribution of spiritual gifts. According to 1 Corinthians 12:7, all believers have been given spiritual gifts for the benefit of the whole body. Paul uses the metaphor of the body to illustrate that all believers are equally indispensable because the body needs every gift.

God the Holy Spirit is clearly the source of these gifts. To examine the dynamic from a social-scientific point of view, God is in the position of patron, distributing gifts for which we rightly owe God honor. But the gifts we receive from God are not for our own benefit. Rather they are for the benefit of the whole body ("for the common good" 1 Cor 12:7). One cannot hoard spiritual gifts.

The beauty of honoring believers for using spiritual gifts is that everyone gets a turn at being honored. Under the usual functioning of patronage, those with material resources use them in exchange for honor. For instance, a wealthy benefactor might build a much-needed bridge for the community, and community members repay the benefactor by offering tokens of honor such as words of praise, invitations to special events, and special attention during community celebrations. Such expressions of honor are normally reserved for those who have accumulated substantially more material resources than the median supply within the community.

But this dynamic is changed when the use of spiritual gifts is honored. Unlike material goods, spiritual gifts are not limited in supply. Therefore, giving honor for their use is similarly unlimited. Spiritual gifts are given from God's inexhaustible supply, with every believer lavishly given gifts to share with others. In exchange, the community honors those who share their gifts.

Looking deeper, it is useful to consider the role of brokers.[15] A broker acts as an intermediary between someone with material resources and someone else in need of those resources. The one with material resources is the patron, and the one who needs resources is the client. The broker facilitates the transfer of material resources from patron to client. Brokers are needed in complex societies where the prospective patron is not personally known to the client. Brokers make the necessary introductions between patron and client.

In small communities where everyone knows everyone else, there is no need for brokers. The client approaches the patron, the patron supplies what the client needs, and in exchange, the patron receives honor from the client. In contexts where honor is considered of higher worth than money, this exchange is viewed favorably by both parties. The patron is always held in higher honor than the client, but because the client's material deficit is addressed through the exchange, the

---

15 The word broker has come to have a negative connotation in some areas because it is associated with human trafficking and sexual exploitation. I beg the reader's indulgence for my use of the term in its sociological sense as described here.

Pneumatikos in Pauline Perspective 111

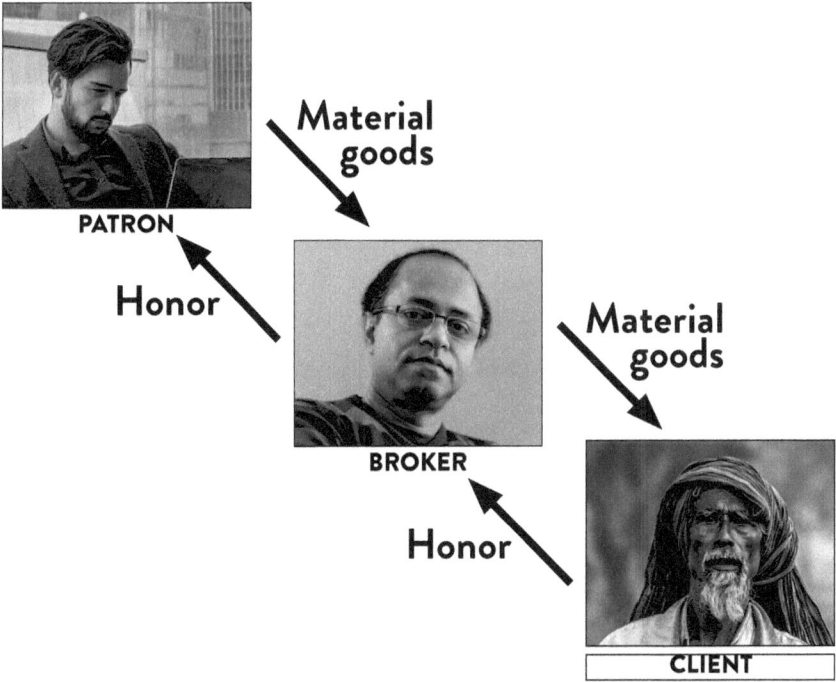

Figure 2: Patronage System with Broker. In typical implementations of the system, the relationships between patron, broker, and client are fixed.

client becomes embedded in the patron's honor and therefore experiences a concomitant increase in honor status, as well.

The situation is similar when a broker is involved. Money or other material resources pass from the patron to the broker to the client. In exchange, the client honors both the broker and the patron. It is easy to see why this scenario would be desirable to the broker since the broker gains honor even in the absence of material resources to leverage for honor.

In the typical functioning of this broker-enabled form of the patronage system, society naturally becomes increasingly stratified. Although there is a connection between patron, broker, and client, the patron is always on top, the broker in the middle, and the client on the bottom (see Figure 2). Since serving as a broker has such clear social benefits, people naturally seek opportunities to serve in this role. As a result, there are increasingly more brokers at every level, and society is increasingly divided into different status levels.

Returning to the scenario with spiritual gifts, the usual dynamic is upended because everyone has a unique gift to share that comes in unlimited supply, and everyone also has need of the unique gifts that others possess. No one stands in the position of patron since no one owns his or her gift. The gift comes from the Holy Spirit. The one who has a spiritual gift is only a broker of that gift. Nevertheless, as with brokers in the typical patronage system, the broker deserves honor when he or she uses a Spirit-given gift for the benefit of the community.

Moreover, because every believer has a gift from the Holy Spirit, every believer can serve as a broker. In the typical patronage system, some relationships between patron and client are fixed—once a client, always a client. In contrast, through the wisdom and generosity of the Holy Spirit, all believers can be in the position of a broker when their gift is needed and in the position of a client when they need the gifts of others. For instance, Person A, who has the gift of wisdom, serves as a broker to Person B when he or she needs God's wisdom. But Person B, who has the gift of healing, serves as a broker to Person A when he or she has need of God's healing. God is always the patron, but believers rotate roles of broker and client, depending on the need of the moment.

This circumstance, where God is the source of everything good, and individuals take turns distributing God's goodness as brokers of God's gifts to his people, is illustrated in Figure 3. Notice, especially, the circular arrows, wherein believers are sometimes in the role of broker and other times in the role of client. This picture illustrates Paul's observation about God's indescribable gift in 2 Corinthians 9:15.

Returning to the earlier observation that every gift is a spiritual gift because it comes from the Holy Spirit, it becomes clear that God's

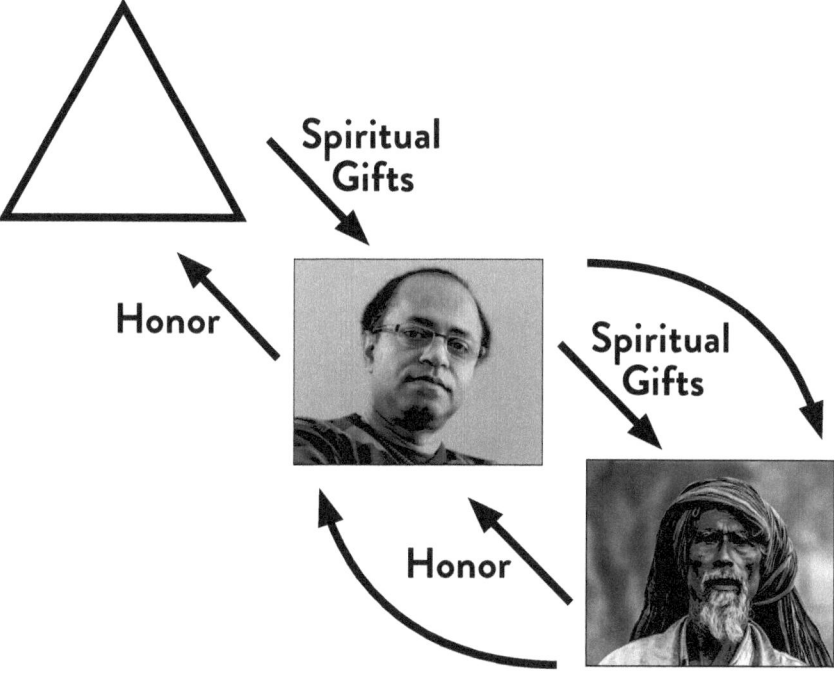

Figure 3: Patronage System for Spiritual Gifts. Note that every believer sometimes stands in the role of broker and sometimes in the role of client.

intention is for this modified patronage system to incorporate all of life. Some believers are Spirit-gifted with material resources. It is proper for such individuals to stand as brokers of these material resources with the wider community as clients. It is easy (and proper) for people who have received material benefit from brokers of God's material gifts to honor those brokers. It is equally proper, but less common, for people who have received an immaterial benefit from brokers of God's immaterial gifts to honor these brokers. When every gift is celebrated as a spiritual gift, and every broker is honored for sharing God's gifts, the body of Christ is knit together through the realization that we all need each other. This is the basis for what missiological researcher,

Eric Spangler, describes as biblical interdependence.[16] Such interdependence thrives when every believer seeks to outdo one another in giving honor for their brokerage of God's pluriform gifts for the common good, as Paul describes in Romans 12:10 and 1 Corinthians 12:7.

Pauline Spirituality as New Creation Living

Paul uses the term *pneumatikos* frequently to describe both abstract ideas and people. In both cases, *pneumatikos* is related to the Holy Spirit and the new way of living the Spirit enables. People are spiritual, *pneumatikoi*, when they live in the grace-produced holiness God desires. Spiritual people receive gifts from the Holy Spirit to use for the benefit of the body of Christ, and they receive honor from the community when they share their gifts as God intends. Through his use of *pneumatikos*, Paul promotes a worldview that is distinctively different from the old way of the flesh. Instead of a world characterized by self-centeredness and sin, the new spiritual (*pneumatikos*) world celebrates the patronage of the Holy Spirit, who calls us beyond ourselves and guides us into the fullness of new creation living in Christ.

Therefore, if anyone is in Christ, the new creation has come:
The old has gone, the new is here! (2 Cor 5:17)

Bibliography

Conzelmann, Hans. *1 Corinthians: A Commentary on the First Epistle to the Corinthians*. Edited by George W. MacRae, translated by James W. Leitch. Accordance electronic ed., vol. 67, Hermeneia: A Critical and Historical Commentary on the Bible. Minneapolis: Fortress, 1975.

Ekem, John D. "'Spiritual Gifts' or 'Spiritual Persons'? I Corinthians 12:1a Revisited." *Neotestamentica* 38, no. 1 (2004): 54–74.

---

16 Spangler, "Better Together."

Jones, Peter. "Paul Confronts Paganism in the Church: A Case Study of First Corinthians 15:45." *Journal of the Evangelical Theological Society* 49, no. 4 (2006): 713-37.

Kuwornu-Adjaottor, Johnathan E. T. "Spiritual Gifts, Spiritual Persons, or Spiritually-Gifted Persons? A Creative Translation of ΤΩΝ ΠΝΕΥΜΑΤΙΚΩΝ in 1 Corinthians 12:1a." *Neotestamentica* 46, no. 2 (2012): 260–73.

Land, Darin H. "Just as He Determines: Spirit Baptism in the New Testament." In *Holy Spirit: Unfinished Agenda*. Edited by Johnson T. K. Lim, 115–19. Singapore: Word N Works, 2015.

Porter, Stanley E. "The Holy Spirit in the New Testament." In *Holy Spirit: Unfinished Business*. Edited by Johnson T. K. Lim, 46-51. Singapore: Word N Works, 2015.

Pretorius, Stephan P. "Understanding Spiritual Experience in Christian Spirituality." *Acta Theologica Supplementum* 11 (2008): 147–65.

Sheldrake, Philip F. "Christian Spirituality as a Way of Living Publicly: A Dialectic of the Mystical and Prophetic." *Spiritus* 3, no. 1 (2003): 19–37.

Soards, Marion L. *1 Corinthians*. Accordance electronic ed. Understanding the Bible Commentary Series. Grand Rapids: Baker, 2011.

Spangler, Eric. "Better Together: Upgrading the Cultural Operating System of the Free Methodist Church Vietnam to Reinforce Biblical Interdependence." DIS Dissertation, Fuller Theological Seminary, 2022.

Sumney, Jerry L. "The Holy Spirit in Paul." In *Holy Spirit: Unfinished Business*. Edited by Johnson T. K. Lim, 67–70. Singapore: Word N Works, 2015.

For Further Reading

Kuwornu-Adjaottor, Jonathan E. T. "Spiritual Gifts, Spiritual Persons, or Spiritually-Gifted Persons? A Creative Translation of ΤΩΝ ΠΝΕΥΜΑΤΙΚΩΝ in 1 Corinthians 12:1a." *Neotestamentica* 46.2 (2012): 260–73.

Lim, Johnson T. K., ed. *Holy Spirit: Unfinished Business*. Singapore: Word N Works, 2014.

Spangler, Eric. "Better Together: Upgrading the Cultural Operating System of the Free Methodist Church Vietnam to Reinforce Biblical Interdependence." DIS Dissertation, Fuller Theological Seminary, 2022.

5

JESUS, THE FOUNDER AND PERFECTER OF FAITH: SPIRITUALITY IN HEBREWS

David A. Ackerman

The Epistle to the Hebrews offers important insights into the person and ministry of Jesus Christ. This letter given in sermon form is a call to look to Jesus as the source of victory over sin and hope for eternal life. We owe much to the unknown author of this document for the development of Christology in the early church.[1] The author seems to have been an educated Hellenistic Jewish-Christian who knew both Greco-Roman rhetoric and rabbinic methods of interpreting Scripture. He was a creative theologian trained in biblical exegesis, mainly using the Septuagint as his text and focusing on four key Old Testament passages: Psalm 8:4-6; 95:7-11; 110:1-4; and Jeremiah 31:31-34. He was a pastoral theologian who adapted early Christian traditions to appeal to a community in crisis. The many references to Jewish worship

---

1 A summary of positions about the author is given in Anderson, *Hebrews*, 31-38.

practices imply that the author was a Jewish Christian.[2] He was able to bridge the Old Testament to the New Testament. Hebrews is "a unique blend of Christology and primitive Christian eschatology within a cultic frame of reference."[3] Although such historical background information can be helpful for exegesis and exposition, this document has a timeless quality that speaks to many issues believers have faced throughout time.

The epistle gives little historical information about the audience. Interpreters must "read between the lines" to understand the situation of the readers, who appear to be experiencing two related sources of stress upon their faith in Christ: external pressure from persecution and an internal lack of commitment. The community had grown lax in its commitment to the Christian message (2:1-4). The author appears concerned that the community could falter in its response to the spoken word of God (3:12, 13; 4:1, 11; 6:11; 12:15). Their weak faith was partly due to social pressures (10:32-39; 11:24-28, 32-38; 12:1-11).

The Cruciality of Spirituality

The spirituality of the readers is of utmost concern to the author. He uses the rhetorical style of parenesis to call them to renew their faith commitment to Christ. He supports this call with biblical exposition and theological argument. Lane comments, "Hebrews was written to arouse, urge, encourage, and exhort those addressed to maintain their Christian confession and to dissuade them from a course of action that the writer believed would be catastrophic."[4] The author addresses the sagging faith of the readers and exhorts them to hold firm to their confession of Jesus Christ. They were no longer listening to the voice of God in Scripture and the preaching of the gospel (2:1; 3:7-4:13; 5:11;

---

2 Lane, *Hebrews 1-8*, l.
3 Lane, *Hebrews 1-8*, li.
4 Lane, *Hebrews 1-8*, c.

12:25). Their commitment had faded (10:32–34) and was replaced by spiritual laziness (5:11; 6:12; 12:3, 12–13). Some of the group had left (10:25). As second-generation Christians, they had come to believe in the gospel, but their hope was faltering because of their spiritual laxity (3:6; 6:18–20; 10:23–25). They were even in danger of apostasy (3:12; 6:4–6; 10:26–31). Hebrews is written as a sermon to early Christians who had allowed their challenges and circumstances to take their eyes off Jesus. It is a sensitive response to sagging faith.

At the core of Christian spirituality is relationship with God, which influences and determines a person's worldview. Spirituality connects being, knowing, and doing. Peter Toon comments, "The addition of the suffix 'ity' to a word usually has the effect of causing that word to express a state or condition. Thus, spirituality is the state/condition of being spiritual, that is of being indwelt and guided by the Holy Spirit."[5] There are three crucial components to early Christian spirituality: one's faith in Jesus Christ, the charismatic experience of the Holy Spirit, and agreement with the orthodox interpretation of the gospel. This spirituality was not simply to be kept internally, within one's mind, but was to be expressed as authentic and active faith. The readers of this epistle faced the danger of failing to move forward in their faith with the result that they could fall back into their old empty life of Judaism.

The purpose of spirituality in Hebrews is to call the readers to "perfection." The Greek word *teleios* and its derivatives are important in the epistle.[6] The word's basic meaning is something that has reached its highest standard or what it was meant to be. When used for spiritual development, it can mean maturity or not lacking anything.[7] It

---

5   Toon, *What Is Spirituality?*, 13.
6   The root *tele-* is used in various forms in 2:10; 3:14; 5:9, 14; 5:14; 6:1, 8, 11; 7:3, 11, 25; 9:9, 11; 10:1; 11:22, 40; 12:2.
7   Arndt et al., *A Greek-English Lexicon*, 995–96.

can be used in different contexts for different types of maturity and completion, including moral, physical, temporal, spiritual, and cultic situations.[8] Theologically, it is closely linked to holiness and being restored into the image of God.[9] Spirituality in Hebrews is a journey towards perfection.

The key exhortation in 6:1 captures the intent of the author and expresses the focus of the epistle: "Therefore, since we have moved on past the elementary teachings about Christ, let us be taken forward to maturity, not laying again the foundation of repentance from acts that lead to death, and of faith in God."[10] This epistle is a call to spiritual growth into "perfection." If the readers did not change their ways and grow in their faith, they were in danger of slipping back into disobedience. The author gives the strong and stern warning in 6:4-5 that it is "impossible for those who have once been enlightened, who have tasted the heavenly gift, and have shared in the Holy Spirit . . . and have fallen away . . . to be restored again to repentance."

There was only one way the readers could grow into perfection, and that was through faith in Jesus Christ. The spirituality in Hebrews is Christocentric. The author offers the life, death, resurrection, and exaltation of Jesus Christ as the answer to the readers' problems. The message about Jesus demands the response of faith. The author describes faith in 11:1 as believing in things that cannot be seen. The readers could not see Jesus in the flesh, so they had to trust in the author's words. They had experienced the power of the gospel but needed to look to Jesus, the author and perfecter of their faith (12:1-2). The only way they could strengthen their drooping hands and weak knees (12:12) was to put their complete trust in Jesus, which would require

---

8   Ackerman, "The High Priesthood of Jesus and the Sanctification of Believers," 230.
9   See also Peterson, *Hebrews and Perfection,* McCown, "Holiness in Hebrews," 58–78.
10 All translations of the Bible are the author's own.

total consecration, not a wavering faith. They needed to be *entirely* sanctified, not partially or initially. The salvation Jesus brings is not partial and should not leave people wandering in the desert of doubt. As 7:25 states, "He is able to save completely those who come to God through him because he always lives to intercede for them."

Spirituality in Hebrews sets the direction for how believers ought to live. With eyes focused on Jesus, their worldview and behavior would also change. They would have a new vision of God through the mediator, Jesus. Through Jesus, this community of believers could be transformed. No one would be left behind in the desert of doubt. They would find strength together to face persecution. Their love for one another would secure them against heresy. Their vision would be clear and their faith unshaken.

The Foundation: A Spirituality Based on Scripture

The symbolic world of the author appears to be heavily influenced by the Hebrew Scriptures. Since the author bases so much of his argument upon Scripture, it could be assumed that the readers shared in this symbolic world to some extent if this epistle was to have any impact upon them.[11] At the very core of this worldview was the problem of sin that separates humanity from God. God is holy, and only that which is holy can be in God's presence. Sin causes humanity to miss out on the salvation God offers. The only answer to the problem of sin is a sacrifice (9:14, 22, 26; 10:12, 14). Much understanding of Hebrews would be lost to the modern reader without entering into the world of the Old Testament. Many aspects of the author's rhetoric are lost without some prior understanding, particularly of Leviticus and the sacrificial system of Israel.

---

11 See Miller, "Paul and Hebrews," 246–47.

An Old Word as Witness

The Hebrew Scriptures are the author's key sources for supporting and developing his argument. He begins his sermon with a clear statement of belief that the Scriptures point to Jesus Christ. God spoke in the past through the prophets, but God has a new word for humanity. The "prophets" in 1:1 refer to Israel's prophets in the Old Testament. Like many early Christians, the author believed Scripture to be a witness to God's plan of salvation through the coming Messiah (2 Tim 3:15). There are seven statements about God's Son in 1:1—4: 1) he was appointed heir, 2) the world was created through him, 3) he is the radiance of God's glory, 4) he is the exact imprint of God's nature, 5) he upholds the universe by his powerful word, 6) he has made atonement for sin through his blood, and 7) he has been exalted to the right hand of God's throne.

The author's first proof in 1:5 is from Psalm 2, which was an important messianic psalm to early Christians (Acts 4:25-28). The emphasis in the first proof (vv. 5-14) highlights the Incarnate Son's superiority in his mediatorial work. This section contains seven quotations of Scripture that show the superiority of the Son, particularly over the angels: 1) Ps 2:7 in v. 5; 2) 2 Sam 7:14 in v. 5; 3) Deut 32:43 in v. 6; 4) Ps 104:4 in v. 7; 5) Ps 45:6,7 in vv. 8-9; 6) Ps 102:25-27 in vv. 10-12; and 7) Ps 110:1 in v. 13.

The author believed Scripture to be inspired by God and, therefore, quotes his selected texts with confidence, knowing that these words are from God. For example, the citation of Psalm 2:7 in 1:5 asks, "did God ever say?" Each of the quotations in ch. 1 refers to God speaking about the Son. In 1:7, the quotation of Psalm 95:1-11 attributes the text to the Holy Spirit. God spoke "through David" in a repeat of Psalm 95:11 in 4:7. God's word communicated through Scripture was not simply spoken to ancient Israel but was relevant to the readers of this epistle. Moreover, the word of God is described as "living and active" (4:12) because its message still applies to believers.

A New Word from God

The author views the Old Testament as valid and trustworthy, yet pointing to something even greater. The many citations and allusions to the Old Testament are not simply looking back in time at what happened long ago. These ancient words point ahead to something greater. The author uses the rabbinical method of *Qal wahomer*, from the lesser to the greater, to develop his argument. What was true in the Old Testament for Israel is even more true for believers today. The author will cite or reference certain events, people, or ideas from the Old Testament and show how Jesus and the salvation he brings are even greater. God's new word speaks even more loudly to the human need for redemption from sin.

One of the central themes of the Old Testament was fellowship with the Holy God. This relationship was broken in the garden of Eden when Adam and Eve ate the forbidden fruit. Later, God revealed himself to Israel through the exodus event and the revelation of the law. Part of the law included sacrifices intended to teach the people about God's holiness, love, and redemption. The sacrifices were how Israel could express their faith and dependence upon God's grace. The high priest could enter the holy of holies within the tabernacle only after his own sins and the sins of the people had been atoned for through sacrifice (5:3). This sacrifice was effective only as long as it was accompanied by faith. And this ritual had to be repeated every year (9:25). The sacrificial system was unable to perfect the consciences of the worshippers (9:6). By the end of the Old Testament, a separation still existed between the Holy God and sinful humanity.

The author builds his argument on the premise that Israel's sacrificial system was inadequate to deal with the deep human problem of sin. A greater sacrifice had to be offered. This sacrifice had to be on the human level—but without sin. There is only one person who has ever lived without sin, and that was Jesus, who became the perfect sacrifice by offering himself in obedience to the Father (7:27). Jesus is both the atoning sacrifice (2:17; 1 John 2:2; 4:10) and the one who offers the sacrifice. In 7:26, the author lists what qualifies Jesus to be the perfect high priest: "holy, innocent, unstained, separated from sinners, and exalted above the heavens." What was true only in part in the Old Testament has been fully fulfilled in Jesus Christ.

The author also uses typology alongside the *Qal wahomer* methodology. R.T. France defines typology as "the recognition of a correspondence between New and Old Testament events, based on a conviction of the unchanging character of the principles of God's working."[12] Three key personages serve as types for Jesus. The first is Moses in 3:3-6. Undoubtedly, Moses was one of the most significant persons in the Old Testament and a key figure for Jews as the giver of the law. The author emphasizes Moses' faithfulness "in all God's house," referring to the people of Israel. Moses was faithful as a servant, but Christ was faithful as a son. Moses was allowed to see God's fading glory, but Jesus has been exalted to the highest place of honor at the right hand of glory (1:13). The author uses this idea in transition to urge the readers to be faithful to God's promise of full salvation.

The author devotes significant attention from 6:20—7:28 to the typology of Melchizedek, the priest-king mentioned in Genesis 14:18-20 and Psalm 110:4. The author mentioned Melchizedek three times before this (5:6, 10; 6:20). Melchizedek was the king of ancient Salem (early Jerusalem) and the one to whom Abraham gave a tithe of the spoils that he won after defeating four kings and freeing his nephew Lot. The author reflects on the symbolism of this name in 7:2 as "king of righteousness" and "king of peace." The author builds his argument

---

12 France, *The Gospel According to Matthew*, 40, quoted by Klein, Blomberg, and Hubbard, *Introduction to Biblical* Interpretation, 182.

on what Scripture does not say about Melchizedek: he was without father or mother, without genealogy, without beginning of days or end of life, and remains a priest forever (7:3). All of these set him apart as a unique priest and king.

Melchizedek is a perfect person to compare to the limited Levitical priesthood and the sacrificial system they administered. The Levitical priests collected a tithe from the people, which represented the old covenant under the law. Melchizedek collected a tithe even though he was not a descendent of Levi (7:4, 6). This act of worship qualified him to be a forerunner of the new covenant and a "priest forever." He serves as the example of a new order of priesthood. The author uses logical argumentation to show that even Levi, in a sense, paid tithes and acknowledged the greatness of Melchizedek (7:9-12). The Levitical priests all died, but Melchizedek remains a priest forever (7:8). Everything the Levitical priesthood and the old system did was temporary. Something needed to happen, or someone greater had to come to solve the sin problem. Using Melchizedek in this way allows the author to do a "how much more" argument for the superiority of Jesus, who is in the unique priesthood of Melchizedek.

The readers were tempted to give up their faith in Jesus and return to Judaism. The author shows that Jesus is a better high priest than Judaism could provide. The Levitical priesthood was inadequate and could not bring perfection (7:11). It could not qualify one to draw near to the Holy God. If God's goals could have been accomplished through the Levitical priesthood, nothing else was needed. Psalm 110:4, however, shows that God's goals could not be met through the Levitical priesthood. A new priesthood was needed to open the way to God and make being in his presence possible. A changed priesthood needs a changed law. So, Jesus becomes the mediator of a new covenant that makes it possible to approach the very throne of grace in the presence of God (4:14-16). The author urges the readers to trust in this message and "draw near with a true heart in full assurance of faith with our hearts sprinkled clean from an evil conscience, and our bodies washed with pure water" (10:22).

A third notable rhetorical method is the repetition of various words translated as "therefore" in English. These words occur at critical points as the author moves from exposition or explanation to exhortation. For example, after quoting seven different Old Testament passages in ch. 1, the author applies the idea of the exaltedness of the Son in 2:1 with, "Therefore, it is necessary all the more to pay attention to the things we have heard so that we do not drift away." "On account of this" (*dia touto*) links the readers' situation to the words from God just quoted. "The things we have heard" refers to the message of salvation found in Jesus Christ (v. 2). An infinitive with its subject in the accusative carries an imperatival force with *dei:* "it is necessary . . . for us to pay attention." The danger of not heeding the words about the Son could cause the readers to drift away from salvation. Attention to the witness of Scripture about the Son is essential for maintaining salvation.

Another significant application is marked in 3:1 with "therefore" (*hothen*). This time, the author builds on his interpretation of Jesus' suffering and sacrificial death in 2:10–18 before making the application. This verse serves as a transition to the typology of Moses and exposition of Psalm 95. The key exhortation is simple but again identifies the central theme of the epistle: "Consider Jesus." Since Jesus became like we are through suffering, temptation, and death, we need to think more seriously about why he came. We must not turn away from him towards other beliefs or abandon our faith in him, and we must also grow in our understanding of the claims the Bible makes about him. This type of commitment is exactly the answer to all the readers' problems.

Another noteworthy application is made in 4:1 in the midst of the exposition of Psalm 95, which describes how the desert generation failed to enter the rest of God because they hardened their hearts. God's promise in Scripture of the "rest of faith" was available to the readers, but they were in the same position as the desert generation of not believing this promise. The author this time uses a hortatory subjunctive, "let us fear" (*phobēthōmen*), which has the force of a command. The focus of this fear was that some of the readers would fail to reach this promise, which was serious business and a real danger. This exhortation is repeated in 4:11, showing the importance of this idea to the author. The danger of not maturing into the sanctified life was real because of a lack of faith in Jesus.

With a fourth method, the author uses rhetorical questions at important locations to advance his argument and apply it to the readers. After the prologue, the author begins in v. 5 with two questions using Psalm 2:7 and 2 Samuel 7:14 that have the obvious answer that God has not said these things about anyone except the Son. A similar question is asked in v. 13, which right away challenges the readers to begin to think about the awesomeness of Jesus. One of the uses of rhetorical questions is to engage the listeners or readers in self-introspection. This self-analysis starts to build with the crucial question in 2:3, "How shall we escape if we ignore so great a salvation?" If the readers could not yet answer that, they should have had no doubt about the matter by the end of this epistle. There is no escape from God's judgment unless one puts his or her faith in Jesus Christ.

After citing Psalm 95 and using the rebellion of the desert generation at Kadesh Barnea as an example, the author asks a series of questions in 3:16–19. He asks three questions in these verses and then answers each in the form of another question. This string of questions moves the discussion along so that the author can emphasize the disobedience and unbelief of the Israelites (vv. 18b, 19), which were the very problems facing the readers. This concern becomes apparent as the author concludes this section with the assertion in 4:11, "Let us strive, therefore, to enter that rest, so that no one may fall by the same type of disobedience."

Another question at a turning point in the letter occurs in 7:11, where the author asks, if perfection (*teleiōsis*) could be obtained by the old priesthood and the old system of sacrifices, why would another priest need to come? The logic is that since another priest did come, namely Jesus, a new way has opened to perfection. The author shows that since the old covenant is obsolete and passing away, Jesus is the only way through a new covenant to experience this perfection. The issue becomes more critical with another serious question in 10:29, where the author warns about the severe danger of spurning the Son of God, profaning the blood of the new covenant, and outraging the Holy Spirit. The readers needed to look deeply within themselves to ensure there was no intentional sin (v. 26) that would bring judgment and keep them from salvation.

As the author begins to wind down the letter after having made a clear case for the superiority of Jesus and the need to put one's faith in him, he asks two more key questions in ch. 12. In 12:5, he includes the readers in his discussion of God's discipline. Since they are "sons," they should be prepared for God's love to be expressed as discipline if they do not reject sin and look to Jesus to perfect their faith (12:1–2). In a second question in the same section, the author shows that if the readers submit to God's plan, they will experience life.

There is continuity and discontinuity between the Son and the old system. The first covenant was spoken to us. The second covenant was spoken in us. The second covenant accomplishes what the first could not: a change of heart through purification from sin. The reference to "in these last days" in 1:2 gives a sense of finality. There is nothing more that needs to be said. Jesus is the last and perfect word God has been spoken and is all we need. This phrase also creates an eschatological sense of urgency that marks a decisive turning point in history. As 9:26 notes, Jesus has appeared "once and for all at the end of the age" as the final revelation.

At the heart of Hebrews' Christology is the affirmation that Christ is God's definitive word to the world because of his salvific death. Even though the author appeals to the authority of Scripture, there is an even more important word from God. The Son came as God's ultimate form of communication to us. The Son sustains everything through "his word of power" (1:3). This descriptive genitive mirrors a Hebraic construction and means "his mighty word." The Son sustains everything simply by his word. The infinite power and energy of God are present in the Son. This same power is now available to those willing to put their faith in Christ.

The Means: A Spirituality Focused on Christ

Spirituality in Hebrews is connected to Christology. The author argues that Christ is the only way to perfection. Perfection is growth into holiness by cleansing from sin and total commitment to Jesus Christ as the focus of faith and devotion. The importance of this journey of faith is expressed in the often quoted 12:14: "Pursue peace with everyone and the holiness without which no one will see the Lord." The question becomes, how can a person be made holy in order to be in the presence of the Holy God?

The answer is found in who Jesus is and what he has done. Jesus' redemption follows the pattern of a parabola, beginning with the high point of his divinity, followed by his descent to humanity, and finally ending with his exaltation. The pre-existent, eternal Son was one with the Father, highlighted particularly in ch. 1. The divinity of the Son is an important starting point because it stresses that what the readers heard had its origins with the eternal, almighty God. Chapter 2 begins the descent as the Son suffered death so that everyone might experience redemption (2:9). The theme of Jesus' humanness runs throughout the heart of the epistle. It is important in the author's argument to demonstrate that Jesus qualified as a high priest who can identify with us in our weaknesses (4:15). Through his victory over sin and death while on earth, Jesus opened the way to the Father and is exalted at the right hand of the throne of God, where he makes intercession for the people of God (7:25).

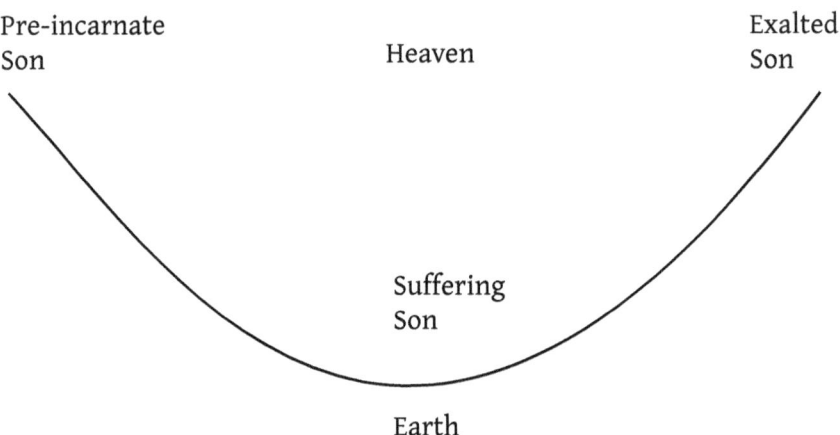

Jesus as the Perfect Human High Priest

Beginning in 2:5–18, the author focuses on Jesus' earthly life. He brought many people to "glory" through his suffering (v. 10). There is strong unity between Jesus and believers because both live in the flesh and face death. Jesus is first described as a "high priest" in 2:17, where the adjectives "merciful and faithful" emphasize the grace available through trusting in his atoning death and his obedience necessary to make this atonement worthy of what it seeks to accomplish. His suffering to the point of death secured for all time the forgiveness of sins. This theme is developed in more detail later in ch. 7. The image of a high priest would have been familiar throughout the Greco-Roman world, but the author chose his imagery from the Jewish Scriptures.

A priest's essential duty was to mediate between God and sinful humanity (Exod 29:44–45). To highlight the significance of Jesus as high priest, the author must show how the priesthood under the old covenant was problematic, inferior, and unable to bring people to perfection. There are several problems in appealing to the old system of sacrifices administered by the Levitical priesthood. For one, the author compares the inadequacy of the old covenantal system with the new way inaugurated by Jesus. A person became a priest by heredity and not merit (7:20). Jesus became high priest by an oath from God because he was perfect and the only one fit for this position (5:5; 7:21). Another problem is that the high priest was human and sinful and so had to offer sacrifices for his own sins (5:3; 9:7). Jesus did not offer a sacrifice for his sins but for the whole world (7:27). Third, the ministry of the priests was temporary because they each eventually died (7:23–24). Their ministration of sacrifices was only temporary and good for one year (9:7, 25), but Jesus' sacrifice was good for eternity (7:27). Fourth, the Levitical priests ministered in the earthly tent, but Jesus' ministry is in the heavenly tabernacle at the right hand of God, where he intercedes on behalf of humanity (8:1–6). Fifth, the sacrifice for atonement made by the high priests never allowed the people to go into the holy of holies (9:6–8). Sacrifices never took care of the real problem of sin and could not perfect the conscience (9:9). A better and sufficient sacrifice had to be made. Nothing on earth filled this void until Jesus came.

The author spends significant effort in the epistle demonstrating that Jesus is the only true and adequate solution to the problem of sin. The author builds on the imagery of the cultic system under the old covenant of Israel. Jesus is qualified as a high priest to represent humanity because he himself was fully human. The importance of this in the author's mind and in all of Christian theology cannot be overstated. Hebrews takes the full humanity of Jesus seriously. This premise is essential to the overall logic of the argument. Jesus became one with humanity in solidarity with our weaknesses (2:14, 18; 4:15). He learned obedience through suffering (5:8), which implies that he was not omniscient but had the same limitations as we do.

Jesus' suffering was how the Father made him perfect (2:10). In Hebrews, Christ's perfection was a vocational process by which he is made complete or fit for his office, not moral but existential. How did he become perfect through suffering? This process is the divine paradox because we would expect perfection through self-actualization and personal growth towards the highest attributes of humanity based on intellect and strength. Jesus' death is what made it possible for him to be our founder and was necessary for our salvation. What made him different was his complete trust in and reverence for the Father (5:7). He was holy and blameless (7:26), which qualified him to be exalted to the very throne of God. He is in a special category far beyond any human high priest. Such a high priest was needed who could bridge sinful humanity—but yet not tainted with human sin—and the holy God. Jesus' testing proved him to be God's Son and perfect advocate for humanity.

His perfection was consummated with his death and exaltation. His suffering opened the way to his exaltation. His journey to the cross conformed him to the will of the Father. The author's reflection on this in 5:5-10 echoes the same thought as Philippians 2:5-11. Jesus' journey to the cross is the same one we must take. The readers were experiencing increasing hardship and persecution. This epistle should have assured them that if they looked to Jesus, they would be able to endure these trials and temptations. McCruden comments, ". . . the reigning Lord who ministers in the heavenly sanctuary is also the human exemplar of what the shape of the journey to perfection looks like on this side of the age to come."¹³ Koester adds, "The exaltation that followed Jesus' passion gives listeners confidence that their own suffering is not the final word, but part of the way in which God is bringing them to glory."¹⁴ It is in the position of the right hand of God's throne that Jesus, the Son, makes intercession for humanity (7:25; 8:1). In the old system, only the high priest had access to God in the holy of holies, only on rare occasions. Jesus' access to God is continual and eternal. His priesthood is bound up in his heavenly status. His effectiveness as redeemer can be seen in the phrase, "passage through heaven" (4:14). For a relatively short book in the New Testament, Hebrews has a significant number (16) of references to heaven. Heaven is our goal, and the only way to get there is through the way opened by the Son (6:19–20). Bruce comments, "What God essentially is, is made manifest in Christ. To see Christ is to see what the Father is like."¹⁵ The Son's sacrifice qualifies him to be the mediator of the spiritual world. Our communion with the Father is channeled through the Son.

The Goal: A Spirituality Experienced through Active Faith

Undoubtedly, Jesus is at the center of this epistle. The author calls the readers to respond to Jesus in appropriate and needed ways. This response will be evident in active faith. The author highlights this need in the famous "faith" chapter 11. It was common Jewish practice to summarize Old Testament history to teach a lesson or give encouragement (see Acts 7). The author has an important lesson to teach his readers. They had faith, but this faith was weak and misdirected (10:39). "Faith" is defined in two ways in 11:1. First, it is "the assurance of things hoped for." The word "assurance" (*hypostasis*) first appears in 1:3 in reference to the Son being the exact "representation"

---

13 McCruden, *A Body You have Prepared for Me*, 63.
14 Koester, *Hebrews*, 236.
15 Bruce, *The Epistle to the Hebrews*, 6.

of the Father. The word is repeated in 3:14 for the "confidence" we can have because we have put our faith in Christ. The sense of this word is broad, and its meaning depends on its context. In a philosophical context, like 11:1, it refers to the reality or essence of something otherwise abstract or unseen.[16] Faith is hope put into action in the present in anticipation of things yet in the future. The readers hoped in heaven and could experience this hope in the present by faith in Jesus Christ.

Second, faith is "the conviction of things not seen." "Conviction" (*elengchos*) can be translated as "proof." Faith is believing that things that have not yet happened will indeed happen. "Faith does not do the convincing, but God, for the whole point in Hebrews is that faith stands on the revelation, word, and promise of God. Faith is the divinely given conviction of things unseen and is thus the assurance of what is hoped for."[17] Faith is assurance that God's promises in Scripture will come to pass because history has proven this to be true. This description of faith leads the author to give a brief account in the rest of ch. 11 of just how God's promises have come true throughout Israel's history.

One of the key messages of the whole epistle is the author's charge to the readers to stay true to the call of faith in Jesus Christ. Because of what Jesus had done for them and the claims about who he is, they needed to stay the course and not waver from their "confession" (4:14). Faith is the required response to the revelation of Jesus as the Messiah. The high point of the epistle comes at 12:1-2. The readers could look to the "great cloud of witnesses" for inspiration (12:1), but their focus needed to be on Jesus (12:2). The author calls the readers to "lay aside every weight and sin that easily causes tripping." The word "lay aside" is an aorist participle that has an imperatival force picked up in many translations. As an aorist, it indicates decisive action taken before the real imperative of the verse, "let us run." A person must set aside the

---

16 Kittel, Friedrich, and Bromiley, *Theological Dictionary of the New Testament*, 1237.
17 Kittel, Friedrich, and Bromiley, *Theological Dictionary of the New Testament*, 222.

old life of sin in the act of consecration and then run the race of holiness with eyes fixed on Jesus. The only way to run the race with confidence and success is to look to Jesus, who gives complete victory over sin. He is the only source of the sanctified life that qualifies us to be in God's presence and, thus, to get into heaven. This journey requires consecration, shown by rejecting and "taking off" (*apothemenoi*) the old ways (see Eph 4:22) of immaturity (6:1), which include rebellion and doubt. Looking to Jesus is the only way to run our race with *endurance* (*hypomenēs*), patience, and steadfastness. The participle "fixing one's eyes" (*aphorōntes*) is present tense, indicating that looking to Jesus is the way the race must be run. There is no other option for victory. If we take our eyes off him, we will get tripped up, discouraged, and even fall away. This shift of focus is essentially what faith is.

Jesus is the only solution to separation from the Holy God caused by sin. There is no other way any person can approach the throne of grace in the heavenly temple outside of the mediation of Jesus (8:6; 9:15; 12:24). That is because he is the "founder and perfecter of faith." This phrase in 12:2 is significant for the whole epistle and summarizes many important ideas of the author. As the founder, Jesus is the one who makes faith possible. In 2:10, the author calls Jesus, the "founder of our salvation." As the "founder" (*archēgon*), Jesus "began" or "initiated" the possibility for us to have faith. He set the pattern for us by his faithfulness to the point of death (2:14; 3:2) and makes it possible for us to have faith because he opened the way to the Father's throne of grace for us (10:19–20).

In addition, Jesus is the "perfecter" (*teleiōtēn*) of faith. It may be tempting to interpret the word "perfecter" in the sense of "completer," but in light of the important and frequent use of cognates of this word in this epistle, there is more implied here. Humanity's real problem is "easily besetting sin" (12:1). Sin is deceitful and results when persons reject faith and harden their hearts against God's conviction

(3:13). This problem is not new. In their trial in the desert and their rebellion against God, ancient Israel faced the same problem the readers faced. The account of Kadesh Barnea, summarized from Psalm 95 in chs. 3—4, is a timeless truth that gets deep into the human predicament. Jesus' sacrifice of his blood upon the cross is the only means of atonement (2:17). His blood inaugurated the new covenant through which God promises those who believe, "I will be merciful toward their iniquities, and I will remember their sins no more" (8:12). It is only through the perfect sacrifice of Jesus that the penalty of sin is removed, and the problem of sin is cleansed. Jesus provides the means for holy living through his sacrificial death and the model by his victory over temptation. It is noteworthy that the author uses the singular for *sin* (*hamartian*) in 12:1. Wiley comments, "The word has reference to 'sin' itself, the heart condition from which all sins flow."[18]

Verse 2 continues with how this change in the human situation is possible and in whom we must put our faith. There are four significant statements about what Jesus did to remove the problem of sin from the human condition. First, he joyfully went to the cross. We often think of the pain of the cross. The author focuses on Jesus' joy as he bore the sins of the world upon himself. He saw the final outcome. This joy was driven by his love for the Father and every person. He embodied the love of God and trusted in the Father for resurrection and exaltation. Second, with this joy and its implied love, he endured the cross. The author emphasizes Jesus' humanity and the real suffering and blood shed on the cross. The historical event of Jesus' death is paramount to the theology and message of this epistle. Third, Jesus despised the shame that came with dying on a Roman cross. He died in one of the most humiliating fashions of that time. It was not his own shame that he bore on the cross—because he had perfect faith in the Father, but it was our shame. Finally, he was exalted by the Father. The

---

18 Wiley, *The Epistle to the Hebrews*, 342.

verb "sat down" is aorist and shows the finality of Jesus' salvific work. His exaltation to "the right hand of the throne of God" shows the final outcome and ultimate goal: that God as Father and Jesus as Son might both be glorified. The ultimate goal of Jesus' descent to earth was to point people to the Holy God from whom they would find mercy and help.

In the next verse, the author brings this great message of salvation home to the readers with the imperative "consider carefully" (*analogisasthe*). The responsibility for spiritual growth and eternal life was in their hands. They had clearly heard the gospel presented in this epistle, and there should be no doubt about what their problem was. Whatever temptation, persecution, or questions they faced, they could turn to Jesus, where they would find answers to their greatest needs. Jesus showed a total dependence upon God. At the heart of the temptations he faced in the wilderness was the option to lessen his confidence in the Father. However, he was victorious over temptation because he looked to the Father for his source of strength. This total faith in God is at the heart of the call to holiness.

Jesus' atoning sacrifice purifies our hearts through our faith in him. In one of the last major theological imperatives, the author writes in 13:12–13, "And so Jesus also suffered outside the city gate in order to make the people holy through his own blood. So then, let us go out to him outside the camp, bearing the disgrace he bore." The call to "go out" challenges the decisive choice of faith. Jesus' blood makes the removal of sin and the cleansing of an evil conscience possible. McCruden comments, "What Hebrews rather enigmatically describes as the assurance of a cleansed conscience (9:14; 10:2, 22) stems from the religious experience of appropriating the response of faith in the power of the death and exaltation of Jesus."[19] There is no shortcut to this spirituality. As Long writes, "The weary congregation of Hebrews

---

19 McCruden, *A Body You have Prepared for Me*, 43.

longed for a gospel without a cross, a redemption without sacrifice, a faith without pain—something pristine and holy, something that does not exhaust the faithful with calls to put one foot in front of the other in daily obedience, something beautiful like an image of God in an unspoiled heaven surrounded by lovely angels singing untroubled hymns."[20]

The requirement for "perfection" (holiness) is the act of faith by drawing near to the throne of grace, coming "in our time of need" with boldness and confidence (4:16). This confidence is not in our own ability but in the blood of Jesus Christ. We have free access to mercy and grace, but we must yield to God's word in our lives so that we might take our eyes off of the world and look unto Jesus. God's mercy remains only a distant promise, like the land of Canaan, unless we act in the obedience of faith and accept this promise of full salvation. The path to the glory of God's presence is sanctification. Sanctification on earth leads to the glory of heaven. The infinite Son has become one of us so that we might share in his glory. Jesus is our leader in faith who has shown the way. He is the model of perfect faith and opens up the way of faith for us.

Bibliography

Ackerman, David. "The High Priesthood of Jesus and the Sanctification of Believers: New Covenant Possibility in Hebrews 7–10." *Wesleyan Theological Journal* 45:1 (Spring 2010): 226–45.

Anderson, Kevin L. *Hebrews*. New Beacon Bible Commentary. Kansas City: Beacon Hill, 2013.

Arndt, William, et al. *A Greek-English Lexicon of the New Testament and Other Early Christian Literature*. Chicago: University of Chicago Press, 2000.

---

20 Long, *Hebrews: Interpretation*, 22.

Bruce, F. F. *The Epistle to the Hebrews*. Grand Rapids: Eerdmans, 1997.

Eusebius, *Church History*, Translated with Prolegomena and notes by Arthur Cushman Mcgiffert. Lane Theological Seminary, 1890. Available online at http://prenicea.net/doc4/40201-en-01.pdf.

France, R.T. *The Gospel According to Matthew*. Grand Rapids: Eerdmans, 1985.

Kittel, Gerhard, Gerhard Friedrich, and Geoffrey William Bromiley, eds. *Theological Dictionary of the New Testament* abridged. Grand Rapids: Eerdmans, 1985.

Klein, William W., Craig L. Blomberg, and Robert L. Hubbard. *Introduction to Biblical Interpretation*. Nashville: Thomas Nelson, 2004.

Koester, Craig R. *Hebrews*. New York: Doubleday, 2001.

Lane, William L. *Hebrews 1-8*. Word Biblical Commentary. Dallas: Word, 1991.

Long, Thomas G. *Hebrews*. Interpretation: A Bible Commentary for Teaching and Preaching. Louisville: John Knox, 1989.

McCown, Wayne G. "Holiness in Hebrews." *Wesleyan Theological Journal* 16 (1981): 58–78.

McCruden, Kevin B. *A Body You have Prepared for Me: The Spirituality of the Letter to the Hebrews*. Collegeville: Liturgical Press, 2013.

Miller, James C. "Paul and Hebrews: A Comparison of Narrative Worlds." In *Hebrews: Contemporary Methods—New Insights*, edited by Gabriela Gelardini, Biblical Interpretation Series 75, 245–264. Leiden: Brill; reprinted Atlanta: Society of Biblical Literature, 2008.

Peterson, David. *Hebrews and Perfection: An Examination of the Concept of Perfection in the Epistle to the Hebrews*. Cambridge: Cambridge University Press, 1982.

Toon, Peter. *What Is Spirituality? And is it for Me?* London: Daybreak, 1989.

Wiley, H. Orton. *The Epistle to the Hebrews*. Kansas City: Beacon Hill, 1984.

PART II

THEOLOGICAL FOUNDATIONS

6

CHRISTLIKENESS AND SPIRITUALITY

Diane Cunningham Leclerc[1]

"Who do you say I am?" asked Jesus to his disciples. Even though Peter was able to articulate that Jesus is the Messiah in Matthew 16, it is only verses later that Peter is depicted as misunderstanding what kind of Christ Jesus would be, requiring Jesus' strong rebuke. It is further in the same chapter that we find Jesus' hard words about his own suffering and death and his address about disciples losing and saving their lives, the basis of spiritual discipleship. We can say that Peter misread the real need of his own culture and missed that Jesus would be the Savior of the whole world, not through political overthrow but through his own shame, degradation, and abandonment. At Pentecost, it is clear that Peter then fully understood the identity of Jesus and preached a sermon that resulted in thousands being baptized. He was preaching to a crowd made up of at least fifteen different cultures.

---

1   Floyd Cunningham's sister; Professor of Historical Theology at Northwest Nazarene University.

They heard the witness of Jesus' disciples in their own language and cultural paradigms.

To say that Jesus Christ transcends cultural differences, while certainly true, misses the deeper truth that he meets people *in* their cultural situations and that the gospel is culturally germane, always. "All human beings are cultural beings. Jesus must be culturally relevant if he is really to be understood and appreciated. This is a most obvious fact, unfortunately only too often overlooked."[2] Culture had been largely neglected in the past when it came to evangelizing people and communicating theology.[3] In other words, the gospel that was disseminated by European and North American missionaries was non-contextualized.[4] This was certainly the case in Asia, as in all non-Anglocentric cultures in the world during western expansion. The failure to contextualize the message was, unfortunately, only one of the outrageous sins of imperialism. "It was largely colonization and evangelicalism in tandem that brought and propagated the Western understanding of Jesus in Asia. Not only was it foreign to Asia, but it was also an understanding which was polemical against non-Christian religions, disrespectful of indigenous cultures, and insensitive to the injustices which colonization brought about."[5] While most Christian denominations have now recognized the egregious nature of such an aggressive and domineering Christianity that was tied to colonialism, we can look back and see disturbing aspects of a non-contextualized message going out in the relatively short history of the Church of the Nazarene.[6] While it is not the point of this chapter to outline such offenses, caution must be taken not to revert to the sins of our forefathers and mothers. A key way to avoid this is to do theology with the

---

2   de Mesa, "Making Salvation Concrete and Jesus Real," 1.
3   de Mesa, "Making Salvation Concrete and Jesus Real," 1
4   Phan, "Jesus the Christ with an Asian Face," 399.
5   de Mesa, "Making Salvation Concrete and Jesus Real," 2.
6   See Cunningham, *Holiness Abroad*.

context in full view, allowing it to inform the process and even to form its theological and practical conclusions.

The chapter here seeks to offer insights and suggestions for doing Christology in an Asian context, all the while confessing that mine is not an Asian voice. It seeks to address three major questions. First, what have Asian theologians been intuiting and construing about Christology recently? Second, are there potentially contextual Wesleyan-Holiness-Nazarene Asian theological methodologies and Christologies to be had today? And third (and most important), what connections can we make between such a theology and spirituality in light of the holiness message of Christlikeness as the goal of perfect love?

Asian Christology

The fact is Christianity in Asian countries is still very small in contrast to the plethora of other Asian religions and their adherents. There are many reasons for this, some hypothetical, others more tied to statistics and concrete realities. Timoteo Gener, an evangelical Filipino scholar, suggests this: "The close identification in Asia with Euro-American colonization and the church's corresponding lack of rootedness in Asian cultures is likely a major factor for the persistence of this minority status."[7] He also believes that a lack of authentic contextualization can make Asian Christians look like (Western) missionary clones.[8] Peter Phan intimates that Asian Christologies must produce peculiarly Asian Christian lives. To counter the westernized flavor, he says that Christian praxis needs to be found not only in the conclusions of a specific Christology but also in the very method used to attain such Christology. "Insistence on praxis as part of the theological method, along with social and psychological analysis, assures the

---

7   Gener, "Christologies in Asia," 150.
8   Gener, "Christologies in Asia," 150.

adequacy of an Asian Christology for Asia."[9] Gener concurs. "The true test of any Christology is in how it assists authentic following of Christ in one's own context."[10] Adonis Gorospe emphasizes that "All authentic mission flows from a spirituality that fosters Christlikeness in the believer . . . thus spiritual formation is the spring from which mission flows."[11] If as Wesleyans we are searching for the call to Christlikeness as the goal of spirituality as Wesleyans, contextualization both feeds a specific culture's expression of spirituality while also aiding the goal of spirituality: contextualized mission.

And so, what are the contextualized Asian sources for Asian theology? The first thing to recognize, of course, is that Asia is not a monolithic culture. "Given [the] cultural and linguistic diversity, 'Asian' theology defies description and neat categorization. Nevertheless, there exists throughout Asia . . . a common religio-cultural heritage and similar sociopolitical context"[12] necessary to do more generalized theologizing. Several scholars agree that the two most important factors to consider are: 1) the deep, widespread poverty in Asia and 2) the tremendous religious plurality, whether coming from a liberationist or an evangelical perspective.[13] Each Asian country is filled with severely impoverished people, indeed the poorest of the poor. In order to be pertinent to Asian realities, any valid theology must take extreme poverty into account. Likewise, Asia is home to multiple religions that are embedded in Asian culture and not easily extracted. Religious symbols, icons, figures, thought forms, language, and idioms flow freely, are easily exchanged, and permeate culture itself. In other words, syncretism between culture and religion is not only unavoidable; it is made up of multiple religions at once. Other sources

---

9 Phan, "Jesus the Christ with an Asian Face," 425.
10 Gener, "Christologies in Asia," 16.
11 Gorospe, "Spiritual Formation and the Contextualization of Christology," 48–49.
12 Phan, "Jesus the Christ with an Asian Face," 400.
13 See de Mesa, Phan, and Gener.

for doing Christology in an Asian context include a history of violence from outside and between Asian countries; the often cruel subjection of women; the monastic tradition of Buddhism; the quest for freedom from political oppression; the communal nature of culture over against Western narcissism; and the existence of Han throughout Asia (not just in Korea), to name a few.[14] The following Christological images are variations on the desire to take Asian contextualization seriously.[15] Each of the Christologies listed below finds commonality in how Jesus can speak to, but also very much live within, a suffering people.

Jesus as the Poor Monk

It has been said above that one of the main two sources of Asian contextualization is the categorical and unrelenting experience of the poverty of the masses. This widespread and debasing poverty is the product of oppression and injustice that can be traced back to centuries of strife, as well as to present-day sociopolitical factors that continue to foster such subjugation. "What can Christianity and Christian theology do with and say to teeming millions of Asians, most of whom are crushed by abject poverty and live in dehumanizing squalor?"[16] A more incisive question might be, "What can Christian theologians who are not poor say to billions of Asian poor who are not theologians?"[17] Peter Phan answers these questions by pointing to a cultural symbol that has non-Christian but strongly religious roots. Voluntary poverty has been embraced by some of the religious as a means of true empathy and seeks to enter into the suffering of the poor for the purposes of solidarity and liberating activity. This brings us to the image of the

---

14 See Phan, "Jesus the Christ with an Asian Face," Moon, "Genealogy of the Modern Theological Understanding of Han," 419–35. Moon suggests strongly that Han be utilized by all Asian countries as a means of defining suffering.

15 I am mostly dependent on Peter Phan for these suggestions. Also See Gener's discussion in "Christologies in Asia: Trends and Reflections."

16 Phan, "Jesus the Christ with an Asian Face," 402.

17 Phan, "Jesus the Christ with an Asian Face," 402.

"poor monk." Buddhist monks are a very public symbol. The monk is the "quintessential renouncer of mammon for religious reasons. . . . so that he may help the poor."[18] Aloysius Pieris suggests that Jesus was/is also a poor monk who can radically transform the oppressive social structures operated by "mammon." According to Pieris, "Only the Jesus who has been baptized in the Jordan of religiousness and on the cross of poverty can acquire an authentically Asian face."[19] "The door once closed to Jesus in Asia is the only door that can take him in today, namely, the soteriological nucleus or the liberative core of various religions that have given shape and stability to our cultures."[20] The Christology of the poor monk represents the goals of most religions, love, and wisdom. Such a view of Jesus must be followed by Christians as well. Only as the church embraces voluntary poverty and a more generalized religiosity will it be able to speak into the sociopolitical oppression of mammon, which continually keeps the poor oppressed.

Jesus as the Marginal Person Par Excellence

This image, as well as the next two, are very similar in what they are trying to communicate. The common theme is that Jesus has unlimited capacity for empathy for the oppression of the masses; he identifies with and represents the people to both God and evil oppressors. Jung Young Lee combines a Taoist philosophical model with his own experiences as an immigrant in the U.S. He describes this experience as being on the margin of society rather than in the center. But it is crucial to his work to distinguish between the definition of marginality imposed on the people by those in the center and the definition that comes from the marginalized people themselves. "The people-on-the-margin as described by the central people . . . have been diagnosed as products of an inferiority complex . . . with its symptoms

---

18 Phan, "Jesus the Christ with an Asian Face," 409.
19 Phan, "Jesus the Christ with an Asian Face," 408.
20 Pieris, *An Asian Theology of Liberation*, 59.

of ambivalence, excessive self-consciousness, restlessness, irritability, moodiness, lack of self-confidence, [and] pessimism."[21] This is, of course, an explanation imposed on them by the more powerful, which seems almost necessary to marginality—having others define the people rather than allowing for self-definition. But when the marginalized do define themselves, a certain amount of power emerges. When it comes to Christology, Lee "points out that Jesus' question, 'Who do you say that I am?' has been consistently wrongly answered in the history of Christianity because Jesus was understood from the perspective of centrality. Traditionally he was regarded as the 'center of centrality.' On the contrary, Lee argues that Jesus is 'a new marginal person par excellence.'"[22] In this model, we not only have Asian contextualization at play, but we also have the facts of history. Jesus *was* marginal as a Jew under Roman occupation, as a Jew from Nazareth rejected by his own people, and ultimately as a shamed criminal nailed to a cross outside the city. His empowerment came, ironically, from his willing *kenosis*—self-emptying—to accept his position as a slave who experienced harassment and humiliation. "Jesus' death symbolizes tragedy, failure, disappointment, and darkness."[23] But this is not the end. His resurrection "symbolizes hope, joy, and life," and "With resurrection . . . Christ transcends all marginality. . . . With resurrection, Jesus-Christ is a new humanity."[24]

Jesus as the Crucified People

In his article, "Jesus the Christ with an Asian Face," Peter Phan offers images of Christ that are relevant for the Asian context by discussing Choan-Seng Song's portrait of Jesus as the rejecter of wrong views about God. Song argues that Jesus had a "people hermeneutic"

---

21 Phan, "Jesus the Christ with an Asian Face," 414.
22 Phan, "Jesus the Christ with an Asian Face," 415.
23 Phan, "Jesus the Christ with an Asian Face," 416.
24 Phan, "Jesus the Christ with an Asian Face," 416.

that saw the plight of the people as they were and thus communicated to them that God is a God who loves them. According to Phan, "Song discovers that central to Jesus' teaching and experience is his rejection of a God of retribution, the God defended by Job's friends, and his affirmation of God as Abba, the God of merciful love."[25] Further, "Choan-Seng Song derives much of his inspiration from the stories, real and mythological, of the people oppressed by both church authorities and sociopolitical powers."[26] Song says, "The cross is the suffering of Jesus of Nazareth and it is the suffering of humanity. . . . The cross is the plot of an organized religion blinded by its own power and orthodoxy and unable to tolerate those deeply and sincerely religious persons. . . . The cross discloses the complicity and sociopolitical powers ready to defend their self-interest at any cost."[27] The cross then represents the killing of the people along with the killing of Jesus. Jesus' God is inclusive of all those who are rejected and abandoned by others. The most important question is not who Jesus is, but with whom does Jesus identify? In sum, to know Jesus is to know crucified people—the most exploited and oppressed—and to work against such exploitation.

Jesus as the Minjung within the Minjung

Chung Hyun Kyung writes an Asian theology for Asian women. She points out that within the oppressed people of Asia, Asian women are further oppressed. They are the "minjung *within* the minjung." They are dominated and suppressed by others of the minjung and take the lowest rung of the low rungs of oppression. And therefore, common images of Christ in Asian women's theology include that of a liberator and revolutionary; the compassionate mother; as a priestess who helps them with their pain; and "Finally, because Asian women are often forced to bear an overwhelming share of back-breaking labor,

---

25 Phan, "Jesus the Christ with an Asian Face," 418.
26 Phan, "Jesus the Christ with an Asian Face," 418
27 Phan, "Jesus the Christ with an Asian Face," 418

not only in the home but also in factories, Christ is also depicted as a worker enduring the despair and humiliation of unskilled laborers."[28]

If not already evident, it should be pointed out that the images of Christ given thus far come out of the premises of liberation theology that preference the context even over tradition. Liberation theologies have proclaimed for decades that context deeply affects theological conclusions. Yet, even after presenting and advocating for these Asian liberation Christologies, Peter Phan can still say that "A cavalier dismissal of patristic and medieval Christologies would impoverish Asian Christologies by neglecting their genuine insights . . . a thorough knowledge of them may spare Asian Christology the mistakes and deficiencies for which Asian theologians have criticized Western Christologies."[29]

Timoteo Gener reflects on the trends of Asian Christologies, especially pointing out dozens of images that come from other Asian religions. He offers over a dozen Christologies that are directly connected to Hinduism, then Buddhism, then Islam, where the religious ideas of each directly inform varying metaphors for Christ; for example, Jesus as *Jivanmukta* (One who has attained liberation while alive). He acknowledges the great benefit of the liberationist lens but also believes that Evangelical theologians avoid Marxist-driven liberation theologies by developing Christology that takes Scripture as its foundation but utilizes experience as a conversation partner, namely Asian experience.[30] He advocates for what he calls "missional Christology." In this type of Asian Christology, context is on more equal footing with Scripture/tradition, if not ultimately more important.

---

28 Phan, "Jesus the Christ with an Asian Face," 423.
29 Phan, "Jesus the Christ with an Asian Face," 430.
30 Gener, "Christologies in Asia," 153.

Missional Christologies

In 1991, Floyd T. Cunningham published an article entitled "Christ, the Word, the Light, and the Message" (parts of which he also preached on several occasions). In it, he models such a missional Christology. What we find in the article is an overview of classical doctrines such as sin and salvation. He avoids an exclusivist position in regard to the gospel, planting his missiology firmly in the *via media* of Wesley while also avoiding a type of pluralism sometimes found in liberationist paradigms. What Cunningham focuses on most is the doctrine of prevenient grace in a Wesleyan framework; here, we find his answer to the question of the usefulness of other world religions. God can work through them to draw people toward God's redeeming love. We also find keen insights regarding the life to which missionaries are called, and he extends his Christology appropriately to a theology of spirituality. "The Wesleyan tradition stands to offer an evangelical theology of mission which takes into serious and sympathetic account the cultural predicaments of human beings. And while vitally concerned with the 'telling' of the gospel well, historically it has been as equally committed to the 'living' of the gospel."[31]

Jesus Christ the Word

When offering his readers the image of Jesus as the Word, Cunningham is making direct reference to the first chapter of John. The Word is God and was with God in the beginning. And it was through the Word that the world was created. The world, or earth, has the ability to reveal God. Although he does not name it, his thoughts are very attuned to Aquinas' idea of natural revelation: "Even those not privy to the stream of revelation in the Hebrews' history of salvation are enabled by grace to perceive something of God."[32] But even beyond the

---

31 Cunningham, "Christ, the Word, the Light, and the Message," 10.
32 Cunningham, "Christ, the Word, the Light, and the Message," 11.

existence of God as revealed in nature, the Word is the one all persons have longed and yearned for; we see this in the quest for truth—as in religious philosophies—or in the searchings of the common person's heart. This is the evidence of God's prevenient grace. And so is humanity's moral center, seen in both law and conscience.

Cunningham highlights that Wesley asserts that God is at work among those who are not explicitly Christian, among those who do not know Christ's name, through the law; for Wesley, the restoration of the law was God revealing his own heart—that God is still compassionate toward the lost.[33] Prevenient grace also enlightens the human conscience. Here Cunningham shows how Wesley counters Augustine, although not naming him. Wesley affirms the doctrine of original sin, no doubt. But according to Augustine, human nature and will are totally depraved, and the person has no option but to sin. Here the question can be raised, if original sin causes us to sin necessarily, how can God justly condemn us for what we cannot help but do? Wesleyans have an answer. "Prevenient grace enabled individuals to keep the law, so that everyone was accountable for the moral insight received. No one, not even non-Christians, has any excuse for sinning"[34] because they have been given, as a gift, what is needed to obey the law. Both the external law of one's culture and the internal law of one's conscience offer enough to make a person accountable for sin, thus maintaining God's justice. The Word, then, is manifested in the creation, in law, and in the conscience.

Jesus Christ the Light

Jesus is the light of the world. "There is a radiance from the Light sufficient to account for the impulses in the religions and cultures of the world which seem to be in some accord with [special] revelation."[35]

---

33 Cunningham, "Christ, the Word, the Light, and the Message," 14.
34 Cunningham, "Christ, the Word, the Light, and the Message," 14.
35 Cunningham, "Christ, the Word, the Light, and the Message," 18.

Here Cunningham moves from the individual to collective religions and cultures as being places where partial truth can indeed be detected. "If the Holy Spirit is active preveniently on an individual basis, then the Holy Spirit must also be active collectively. The 'collective conscience' of a culture may reflect in some ways how the Holy Spirit has been at work."[36] The same can be said of a particular culture's religion(s). Cunningham moves from a descriptive to a prescriptive tone: "Cross-cultural ministers must not evangelize by opposing cultures, if the Holy Spirit has already been at work in them, but must find continuities between the revealed gospel and the structures of society. By listening to culture, by attentively understanding its form and depths of meaning, they may discover just how the Holy Spirit has been working."[37] Here Cunningham quotes Nikolas Zinzendorf, who wrote in the 1700s and was influential on the spiritual life of John Wesley: "If we tell a savage of his Savior, the Holy Spirit has surely been there ten years before; and if we get so far as to speak one intelligible word, we are witnesses of the Holy Spirit. We assure them of that which they had long ago, only they could not read it or express it; we emphasize it, we put the seal upon it. We simply assist the Holy Spirit in his work."[38] This is an expression of Jesus as the light of the world. It is Jesus' Holy Spirit who shines into the heart of all people and who can also be found in the world's religions, although incompletely. Prevenient grace is drawing persons to God, even if God remains veiled. When the gospel is then spoken, prevenient grace reveals that Jesus is the Life they have been seeking and the cure for the curse of their sin. Christ is then accepted or rejected. But it is crucial to remember that this acceptance of Christ is not an acceptance that displaces a person's cultural realities and replaces them with the cultural assumptions of

---

36 Cunningham, "Christ, the Word, the Light, and the Message," 21.
37 Cunningham, "Christ, the Word, the Light, and the Message," 22.
38 Cunningham, "Christ, the Word, the Light, and the Message," 22.

those presenting the gospel. Wesleyans cannot stand in a position, to use Richard Niebuhr's model, of Christ against culture.

Jesus Christ the Message

In Cunningham's final section, he turns more directly to the subject of holy living. Jesus, as Word and Light, is obviously the Message—Jesus is the answer to all philosophical, religious, and personal seeking. But, in closing, Cunningham focuses on the messengers of the message, namely Christians who are ministering in cultures other than their own, namely missionaries. Keeping to the first chapter of John, he reminds us that the attitude of John the Baptist is important as a model. "John the Baptist's humility is an example. Ministers and missionaries must have the same spirit of honesty and humility, letting those among whom they minister know that they are unworthy servants of the one about whom they witness. Unfortunately, this is not always the case, and it is too easy to allow hearers to think of them too highly."[39] He says that there is already a sense of inferiority in the Two-Thirds world to those who come from the First-World West. Cunningham is appropriately incisive here: "Missionaries arrive out of the sky in jets, drive up to shacks and bamboo churches in airconditioned cars and live lives which seem to most of the people among whom they work luxurious, lavish, and wasteful."[40] Instead, the minister or missionary must "exhibit a 'crucified mind, emptied of self.' . . . There must be an incarnation theology of mission wherein missionaries lose themselves for the sake of others as they take up the cross of Christ."[41] Indeed, telling the gospel must be matched by living the gospel. In terms of "spirituality," the kenotic life of the messengers will verify the message of the Crucified One. Floyd Cunningham wrote the article just discussed when he was thirty-seven years old and not ten years into his career as

---

39 Cunningham, "Christ, the Word, the Light, and the Message," 24.
40 Cunningham, "Christ, the Word, the Light, and the Message," 24.
41 Cunningham, "Christ, the Word, the Light, and the Message," 24.

a missionary. His words still ring true, especially in his call for living a truly holy and Christlike life.

Nazarene Christologies and Spiritualities for Asia

While it is theologically and historically based and prophetically spoken, in light of the fact that Cunningham wrote the above-quoted article in 1991, it is a legitimate question to ask if we might develop other evangelical, missional, Wesleyan, Holiness, and Nazarene Christologies presently to aid in our quest toward a Christologically-formed practice of spirituality. The following are simply proposals that seek to harmonize missional ideals with liberationist perspectives (which many scholars believe are attuned to Wesleyan principles). Hopefully, it will be evident how connected these proposals are to practical Christian living, that is, as examples of theological and spiritual praxis.

The Christ of the Poor

The images of Jesus as the poor monk, Jesus as the par excellent marginal person, Jesus as the crucified people, and Jesus as the minjung within the minjung, all share in the common concern of *abject poverty* and oppression, which has been named as one of the main cultural realities to consider in the development of pertinent Christologies for Asia. Every Asian country has experienced the veracity of masses of poor people as a historical and present problem. Does Christ have anything to say in the midst of this dire situation? These liberation Christologies share the sense of Christ's solidarity with the situation. But more so, while it is possible to stand in solidarity from a distance, Christ, in his condescension and incarnation, entered into human life and experienced poverty for himself. And in his death, he shows his unrelenting capacity for true empathy toward those who suffer. But an implicit spirituality in these Christologies is what can be explicitly seen in the original vision of the Church of the Nazarene. From the

Covenant of Christian Conduct section of the *Manual,* we find these words:

> The Church of the Nazarene believes this new and holy way of life involves practices to be avoided and redemptive acts of love to be accomplished for the souls, minds, and bodies of our neighbors. One redemptive arena of love involves the special relationship Jesus had, and commanded His disciples to have, with the poor of this world; that His Church ought, first, to keep itself simple and free from an emphasis on wealth and extravagance and, second, to give itself to the care, feeding, clothing, and shelter of the poor and marginalized. Throughout the Bible and in the life and example of Jesus, God identifies with and assists the poor, the oppressed, and those in society who cannot speak for themselves. In the same way, we, too, are called to identify with and to enter into solidarity with the poor. We hold that compassionate ministry to the poor includes acts of charity as well as a struggle to provide opportunity, equality, and justice for the poor. We further believe the Christian's responsibility to the poor is an essential aspect of the life of every believer who seeks a faith that works through love. We believe Christian holiness to be inseparable from ministry to the poor in that it drives the Christian beyond their own individual perfection and toward the creation of a more just and equitable society and world. Holiness, far from distancing believers from the desperate economic needs of people in this world, motivates us to place our means in the service of alleviating such need and to adjust our wants in accordance with the needs of others.[42]

What we first find here is the ministry of Jesus to the poor. Indeed, "God identifies with and assists the poor, the oppressed, and those

---

[42] Church of the Nazarene *Manual,* 28.3.

in society who cannot speak for themselves. But Jesus intended such ministry to continue on by his disciples. In the same way, we, too, are called to identify with and to enter into solidarity with the poor." This manifests itself in working in compassionate ministry but also in working toward equality and justice. Perhaps the most challenging but absolutely true point is that "Christian holiness [is] inseparable from ministry to the poor." In other words, one cannot claim to be holy and neglect the needs of the world, which includes economic needs. This should motivate us "to place our means in the service of alleviating such need and to adjust our wants in accordance with the needs of others."

I would venture to say that most Nazarenes do not even realize this is part of the *Manual*, let alone in the section on exactly what holiness ethics look like. "Living simply" and "adjust[ing] our wants in accordance with the needs of others" are severely neglected if we believe "Christian holiness [is] inseparable from ministry to the poor" to be true. Financial giving is, of course, only one way to measure the self-sacrificial nature of Christ and the holy life to which he has called us. But it is an important part. If a potential Asian Christology of the "Christ of the poor" is to be worth anything, Nazarenes need to grasp a vision of Christ's ministry to the poorest of the poor and to all who were oppressed by others and understand that a holiness without self-sacrifice is a "cheap grace" indeed. But a true and authentic holiness spirituality that is nurtured in the life of a believer breaks open in solidarity with, empathy for, and action toward the poor and oppressed, as it did in Wesley's day, in the radical ethics of the Holiness Movement and in the original principles of the Church of the Nazarene.

The Christ of Full Salvation and Ultimate Healing

Filipino scholar, Jose M. de Mesa, outlines a contextual methodology to help individual communities name their image of the Christ of salvation. He wants to encourage Christian churches, culturally situated, to find a contextualized understanding of Christ's salvation that they will follow through spiritual devotion because it speaks into their cultural imagination. In order to find their image of Christ, de Mesa shows how important images are in the process. If the good, the delightful, and grace-filled can be imagined as a "rooster who brings back the sun to this dark world" by the community of Pangasinan, Philippines, and "clean, fresh water" as that which enables people to live and be supported by their livelihood, "Then Jesus, perhaps, would be indeed real to people of the cultural contexts" as light and as living water. "Christology needs to be intimately linked with the culture, the particular way of feeling, thinking and behaving of a given people."[43] He continues, "Would the significance of Jesus not be more intelligible and meaningful to women who are battered or physically abused and who perceive their condition as 'being asphyxiated' or strangled . . . if Jesus and the 'salvation' he brings are presented in terms of being able to breathe well?"[44] De Mesa's methodology, then, is to have each community give a picture or image to the evil they are suffering and to a corresponding saving image. This might be a good practice to follow as missionaries to Asia attempt to spread the gospel. To generalize what de Mesa wants to specify in each community, Nazarene theology and spirituality affirm that *Christ is the God of Full Salvation.*

Not only does Jesus save us from sin by forgiving our transgressions, but he sanctifies us by his Spirit, making our salvation full or "complete." The sin nature is cleansed and no longer in control; love now reigns. John Wesley's imagination led him to see sin as a malady through "Inbeing Sin" and as a disease or plague that needs to be healed. "If the crucial problem of sin is not just guilt but the spiritual debilitation and affliction of the human person, then salvation

---

43 de Mesa, "Making Salvation Concrete and Jesus Real," 1.
44 de Mesa, "Making Salvation Concrete and Jesus Real," 1.

must involve more than pardon; it must also be healed."[45] In this sense, *Christ is our Ultimate Healer*.

But there is another sense in which we can be healed. Pertinent to Asian oppression, we can ask the question, "Does Christ have anything to say, not only to the sinner, but also to the sinned-against?" According to Korean theologian Andrew Sung Park, the *sinned-against* are victims who experience Han.[46] Victims of violence, abuse, poverty, and various forms of oppression come in all shapes and sizes, and victims stand in need of "salvation"—as healing, redemption, and liberation—often desperately. All victims need liberation in some way, in the sense of being freed from a disempowering and dehumanizing woundedness. All need the liberation of being re-humanized and re-dignified. This is no less a need for *full salvation* and *ultimate healing* than those who seek forgiveness.

It is crucial to realize that to address the needs of victims, we do not have to find another salvation narrative. The cross retains potent capacity as a strong metaphor for the sinned-against. Yet the narrative of the cross needs to be told differently and reimagined differently. The symbolism is there; it needs to be "brought to bear" (up under) the victimized. At Golgotha, Jesus was abused. His hands and feet were nailed. His muscles and sinews tore under the weight. His "crown" bled. He suffocated slowly. He refused any analgesic. He died there an excruciating death so that he might fully enter into human suffering.

In the shadows, we "see" hidden Asian people look on with keen perception of the pain, for they are familiar with its visceral reality. They truly understand. Who are they? They are the children huddling in their closets, praying that their father will not come tonight and do

---

45 Maddox, *Responsible Grace*, 145.
46 See Park, *The Wounded Heart of God*. Han is an untranslatable word that means deep pain and suffering, mixed with despair and bitterness. It is a concept used in Korean theology but can be used more broadly.

unspeakable, truly violating things to them. We see the woman in the mirror trying to cover the bruises with makeup, to no avail. We see an Asian young woman running naked down a back road in Vietnam. We can see a man instantly incinerated by nuclear fire in Hiroshima. We see in skeleton people intense Han that needs to be healed. We see beaten children, rape victims, the dismembered and neglected bodies of veterans, the elderly who die alone in rank conditions, slaves of all kinds, the diseased, the desperate, and the despised. We see people—intermingled yet solitary—who tentatively and slowly dare to move toward the front, toward the foot of the cross, and quietly beckon: "Speak to *me*!" Jesus is the Christ of Full Salvation and Ultimate Healing for those at the "backside of the cross." Do Nazarenes have anything to say or do here?

Phan is clear that "There are . . . essential steps that must be performed as constitutive parts of an Asia theology: personal commitment to and active solidarity with the teeming masses of poor and oppressed Asians in their struggle for justice and liberation." What is constitutive of theology is even more essential in how we are to live out of our holiness spirituality. Our theology must be practiced! Have we experienced our own full salvation and anticipate our ultimate healing? Are we walking with the Christ who sanctifies us to love? If so, Cunningham's words will ring fresh in our ears today: "The Word became flesh and dwelt for a while among men and women. He forms the model and pattern of ministry. The servant model of ministry . . . must also be the model [for us]. There must be an incarnational theology of mission wherein [we] lose [ourselves] for the sake of others as [we] take up the cross of Christ. . . . The ideal of past generations, of going to the lost world no matter the cost materially and of being willing to suffer, is not outdated."[47]

---

[47] Cunningham, "Christ, the Word, the Light, and the Message," 25.

Conclusion

If we follow Cunningham's advice and agree that the kenotic life of the messenger verifies the gospel, we must also recognize that he himself has been an excellent model of a holy, self-emptying, gentle, generous, and Christlike messenger, as he has poured his life into his students, colleagues, and Filipino communities. "All authentic mission flows from a spirituality that fosters Christlikeness in the believer."[48] Cunningham displays such Christlikeness as a result of a deep and abiding holiness spirituality. He is a "living reminder"[49] of what God can do with a life fully devoted to him. In a sense, Cunningham *is* APNTS, having been there from the beginning of its nearly 40-year history and having served as professor, dean, VPAA, and President. Anyone who knows him would readily speak of his Christlike humility. The Philippines has become his country and his culture as he has lived among the people in mutuality and love for decades. How does one retire from this? We'll have to watch him.

Bibliography

Cunningham, Floyd T. "Christ, the Word, the Light, and the Message: A Wesleyan Reflection on World Mission." *Evangelical Review of Theology* 16 (June 1992):10-27.

―――. *Holiness Abroad: Nazarene Missions in Asia*. Lanham: Scarecrow, 2003.

De Mesa, Jose. "Making Salvation Concrete and Jesus Real: Trends in Asia Christology." *Exchange* 30 (January 2001): 1-17.

Gener, Timoteo D. "Christologies in Asia: Trends and Reflections." In *Majority World Theology: Christian Doctrine in Global Context*, edited by Gene L. Green, et al., 59–79. Westmont: InterVarsity, 2020.

---

48 de Mesa, "Making Salvation Concrete and Jesus Real," 48.
49 See Nouwen, *The Living Reminder*.

Gorospe, Adonis Abelard O. "Spiritual Formation and the Contextualization of Christology." *Journal of Asian Evangelical Theology* 18, no 2 (2014): 47–60.

Leclerc, Diane, and Brent Peterson. *The Backside of the Cross: An Atonement Theology of the Abused and Abandoned.* Eugene: Wipf and Stock, 2022.

Maddox, Randy. *Responsible Grace.* Nashville: Abingdon, 1994.

Moon, Hellena. "Genealogy of the Modern Theological Understanding of Han." *Pastoral Psychology* 63, no 4 (2014): 419–35.

Nouwen, Henry. *The Living Reminder.* San Francisco: Harper One, 1977.

Park, Andrew Sung. *The Wounded Heart of God: The Asian Concept of Han and the Christian Doctrine of Sin.* Nashville: Abingdon, 1993.

Pieres, Aloysius. *An Asian Theology of Liberation.* London: T & T Clark, 1988.

7

NAZARENE AND WESLEYAN SPIRITUALITY: THE INTERPLAY OF SPIRIT AND STRUCTURE

David McEwan

Introduction

At the Nazarene Global Theology Conference held in Guatemala in 2002, one of the key areas of debate that emerged concerned Nazarene ecclesiology. In a later paper given by Thomas Noble, based on his endnote address at the conference, attention was drawn to two conflicting understandings of the nature of the church that emerged at the conference. He described the first one as a "believers church" model that was individualistic and collectivistic, with a focus on the freedom of the Spirit in its worship practices. It rejected any formality or set liturgy because that was evidence of the Spirit's absence in congregational life. He described the second form of ecclesiology as "catholic" (as in universal, not Roman). This begins with the corporate and then moves to the personal, with a focus on participating in the great liturgical traditions and the key importance of the sacraments. The former has been the dominant understanding in the Church of the Nazarene in North America and the United Kingdom and has then been taken by mission personnel to the rest of the world. The latter understanding has remained the preserve of a small number of congregations, predominantly in North America and the United Kingdom.[1]

Nazarene ecclesiology is further complicated by the impact that the Pentecostal/Charismatic movements have had on church life, particularly the understanding of community worship and spiritual formation. Here we meet with a very strong emphasis on the power of the Holy Spirit that will overturn all the forces of evil directed against the believer and the church. Above all, every Christian is to pray for and expect an intense, ecstatic experience of the Spirit's presence that is totally independent of ritual, formal liturgy, and its structures. The emphasis is very much on the freedom of the Spirit to work directly and immediately, to be evidenced by miracles, signs, and wonders.

The focus of this essay is not on ecclesiology as such but on spiritual formation in Nazarene (and the wider Wesleyan) tradition. Any understanding of the process of spiritual formation is very much the product of our often unstated and unexamined ecclesiology. Noble's two categories form an important framework for discussions about spiritual formation. In a Wesleyan understanding, as Kevin Watson reminds us,

> *Christian spirituality involves those disciplines or practices that are purposefully undertaken in order to help Christians become deeply committed followers of Christ who habitually practice their faith. In other words, spirituality, for the Christian, is about growing in*

---

[1] Noble, "Church and Mission", 1–3

holiness. It is about the process by which we participate in God's sanctification of our lives.²

It embraces the whole person in every dimension of that person's life with God. This includes a personal relationship with God and neighbor and stewardship of the whole creation. The goal is a transformation of the individual, community, and environment. This necessarily involves the work of the Spirit engaging with our human capacities and capabilities, as he invites us to deepen our relationship through his indwelling and transformative presence. Our core understanding of the nature of the church impacts the way we believe the Spirit works, both personally and corporately.

The question centers around how liturgical forms and practical spiritual disciplines interact with the power of the Spirit. Some would claim that all we need is the direct, personal work of the Spirit unmediated by any set ritual or practice. Others would claim that certain rituals and practices are essential for spiritual formation. So, is it a choice between the freedom of the Spirit and the long tradition of the church catholic? As Noble pointed out in his paper, it is not actually a matter of "either/or" since both perspectives can be found in the life and ministry of our spiritual forefather, John Wesley.³

"Spirit" and "Structure" in Wesleyanism

Wesley was a life-long High Church Anglican who clearly testified to a "warmed heart" through the work of the Spirit in his life. He embraced the rich tradition of the Church of England, with its formal liturgy and sacramental practice, as well as the freedom of the Spirit in personal and corporate experience. He held them in a healthy, dynamic tension that few of his successors have managed to emulate. Perhaps the problem is summed up best by Rob Staples, who refers to

---

2   Watson, "Wesleyan Spirituality," 4.
3   Noble, "Church and Mission," 2–3.

"The Wesleyan Dilemma: 'Spirit' vs. 'Structure.'"[4] Wesley's embrace of tradition, order in worship, and emphasis on sacramental practice is meant by "structure" in this context. Nazarene tradition has generally underplayed and neglected set rituals and the sacramental life because it is associated with a formalism that is believed to limit the free work of the Spirit in the human heart ("spirit" in this understanding).[5] Staples draws attention to the impact of revivalism and personal conversion on Nazarenes because this was a movement that emphasized a "dramatic, emotion-laden, will-oriented experience."[6] The growth of the Pentecostal/Charismatic movement has elevated the supreme value of the freedom of the Spirit and personal religious experience even further, ensuring that in most settings, "spirit" is placed above "structure." It has also exacerbated the focus on the inner life at the expense of community relationships and stewardship of the created environment.

Spontaneity does not last forever, and if there are no deep links to the great tradition theologically, liturgically, and practically, Christians will inevitably chase an experience devoid of Christlike character. This reduces worship services to little more than lots of singing with limited extemporaneous prayer and minimal scripture reading, with a short homily on a topical issue. Spiritual formation practices are often limited to personal prayer and Bible study, where the focus remains on an experience of the Spirit as the evidence of spiritual growth. Wesley repeatedly affirmed that God's covenant relationship with us is neither unilateral and coercive nor merely free-flowing and spontaneous. It requires the moment-by-moment empowering work of the Spirit

---

4   Staples, *Outward Sign*, 21–39.
5   Staples, *Outward Sign*, 24.
6   Staples, *Outward Sign*, 23. The quotation is from Dunning, *Grace, Faith, and Holiness*, 549–50. The problem was not the conversion experience itself, but the cultural framework that shaped its expression.

and our grace-enabled cooperation with that work.⁷ This implies that authentic and enduring spiritual formation requires both "spirit" and "structure." As Philip Meadows reminds us, "Discipline without Spirit descends into mere legalism. Spirit without discipline descends into mere emotivism."⁸

As we shall see, habits matter for spiritual formation. There is a need to adopt a range of simple but powerful habits to reshape our orientation toward the world and enable us to break free from its pervasive hold on our personal and community life. Such habits are not divinely implanted by the Spirit at conversion so that they are expressed instinctively, but they must be intentionally developed. Seen in this light, everything about our church gatherings—songs, preaching, sacramental practice, prayers, furnishings, calendar—would be oriented toward the kinds of faith-forming practices that help us flourish in a world that is opposed to God and his kingdom. Protestant evangelicals have long emphasized regular Bible reading and prayer, but even these can easily get caught in the emphasis on spontaneity that inevitably results in sporadic practice. What is needed are practices of Bible reading, prayer, and other spiritual disciplines that take place within a community with a specific purpose: to intentionally form sustainable habits that will enable personal and community transformation, as well as godly care for the environment.

The Means of Grace

For John Wesley, healthy spiritual formation requires both the active presence of the Spirit and our grace-enabled active participation in a range of practices that allow the Spirit to work in our personal and community lives more effectively. This can be pictured in terms of the need for plants to have water if they are to live and flourish.

---

7   See Maddox, *Responsible Grace* for a full account.
8   Meadows, *The Wesleyan DNA of Discipleship*, 8.

There is no disagreement with the fact that rain can fall on an area and adequately water all the plants in that location. The rain falls freely and without any human involvement to accomplish the required hydration. In many countries, the climatic conditions are such that the rainfall is both infrequent and inadequate. If the plants are to flourish, then "means" must be found to bring the life-giving water to them, such as the use of a bucket or hose. Neither the bucket nor the hose has any power in itself to water the plant—they are the "means" to convey the water, which is the only source of life and refreshment.[9]

Wesley affirms that God can bless his people in all sorts of non-specific ways (like the rain), but he can also bless them through specific means (like using a hose or a bucket). In this light, we are to understand the vital role of the means of grace in spiritual formation—involving both spirit and structure. For example, the Bible is simply a book with words on its pages and has no power at all to nourish us (like the hose). However, if we read these words open to the grace of God, the Holy Spirit will work in our hearts through the channels provided by these words. It is God alone who changes us because there is no power in the words separated from the Spirit.

In Wesley's sermon, "The Means of Grace," we get our clearest picture of his conviction that spiritual formation is not a matter of either the spontaneous work of the Spirit or blindly following set rituals and practices. As Albert Outler pointed out in his "Introductory Comment" to the sermon, there was a lively debate in the early years of Methodism between those who believed that, with their evangelical experience, they no longer needed any means of grace whatsoever. In fact, they believed that these "ordinances" were now a hindrance to spiritual formation as Christ alone was sufficient. Wesley once believed this himself but had come to realize that the means of grace

---

9 McEwan, *The Life of God in the Soul*, 103.

were not only useful but almost essential in the life of a Christian.[10] He defines them as the "outward signs, words, or actions ordained of God, and appointed to this end—to be the *ordinary* channels whereby he might convey to [us] preventing, justifying, or sanctifying grace."[11]

While we often limit these to such things as the reading of Scripture, prayer, fasting, and the sacraments, Wesley himself understood the term to cover a more extensive set of practices, both within the church gathered and the church in service to its community. Nevertheless, he did not confuse the means of grace with the source of grace. He was adamant that it is God alone whom we trust even though he has appointed these means as channels through which he normally grants us his gifts.

> We allow likewise that all outward means whatever, if separate from the Spirit of God, cannot profit at all, cannot conduce in any degree either to the knowledge or love of God. . . . And all outward things, unless he work in them and by them, are mere weak and beggarly elements. Whosoever therefore imagines there is any intrinsic *power* in any means whatsoever does greatly err, not knowing the Scriptures, neither the power of God. We know that there is no inherent power in the words that are spoken in prayer, in the letter of Scripture read, the sound thereof heard, . . . but that it is God alone who is the giver of every good gift, the author of all grace; that the whole power is of him, whereby through any of these there is any blessing conveyed to our soul. We know likewise that he is able to give the same grace, though there were no means on the face of the earth . . . seeing he is equally able to work whatsoever pleaseth him by any or by none at all.[12]

---

10 Outler, "An Introductory Comment", 376–77.
11 Wesley, *Sermons*, 1:381.
12 Wesley, *Sermons*, 1:382.

Grace is not given at some moment in the past to act like a "slow-release" medication that works for the rest of our lives. The means of grace are efficacious only to the degree that the active presence of the Spirit empowers them because God alone is the source of all grace.[13]

In Wesley's view, the means of grace are vital in spiritual formation and practical discipleship because the Christian life requires active practice, not a passive waiting for the Spirit to work. On the other hand, discipleship is not simply about doing certain actions out of duty or obligation but about increasing receptivity to God's love poured into the heart by the Holy Spirit, increasing the capacity to receive and share God's love as well as increasing the inclination to exercise that love in practical ways as we serve the neighbor. Because the life of faith is a dynamic relationship with God and neighbor, it requires an active involvement in a community of faith, personal and community discipline, and an intense desire for an ever-increasing depth of personal and corporate transformation. It involves every aspect and every moment of daily life—not a set of esoteric practices caried out in an enclosed community. The goal is the formation and inculcation of "habituated practices" that truly reflect the character of Christ. The means of grace are important because of our weakness of faith and our proneness to wander or be easily distracted by the temptations of the world. By nature, we are self-idolatrous and slaves to the things of this world; only the way of discipline can wean us from our worldly attachments and free us for God's service.[14]

Spiritual Formation and the Means of Grace

This section of the chapter focuses not on an exhaustive examination of each of the means of grace but rather on highlighting their range and why they are so important in spiritual formation. Wesley

---

13 Wesley, *Sermons*, 1:382.
14 McEwan, *The Life of God in the Soul*, 102–04.

had a comprehensive awareness that extended well beyond the common evangelical list of prayer, Scripture, worship (both private and corporate), and the sacraments. While these were all important (especially prayer, reading/meditating on Scripture, and the sacrament of the Lord's Supper), they were by no means exhaustive. What follows is largely drawn from the important (and still relevant) book by Henry Knight III.[15]

General Means of Grace

These are more an approach to the practice of faith rather than specific spiritual exercises. They seek to foster an intentional awareness of our motivations, thoughts, words, and actions by calling for a searching self-examination and daily reflection on our attitudes and practices as we live our daily life for Christ. They are identified as keeping the commandments, universal obedience, watching, self-denial, taking up the cross daily, and the exercise of the presence of God.[16] In every case, they involve both personal practice and community accountability. They can be exercised in a wide range of ways and are suited for many different confessional and cultural settings.

Instituted (Particular) Means of Grace

These are more specific acts of worship and spiritual discipline that are appointed by God: private, family, and public prayer; reading, meditating, and hearing the Scriptures; participating regularly in the Lord's Supper; regular fasting or abstinence; and faithful participation in Christian Conference (fellowship and conversations that minister grace).[17] While this is a more specific list, the means themselves can be practiced faithfully in a wide range of settings.

---

15 Knight III, *The Presence of God*.
16 Knight III, *The Presence of God*, 5.
17 Knight III, *The Presence of God*, 5.

Prudential Means of Grace

These are practices that vary from age to age, society to society, or person to person. This variation acknowledges that the spiritual life and practices of each person and community are impacted by their time and place, including such elements as culture, education, language, race, wealth, and social standing. In Wesley's day, they included such things as classes, bands, love feasts; particular rules or acts of holy living; prayer meetings, covenant services, watchnight services, love feasts; doing all the good you can while doing no harm; visiting the sick; reading devotional classics and edifying literature.[18] Whilst some of these are private practices, most of them are set in the community of faith and involve both personal spiritual development and loving community service.

Wesley recognized that within these broad categories, persons could direct their attention to practices that developed their relationship with God as the primary goal. He identified these as "works of piety," which are essentially the instituted means of grace. They could also focus on acts of love that seek to relieve the distress of the neighbor, and these are "works of mercy."[19] Both are necessary for healthy spiritual formation in Christlikeness because there is a pattern of interactivity amongst all the means that must not be set aside to focus on a select number that we personally favor. They provide a holistic context within which the Christian life is formed and shaped as we participate, by faith, in the various rituals and practices.

This opens us up increasingly to the presence and transforming power of divine love, all in the context of God's initiative and our grace-enabled response. They provide the resources and the discipline to respond in love to God and neighbor in a thoroughly Christian pattern. Ministry to the neighbor requires personal involvement because

---

18 Knight III, *The Presence of God*, 5.
19 Knight III, *The Presence of God*, 3.

visiting the sick and providing for their needs cannot be done by proxy if we truly love God. Such ministry is essential, not only for the benefit of the neighbor, but also for our own spiritual welfare.[20] If there is a clash between them, Wesley strongly opts for works of mercy over works of piety when the latter are used as "excuses" for avoiding the practice of love. Wesley reminds his people that both works of piety and works of mercy are "real means of grace and both are essential for spiritual vitality.[21]

The Interplay of Spirit and Structure

The relationship between "spirit and structure" is often set out as an either/or proposition. In our spiritual formation, we either rely on the work of the Spirit or a rigid set of rituals and practices. The genius of Wesley is seen in his ability to find a middle way between two extremes that incorporates the best of both while providing a fresh dynamic for our spiritual life. We can see this very clearly when we compare our options with three forms of skeleton found in nature. The three types are:

- A *hydrostatic skeleton* lacks any structure and relies on fluid pressure to provide the animal's shape. An example of this is the jellyfish.
- An *exoskeleton*: a rigid (or articulated) envelope that provides protection for the animal's soft tissues. These skeletons do not grow and must be discarded to allow a new one to be formed. During this time, the animal is very vulnerable to predators and environmental changes. An example of this is the crab.
- An *endoskeleton*: a bony or cartilaginous structure found within the body that provides structural support and protection for the internal organs and tissues of the animal. As living

---

20 McEwan, *The Life of God in the Soul*, 104. See also Wesley, *Sermons* 3:385.
21 Knight III, *The Presence of God*, 3-4.

tissue, this type of skeleton grows in tandem with the rest of the animal's body. An example of this is the human being. We share a common skeletal structure while exhibiting a vast range of body sizes, shapes, and colors.

Spirituality and Enthusiasm (Hydrostatic Skeleton)

As noted earlier, many Protestant evangelical denominations rising in the late nineteenth century were heavily influenced by American revivalism and the later Pentecostal/Charismatic movement that is defined, above all, by its intense focus on, and valuing of, personal spiritual experience. The goal was to allow the Holy Spirit freedom to impact the lives of people in powerful and transformative ways. Alongside the central importance of the various church services (including Sunday School, prayer meetings, and group Bible studies), spiritual formation was promoted by a time of private devotion each day (prayer and Bible study). For such churches, their vocabulary is not one of ritual, liturgy, or structure, but of freedom and ecstasy. From this standpoint, any stricture, rule, or human imposition that hinders life in the Spirit is, by default, suspect and anathema. The very idea of the means of grace is contrary to their central belief that the unfettered power of the Spirit is sufficient.

Like the hydrostatic skeleton that must be kept pumped full of fluid or it shrivels and dies, the people must have a frequent and fresh experience of the presence and power of the Spirit, or they too will shrivel and die. The problem is maintaining the "power" of the Spirit to keep the church in shape. Just as the jellyfish collapses and dies when stranded out of the water, so congregations collapse and die when the presence of the Spirit is no longer experienced as it once was. Many congregations discover that spontaneity and freedom are soon ritualized in practice, which is equally true for personal devotional practices. Just because it is not written down or formally acknowledged does not mean it is not there. In practice, to be "led by the Spirit" in such settings means that only a limited range of worship and devotional practices are ever adopted, and, consequently, many issues in character formation are never addressed. It can lead to deformation rather than formation because our lives are shaped by our own selfish desires for spiritual experiences and needs that are never questioned.

Spirituality and Traditionalism (Exoskeleton)

Some churches settle on a set of rituals and practices that are rigorously and faithfully followed because they were effective and normed by an earlier generation. It is often strongly linked to the founding emphases and distinctives of the denomination. Sometimes the claim reaches back to the New Testament and the early Christian centuries, or sometimes to the Reformation or a later period in church history. Occasionally, it goes no further than the founding pastor of the local church. It is worth noting that this is true even of Pentecostal and Charismatic churches where the "freedom of the Spirit" has been routinised and follows a set pattern. In every case, the pattern is ossified, and no deviation is allowed. This is not to say that the rituals and practices are necessarily wrong in themselves, but they have become a hard exoskeleton that constricts and limits the growth of the living people of God.

In this understanding, the church stresses the vital necessity of the structure, whether it is formalized in set liturgy and practices, or simply becomes the normed pattern. The congregation is then locked into these forms like the exoskeleton that confines the living animal within. As Bryan Draper reminds us, "The rituals and practices provide security and meaning which tells us who we are, why we are here, and where we are heading. There is security in knowing such things. The problem is that once we're established, we like things to stay that way.

In the face of new challenges, we defend our ways because that's the way we've always done it."[22]

There can be no further growth in spiritual life until the shell cracks and splits, but this leaves the people vulnerable to the temptations and trial around them until a new protective shell has formed. We have seen examples of this when congregations split over worship practices, missional outreach, and social justice issues. Part of the problem for this group is that they mistake traditionalism for tradition. As Jaroslav Pelikan pointed out:

> Tradition is the living faith of the dead; traditionalism is the dead faith of the living. Tradition lives in conversation with the past, while remembering where we are and when we are and that it is we who have to decide. Traditionalism supposes that nothing should ever be done for the first time, so all that is needed to solve any problem is to arrive at the supposedly unanimous testimony of this homogenized tradition.[23]

It is a stark reminder that what was successful in one particular time and place may no longer be effective when situations change.

A Wesleyan Spirituality (Endoskeleton)

Wesley's writings on the Christian life and spiritual formation show a clear concern with the twin dangers of enthusiasm and a dead formalism. This implies that the two models just listed are deeply flawed if they alone are to be relied upon to enable holy living. Looking first at the hydrostatic model, we are faced with two major points of concern. The first issue is the physiological reality that any ecstatic emotional experience diminishes over time, and it requires fresh and more intense experiences to give the same level of satisfaction. This inevitably leads to either seeking more and more extreme experiences or to a

---

22 Draper, "Beyond Segmentation," 10.
23 Carey, "Conversation with Jaroslav Peilikan," 57.

rejection of the faith because it no longer delivers the level of experience being sought.

The second problem is, as Wesley pointed out, the danger of "overvaluing *feelings* and *inward impressions*; mistaking the mere work of *imagination* for the voice of the Spirit; expecting the end without the means; and undervaluing *reason, knowledge*, and *wisdom*, in general."[24] He labelled this as enthusiasm and defined it as "a hope to attain the end without the means."[25] The danger of a narrow focus on a personal experience of the Spirit is that it reduces Christianity to little more than an inward, private experience that removes the need for social interaction and community interdependence. The spiritual life of the believer needs to be regulated and not simply left to personal freedom.

On the other hand, Wesley recognized the danger of replacing a dependency on the work of the Spirit with a mechanical application of the Methodist general rules. He realized there was a need for various safeguards, and these had to be such that they did not deny or stifle the direct work of the Spirit in the heart. Through a sound application of reason, knowledge, and wisdom, the church can discern the value of earlier traditions for their present situation. Both issues are clearly identified in his "Preface" to the *Sermons*:

> I have endeavored to describe the true, the scriptural, experimental religion, so as to omit nothing which is a real part thereof, and to add nothing thereto which is not. And herein it is more especially my desire, first, to guard those who are just setting their faces toward heaven . . . from formality, from mere outside religion, which has almost driven heart-religion out of the world; and secondly, to warn those who know the religion of

---

24 Wesley, *Journals and Diaries*, 21:396. The consequences of all this he outlines on pp. 396–97. For examples of its negative impact on the societies, see *Journals and Diaries*, 21:407, 415, 433, 438.

25 Wesley, *Letters* 25:504.

the heart, the faith which worketh by love, lest at any time they make void the law through faith, and so fall back into the snare of the devil.[26]

There is a clear emphasis on the work of the Spirit ("religion of the heart") while avoiding replacing vibrant faith in Christ with a trust in the ordinances and practices of the church, no matter how "ancient" they happen to be. Wesley's own life and ministry demonstrates the truth of the aphorism: "Tradition is not the worship of ashes, but the preservation of fire."[27]

When Wesley discusses spiritual growth, he is clear that the goal towards which we move is holiness of heart and life, both personally and corporately. As such, it is always centered on encouraging and enabling the presence and growth of love in the heart through an ongoing relationship with God and neighbor.

> From his earliest days at Oxford until the end of his life, John Wesley believed that the essential nature of God is love. . . . We were created in love and for love from the very beginning, placing relationships at the very center of our existence. Scripture makes it clear that the love of God was poured into our hearts [by the Spirit] in the original creative act and it is this quality of love that we are to return to God and share with the neighbor.[28]

This is placed in the context of the means of grace, which are themselves always linked with the work of the Spirit, both personally and corporately. The means must not be substituted for the relationship or become an end in themselves. Encountering God through the means of grace gives objectivity to our otherwise subjective experiences. It is easy to fool ourselves into thinking we are making real progress in Christlikeness because of certain spiritual experiences we have had.

---

26 Wesley, *Sermons*, 1:105–06.
27 Aphorism attributed to Gustav Mahler (1860–1911).
28 McEwan, *The Life of God in the Soul*, 153.

The means of grace provide a range of practices that we (and our fellow-believers) can evaluate and enable us to develop critical self-awareness. "The disciplines for the spiritual life, rightly understood, are time-tested activities consciously undertaken by us as new men or women to allow our spirit ever-increasing sway over our embodied selves."[29] As we continue to faithfully participate in them, they will increase our self-knowledge of the hidden deceptions, mixed motives, and social conditioning that makes us blind to our own shortcomings. We need to break our naturally acquired bad habits and replace them with godly ones. This is not done easily nor simply by an act of the will. It can only be fully realized in a fellowship that encourages accountable discipleship within a community of forgiveness and love.

> Emphasizing accountability will seem like a curse to those who are content with their own private spirituality, or who expect little from the Christian life. People are right to be wary of accountability in the spiritual life if it is associated with forms of evaluation, reward and punishment, rather than sharing, healing and growth. The best way to understand accountability is in the context of spiritual direction, with the goal of helping one another become more attentive to the presence of God, and more responsive to the leading of the Spirit. The challenge of accountable discipleship is grasped as a blessing, albeit with "fear and trembling," by those who long for more of God and desire to fulfil his missional purposes in their lives.[30]

Conclusion

While some nations are more monocultural than others, none of us escape the impact of migration, refugee movements, social media,

---

29 Willard, *The Spirit of the Disciplines*, 86.
30 Meadows, *The Wesleyan DNA of Discipleship*, 10.

education, travel, and economic status. The impact of these on our spiritual life is often underestimated. As society fragments into a multitude of subcultures, we face the danger of simply adopting the dominant perspective of the group to which we belong or retreating into the spiritual practices of an earlier "golden" age when spiritual life in the church seemed to flourish. We then embrace the practices that seem to work best for us but rarely question whether they are in fact robbing us of a much richer life in Christ.

This essay has argued that there is a danger of resolving the tension in ecclesiology to embrace either enthusiasm ("spirit") or formalism ("structure"). In the former case, we must acknowledge that "spontaneity" does not last forever, and if we do not have deep links to the great tradition, we will inevitably settle for less than God desires to give. Likewise, believing that simply using the "right" rituals and practices from an earlier age without the presence of the Spirit is also going to fail. Embracing rituals and spiritual practices that are purely "spirit" or "structure" in isolation from each other is to be reduced to relying on the power of our feelings (hydrostatic skeleton) or to be trapped in forms and practices that have no life in them (exoskeleton).

For Wesley, any suitable model of spiritual formation that is to be embraced must take full account of the indispensable living presence of the Holy Spirit, who normally makes use of the means of grace (but is not absolutely bound to use any or all of them). This eliminates a purely mechanistic adherence to any ritual or practice, as well as over-valuing freedom and spontaneity. The model of the endoskeleton as a living, dynamic, and shared framework that allows for a vast range of bodily shapes, sizes, and colors, fits Wesley's theological understanding. The Spirit's use of the means of grace enables Christians within their community of faith to avoid both enthusiasm (the absence of means) and empty ritual (unaided human effort). The means of grace and the dynamic presence of the Spirit are interconnected, and their mutual relationships are essential for the whole to function in a healthy manner.

Looking at the list of the means of grace, we see that they are tied very closely to community life. Being part of a group who shares this vision helps us to continue when it would be easier to settle for something less. Without the community, personal spiritual formation will always be less than it could be because we are unlikely to be challenged by simply doing what we have always done. Wesley's vision was clear: we need both the instituted means of grace to provide our lives with structure as well as the prudential means of grace to allow for diversity of form as situations change.

With this support in place, a local congregation would then be at liberty, under the guidance of the Spirit, to embrace a range of rituals and practices suited for their place and time. The congregation would be anchored deeply both in the living tradition and the local culture, without being held captive by either traditionalism or the culture. In this understanding, the person/community seeking to be spiritually transformed is never autonomous. It is always the role of the Holy Spirit to enable the church to grow in wisdom and discernment, giving new insight into how to grow faithfully in the current setting. By being open and receptive to the work of the Spirit, a local congregation can recapture, renew, or refresh the rituals and spiritual practices found in the church since its foundation, expressing them in a wide variety of cultural expressions.

Bibliography

Carey, Joseph. "Christianity as an Enfolding Circle [Conversation with Jaroslav Pelikan]." *U.S. News & World Report* 106:25 (June 26, 1989), 57.

Draper, Bryan. "Beyond Segmentation." *The Bible in TransMission* (Autumn 2002): 10–13.

Dunning, H. Ray. *Grace, Faith, and Holiness: A Wesleyan Systematic Theology.* Kansas City: Beacon Hill, 1988.

Knight, Henry H., III. *The Presence of God in the Christian Life: John Wesley and the Means of Grace.* Lanham: Scarecrow, 1992.

McEwan, David B. *Wesley as a Pastoral Theologian: Theological Methodology in John Wesley's Doctrine of Christian Perfection.* Milton Keynes: Paternoster, 2011.

———. *The Life of God in the Soul: The Integration of Love, Holiness and Happiness in the Thought of John Wesley.* Milton Keynes: Paternoster, 2015.

Maddox, Randy L. *Responsible Grace: John Wesley's Practical Theology.* Nashville: Kingswood, 1994.

Meadows, Philip. *The Wesleyan DNA of Discipleship: Fresh Expressions of Discipleship for the 21st-century Church.* Cambridge: Grove Books, 2013.

Noble, Thomas A. "Church and Mission." A paper presented at Nazarene Theological Seminary, Kansas City, USA, February 2003, 1–13.

Outler, Albert C. "An Introductory Comment." In John Wesley, *Sermons 1*, edited by Albert C. Outler, 76–77. Nashville: Abingdon, 1984.

Staples, Rob L. *Outward Sign and Inward Grace: The Place of Sacraments in Wesleyan Spirituality.* Kansas City: Beacon Hill Press of Kansas City, 1991.

Watson, Kevin M. "The Spirituality of John Wesley Pathways of Faith." Paper presented at the McFarlin Memorial United Methodist Church, Norman, OK. September 29, 2007.

Wesley, John. *Sermons.* Edited by Albert C. Outler. Vols. 1–4. Nashville: Abingdon, 1984–1987.

———. *Letters.* Edited by Frank Baker. Vols. 25–26. Nashville: Abingdon, 1980–1982.

―――. *Journals and Diaries*. Edited by W. Reginald Ward and Richard P. Heitzenrater. Vols. 18-24. Nashville: Abingdon, 1988–2003.

―――. *The Letters of the Rev. John Wesley*. Edited by John Telford. Vols. 1-8. London: Epworth, 1931.

Willard, Dallas. *The Spirit of the Disciplines: Understanding How God Changes Lives*. Harper: San Francisco, 1991.

PART III

SPIRITUALITY OF THE PEOPLE

8

PRACTICAL WAYS OF NURTURING CHILDREN'S SPIRITUALITY

Nativity A. Petallar

Introduction

There was once a little girl who asked me, "*Ate Natz, Katoliko diay ka?*" ("Ate Natz, are you Catholic?"). I asked back, "Why?" She then answered, "*Tungod sa imong krus na kwentas*" ("Because of your cross necklace"). Because of that little girl's question, I was able to explain to her the plan of salvation using the cross as my "visual aid." In Exodus 12:24–25, Moses said to the Israelites, "Obey these instructions as a lasting ordinance for you and your descendants. When you enter the land that the Lord will give you as he promised, observe this ceremony. *And when your children ask you, 'What does this ceremony mean to you?' then tell them....*"[1] Moses then instructed the Israelites to tell the children the story behind the Passover ceremony (v. 27).

---

1 Italics mine.

How do we ignite the curiosity of children toward spiritual things? As church leaders, seminary professors, and parents, are we aware of God's stirring in the spirits of the children in our midst? How do we respond when they ask questions about the deep things of God? Will our answers to their questions nurture their sense of "awe" and "wonder," or will we quench the moving of the Spirit in their young hearts by our careless response? The purpose of this paper is threefold: (1) to define children's spirituality and explain why it is important; (2) to give a brief historical sketch on how children have received spiritual nurture; and (3) to identify practical ways of nurturing children's spirituality in the home and the church, the two most important settings where faith can grow. The paper will also identify a few implications on how the seminary can join in this journey of nurturing the spiritual life of children.

What is Children's Spirituality and Why is it Important?

Rebecca Nye, a researcher, consultant, and practitioner in the field of children's spirituality, defines children's spirituality as "like a child."[2] The following are several characteristics of child spirituality as described by Nye:

- It does not usually conform to accepted norms or use conventional expression.
- At first glance, it might sound like babble rather than fluent "Christian." It requires effort (listening) on our part to recognize what is being expressed, and to develop (not impose) shared language.
- It surpasses compartmentalization (gets into and will use everything not just religious material).

---

[2] Nye, *Children's Spirituality*, 6.

- It can be intense one minute and nonchalant the next. Development is rarely in a straight line or under our control.
- And often it feels like it matters to the child but is perceived by them not to matter to anyone else, and not to be part of mainstream values.
- It is vulnerable, and can even die if neglected, ignored or misunderstood.[3]

Nye says that children's spirituality is "God's ways of being with children and children's ways of being with God."[4] This definition portrays the relationship that goes on with God and the child. I especially like how Walter Wangerin, a multi-awarded author of children's books, described this special bond that he calls "faithing" or "coming to faith."[5] About the beginning of this "faithing," Wangerin writes that "no one can say when it has its birth in the child because it is as natural an experience (as early and as universally received) as the child's relationship with the sun or with his bedroom."[6] God, in his special way, is revealing himself to the child in ways that adults cannot fathom. Wangerin continues to write that, at first,

> ... the child has no name for this Someone so Significant, this Other, the Dear or else the Terrible Almighty (*El Shaddai*), yet the holiness and glory, the power and even the righteousness of the Other are real to him—and the love, though kindness and the expression of that love may wax and wane, depending upon the child's own sense of goodness and health. It is the common lot of all children to encounter and to experience the Deity.[7]

---

[3] Nye, *Children's Spirituality*, 6.
[4] Nye, Children's Spirituality, 5.
[5] Wangerin, *The Orphean Passages*, 20.
[6] Wangerin, *The Orphean Passages*, 20.
[7] Wangerin, *The Orphean Passages*, 21–22.

At the earliest stages of life, the "Significant Other" is already extending his hand of love to the tiny infant. Wangerin writes, "We all have danced one round with God. But we danced it in the mists."[8] I am so enamored by this statement by Wangerin: "We all have danced one round with God." It seems mystical and so filled with "wonder." I remember when my daughter was about two or three years of age. She told me, "Ma, when we are sleeping, Jesus kisses us." I want to believe that this consciousness, this "dance" between God and my daughter, would continue throughout her life. What a challenge to the parents and/or caregivers around the child: how to nurture this relationship, so it blossoms. This task might seem difficult, but it is not impossible.

In relation to this connection between God and the child, Logan and Miller challenge their readers to "honor the soul—the sacred space God has already placed within children."[9] Blaise Pascal (1623-1662), a mathematician and philosopher from the 1600s, inspired by Augustine's *Confessions*, wrote, "There is a God-shaped vacuum in every man that only Christ can fill."[10] The verse in Proverbs 22:6, "Start children off on the way they should go, and even when they are old they will not turn from it," might seem "deterministic" to some people's understanding; however, if the significant people around the life of the child are intentional in their approaches to helping the child develop spiritually, this verse in Proverbs is good news! The word "old" in this verse means, literally, "hair on the chin" or "bearded one."[11] Spackman makes this comment, "King Solomon was suggesting that the way our children are trained now seriously affects the direction of their entire lives; indeed, the training sets them in a certain way that will prevail even when they are old."[12]

---

8   Wangerin, *The Orphean Passages*, 22.
9   Logan and Miller, *Child-Centered Spirituality*, 13.
10 Pascal, *Pensees*, 45.
11 Spackman, *Parents Passing on the Faith*, 29.
12 Spackman, *Parents Passing on the Faith*, 29.

Why is spirituality essential? Experts on children's spirituality convey to us that children are as much spirituals beings as are the adults in their lives.[13] In essence, spirituality is the person's capacity and yearning for relationship, that is, for a divine or transcendent being, someone "wholly" other than one's self. There is, of course, no generic spirituality untethered from a historical and particular tradition and community.[14] Asian spirituality, for example, is very community oriented. For many Filipino Christians, we find ourselves exercising most of our spiritual practices in the context of the community, more specifically, the church. Children are no different. Most Filipino children identify with a church that they and their parents are attending. Going back to my anecdote about the little girl, she equated the "cross" that I was wearing with being "Catholic." For most Filipinos, when we say "Catholic," we mean the "Roman Catholic Church." More often than not, a Filipino's faith is directly connected to the church in which they participate.

A child's spirituality is a significant part of a child's thriving. Susan Greener, a catalyst for Children at Risk[15] with the Lausanne Movement, presents this framework called "Interaction of Areas of Human Development with Spirituality at the Center" (Figure 1 below).[16] This would put ministers or caregivers of children in a strategic position to place the child on a positive trajectory towards wholeness.

In this model, Greener discusses how that human development research and theory suggest that four developmental categories best capture holistic child development: spiritual, socio-emotional, cognitive, and physical. These areas of development give child development workers the point of entry towards ushering children to flourish. The

---

13   Ratcliff, *Children's Spirituality*, 7.
14   Phan, "Asian Christian Spirituality, " 221–27.
15   "Celebrating New Lausanne Catalysts."
16   Greener, "A Roadmap for Reflection," 6. Used with permission from the author.

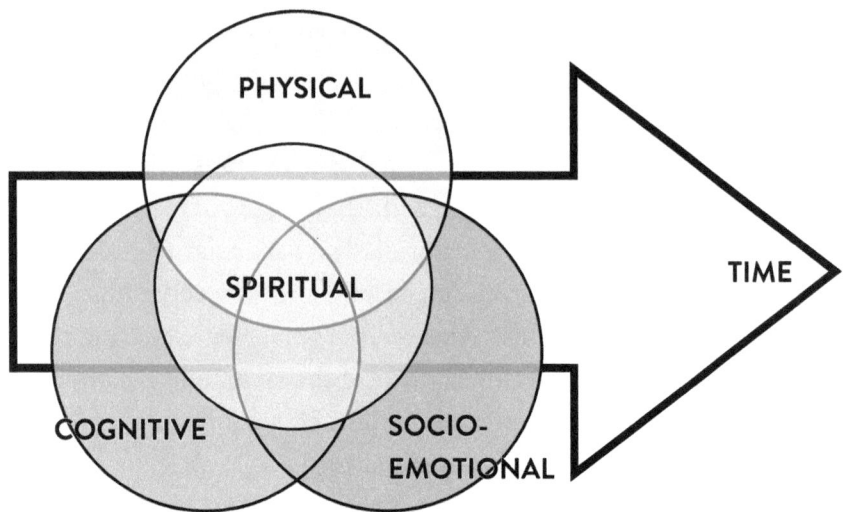

Figure 1. Interaction of Areas of Human Development with Spirituality at the Center

uniqueness of this model lies in its emphasis on the centrality of spiritual development linking the whole person and reflecting the developmental implications of a biblically and theologically grounded model of holistic development. Greener expounds:

> From the Christian perspective, spiritual development is unique among developmental areas because it provides the epicenter that anchors the remainder of human development. In addition, it is distinctive, in that it is not as directly tied to development over time as other areas of growth. For example, physical development follows a fairly specific trajectory and timetable, allowing for comparatively accurate prediction of timing milestones in development (e.g., children across the globe typically take their first steps between 9 and 12 months of age). However, spiritual insight and sensitivity are not necessarily connected to one's chronological age. Children may exhibit a depth of spiritual awareness that may be absent in older persons, even if

that awareness remains framed in developmentally appropriate expressions.[17]

This model combines all the areas of human development plus time but specifically puts spiritual nurture as the glue that binds all the aspects of life. In our homes and churches, therefore, our strategy needs to consider an integrated approach to nurture that meets physical, socio-emotional, and cognitive needs. At the same time, this strategy should also usher children into a vital relationship with God, filling their natural hunger for God with a fresh inquiry of the Scriptures while making God's Word come alive in all our engagements with them.

Spirituality is also a protective factor to one's existence. Sifers, Warren, and Jackson, in their study on the spirituality of children and youth, wrote, "Reliance upon spirituality in the face of challenges allows individuals to cope with pain without emotionally withdrawing, thereby facilitating the processing of difficult life events. For example, difficult events may come to be viewed as challenges that allow the individual to grow in his or her spiritual strength."[18] Similarly, Myers reviewed a wide range of literature suggesting that spirituality is associated with a variety of measures of well-being in a number of populations and theorizes that spirituality provides social support and a sense of meaning and purpose that buffers individuals from the gamut of challenges that may occur, even fostering physical, mental, and behavioral health and happiness.[19] Indeed, spirituality and cultivating it amongst children is an essential component of life.

---

17 Greener, "A Roadmap for Reflection," 6.
18 Sifers et al., "Measuring Spirituality in Children," 210.
19 Sifers et al., "Measuring Spirituality in Children," 210.

A Brief Historical Sketch on how Children Have Received Spiritual Nurture[20]

The Bible writes that children are a heritage from the Lord (Ps 127:3) and that they are part of his atoning work.[21] In the Old Testament, there were no paid teachers specified for the young members of the household. Richards notes that the "Old Testament assumes that children will grow up as participating members of the community."[22] So, the children witnessed their own parents and their neighbors go through the whole year celebrating the festivals, experiencing rituals in worship to Yahweh, and seeing the memorials that the adults erected as symbols of their communal faith. Richards writes that the Old Testament nurture system comes from the "vision of life together as a committed community: a vision embedded in Mosaic law."[23]

When one reads through the pages of the New Testament, especially in looking at Jesus' ministry, one could observe that Jesus placed a high value on children (Matt 9:22-26; 18:1-7, 10; Mark 9:36-37; 10:13-16; Luke 18:16-17).[24] In the Apostle Paul's ministry, children joined in the home-sized groups (Romans 16:5), experiencing intergenerational occasions of spiritual nurture (1 Cor 14:26, 29-31). In more ways than one, the New Testament believers practiced their spirituality as a faith community. Richards identifies the church as a "network of believers" of which children are a part.[25] Below is Richards' a summary of his survey of the Old Testament and New Testament nurture systems:

---

20 This section does not contain an exhaustive discussion on the history of how children are nurtured spiritually through the centuries. For a comprehensive treatment of this topic, see Bunge, *The Child in Christian Thought*.

21 Petallar, "Emerging Themes of Child Theology, " 4.

22 Richards, *Theology of Children's Ministry*, 20.

23 Richards, *Theology of Children's Ministry*, 31.

24 Abecia,"Implications of the Perceived Learning Preferences," 32.

25 Richards, *Theology of Children's Ministry*, 40.

Mosaic Ideal	New Testament Reality
The whole society is envisioned as a loving community.	A loving community exists within the fabric of pagan society.
Children participate in the structured life and worship of the community.	Children participate in the spontaneous life and worship of the community.
Children are given daily instruction by parents in the context of shared family experiences.	Children are given daily instruction by parents in the context of shared family experiences.

Table 1. Comparison of Old Testament and New Testament Nurture[26]

Both the Mosaic ideal and the New Testament reality show how children are considered a part of the family and community circle. There is no nurture apart from the embrace of the family and community bonding as one.

Conceptions of Children in the Middles Ages to the Eighteenth Century

How were children looked at during the Middle Ages? Philip Aries, a French historian in the medieval times, observed, "In medieval society, the idea of childhood did not exist; this is not to suggest that children were neglected, forsaken or despised. The idea of childhood is not to be confused with affection for children: it corresponds to an awareness of the particular nature of childhood, that particular nature which distinguishes the child from the adult, even the young adult."[27] In medieval society, this awareness was lacking. Aries noted that until the twelfth century, medieval art did not attempt to portray childhood, indicating that there was "no place" for it in this civilization. All that artists came up with was the occasional tiny figure resembling

---

26 Richards, *Theology of Children's Ministry*, 47.
27 Aries, *Centuries of Childhood*, 128.

a man on a reduced scale: "horrid little dwarf" as in the case of the infant Jesus.[28]

In the sixteenth through eighteenths centuries, which are considered the Moralistic Period, the concept of childhood was much closer to our perception today. This is when John Locke (1632–1704) espoused his understanding of *tabula rasa* (blank tablet), which discounts the "notion that any 'innate principles' arrived inborn with the infant. Instead, Locke proposed that a child entered the world as a blank tablet upon which would be written the contents of the mind."[29] In addition, Jean Jacques Rousseau (1712–1778) was the most well-admired moralist and propagated the "innocence of childhood"; however, many experts in the twenty-first century have found that both of these notions of childhood are incomplete. While it is true that children have no lengthy "track record" of life experiences and indeed, in some ways, children are innocent, they are not blank slates or without sin. There is a tension that children are both innocent and sinful.[30] Knowing this tension allows parents and church leaders to be perceptive in their approaches to children's spiritual development.

Spiritual Formation of Children in the Nineteenth to Twentieth Centuries

How did the educators in the nineteenth and twentieth centuries engage in the Christian formation of children? When one speaks of the nineteenth century, the Sunday school movement almost always comes to mind in terms of the Christian formation of children. The Sunday school movement started by Robert Raikes (1735–1811) did a lot of help amongst children who worked all week down in the coal mines. They were taught how to read and write using the Bible as the textbook. Sunday school then spread all over the world and is still

---

28 Aries, *Centuries of Childhood*, 31.
29 Winik, "The Demise of Child-Rearing," 44.
30 For more discussion on this tension, read Bunge, "A More Vibrant Theology of Children."

alive and well in many churches until today. In my estimation, in the Philippines, the Sunday school (or its equivalent) is still by far the most effective tool in the spiritual nurture of children.

At the beginning of the twentieth century, one finds the names Montessori and Westerhoff as the prime movers of children's nurture. Maria Montessori advocated for "hands-on" learning. Westerhoff promoted (among others) that children's faith development will be nurtured through rituals, experiences, and the action of the environment.[31] Berryman noted:

> At the beginning of the twentieth century, Maria Montessori had argued that children were inherently spiritual and trained her teachers to guide children's spirituality which includes their educational drive to fulfill itself in their lives. If you ask a Montessori child, "Who taught you that?" She or he is likely to say, "I don't know. I guess I taught myself." This approach encouraged self-direction rather than being other directed which made it especially appropriate to honor children's personal experience of God. Since one must die for oneself learning to live well also needs to be personal. This approach to Christian education recognized that children have an owned faith from the beginning and supported a lifelong journey toward greater maturity based on this. The Montessori approach largely bypassed Westerhoff's "affiliated faith," living by the faith of other people to encourage children's personal quests alongside adult mentors teaching each other mutually across the generations.[32]

Both Montessori and Westerhoff advocated that children become the center of the teaching-learning process. Their approaches call for a challenge to leave behind the assumption that teachers are the center of the universe. Writing about spiritual nurture of children in light

---

31 Westerhoff, *Will Our Children Have Faith?*, 53–65.
32 Berryman, *The Spiritual Guidance of Children*, 18–19.

of curriculum design, Scottie May et al. give this advice: "In the setting where children are the learners, the curriculum pursues to relate with them and their lives because children themselves are part of the curriculum. The content revolves around the necessity for the children to know and love the stories of God and the people of God."[33] This would enable the children to experience the Bible in their everyday life. In the child's educational venture, the teacher serves as "facilitator of experiences and manager of the conditions of learning."[34] As such, the close relationships formed by children with teachers are critical. This also implies that for church leaders to fully design a robust curriculum for children's spiritual development, knowing their needs and preferences is of paramount importance.

Twenty-first Century and the Spiritual Formation of Children

One could observe that, until the twentieth century, little attention was given to children's growth and development. In the past 75 years, however, research has provided a great deal of information about childhood.[35] In the literature of children's spirituality, Rebecca Nye formulated the "six criteria for ensuring spiritual foundations" called S-P-I-R-I-T, which was based on empirical studies with children. S-P-I-R-I-T means Space, Process, Imagination, Relationship, Intimacy, and Trust.[36] Children respond to a prepared environment. For Nye, the process is more important than the product. Children's imagination is often encouraged when they are allowed to explore nature, manipulate various objects, or participate in rituals. Relationship, intimacy, and trust would relate with the children's various engagements with God, others, and the world around them. Nye advises that in every

---

33 May, et. al., *Children Matter*, 196; cited in Karumathy, "Proficiency Level," 35.
34 Gagné, *Conditions of Learning*, 324.
35 Ruppel, "Using Developmentally Appropriate Practice," 346.
36 Nye, *Children's Spirituality*. For a detailed explanation on Nye's S-P-I-R-I-T model, see pages 45–55.

situation, a teacher could use these criteria as a checklist to help take stock of how well children's spirituality is being supported.[37]

The corpus of literature and studies on various instructional paradigms for the development of children's spiritual development is vast. There are a number of educational methodologies[38] that have been developed in the twenty-first century that could be of help to parents and church leaders as they seriously think of engaging children in the nurture of their relationship with God and others and their existential well-being.[39] These methods provide interactive participation of children and the adults around them.

Models in Nurturing Children's Spirituality

In addition to the instructional paradigms that could be used in the nurture of children's spirituality, there are several models in engaging children in the development of their spiritual life. I will identify the following four models very briefly: (1) the contemplative reflective model; (2) the instructional-analytic model number; (3) the pragmatic-participatory model; and (4) the media driven active-engagement model.[40]

First, the "Contemplative-Reflective Model" intentionally creates an environment that enables children to move at a slow place in relative quiet so they can reflect on a Scripture that helps them know

---

37 Nye, *Children's Spirituality*, 41.

38 Appendix A is a compilation of instructional paradigms from recent literature and studies that I have gathered and could be of use for teachers in Sunday school as they think of creative ways of teaching children.

39 These three categories, namely, relationship with God, relationship with others, and existential well-being are enumerated by Sifers, Warren, and Jackson (2012) in their pilot study on measuring spirituality with more than 300 participants who are seven to 15 years old. This study uses literature from Cavalletti (1992), the pioneer of the *Catechesis of the Good Shepherd* and Robert Coles who espoused the moral development of children (1990).

40 I want to acknowledge Wobeni Lotha, PhD in Holistic Child Development candidate for giving me the resources for these four models.

who God is.[41] This approach is espoused by Scottie May. In addition, Catherine Stonehouse's book, *Joining Children in the Spiritual Journey*, also espouses this contemplative-reflective model, allowing children to be in a silent mode and encouraging them to communicate with God while listening to the story as well as in engaging with different objects inside the room. Stonehouse also espouses *Godly Play* by Jerome Berryman.

Second, the "Instructional-Analytic Model" engages children in Scripture memory, Bible instruction, a graduated award system, and a systematic structure for training.[42] This model has the instructional element, the evangelistic element, and the developmental element, as well as Scriptural foundation. This approach is modeled by the "Approved Workmen Are Not Ashamed" (AWANA) clubs all over the world.

Third, the "Pragmatic-Participatory Model," according to Trisha Graves, "is a ministry model that is dependent on a child's thought process that is formed through active participatory learning. This model is known for engaging children in learning while using a variety of different methods to teach them with practical and relevant application."[43] This approach includes large and small groups using a mix of innovative and creative methods such as video, references to pop culture, games, and appealing worship music to capture the children's attention and make the Bible come to life and become relevant to the children of today's culture. In my observation, this model is commonly seen in most of the mega-churches in Metro Manila.

---

41 May, "The Contemplative-Reflective Model," 47. For a video on what this is done, please see https://www.youtube.com/watch?v=wvfVf13GhYA.

42 Carlson and Crupp, "Instructional-Analytic Model," 202–307. For an example on what this model looks like, see, https://www.youtube.com/watch?v=-PCAvOr9OO4.

43 Graves, "Pragmatic-Participatory Model," 308–409. For an example on how this model looks like, see https://www.youtube.com/watch?v=9t4_-p9d4k4.

Finally, the "Media Driven Active-Engagement Model" uses technology and interactive media to emphasize discovery-based and cooperative learning. Based on the assumptions of educational psychologists Jean Piaget, Jerome Bruner, and David Ausubel, this instructional design takes into consideration the unique learning styles of all learners.[44] This approach is also based on the concept that today's children are driven by media and would benefit much from discovery-based and cooperative learning.

The home and the church could look at these different models and decide which one would work in their respective contexts considering resources, space, and time, as well as the characteristics of the children.

Practical Ways of Nurturing Children's Spirituality in the Home and the Church

The home and the church are the two primary settings where the spiritual nurture of children can be done best. This does not mean that the school, community, and other settings are not important. Bronfenbrenner, in his Ecological Theory, espouses that for the child to flourish, every system is needed.[45] When all the systems around the life of the child are working, there is safety, heath, and quality of life. However, for the purposes of this study, I am identifying specific suggestions for the home and the church to consider in developing the children's relationship with God and the people around them.

Nurturing Children's Spirituality in the Home

The "biblical plan for the home" is a divine blueprint for family life culled from the pages of Scripture.[46] Jesus Christ was placed in

---

44 Ellis et al., "Media-Driven Active-Engagement Model," 410–498. For an example on this model, please see https://www.youtube.com/watch?v=14hOxWe_FVU.
45 Bronfenbrenner, *The Ecology of Human Development*.
46 Emily Hunter McGowin, *Quivering Families*, 171.

a family. The family is the first unit of society where love, care, and protection are exercised. This is also the primary place where the faith of children is nurtured. In the research done by the Asia-Pacific Nazarene Theological Seminary (APNTS) Research Team with Dr. Floyd T. Cunningham as one of the research mentors, the 776 respondents indicated that "family" is the number one factor that helps children to thrive.[47] The drawings of the children in that research indicated how their family helps them with their needs and general well-being.

So, how can the home provide this nurture the child needs for spiritual growth? Let me identify at least three practical ways. First, parents have to be spiritually mature themselves and never ignore but be keen in observing the spiritual awakenings of their children. Parents are mandated by God to lead their children in his ways. Second, parents and other people living in the home need to respect the development of the children. Children should not be pushed or forced to memorize verses or be punished for not reading the Bible; instead, other proactive methods should be considered in encouraging the children's love for these spiritual disciplines. Finally, there needs to be a careful plan of nurture that could include the following:

1. Provide a "prepared environment" where children's spirituality can thrive.
2. Engage children in rituals and intergenerational celebrations where their imagination will be kindled toward the goodness of God.
3. If possible, let the children lead the family devotions but make sure to guide them to age-appropriate "leadership."

---

[47] Asia-Pacific Nazarene Theological Seminary Research Team, "Listening and Learning from Various Entities."

4. Go out into the woods once in a while and experience nature. Most children respond to nature and their spiritual sensitivity is heightened.
5. Bring them to church and cooperate with the programs in the church.

Nurturing Children's Spirituality in the Church

The church is a significant place where families gather to receive spiritual feeding as well as fellowship and training for the work of the Lord. The church is a strategic place for the spiritual nurture of children to be reinforced. When the home is not consciously helping the child's growth of faith, the church can come to supplement that lack; however, the collaboration of the home and the church usually yields optimum results. Let me identify some areas where church leaders can help children grow in their faith:

1. Be alert to children's language, thoughts, and actions that reflect their spiritual needs;
2. Like the OT and NT nurture systems, allow the child to participate in church rituals and ceremonies that ignite their sense of "awe and wonder";
3. Provide mentors to children who can come alongside them in their relationship with Jesus;
4. There is a plethora of instructional methodologies on the interactive teaching-learning process; however, the teacher has to exercise wisdom in the choice of activities. Looking at the various contexts of children, including their current social and cultural influences, socio-economic status, stressors, family dynamics, protection issues (is there abuse in the family or outside the family?), their learning styles, the goals of spiritual education, etc. These are some of the essential things to consider in lesson planning and teaching. The more senses

that are engaged, the better the comprehension and application of certain lessons will be. With this in mind, the key is listening to children and including their perspectives in the curriculum design;

5. In worship services (or other related activities) with children, take into account Nye's "six criteria for ensuring spiritual foundations," which are Space, Process, Imagination, Relationship, Intimacy, and Trust (S-P-I-R-I-T).

6. Consider the various models of ministry that could facilitate the spiritual growth of children.

Conclusion

When that little girl asked me if I was Catholic, the state of my own spiritual journey presented itself. I was able to lead her to a deeper understanding of the cross. The growth of children's spirituality is a journey. God has placed in every child his divine image, and he loves to see each child having a relationship with him. When children's spirituality is nurtured by the significant persons around them, they thrive and grow into the persons God created them to be. This task of journeying with children is never easy, but help abounds: from the family, church, and most of all, the Creator of us all, the author and finisher of our faith.

Appendix
Examples of Instructional Paradigms
from Recent Literature and Studies

Paradigm	How it works
"Individual attention"	Teachers would do well to make sure each student is given individual attention to promote "context awareness."[48]
Dialogue or "intersubjectivity"	Bunge espouses that "Children can teach adults, and be moral witnesses, models of faith, and sources of revelation."[49] If this is the case, then one will listen more attentively to children and learn from them, structure religious education programs in ways that honor their questions and insights, and recognize the importance of children in the faith journey and spiritual maturation of parents and other adults
"tactile interfaces"	Projects using art materials or other objects
Teaching strategies that meet the learning styles of students	Discussion groups or buzz groups, recitation oral questions, panel discussion, student reports, debate, bulletin boards (online), choral speaking, choral reading, collecting objects, journaling, reflection from a Bible story, cooking, vocabulary drills, dance, song composition, outdoor sports (quarantine protocols), dressing dolls, art, term papers, biographical reports, research (library or interviews), field trips, quizzes, photographs, experiments, poster making, haiku, case studies, puppets, drama, sand tables, service projects, storytelling, surveys,

---

48 Anderson, "Toward an Understanding of Context-Awareness."
49 Bunge, "A More Vibrant Theology of Children."

	studying local history, preparing an art exhibit, collecting money for a cause, mock newspaper writing, brainstorming
Problem solving and other heuristic methods of teaching	Using a case study, or a story from a newspaper, or any trending story or problem from social media or the news; teacher is a facilitator. This engages the learners in "trial and error," and promotes "self-experience
Role playing	For example, a lesson on bullying—one student will be the bully, another would be the bullied child, the rest could be other characters assigned by the teachers
Discourse with the family	The need for parents and church leaders to be in collaboration towards the holistic nurture of children
Informal learning	Informal learning is "learner initiated, occurs on as-needed basis, is motivated by intent to develop, involves action and reflection, and does not occur in a formal classroom setting."[50] This can be done through daily experiences and exposure to the environment
Games and relays	Interactive games that reinforce a particular biblical truth and allow children to share their inner states
Mind mapping	Mind map assists learners to visualize and classify a structure of ideas.

Bibliography

Abecia, Nativity (Petallar). "Implications of the Perceived Learning Preferences of Intermediate Pupils in the Free Methodist Churches in Northern Mindanao, Philippines to Curriculum Design for

---

50 Noe et al., "Learning in the Twenty-First-Century Workplace," 245–75.

Sunday School." ThD diss., Asia Baptist Graduate Theological Seminary, 2002.

Anthony, Michael J., Scottie May, and Gregory C. Carlson. *Perspectives on Children's Spiritual Formation: Four Views*. Nashville: Broadman and Holman, 2006.

Anderson, Nels Christian. "Toward an Understanding of Context-Awareness and Collaborative Narratives in Mobile Video Creation," 2007. https://search.ebscohost.com/login.aspx?direct=true&db=ddu&AN=6916C8693AD6D088&site=ehost-live.

Aries, Philippe. *Centuries of Childhood: A Social History of Family Life*. New York: Vintage, 1965.

Asia-Pacific Nazarene Theological Seminary Research Team. "Listening and Learning from Various Entities on the Perceived Dynamics that Help Children Thrive." Paper presented at the Lausanne Forum for Children-At-Risk, Manila, August 17, 2018.

Augustine. *Confessions*. https://www.gutenberg.org/files/3296/3296-h/3296-h.htm#link2H_4_0001.

Berryman, Jerome. *The Spiritual Guidance of Children: Montessori, Godly Play, and the Future*. New York: Church, 2013.

Bronfenbrenner, Urie. *The Ecology of Human Development: Experiments by Nature and Design*. Cambridge: Harvard University Press, 1979.

Bunge, Marcia. *The Child in Christian Thought*. Grand Rapids: Eerdmans, 2001.

———. "A More Vibrant Theology of Children." *Christian Reflection: A Series in Faith and Ethics*, 11-19. Waco: The Center for Christian Ethics at Baylor University, 2003.

Carlson, Gregory C., and John K. Crupp. "Instructional-Analytic Model." In *Perspectives on Children's Spiritual Formation*, edited by Michael J.

Anthony, Scottie May, and Gregory C. Carlson, 202–307. Nashville: Broadman and Holman, 2006.

Cavalletti, Sofia, et al. *The Religious Potential of the Child: Experiencing Scripture and Liturgy with Young Children*. Mt. Rainier: Catechesis of the Good Shepherd, 1992.

"Celebrating New Lausanne Catalysts." Lausanne Movement. https://lausanne.org/about/blog/celebrating-new-lausanne-catalysts.

Coles, Robert. *The Moral Life of Children*. New York: Atlantic Monthly, 1986.

Deganis, Isabelle. "A Dialogue across Paradigms: The European Commission's Autonomous Power within the Open Method of Coordination." PhD diss., University of Oxford, 2011. https://search.ebscohost.com/login.aspx?direct=true&db=ddu&AN=8723DE370D115AD&site=ehost-live.

Ellis, Tim, Bill Baumgart, and Greg Carper. "Media-Driven Active-Engagement Model." In *Perspectives on Children's Spiritual Formation*, edited by Michael J. Anthony, Scottie May, and Gregory C. Carlson, 410–98. Nashville: Broadman and Holman, 2006.

Gagné, Robert M. *Conditions of Learning*. 2nd Revised edition. London: Holt, Rinehart and Winston, 1970.

Graves, Trisha. "Pragmatic-Participatory Model." In *Perspectives on Children's Spiritual Formation*, edited by Michael J. Anthony, Scottie May, and Gregory C. Carlson, 308–409. Nashville: Broadman and Holman, 2006.

Greener, Susan. "A Roadmap for Reflection: The Vision of the Lausanne Movement and Mission 'To, For, and With Children at Risk.'" Paper Presented at the Lausanne Consultation on Children at Risk, Quito, Ecuador, November 17–19, 2014.

Leasure, June Ruff, and Laura Sanchez-Fowler. "Teaching Strategies for Students with Low Achievement in a Christian School Classroom." *Journal of Research on Christian Education* 20 no. 2 (May 2011): 155–81.

Karumathy, Ponelyn D. "Proficiency Level of Selected Early Childhood Teacher-Education Graduates of Harris Memorial College: Implications to Curriculum Enrichment." PhD diss., Asia-Pacific Nazarene Theological Seminary, 2020.

Logan, Janet, and Tara Miller. *Child-Centered Spirituality: Helping Children Develop Their Own Spirituality*. Scotts Valley: CreateSpace Independent Publishing Platform, 2017.

Lotha, Wobeni. "Children's Spirituality." Class Lecture, Approaches to Holistic Nurture of Children. 2021.

McGowin, Emily Hunter. *Quivering Families: The Quiverfull Movement and Evangelical Theology of the Family*. Minneapolis: Fortress, 2018.

May, Scottie. "The Contemplative-Reflective Model." In *Perspectives on Children's Spiritual Formation*, edited by Michael J. Anthony, Scottie May, and Gregory C. Carlson, 45–102. Nashville: Broadman and Holman, 2006.

May, Scottie, et al. *Children Matter: Celebrating Their Place in the Church, Family, and Community*. Grand Rapids: Eerdmans, 2005.

Noe, Raymond, Alena Clarke, and Howard Klein. "Learning in the Twenty-First-Century Workplace." *Annual Review of Organizational Psychology and Organizational Behavior* 1 (March 21, 2014): 245–75.

Nye, Rebecca. *Children's Spirituality: What It Is and Why It Matters*. London: Church House, 2009. http://public.eblib.com/choice/PublicFullRecord.aspx?p=6189828.

Pascal, Blaise. *Pensees,* translated by A. J. Krailsheimer. London: Penguin, 1993. https://library.iusb.edu/search-find/archives/gcarchive/docs/writ-god-shaped.pdf.

Petallar, Nativity. "Emerging Themes of Child Theology and the Context of Filipino Children: Implications to Engaging Children in Missions." *Journal of Asian Mission* 14 no. 2 (2013): 3–15.

Phan, Peter C. "Asian Christian Spirituality: Context and Contour." *Spiritus: A Journal of Christian Spirituality* 6 no. 2 (2006): 221–27.

Ratcliff, Donald. *Children's Spirituality: Christian Perspectives, Research, and Applications*. Eugene: Wipf & Stock, 2004.

Richards, Lawrence. *Theology of Children's Ministry*. Grand Rapids: Zondervan, 1983.

Ruppel, Joyce Ruppel. "Using Developmentally Appropriate Practice in Faith-Based Early Childhood Settings." In *Children's Spirituality: Christian Perspectives, Research, and Applications*, edited by Donald Ratcliff, 347–62. Eugene: Wipf and Stock, 2004.

Sifers, Sarah K., Jared S. Warren, and Yo Jackson. "Measuring Spirituality in Children." *Journal of Psychology and Christianity* 31 no. 3 (January 2012): 209–18.

Spackman, Carl K. *Parents Passing on the Faith*. Wheaton: Scripture Press, 1989.

Wangerin, Walter, Jr. *The Orphean Passages: The Drama of Faith*. Grand Rapids: Zondervan, 1986.

Westerhoff, John H. III. *Will Our Children Have Faith?* Revised Edition. Harrisburg: Morehouse, 2000.

Winik, Lyric Wallwork. "The Demise of Child-Rearing." *Public Interest* 141 (Fall 2000): 41–54.

Youtube Videos

https://www.youtube.com/watch?v=9t4_-p9d4k4.

https://www.youtube.com/watch?v=14hOxWe_FVU.

https://www.youtube.com/watch?v=wvfVf13GhYA.

https://www.youtube.com/watch?v=-PCAvOr9OO4.

9

SPIRITUALITY OF ADULTS

Clark G. Armstrong

Introduction

Human beings are wired with a spiritual dimension. Twenty-first-century adults are keenly interested in exploring the possibilities of spiritual meaning, and Christianity does not have a corner on the market. Michael Slaughter writes, "Postmodern people sense that the core of life and existence is spiritual.... Postmoderns are open to the supernatural. They believe in gods, but they are not sure which one. The harvest is ripe with seekers.... Communicators [are needed] who understand how to connect biblical truth with their felt needs."[1] In our time, we can confidently say that spirituality is "in" even if religion is not.

It is difficult to define an adult. Not every person who reaches a certain age or achieves a certain milestone can be identified as an adult just because he or she turned eighteen or graduated from high school.

---

1 Willimon, *The Pastor's Guide*, 79.

Getting married, taking on a job, or living independently is closer to what it means. An adult is *someone of legal age who is functionally responsible and capable of loving.*[2]

The brain is not fully developed until approximately age twenty-five. Yet, we make most of our major life decisions during the first stage of "adulthood."[3] Daniel Levinson divided adulthood into three stages: young adulthood, middle adulthood, and late adulthood.[4] Gail Sheehy broadened these to include many other *passages.* "Life Passages are the external phases of accomplishment or achievement that occur as we progress through the biologic life cycle."[5] Sheehy also coined the term "mid-life crisis," describing a stage of re-evaluation and re-charting of one's life.

Transitions are important in understanding the spirituality of adults because growth is incremental. Without these markers, those who study the spirituality of adults would have no way to measure any progress. The spirituality of adults must be understood along their normal developmental stages after late adolescence.

Development psychologist Erik Erickson introduced his theory of eight psychosocial developmental stages of life. The four stages related to adulthood should be considered in the adult's spirituality and search for meaning in life:

Intimacy vs. Isolation	Young Adulthood	22-35
Generativity vs. Stagnation	Middle Adulthood	34-60
Integrity vs. Despair	Late Adulthood	60-75
Immortality vs. Extinction	Older Adulthood	75 to Death

Stages like these define tasks within the normal development of adults.

---

2 Leypoldt, *Learning is Change,* 7–13.
3 Brown & Strawn, *The Physical Nature of Christian Life,* 18–25.
4 Wilber, *Life Passages Chart.*
5 Wilber, *Life Passages Chart.*

The latter two stages of adulthood become a grappling with the successes/failures of one's life with a hopeful view toward integrity.[6] These become the stages of passing the baton, discerning one's significance, and leaving one's legacy. Communicating experience and wisdom to the next generations becomes prominent.[7]

Contemporary studies identify further passages like Elderhood (75-95) and Senescence (95-100+). Elderhood overlaps with the Immortality/Extinction stage relating to debility, illness and infirmities, diminished capacities, and loss of control. Senescence may include some celebration(s). Among those who retain self-awareness, there is a universal task of coming to acceptance of one's life and death.

Spirituality in Asia

Ken Wilber has done an interesting study and named a stage Beyond Consciousness/Divine *Bardos* (plural). *Bardo* (singular) is a Tibetan word that simply means a "transition" or a gap between the completion of one situation and the onset of another. In the Tibetan view of spirituality, the term refers to the intermediate state or gap we experience between death and our next rebirth.

However, more generally, the word *bardo* refers to the gap or space we experience between any two states, including the *bardo* of sleeping/dreaming, the *bardo* of meditating, and even the *bardo* of this life itself, which is the intermediate state between birth and death.[8] Spirituality is seen as a series of multiple points of letting go and reinventing oneself (reincarnating), even within the journey of living this life.

While this book is essentially a Christian text, it can be helpful to consider the non-Christian understandings of the spirituality of adulthood (and of life itself) in order to understand best the Christian

---

6 See the last stage of Erik Erikson's stages of psychological development (*Identity and the Life Cycle*).
7 Wilber, *Life Passages Chart*
8 "Bardo," *Encyclopedia of Buddhism*.

position among the wisdom and understanding of the world. My own experience in Asia has helped me gain perspective about the Buddhism I encountered primarily in Korea and Myanmar (where I have taught), the Islamic views found in Mindanao, Pakistan, and Indonesia, the animism and Catholicism of the Philippines, the Taoism and Confucianism in China, the Shintoism of Japan, and the Hinduism, Jainism, and Sikhism of India. Many other major world religions or belief systems are also found in Asia: ancestor worship, secular atheism or humanism, Bahai religion, Hare Krishna, Judaism, Mormonism, and even evangelical Christianity.

Spirituality Defined

Spirituality is simply the giving of concern or attention to the non-materialistic parts of our human being-ness. Some views represent a religious pattern of *doing* things, while others represent a philosophical approach. Some see it as an exploration into the meaning of our existence; others teach that it is a path toward superseding the self and its consciousness. For some, there is a personal God; others acknowledge multiple gods or no god at all. Some hold a belief in a mysterious world of spirits, while others take a rational approach. Some systems have a very organized series of steps, rituals, or observances to follow. Some have a destination like heaven, enlightenment, or Nirvana; for others, it is about the journey (even into extended lives). Some see spirituality as preparation for the afterlife; others present a system of harmonious living within our current existence.

Bereavement helps us to appreciate, while still alive, what it means to die. The Tibetan term *bardo* ("intermediate state") is not just a reference to the afterlife transition but also refers more generally to any moments when gaps appear, interrupting the continuity that otherwise guides our lives. Counselors sometimes refer to this as feeling "ungrounded." These interruptions in our normal sense of equilibrium (*bardos*) refer to whenever we have lost our old reality, and it is no longer available to us.

The spirituality of adults is not that different from that of children or youth and builds as a direct extension of that foundation. For instance, Swiss psychologist Jean Piaget propounded a theory that cognitive development shifts from concrete operations to abstract thinking at around age 12.[9] It is then that concepts such as Jesus as the Lamb of God can be understood.

Adult spirituality expands the earliest trust levels of childhood by evaluating how our parents have shaped our views of God. Our generational influences (grandparent, teacher, pastor/priest, mentor, and "gurus") form our ideas of wisdom as we develop. Our journey from dependence to independence guides us hopefully into a healthy interdependence.

The shift in spirituality from youth to adulthood is also accompanied by the ability to fully use the brain's mirror neurons (neurotransmitters relayed through brain synapses) for contemplation and reflection. In Christian terms, we can deeply reflect on how Jesus could be both the Good Shepherd and the Sacrificial Lamb and the meaning of Jesus telling Peter, "Feed my sheep" after his resurrection.

Unfortunately, major "adult" decisions in many cultures are often made before the brain has developed to be able to evaluate their ramifications fully. More favorable conditions exist in cultures that are community-based rather than individualized. In those contexts, the autonomy and growth of the young adult can be maintained while the needed structural guidance can be sustained through family, culture, or religious traditions and practices.

---

9 Piaget.

Characteristics of Adult Spirituality

The idea of community in any context becomes a quest of adult spirituality. In the early adulthood stage, the task of fitting into one's own community overlaps the psychosocial stage of intimacy versus isolation and traverses the holistic move toward interdependence. Nevertheless, it could be stated that the move toward a monastic community or dedication toward a celibate priesthood (or its equivalency) can be a healthy resolution of this stage in terms of adult spirituality if the lifestyle rises from a deep devotion to an intimate relationship with God or the divinity. In some views, it may be considered the "healthiest" resolution of all in terms of spirituality.

If one task of adult spirituality is *"finding one's community,"* another is *"developing one's narrative"*—otherwise called "metanarrative" in post-modernism. In this grand idea, three strands are woven for adults: their **purpose** to live (and/or die) for; their **pilgrimage** (where it is headed, if anywhere, and who is traveling with them); and the **personal story** one writes or tells (of what is happening and the meaning of what is happening) on the way. All of these give our life its center and meaning.

These tasks are not ones that, upon completion, remain in a fixed state. In a vital adult spirituality, these tasks are alive, dynamic, and constantly growing, developing, and being revised as much as possible. The opposite in Erikson's psychosocial model would be stagnation. Some who appear to have "it all together" in a permanent condition may only reflect a more beautiful form of concrete existence.

Adult spirituality is not task-oriented at all but is *relational* in three dimensions: a) toward a spirit world, God, gods, or Godhead outside of ourselves, b) toward the spiritual being (or center) within us, and c) toward the spirituality we encounter within others. This relationship was echoed when Jesus summed up all the Old Testament law(s) in the two Great Commandments: to love *God* with all our heart, soul, mind, and strength; and to love our *neighbor as ourselves*.

It can be said, then, that another characteristic of adult spirituality is *making spiritual connections of love*. Christianity distinctly adds "of love," while the general description would simply be "making spiritual connections"; however, this is not unique to Christianity. Both Jews and Muslims look to the story of Abraham sacrificing his son Isaac (Ishmael, for Muslims) as an example of the highest form of love Abraham showed to God and the love that the son Isaac showed for his father. Love is such an endeavor in the contemplation of adult spirituality that the greatest writers of the ages, such as Søren Kierkegaard, have studied the account of Abraham's sacrifice of his son with "*Fear and Trembling.*"[10]

Another characteristic of the spirituality of adults is that it is *heuristic*. The dynamic and developing concept assumed with this word implies its synonyms (experiential, exploratory, investigative, empirical, and experimental). We know from psychology that we often grow by moving from equilibrium to disequilibrium and then finding a way to return to a new sense of equilibrium. What is true physically, mentally, and socially in our development is also a characteristic of our spiritual development.

Many people ask others, "How is that working for you?" If the narratives we develop (in our faith journey) are not working, it may be an opportune time to make some adjustments, resulting in a "conversion." Conversion indicates a complete turning. It may appear to be a climactic moment or event, or it may manifest itself in an almost imperceptible and gradual manner; nevertheless, it is one that eventually results in a completely new direction.

---

10 Kierkegaard, *Fear and Trembling and the Sickness unto Death*.

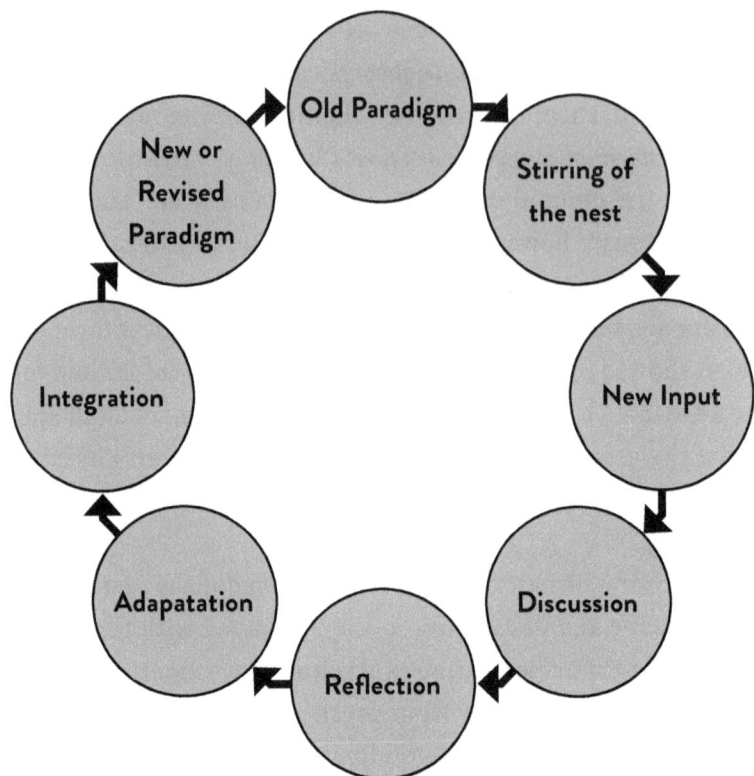

Figure 1: Adult Learning Path

The Adult Learning Path

Adult growth in spirituality comes mysteriously (the divine part) and through normal development and problem-solving. *For Christians, we synergistically cooperate with the grace of God at work primarily by his Spirit in our lives.* Overall, adults learn in a cyclical pattern. If the cyclical pattern were viewed as a clockwise circle, it would include the stages in Figure 1.[11]

---

11 This was an original framework of mine that I developed for my Master's in Religious Education, 1977-1981. It bears similarity to the ten-point pattern of Jack Mezirow the acclaimed founder of the field of Transformative Learning who came out with it in 1978. But I did not learn of how closely they compared until my doctoral studies in education when I was introduced to his work (2004-08).

Starting with our original paradigm, a stirring of the nest or "disorienting dilemma" occurs.[12] Learning results from a "disorienting dilemma" triggered by a life crisis or major life transition. Less dramatic predicaments, such as those created by a teacher, also promote transformation.[13] It may be a crisis, loss (*bardo*) moment, or a sense of inadequacy or need. Sometimes, it is an ongoing reflection, penetrating question, or fact of reality. An effective shift results in wanting or needing to learn.

Martha Leypoldt identified that "Learning is Change" for adults. Thus, learning and conversion are similar. In the next step, new information is gathered by various means. The learner may engage in reading, researching, or experimenting. New information may be the cause of an investigation. The person may participate in continuing education or seek knowledge from other sources. Adults combine discussion and reflection while processing new information. These stages are more heavily weighted toward discussion in the case of extroverts, while introverts are more reflective. The mixture of how much discussion and reflection is involved in any individual case may also be dependent upon personality types (Myers-Briggs) and multiple intelligences (Gardner and Hatch).

Either way, in whatever proportion they are engaged, the stages of discussion and reflection lead to the ensuing stage that becomes an adaptation of the persons' old beliefs, lifestyles, or even their whole faith. The adapted paradigm is integrated into persons' lives, either all at once or gradually in a series of steps resulting in a new or revised paradigm. The field of transformative learning calls this the process of "perspective transformation" and teaches that it has three dimensions: psychological (changes in the understanding of the self),

---

12 Mezirow, "Transformation Theory of Adult Learning," 39–70.
13 Torosyan, *Teaching for Transformation*.

convictional (revision of belief systems), and behavioral (changes in lifestyle).[14]

Jack Mezirow posits that all learning is change, but not all change is transformation. He shows a difference between transmissional, transactional, and transformational education. One of the difficulties in defining transformative learning is that it overlaps the constructivist view (meaning is constructed from knowledge) based on the work of educators such as Dewey, Montessori, Piaget, Bruner, and Vygotsky. The teachings of these theorists intersect with the adult learning path.

"However, learning is life—not a preparation for it. Therefore, transformational learning requires authenticity, a commitment to focus on the here and now, and awareness of feelings and emotions within the learning setting."[15] According to Stephen Brookfield, learning can only be considered transformative in the end if it involves fundamentally questioning or reordering how one thinks or acts.[16]

The new information is then integrated into the adult's belief systems and life resulting in a new or revised paradigm. They enjoy a new sense of equilibrium in their growth, faith, or life for an extended period. Later, another "stirring of the nest" may occur again. Embedded in this process is the reality that adult spirituality is not linear.

Formed, Conformed, Reformed, and Transformed

Guided by the Holy Spirit, Christians are constantly being formed, conformed, reformed, and transformed. Spiritual formation describes the overall process of God at work in terms of the person's growth:

- knowledge of and about God
- intimacy with God

---

14 Miller & Seller, *Curriculum*.
15 Dirkx, "Nurturing Soul in Learning," 79–88.
16 Brookfield, "Transformative Learning as Ideology Critique," 125–150.

- character development in the fruit of the Spirit and in Christlikeness
- ethical decision-making
- and right relations with self and others.

One image of spiritual formation is God as a potter at the wheel, *forming* a clay vessel fit for his purposes (Isa 29:16; 45:9; 64:8; Jer 18:1-6; Lam 4:2; Rom 9:21). Even when that vessel becomes broken, God still intends to repair and repurpose it (Jer 29:11; Phil 1:6).

Robert Mulholland gives a road map for spiritual formation. *He defines spiritual formation as the process of being conformed to the image of Christ for the sake of others.*[17] All four parts of his definition are important. It is a) a process. The process is one of b) "being conformed." The phrase "conformed to c) the image of Christ" is directly from Romans 8:29. Christlikeness is the goal. And it is not for our lives alone, but also d) for the sake of others.

Reformed can have two meanings. It can refer to being made over again a second time with a new beginning. That would be spelled "462re-formed." Reformed (without the dash) refers to the changes in our lives made of our own effort, as in, "he really has reformed his ways." There are changes on the road of adult spirituality that God leaves to measured and redeemed self-discipline in order for these changes to transpire in one's life.

The locus of control is internal and external for our spiritual formation. Reformation has an internal locus; conformation has an external locus. *Conformed* indicates action from outside the person, such as an action taken or a practice required by the religion or faith that one joins. Becoming part of that faith implies conformation to certain lifestyles, beliefs, or standards. In the biblical sense, a personal

---

17 Mulholland, *Invitation to a Journey*, 15.

God is intently interested in conforming his followers to the image of Christ. As a holy God, he seeks to have a holy people. Holiness is Christlikeness.

We cannot conform ourselves to his image. It is God who is committed to doing this work in his people. He does this by Christ dwelling/living inside our hearts (ontological center). We work out what he works in (Phil 2:12-13). The song, "Lord, I Need You," by Matt Maher, is correct in saying, "Holiness is Christ in me."

God is continually doing his conforming work in our lives through the amazing process of transformation. Second Corinthians 3:18 says, "And we all, who with unveiled faces contemplate the Lord's glory, are being transformed into his image with ever-increasing glory, which comes from the Lord, who is the Spirit." Transformation denotes metamorphosis like the caterpillar to cocoon to butterfly process. The process of *transformation* is not a reshaping of something old but is the Lord recurrently making something continually new, from one glory to another; it is a process. We are *being* transformed and are *contemplating* the Lord's glory (with mirror neurons fully engaged and involved in the process).

This transformation is synergistic: we cooperate with God and are involved in the process of being transformed. An illustration may help. Michael Jordan, a professional basketball player, once scored 70 points in a victory for his team. It was a phenomenon that had never been accomplished before. After the game, numerous reporters outside his locker room wanted an interview. Jordan pushed his teammate, Horace Grant, who had scored only two points near the end of the game, outside the door to be interviewed.

The nation watched the commentator ask Grant how he would remember such a historic night. His answer surprised everybody, "I shall always remember this night as the night that Michael and I combined for 72 points!" That captures the gist of it. God is continually transforming us from one glory to another in the process of our spiritual formation, reformation, and conformation. We must never forget that in this process, he is Jordan, and we are Grant.

The Holistic Nature of Adult Spirituality

The spirituality of adults is also holistic. Our spiritual lives are not something separate from our physical, mental, or social existences. We are an integral unity as persons. Jesus grew in wisdom (mentally) and stature (physically) and favor with God (spiritually) and humankind (socially; Luke 2:52).

The Greeks were trichotomists (body, soul, and spirit), which is reflected in Paul's writings in the Scriptures. The Romans were dichotomists (just corporeal and non-corporeal components). Most Middle Eastern cultures believed in the essential unity of human existence. Therefore, when someone died, people would often bury with the deceased person all the things he or she would need in the afterlife. Sometimes this even included killing the person's loved ones so that the person could have his or her meaningful relationships continue.

Scholars no longer adhere to these tri-, di-, or mono-chotomistic views. The study of humankind has consistently led to a more holistic view of our existence, especially our health and happiness. Much has been discovered about the connections between the mind and body. Direct connections have been made between prayer and health or between meditation and psychological well-being. If one area of our life is out of balance, unhealthy, or disconnected from the other areas, then all areas will be affected unfavorably.

The most fundamental way adult spirituality functions is through seven dimensions relevant to people's fullest health and growth. These dimensions form a helical model which contrasts with many traditional views that have focused only on the spiritual, psychological, and relational dimensions of people's lives. In this model, imagine three orbits intertwined with labels of different dimensions. The first has the physical dimension on one end and the play dimension opposite. The second has the mental dimension on one end and the work dimension opposite. The third has the relational dimension with the dimension of society/ nature opposite it. The seventh dimension is the spiritual/ethical dimension, at the center of where the three orbits intersect.[18]

Figure 2: Seven Dimensions for Cultivating Wholeness in People's Lives

This diagram was originally Nelle Morton's theoretical framework. She drew it to resemble the heart of an atom (in Clinebell). All facets must be fully and actively functioning together in a healthy operation. They should also be in a balanced orbit with all the others. This model adds four dimensions to the traditional approach: physical, play, work, and the world. The world has two parts: the social world (society/culture) and the physical world (nature). The spiritual dimension is enhanced by including the ethical element. Moral and faith development stages[19] should be studied as part of the spiritual/ethical dimension. In her diagram, the psychological aspect is listed as the "mental dimension." It would be better to name it "psychological" since that would be a more holistic term. It would include cognitive (mental) and affective (emotional) health.

A strength of the model in terms of the spirituality of adults is that the spiritual/ethical dimension is placed at its center. Most religious

---

18 Clinebell, *Basic Types of Pastoral Care & Counselling*, 30.
19 Fowler, *Stages of Faith*, 113.

approaches or discussions of adult spirituality would agree with that. In many Eastern religions or faiths, *"centering" is a main purpose for the daily practice of healthy adult spirituality.* Even in Christianity, centeredness, balance of all dimensions, and orbit around the center would be considered holistic health in adult spirituality. Having Christ at the center of one's life would be seen as the ideal template for cultivating wholeness in a person's life.

Spiritual Disciplines and Practices

The wholeness of adult spirituality can be experienced through meditation, prayer(s), or the observance of practices/disciplines that are a part of each approach. Some of the disciplines of the Christian approach may include prayer, Bible, church, baptism, worship, and witnessing.[20] Richard Foster's classical disciplines on the path of adult spirituality are in three categories: inward (meditation, prayer, fasting, study), outward (simplicity, solitude, submission, service), and corporate disciplines (confession, worship, guidance, celebration).[21] Donald Whitney adds to these: evangelism, stewardship, journaling, learning, and perseverance. He adds to the reading, hearing, or studying of the Bible—memorizing the word of God and applying the word of God.[22]

There is a major difference between transcendental meditation and Christian meditation. Transcendental meditation aims to empty one's mind completely of all thoughts or cares and to rest in that fixed place for a certain or indefinite length of time. Christian meditation is centering upon a particular scripture (Josh 1:8; Ps 1:2; 119:23, 48, 78, 97, 99, 148) or upon God himself:

- his character (Ps 19:14),

---

20 *GLC Essentials*, 3.
21 Foster, *Celebration of Discipline*, v.
22 Whitney, *Spiritual Disciplines*, 5.

- his being (Ps 77:3),
- his attributes (e.g., his love—Ps 48:9),
- his ways (Ps 119:15; 143:5; 145:5),
- or his deeds (Ps 77:12; 119:27).

In the Christian Scriptures, an empty mind is seen as a dangerous thing (Matt 12:43-45). It is like an unoccupied house into which any evil spirit could move. Instead, it should be filled with God's Spirit and thoughts of God and godly things (Phil 4:8).

Eventually, growth in adult Christian spirituality will come down to some inner and personal things:

- making things right with others
- releasing grudges
- forgiving those who have hurt you
- overcoming impure thoughts
- winning the battle against pride (humility)
- abandoning selfish ambition
- learning to be totally honest and transparent
- and living as a peacemaker in a broken world.

It may address interpersonal disciplines such as making restitution, restoring a fallen Christian, speaking truthfulness, or mending broken relationships.[23] By following Jesus and his ways (and with his power at work within a person), ordinary people can actually make progress in becoming like Christ.

The *Ordo Salutis* and "Taking the Next Step"

Post-modernism has taught us that spirituality is about "taking the next step." As far as the progress in becoming like Christ, theological approaches have taught a certain order of salvation. A Wesleyan

---

23 Drury, *Spiritual Disciplines for Ordinary People*, 9.

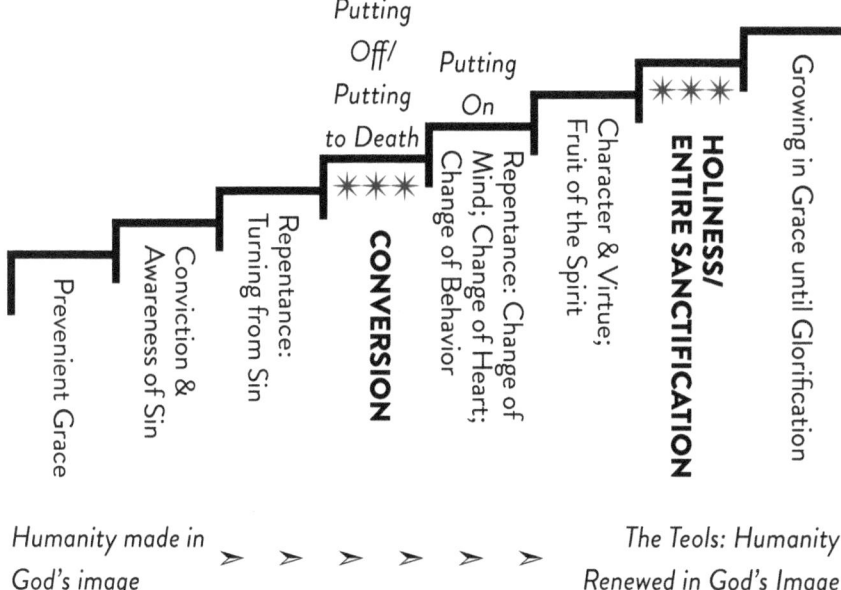

Figure 3. How God Changes Us: A Wesleyan
Way of Looking at Spiritual Formation

Ordo Salutis is demonstrated in a diagram by Keith Drury titled "How God Changes Us: A Wesleyan Way of Looking at Spiritual Formation." Becoming like Christ is equivalent with being renewed in God's image, which is taken from the idea of the *Imago Dei* in Genesis 1:26-27 and that humankind was originally made in the image of God, fell from grace and subsequently needs salvation, reconciliation, and restoration to God's image. The series of steps in Figure 3.

Catalysts toward progress in our formation include personal ministry, the Christian community, pivotal circumstances and suffering, spiritual disciplines, and the means of grace.

Discipleship and Disciple-Making

Since adult spirituality is a process of discipleship and disciple-making, the concern is not only for "converts." Christ's Great Commission that he gave his followers demonstrates his intentional goal (Matt 28:18-20) to make disciples. Therefore, it is important that a disciple-maker knows what a disciple is, what discipleship is, and how to make a disciple of Jesus Christ. The word "disciple" in Greek means a learner or follower. *Discipleship is a lifestyle transfer.* This definition would be true in any religious affiliation. Buddhist monks or devotees who wish to advance in spirituality enter an extended process of discipleship.

Much like the social learning theories, which emphasize the importance of modeling or emulating in the education process, the Peripatetics (like Jesus) of the first century did their teaching by walking around the countryside with a band of disciples who were "learning" from them. According to Albert Bandura, learning can occur by watching others and emulating what they do or say, known as observational learning. There are specific steps in the process of emulation that must be followed if learning is to be successful. These steps include attention, retention, reproduction, and motivation.[24]

Jesus was one of those who chose this method of training and fostering growth in the Way (or Tao). In fact, he said that he himself *was* the Way (Eastern religions), the Truth (Greco-Roman/Western religions), and the Life (zoē of the Middle Eastern/Hebrew religions). Whether discipleship is an intentional process or not, students will, for ebetter or for worse, become like their discipler, for better or for worse, whose life teaches far more than his or her words.

The medium *is* the message,[25] and the teacher *is* the final curriculum.[26] Early in my ministry, I designed a definition of a Christian disciple. It guided me in how to produce a disciple. It was adapted from a definition of a disciple taught by James Kennedy. A disciple is

---

24 Bandura, "Modeling Theory," 35–61.
25 McLuhan, *Understanding Media.*
26 Armstrong, "Choosing a Path."

- a fully devoted learner and follower of Jesus Christ who is
- functionally mature, responsible, and reproducing,
- and meaningfully connected to a cell group of a local church.

This definition has proven helpful over time. Within it are included Jesus' words in Luke 9:23 ("Whoever wants to be my disciple must deny themselves and take up their cross daily and follow me") as a part of what it means to be "fully devoted."

Conversion and Adult Spirituality

What does conversion mean in the discussion of discipleship and of transformation? William James conducted an extensive study of conversion. His work stands as formational. He wrote:

> To be converted, to be regenerated, to receive grace, to experience religion, to gain an assurance, are so many phrases which denote the process, gradual or sudden by which a self hitherto divided, and consciously wrong inferior and unhappy, becomes unified and consciously right superior and happy, in consequence of its firmer hold upon religious realities. This at least is what conversion signifies in general terms, whether or not we believe that a direct divine operation is needed to bring such a moral change about.[27]

Keith Drury describes how salvation occurs both inside and outside a person. He writes:

> Becoming a Christian is a life-changing event. In a single moment, you are brought to life inside. In an instant, God changes areas of your life at the crisis of conversion. However, most Christians recognize that they still have things in their lives that

---

27 James, *The Varieties of Religious Experiences*, 171.

do not measure up to the ideal. Your position may be "perfect in Christ," but your performance is obviously less than perfect.[28]

This change addresses also the work of God's sanctification, which begins at conversion but is a progressive process of God bringing to completion the good work that he has begun. Drury writes, "Sanctification is God's work inside us to transform us into Christlikeness."[29] According to Drury, there are five stages to God's changing process that describe how Christians change as God continues his work of moving us toward perfection (2 Cor 13:9):

1. Dawning Awareness
2. Growing Conviction
3. Crisis Decision
4. Changing Grace
5. Disciplined Obedience.[30]

It is not unusual for people to have multiple testimonies of small conversions throughout their spiritual journey, nor for them not to have a testimony at all of a crisis-like conversion experience. Horace Bushnell taught "that the child is to grow up a Christian, and never know himself as being otherwise."[31] The main goal of Christian nurture is to avoid the need ever to experience a conversion. George Coe wrote, "The term 'conversion' should be used only in the New Testament sense of a reversal, 'about face,' in the principle or policy of one's life."[32] Within a nurturing environment, change is small and in little increments in keeping with the age and development of a child.

---

28 Drury, *Spiritual Disciplines for Ordinary People*, 13.
29 Drury, *Spiritual Disciplines for Ordinary People*, 16.
30 Drury, *Spiritual Disciplines for Ordinary People*, 19–27.
31 Bushnell, *Christian Nurture*, 4.
32 Coe, *A Social Theory of Religious Education*, 181.

It need not be melodramatic like the revivalists prescribed. Bushnell says,

> It is a delicate matter for children to navigate in this rough sea of conversional tossings, where the stormy wind lifteth up the waves, and they go up to the heaven, and go down again to the depth, and their soul is melted because of trouble. For the little ones, there is a more quiet way of induction. Show them how to be good, and then, when they fail, how God will help them if they ask him and trust in him for help. In this manner they will be passing little conversion-like crises all the time.[33]

Coe propounded a theory that everyone (including adults) educationally and spiritually grows through multiple small conversions.[34] He originated the "caught versus taught" concept. For Bushnell, nothing needs to be caught if it is properly taught, but religion certainly must be taught for it to be caught. Augustine was the first to teach (AD 400) that all people should have a testimony of finding their heart's rest in God. "You have made us for yourself, and our heart is restless until it finds its rest in you."[35] His own conversion story has been viewed as an example of the Prodigal Son (Luke 15:11-32).

Comparison of Conversions

A comparison of the conversion testimonies of Augustine and Horace Bushnell finds similarities that fortify our teaching on adult spirituality. There is more than one conversion account for both![36]

---

33 Bushnell, *Christian Nurture*, 62.
34 Archibald, "George A. Coe."
35 Coe, *Can Religion be Taught?* 43.
36 Armstrong, "Choosing a Path," 289.

Figure 3: Comparison of Conversions

Augustine	Bushnell
His conversion to Manichaeism after reading Cicero's *Hortensius*	His "Saved as a Record of Dates" conversion when joining the New Preston Congregational Church
His conversion to Platonism after reading the Neo-Platonist writings of Plotinus	His "Dissolving of Doubts" conversion when pressed by the power of his influence at the time of a revival in New Haven (Yale)
His conversion to Christ after reading Romans 13:13-14 in the Garden of Milan ("Tolle Lege")	His "I Have Seen the Gospel" conversion shared alone with his wife in 1848 after the death of his son
His Heavenly Vision with his mother in Ostia days before her death	His "Laying Hold of God's Vicarious Character" and his identification with it in Christ as a follower

Confessions is a phenomenal book and represents a premier understanding of adult Christian spirituality. It includes the testimonies of at least fifteen other types of conversion than Augustine's. Augustine gives actual examples for most of these types. Our list also includes many contemporary types of conversions. Most people have experienced at least one, even if they are unaware of it.

Many who teach that having a conversion experience is not necessary rethink this after learning about them. Such knowledge brings new awareness that testimonies of multiple conversions are in keeping with adult spirituality and human growth. This diversity should free Christians to admit to experiencing various kinds of conversions during their pilgrimage with God. Moreover, these testimonies need not contrast with the *Ordo Salutis* but could be in step with it.

Figure 4: Types of Conversions

Lost Sheep	Aversio-Type Conversions
The Prodigal Son	Restoration of the Fallen

Spirituality of Adults 235

Odysseus (in Greek Mythology)	Example of Simon Peter
Other Themes	
Garden & Trees	Blossoming/Flowers/Seeds-Growth
Dreams & Visions	
Cataclysmic Event (St. Paul)	Hit by 2x4/Foxhole/Divorce
Romantic/Love	
Teacher/Student	
Death/New life	Death-Bed Conversion
Born Again	Nicodemus
Restless Heart	Augustine/"Confessions"
Sleeping/Waking	
Sobriety/Drunkenness	Addiction
Metanoia	Repentance/Turning (Zacchaeus)
Night/Day	Darkness/Light
Taking off/Putting on	Changing Clothes/Metaphor
Wrestling with God	Jacob
Cocoon-Type	Metamorphosis
Vicarious Conversion	Alyppius/Bushnell
"Little conversion-like crises"	Bushnell/Coe (gradual turning)
Call to Discipleship	Early Disciples
Change of Aspect	Wittgenstein
Transforming Moment	James Loder
Self-Integration	H. Richard Niebuhr
Paradigm Shift	Stephen Covey
Varieties of Religious Experiences	William James (Coe also had an extensive Questionnaire on Religious Experience that appears as Appendix A, The Spiritual Life, 261.)
Characters in the "*Confessions*"	
Augustine, Alyppius, Adeodatus, Valentinus, Security Guys, Comatose Guy, Simplicianus	

Conversion or sanctification can (either or both) be more of a gradual process than a crisis event. John Wesley explained the nature of this to be like a man a long time in dying versus when death occurs:

> Q. Is this death to sin, and renewal in love, gradual or instantaneous?
>
> A. A man may be dying for some time; yet he does not, properly speaking, die till the instant the soul is separated from the body; and in that instant he lives the life of eternity. In like manner, he may be dying to sin for some time; yet he is not dead to sin till sin is separated from his soul; and in that instant he lives the full life of love. And as the change undergone when the body dies is of a different kind, and infinitely greater than any we had known before, yea, such as till then it is impossible to conceive; so the change wrought when the soul dies to sin is of a different kind, and infinitely greater than any before, and than any can conceive till he experiences it. Yet he still grows in grace, in the knowledge of Christ, in the love and image of God; and will do so, not only till death, but to all eternity.[37]

James Loder describes four dimensions to every "transforming moment": the Lived World, the Self, the Void, and the Holy. He calls these the Four-Fold Knowing Event. We are transformed by their intersection. He states, "Under authentic conviction, all four dimensions become mutually supportive of human being, that is, they become consciously and intentionally dimensions of being human."[38]

We go from one *bardo* (passage) to another as we move through this lived world and are not lost into the void but are continually formed, reformed, conformed, and transformed by our contact with the Holy. Transformation is holistic and heuristic. As Paul said, "And we all,

---

37 Wesley, *A Plain Account of Christian Perfection*, 62.
38 Loder, *The Transforming Moment*, 68.

who with unveiled faces contemplate the Lord's glory, are being transformed into his image with ever-increasing glory, which comes from the Lord, who is the Spirit" (2 Cor 3:18).

This spiritual formation is not for us alone but remains ever for the sake of others. We are to impact the lived world with our compassion. Phineas Bresee said, "We are indebted to give to each man the gospel in the same measure in which we have received it."[39]

Bibliography

Archibald, Helen Allan. "George A. Coe." Retrieved July 5, 2010, from http://www2.talbot.edu/ce20/educators/view.cfm?n=george_coe.

Armstrong, Clark. "Choosing a Path: A Study of the Theories of Christian Conversion and Christian Nurture in the Confessions of St. Augustine and in Christian Nurture by Horace Bushnell." Ann Arbor: ProQuest LLC—UMI Dissertation Publishing, 2010.

Augustine. *The Confessions*. New York: Image Books Doubleday, 1960.

Bandura, Albert. "Modeling Theory: Some Traditions, Trends, and Disputes." In *Recent Trends in Social Learning Theory*, edited by Ross D. Parke, 35–61. Amsterdam: Elsevier, 1972, 2021.

Brookfield, S. A. (2000b). "Transformative Learning as Ideology Critique." In *Learning as Transformation*, edited by J. Mezirow & Assoc, 125–148. San Francisco: Jossey-Bass, 2000.

Brown, Warren S., and Brad D. Strawn. *The Physical Nature of Christian Life: Neuroscience, Psychology, and the Church*. New York, Singapore: Cambridge University Press, 2012.

Bushnell, Horace. *Christian Nurture*. New Haven: Yale University Press, 1888.

Clinebell, Howard. *Basic Types of Pastoral Care & Counseling: Resources for the Ministry of Healing & Growth*. Nashville: Abingdon, 2011.

---

39 *Preacher's Magazine*, "Paul's Guideposts," 1.

Coe, George Albert. *A Social Theory of Religious Education.* New York: Arno, 1969. A revision of *A Social Theory of Religious Education.* New York: Charles Scribner's Sons, 1917.

———. *Can religion be taught?* The Inauguration of George Albert Coe, Ph.D., LL.D., as Skinner and McAlpine Professor of Practical Theology. New York: Union Theological Seminary.

———. *The Spiritual Life.* New York: Eaton & Mains, 1900.

Dirkx, J. M. "Nurturing Soul in Learning." *New Directions for Adult & Continuing Education,* Volume 1997 Issue 74 (Summer 1997): 79-88.

Drury, Keith. *Spiritual Disciplines for Ordinary People.* Valenzuela City: CLC Publications, 2004.

Duska, Ronald, and Mariella Whelan. *Moral Development: A Guide to Piaget and Kohlberg.* New York: Paulist, 1975.

Encyclopedia of Buddhism "Bardo." https://encyclopediaofbuddhism.org/wiki/Bardo. Accessed on 12/7/21.

Erikson, Erik H. *Identity and the Life Cycle.* New York: Norton, 1980.

Foster, Richard J. *Celebration of Discipline: The Path to Spiritual Growth.* San Francisco: Harper & Row, 1978.

Fowler, James W. *Stages of Faith: The Psychology of Human Development and the Quest for Meaning.* San Francisco: Harper and Row, 1981.

Gardner, Howard, and Thomas Hatch. "Multiple Intelligences Go to School: Educational Implications of the Theory of Multiple Intelligences." *Educational Researcher,* Vol. 18 No. 8 (November 1989): 4-10.

GLC Essentials: Book 2—Spiritual Disciplines. Pasig: Christ Commission Fellowship, 2015.

James, William. *The Varieties of Religious Experiences: A Study in Human Nature.* New York: Barnes & Noble Classics, 1902, 2004.

Kennedy, D. James. *Evangelism Explosion*, Fourth Edition. Carol Stream: Tyndale House, 1996.

Kierkegaard, Søren. *Fear and Trembling and the Sickness unto Death*. Translated by Walter Lowrie. Princeton: Princeton University Press, 1954.

Levinson Daniel J. "A Conception of Adult Development." *American Psychologist*, vol. 4 (1986): 3–13.

Leypoldt, Martha. *Learning is Change: Adult Education in the Church*. Valley Forge: Judson, 1971.

Loder, James E. *The Transforming Moment: Understanding Convictional Experiences*. San Francisco: Harper & Row, 1981.

McLuhan, Marshall. *Understanding Media: The Extension of Man*. London: Routledge & Kegan Paul, 1975.

Mezirow, Jack. "Transformation Theory of Adult Learning." In *In Defense of the Lifeworld*, edited by M. R. Welton, 39–70. New York: SUNY, 1995.

———. *Transformative Dimensions of Adult Learning*. San Francisco: Jossey-Bass, 1991.

Miller, J. P., and W. Seller. *Curriculum: Perspectives and Practice*. Toronto: Copp Clark Pitman, 1990.

Mulholland, M. Robert. *Invitation to a Journey*. Downer's Grove: InterVarsity Press, 1993.

Myers-Briggs Type Indicator® (MBTI®) | Official Myers Briggs Personality Test). www.themyersbriggs.com. Archived from the original on August 26, 2019. Retrieved October 31, 2021.

Preacher's Magazine, Volume 45 Number 03 (March 1970): 1. Quote by Phineas F. Bresee in an article titled "Paul's Guideposts," by D.I. Vanderpool. Retrieved January 26, 2022, from https://

digitalcommons. olivet. edu / cgi / viewcontent.cgi ? referer = & httpsredir = 1 & article = 1512 & context = cotn_pm.

Sheehy, Gail. *Passages: Predictable Crises of Adult Life.* New York: E. P. Dutton, 1976.

Torosyan, Roben. *Teaching for Transformation: Integrative Learning, Consciousness Development and Critical Reflection.* 2007. Unpublished manuscript.

Wesley, John. *A Plain Account of Christian Perfection.* Kansas City: Beacon Hill, 1971.

Whitney, Donald S. *Spiritual Disciplines for the Christian Life.* Colorado Spring: NavPress, 1991.

Wilber, Ken. *Life Passages Chart*—Appendix A. "Table 3: STAGES OF DEVELOPMENT—Life Passages." Taken from www.kenwilber.com. Accessed on August 22, 2018.

Willimon, William, et al. *The Pastor's Guide to Effective Ministry.* Kansas City: Beacon Hill, 2002.

10

TOWARDS COHERENCE: EXPLORING SPIRITUALITY AS A UNIFYING LINK IN THEOLOGICAL EDUCATION

Bruce G. Allder

Introduction

The Church of the Nazarene, Asia-Pacific, lists nine regional priorities that form the lens through which all strategic initiatives are viewed.[1] The third of the nine relates to *Cohesive Education and Ministerial Preparation.* The statement equates coherence with the integration of education across the whole Asia-Pacific region. A classic definition of coherence is "the situation when parts of something fit together in a natural or reasonable way."[2] As such, the term integration is appropriate. However, understanding the basis for this coherence can help in developing the intentionality of this strategic priority. This chapter explores how such coherence can be expressed in

---

1 https://asiapacificnazarene.org/about-us/regional-priorities
2 https://dictionary.cambridge.org/dictionary/english/coherence

theological education. Several implications are then suggested based on taking this strategic priority seriously.

Coherence

There are several different aspects of coherence in theological education that can be considered. Firstly, coherence can be thought of in structural terms, especially when thinking of the 13 educational institutions that are a part of the educational system in the Church of the Nazarene, Asia Pacific. An important challenge to face is determining how these institutions can collaborate, function, and share resources to avoid the siloing effect contextual issues of language, culture, and educational processes tend to create. However, before addressing the structural issues, more fundamental aspects of coherence can shape the structural conversation.

Secondly, coherence can be thought of in terms of a common program (such as a course of study for ordination) that brings curriculum issues to the fore. How might a particular curriculum cohere and flow? In a global denomination such as the Church of the Nazarene, there is a strong desire to have core material within an overall program common to many different contexts. This similar content can provide a basis for coherence. Within this common core is a theological perspective that is identifiable as an essential part of the identity of a global denomination like the Church of the Nazarene.

Thirdly, coherence can be found by using a common lens through which educational experiences are directed. Woodruff understands this common lens to be outcomes toward the focus or purpose of the educational program.[3] The inputs are described in terms of the "4Cs" of ministry preparation: Content, Competency, Character, and Context.[4] While the inputs are broadly defined in these four catego-

---

3   Woodruff, *Education on Purpose*, 9.
4   Church of the Nazarene *Manual 2017–2021*, para. 529.3.

ries, Woodruff emphasizes the need for these inputs to be integrated rather than parallel to each other. Without integration, he sees a risk of tension and competing priorities.[5] Such lack of integration can result in confusing and, perhaps, rather fuzzy outcomes. These are important distinctions, and building on this understanding can help provide a strong and nuanced ministry preparation program.

Fourthly, coherence can be established if the core at every level of the denomination (not just the educational enterprises) is acknowledged as having the same focus. This unity is found in commitment to the denomination's mission, which is making Christlike disciples, who in turn make Christlike disciples. This aspect is a powerful vehicle for coherence as this common calling is acknowledged and expressed at every level of the church. In the case of the Church of the Nazarene, this means observing this commitment at the local, district, regional, and global levels.

This fourth element of coherence provides a solid, unifying base for the educational ministry of the Church of the Nazarene. The denominational mission is to make Christlike disciples in the nations.[6] Such a focus for the whole church points to the necessity of an integrated approach. At this point, we could choose to enter the conversation from a variety of perspectives. For example, we could look through the eyes of church leadership and at the various administrative levels of the church. Alternatively, we could approach the conversation from a local church perspective and explore the contextual nature of this calling. However, this chapter enters the conversation from the perspective of ministry preparation and theological education. I hope that by so doing, we can take the strategic priority of coherence in theological education seriously.

---

5   Woodruff, *Education on Purpose*, 12.
6   Church of the Nazarene *Manual 2017–2021*, para. 529.3.

The Relational Nature of Discipleship

It is very easy to think of discipleship as a program, a set of doctrines to be learned, or a set of practices to be involved. With these emphases, making disciples is a process of attending programs and learning required doctrines. Often a sense of "safety" accompanies this as we attempt to manage the content. While we may be well-intentioned in using such approaches, discipleship is gradually reduced to a cerebral acknowledgment of a set of premises that may or may not shape behavior or experience. Alternatively, such an approach can drift into a set of behaviors that do not impact the heart and become dry, disconnected activities. Either way, we lose the sense of mystery and open-endedness that comes with a deepening relationship.

I suggest that discipleship is cultivating a spirituality that nurtures a relationship with God and others. This unfolding relationship leads to Christlikeness in mission. Discipleship is deeply relational and, as such, is expressed in practical, tangible ways. The essence of discipleship needs to be embedded in our theological education: the nurturing and forming of a relationship with God and others. As we encounter the trinitarian God, we cannot help but be astounded by the gracious invitation to join in the divine dance of Father, Son, and Holy Spirit.[7] Jesus prayed, "as you, Father, are in me and I am in you, may they also be in us" (John 17:21a, NRSV). Critical to this understanding of discipleship is the re-appreciation of the Trinity.

But we are a product of our own context and educational experiences. In most cases, we have moved away from a relational focus and a relational knowing. Perhaps it is more accurate to say that we have been distracted by what appears safer or more comprehensible. Bennett speaks of the emergence of objectivism by way of "a widespread epistemology and implicit ontology and ethics that elevate a

---

7   Rohr, *The Divine Dance*.

spirituality of fragmentation and isolation over one of community and collaboration."[8]

Rohr suggests this drift began as far back as Aristotle, who distinguished between "substance" and "relationship":

> What defined substance was that it was independent of all else—so a tree is a substance, whereas a "father" is a relationship... Aristotle ranked substance the higher.... So, what the West found itself doing in the earliest traditions ... was trying to build on Aristotle to prove that this God whom we had come to understand as Trinitarian was a substance. We didn't want an ephemeral old relationship God.... We wanted a substantial God whom we could prove was as good as anybody else's God! ... Yet when this Jesus is revealed to us Christians by calling himself the Son of the Father and yet one with the Father, he is giving clear primacy to relationship.[9]

Because we are so steeped in this Aristotelean thought from our educational upbringing, it is difficult to think carefully about a different way of knowing. Rohr goes on to say:

> All authentic knowledge of God is *participatory knowledge*....
> It should be the unique, open-horizoned gift of people of faith. But we ourselves have almost entirely lost this way of knowing, ever since the food fights of the Reformation and the rationalism of the Enlightenment, leading to fundamentalism on the Right and atheism on the Left. Neither of these knows how to know! We have sacrificed our unique telescope for a very inadequate microscope.[10]

---

8   Bennett, "Educational Spiritualities."
9   Rohr, *The Divine Dance*, 44–45.
10 Rohr, *The Divine Dance*, 49, emphasis mine.

Edgar picks up a similar theme in his book, *God is Friendship: A Theology of Spirituality, Community and Society*. Using John 15:15[11] as the springboard for his theology of spirituality, Edgar sketches the movement from lordship to servanthood to friendship.

> When friendship becomes a dominant image of the form of diving-human relationship, then it is as though the old structures have been done away with, and everything shifts into a new way of being. . . . Not only is lordship or "greatness" to be interpreted in the light of servanthood, but servanthood is to be interpreted within the context of friendship.[12]

This shift is profound. When Jesus says, "you are my friends if you do what I command you" (John 15:14, NRSV), we may have thought previously that this was a command to servitude. However, Edgar points out that this is "best understood as consequential rather than conditional."[13] There is a freedom and dynamism to this relationship that is transformative. There is a positive "going the second mile" in relationships based on a love that grounds the connection. We follow the law not out of a sense of duty but out of a love for and friendship with the Triune God and humanity.

If we are to make this shift in our discipleship to a deeply relational engagement with God and others, then the point of friendship is to develop virtue. With the development of character, the fruits of the Spirit (Gal 5:22) are all expressed within community. "The fruit of the Spirit simply cannot be learned in isolation; they are essentially relational,

---

11 "I do not call you servants any longer, because the servant does not know what the master is doing; but I have called you friends, because I have made known to you everything that I have heard from my Father" (John 15:15, NRSV).

12 Edgar, *God is Friendship*, 21.

13 Edgar, *God is Friendship*, 22.

and growth in Christian life depends on having close companions who can help develop them. . . . The road to holiness is not taken alone."[14]

Is not this the heart of discipleship? The meaning-making that moves beyond substance to relationality accommodates the former because of the latter.

Relational Learning

As we suppose that discipleship is a spirituality of relationship with God and others, formal engagement in the educative process must embrace a way of learning that nurtures this. There is a need to break out of our embedded "objectivism," which Bennett describes as destructive to community because of its misleading picture of ourselves as independent and self-sufficient.[15] There is an open-endedness to the learning experience that takes us to a new way of knowing.

The categorization of the forum where learning can take place in the educational setting is worth noting. Formal learning is intentional and done in the formal relationships between teacher and student. We think in terms of a set curriculum and assigned tasks and learning hours. However, just as important is the non-formal learning that engages the students. This may happen in a classroom setting coincidentally or, more likely, outside of the formal setting of the classroom. This non-formal setting is no less important as it inculcates the ethos of the learning environment and the values of what we seek to impart. In theological settings, this may be the attendance at chapel, spiritual enrichment exercises entered into voluntarily, and the conversations that may happen during morning tea or lunch with fellow students and faculty. In the case of remote learning, it may be the time spent before and after class online where teachers and students interact informally or engage in blogging. The third kind of learning is informal

---

14 Edgar, *God is Friendship*, 75.
15 Bennett, "Educational Spiritualities," 177.

or casual learning that takes place in all different settings and quite serendipitously. Many times, under the pressure of formal learning, these non-formal and informal learning experiences are perceived as interference or pushed aside as suspect.[16] However, in ministry preparation and formation, the intentional creation of space for all three forums will enrich and strengthen the educational experience.

Once participative knowledge is understood as an important dimension of spirituality, Wenger's implications for learning are relevant.

> For individuals, it means that learning is an issue of engaging in and contributing to the practices of their communities.
>
> For communities, it means that learning is an issue of refining their practice and ensuring new generations of members.
>
> For organizations, it means that learning is an issue of sustaining the interconnected communities of practice through which an organization knows what it knows and thus becomes effective and valuable as an organization.[17]

Such participative learning (knowledge) suggests an approach to ministry preparation that embraces a holistic pedagogy. Fuertes and Dugan conclude from their study of undergraduate and graduate students that non-formal learning opportunities for expression need to be integrated with formal opportunities. These opportunities include experiential learning that expands a range of desired outcomes, including

> expanded cultural fluency, critical and reflective thinking, well-being, [and] interpersonal relationships. . . . Forms of experiential learning may include local community immersion or integration where students live with the local people, experience their cultures, and are part of the community's interpersonal

---

16 Mullino Moore, "Nourishing Relationships," 104.
17 Wenger, "A Social Theory of Learning," 223.

and social interactions, which forge deep bonding and meaningful, sustainable relationships.[18]

The challenge for theological education is to intentionally move the locus of formal education to include places outside the classroom. This can include local community immersion, where students become part of local faith communities and all the relationships that they hold. Connectionalism and intentional partnership across all levels of the denomination that ensure that such formation is the responsibility of the whole church are critical elements to ministry formation within the Church of the Nazarene.[19] This relocation to embrace more than a

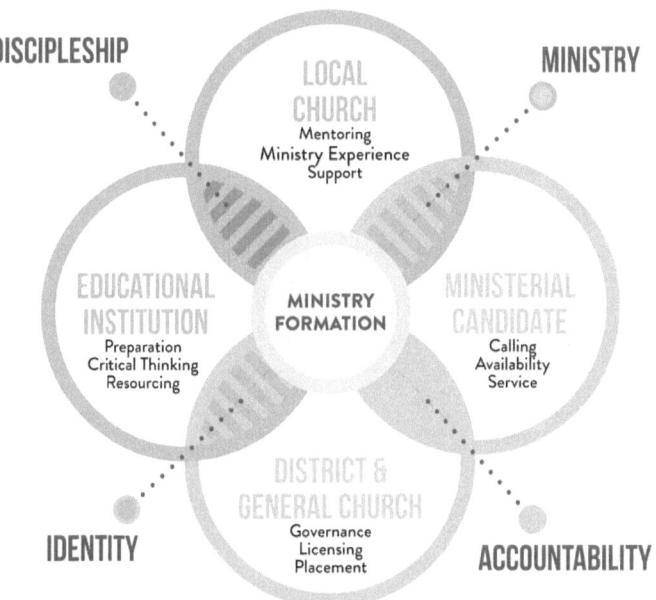

Figure 1: Essential Partnerships in Ministry Formation in the Church of the Nazarene

---

18 Fuertes and Dugan, "Spirituality through the Lens of Students," 10.
19 Allder, "Leveraging Wesleyan Connectionalism," 351–65.

formal classroom setting is challenging on many fronts but a move that is being suggested more broadly than the Church of the Nazarene.[20] The intentional partnerships illustrating the mutual responsibilities at all levels of the Church of the Nazarene are given in figure 1.

Without all areas of the process engaging collaboratively, ministry preparation is less than it ought to be. The natural tendency is to get busy with our own areas of unique activity and drift into a silo that loses the collaborative element so essential in relational and participative learning. These partnerships model an outcome in ministry formation that gives the process inherent dignity and power.

The Emmaus Model[21] for Ministry Formation

Several different approaches to ministry formation have emerged over the centuries, and in recent times, several have been a response to challenges in educational effectiveness. Das has summarized many of these attempts with helpful insights into the theological and missional motivations for different models.[22] To respond to the context of the Church of the Nazarene in the Asia-Pacific Region, the Emmaus Model seeks to synthesize the Athens (Classical)[23] model and Jerusalem (Robert Banks)[24] model. Table 1 summarizes the features compared to the classical and missional models.

Symbol	Athens	Jerusalem	Emmaus
Model	Classical	Missional	Journey in the company of others

---

20 See Harkness, "De-Schooling the Theological Seminary," 103–128.
21 This title is not unique. For example, Spencer ("Seminaries and Discipleship") uses the same connection between discipleship and Luke 24. See our first representation of the Emmaus Model in Allder and Ackerman. *The Emmaus Model.*
22 Das, *Connecting Curriculum with Context*, 17.
23 Kelsey, *Between Athens and Berlin.*
24 Banks, *Reenvisioning Theological Education.*

Context	Academy	Community	Community of faith living in the wider diverse world
Goal/ Purpose	Transforming the individual	Converting the world	Discipled "disciple-multiplier" as a lifelong learner
Emphasis	Personal formation: knowing who ...	Mission, partnership: knowing for ...	Personal and group formation toward Christlikeness in the *missio Dei*
Formation	Individualized and focused on inner personal, moral and religious transformation	Learning has to have reference to all dimensions of life, family, friendships, work, and neighborhood	Shaped by an encounter with Christ and His community
Theology	Theology is the knowledge of God, not about God	Missiology is the mother of theology. It involves action - mission.	A theology of embodiment of the gospel, i.e., Incarnation of Kingdom of God principles and servanthood
Teacher	Provider: of indirect assistance through intellectual and moral disciplines to help students undergo formation	Practitioner/ missionary: the teacher is not removed from practice; teaching involves sharing lives as well as truth	Discipler / Mentor / Coach/fellow learner - sharing life as well as knowledge

| Student | Cultivates the mind, character, and spirit | Discipled to become a disciple-maker | Discipled to be a disciple-maker and shaper of culture |

Table 1: Comparison of the Athens and Jerusalem Models in Ministry Formation

Based upon Luke 24:13–35, the Emmaus Model seeks to bring an outcomes-based perspective on learning to an approach that embraces participative (relational) knowledge (learning). There are at least four key elements to the Emmaus Model. The first is understanding ministry formation and theological education as a journey. In Luke, two disciples made the sad journey homeward, thinking that their hopes and dreams had been shattered by the recent event of Jesus' crucifixion. What had been anticipated had not been fulfilled. Confusion, depression, and bewilderment were all features of their journey. Their journey had not always been like this. They connected with Jesus and his other disciples and witnessed many great things. It was a thrill to engage with the Messiah! However, circumstances changed their perspective.

The concept of journey is not particularly a revolutionary thought in terms of discipleship, but if we place this in Fowler's faith development schema,[25] "journey" suggests a particular pedagogy. Figure 2 illustrates these stages of faith in terms of steps in the discipleship process. Encountering "The Wall" is a significant element in this process.

In describing transformational learning, Mezirow speaks in terms of a *disorienting dilemma* that leads to critical self-reflection and the examination of assumptions along with feelings.[26] This disorientation can be understood in terms of hitting "The Wall," as illustrated in Figure 2. The temptation for the one encountering this disorienting

---

25 Fowler, *Stages of Faith*.
26 Mezirow, "Transformative Learning Theory," 118.

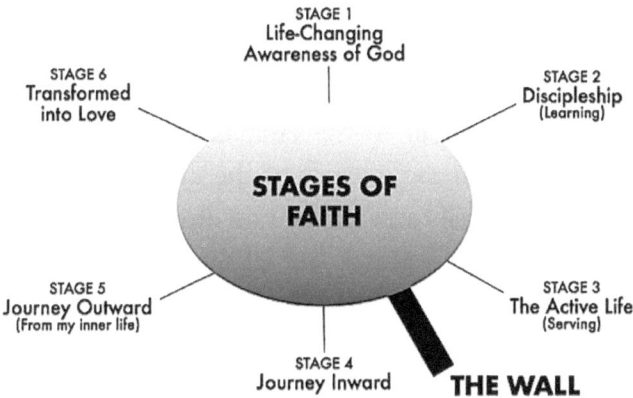

Figure 2: An Interpretation of Fowler's Stages of Faith

experience is to recoil from it and stay at a superficial level where surety and safety appear to exist. However, if there is the cultivation of a safe place for such for a person to explore the reasons for the disorienting experience, significant learning can take place. This is a challenging part of the journey. Dean Smith speaks in terms of an epistemological crisis where

> the breakdown in one's interpretive framework can lead to tremendous personal and existential suffering. . . . In some conservative circles where faith is reduced to a belief in a set of propositions, [this kind of crisis] can be interpreted as a failure of faith. Backsliding, if you will. But what if such a crisis can be interpreted as not a failure of faith but rather the signaling of progress in faith development? [27]

One can envision, especially in ministry formation, that such a journey may result in numerous epistemological crises in which the teacher becomes the relational guide through the existential mire of a

---

27 D. Smith, "Growing Pains," 5.

different way of knowing. Creating a safe place required for this journey is imperative, and the pedagogical strategy requires a relational base.

The second key element in the Emmaus Model appears in how the role of Scripture in the journey of the disciples was critical. As Jesus explained the Scriptures to the two disciples while walking to Emmaus, "Beginning with Moses and all the prophets, he interpreted to them the things about himself in all the Scriptures" (Luke 24:27 NRSV). While there were, no doubt, several "aha!" moments, it was not just about getting the content and understanding correct. On reflection of their encounter with Jesus, the disciples said, "Were not our hearts burning within us?" (Luke 24:32a NRSV). The Scriptures played a formative role in the lives of these disciples. Such formation might appear more nebulous in a pedagogy, but the re-emphasis in recent times on such activities as *Lectio Divina*, small groups, and online discussions all create opportunities to engage with Scripture in a transformative way. Maddix and Thompson speak of this formative nature in the development of the canon but also in the shaping of the church in modern times.[28] Being exposed to Scripture in a regular and systematic way has a way of shaping the people of God. Small groups, involvement in the practice of *Lectio Divina*, and hearing Scripture in times of corporate worship all provide the opportunity for transformation. James K. A. Smith expresses it:

> There is something about this reality that I can only know in the practice itself. I learn something in the doing that can't ever be put into words and yet is its own irreducible sort of understanding. . . . Carried in the practices of Christian worship is an understanding of God that we "know" on a register deeper than the intellect, an understanding of the gospel on the level of imagination that changes how we comport ourselves in the

---

28 Maddix and Thompson, "Scripture as Formation," 79–93.

world, even if we can never quite articulate it in beliefs or doctrines or a Christian worldview.[29]

The challenge is to allow Scripture to shape us rather than for us to shape the Scripture to our own cultural and personal images. Such readings are best conducted in a group setting. This way, we get to hear, probe, and challenge our own preconceived ideas in the interpretive process.

Third, hospitality was an important aspect of the experience of the disciples in Luke 24. It was around the meal table that space was created for grace, conversation, and the demonstration of connectedness to a past that brought recognition of Jesus (Luke 24: 30, 31). The disciples' recognition of Jesus was linked to them seeing him bless the bread, break it, and give it to them. This sacramental action drew together several of what seemed like disconnected events into the person of Jesus. In our time, poor cultures of rushing, pragmatism, and the demand for outcomes (usually focused on self), taking time to rehearse events of the past (remembering), and pausing to sense (or perhaps see for the first time) connections are neglected aspects to ministry formation that need to be recovered. Hearing each other's stories and identifying God at work in unlikely and seemingly disparate ways provide a sense of presence, space, and connection that would otherwise be missed. Marva Dawn's book on worship is beautifully entitled, *A Royal "Waste" of Time: The Splendor of Worshiping God and Being Church for the World*.[30] It may feel like wasting time, but slowing down enough to listen to each other and to God is an important element of ministry formation.

Whetham and Eaton extend this process of journey to the task of evangelism, which can be understood as disciple making:

---

29 J. Smith, *You Are What You Love*, 85–86.
30 Dawn, *A Royal "Waste" of Time*.

> Part of the answer is to say that as a person living in a co-learning community (missional community) [is] listening to God . . . , then essentially the role of the gospel-sharer is to simply invite people into that listening space with you, either one on one or in a small group. This means you don't have to have a script memorised as to the essential truths of the gospel, but rather you are freed up to have real conversations leading to co-learning.[31]

Apart from the time invested, there is also a physicality to this hospitality that engages learning. To use James K. A. Smith's terminology, we enter God's story.

> To do by "feel" what cannot be done by regular conscious thought: that's not a bad description of the goal of discipleship. To conform to the image of the Son is to have so absorbed the gospel as a "kinesthetic sense," a know-how you carry in your bones, that you do by "feel" what cannot be done by conscious thought. You have been remade in Christ such that there are ways you love him that you don't even know. You have a Christlike "feel" for the world, and you act accordingly without thinking about it.[32]

This physicality is expressed in relationships with real people in real time. The gospel is incarnated and touches us in our life circumstances. We laugh together, cry together, eat meals together, and converse with each other—even though we are so different from each other. In vulnerability, we lose the barrier-forming habit of objectifying the other to learn to "know" relationally in a physical world that is far from perfect. "The basic 'sacramental principle' is this: we can know spiritual things through the physical world and bodily actions."[33]

---

[31] Whetham and Eaton, *Lighthouses*, 39.
[32] J. Smith, *You Are What You Love*, 108.
[33] Rohr, *The Divine Dance*, 105.

Fourth, transformation is the consequence or result of this engagement. The disciples had initially persuaded Jesus to stay overnight with them because it was late in the day. Presumably, night travel was dangerous, and it would be safer to accept the hospitality of the two disciples and move on the next day. Yet, once they had recognized Jesus and he had left them, "that same hour, they [the disciples] got up and returned to Jerusalem" (Luke 24:33, NRSV). These discouraged, confused disciples, who were cautious of the night, were now excited and motivated with a mission to go and tell their fellow disciples that they had met with Jesus. Night was no longer an issue.

A new understanding of Scripture in the light of Jesus' life, death, and resurrection (a connecting of the dots, if you will) and a burning heart from an encounter with Jesus became the raw material for transformation. This change was both an existential change as well as a change in behavior. In the light of what Christ has done, Paul writes:

> From now on, therefore, we regard no one from a human point of view; even though we once knew Christ from a human point of view, we know him no longer in that way. So, if anyone is in Christ, there is a new creation: everything old has passed away; see everything has become new! (2 Cor 5:16–17, NRSV)

In addition to the four key elements of journey, the important role of Scripture, hospitality, and transformation—the lens through which everything flows also has implications for our pedagogy. The Emmaus Model envisages the lens as Christlikeness *in* mission (see Figure 3). It is this lens and the focus of the lens toward a Christlike disciple-maker that suggest a pedagogical perspective that places demands upon the teacher.

The teacher's role shifts to one who comes alongside and is more than the deliverer of content. The teacher is one who models the transformative process. Terms such as relational learning, mentor, coach, student-centered learning, experience, empowerment, communities

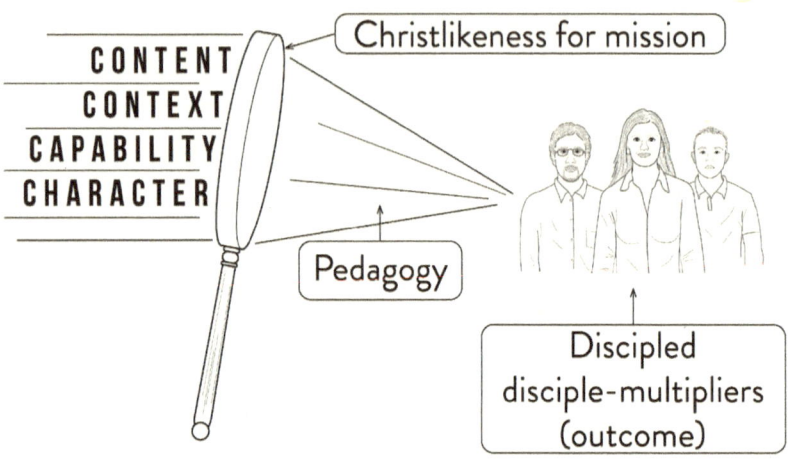

Figure 3: The Emmaus Model

of practice, values, identity, application, and formation become important as pedagogical vehicles for ongoing transformation.

Ministry formation in this model takes place while the student is in some form of ministry. From the moment persons become Christ's followers, they are to become disciple makers. This is the core of ministry. If this is taken seriously, then all students have a learning environment in multiple places other than the classroom. To ignore this is to take away spheres of learning, both non-formal and informal, that are rich in both content and experience.

Applying the Emmaus Model

A trend in the demographic of students preparing for formal ministry has been toward mature age, already employed, and part-time students. This has required a re-evaluation of education delivery systems to allow for accessibility. Further complicating the provision of theological education is the changing contexts into which graduates will minister. Bi-vocational ministry, team ministry, and the need to work from the margins of society now add a "normative" edge to what was previously left to missiologists to ponder. In many cases, theological colleges continue to provide for the traditional full-time student who moves to a campus, but opportunities provided by technology and effective partnerships between education providers and local faith communities have resulted in alternative creative approaches. Scholars and practitioners within the ICETE[34] family have been a part of this creative edge. Of interest in this conversation is the work being done addressing quality assurance in theological education by extension (TEE).[35] The structure of TEE curricula, as represented in Figure 4[36], lends itself to employing the Emmaus Model.

The benefits of TEE's decentralized approach, the focus on the local faith fellowship as a locale for learning, its flexibility in delivery, and the focus on discipleship make this very attractive. However, much of the work of TEE has been through the lens of the local community of faith and mission, but Aylett *et al.* have usefully applied a quality assurance lens appropriate for academic institutions and the rigors of accrediting agencies.[37] While there is much more work to be done in this arena, as the TEEs delivery mechanism has become more accessible to accredited theological institutions because of this work. The potential to formalize the partnerships and relationship between the education provider and the local faith fellowship is enormous. This potential, however, raises the thorny question of quality assurance. In settings

---

34 ICETE is the International Council for Evangelical Theological Education https://www.icete-edu.org/ and has published a number of useful volumes as a result of international consultation gatherings that attract evangelical scholars from around the world.
35 See Van Wingerden *et.al, TEE for the 21st Century,* and Van Wingerden *et. al, TEE in Asia.*
36 Green, "Equipping Disciples and Leaders through TEE," 18.
37 Aylett, Green, and Weymouth, "TEE and Quality Assurance," 237–267.

Figure 4: TEE Structure in "Equipping Disciples and Leaders through TEE" by Tim Green

where educators exert less control than in the formal classroom, ways need to be developed that embed regular feedback, sustainable processes, and evaluative tools that assess the outcomes that we seek. The Asia Theological Association, in its accreditation documents, has begun to address this in a systematic way.[38]

Additionally, skills and learning that have been overlooked or assumed to take place in the formal classroom are confronted in the real-life laboratory. For example,

> Most campus-based seminaries include a course on homiletics to prepare graduates to rightly handle the word of God from the pulpit. But many seminaries give less thought to preparing

---

38 *Asia Theological Association Manual for Accreditation, January 2021*, 22f.

graduates to rightly handle the word of God in small groups, or to helping equip their future congregations to do so.[39]

The Emmaus Model seeks to have these relational skills modeled in the student-teacher interaction so that these abilities are as caught as they are taught. This need is also extended to the development of mentors and coaches, particularly if grounded in the local community of faith. The need for the development of relational intelligence is clear, as the dual emphasis of content specialty with spiritual formation is the bedrock of the Emmaus Model.

Conclusion

In this exploration, it is posited that Christian discipleship, expressed as an ever-deepening relational spirituality, can form the core of theological education across the diverse Asia-Pacific region. This core is found at every level of the church, thus providing a substantial common base for an integration of theological education with the mission of the church. This core is deeply relational so that a participatory knowledge provides an open-ended sphere in which love and friendship are expressed in tangible ways. The Church of the Nazarene, with its connectional structure at all levels of the church, is suited for such a mission. It is also suggested that a TEE-type structure with quality assurance in place may be a suitable vehicle for the Emmaus Model. Such a model engages formal, non-formal, and informal learning that intentionally bring the local faith fellowships into direct partnership with the provider of formal theological education. The challenge for the church will be to embrace this open-endedness and celebrate diversity within a profound unity and coherence as we journey toward Christlikeness.

---

[39] Julius, "TEE and Campus-Based Training in Partnership," 277.

Recommended Reading

Allder, Bruce G., and David A. Ackerman. *The Emmaus Model: Discipleship, Theological Education, and Transformation.* Lenexa: Global Nazarene Publications, 2019.

Burke, David, Richard Brown, and James Qaiser, eds. *TEE for the 21st Century: Tools to Equip and Empower God's People for His Mission.* London: Langham Global Library, 2021.

Das, Rupen. *Connecting Curriculum with Context: A Handbook for Context Relevant Curriculum Development in Theological Education.* London: Langham Global Library, 2015.

Harkness, Allan. "De-Schooling the Theological Seminary: An Appropriate Paradigm for Effective Pastoral Formation." *Tending the Seedbeds: Educational Perspectives on Theological Education in Asia*, 103–28. Manila: Asia Theological Association, 2010.

Bibliography

Allder, Bruce G. "Leveraging Wesleyan Connectionalism to Nurture Partnerships in Learning." 2022.

Allder, Bruce G., and David A. Ackerman. *The Emmaus Model: Discipleship, Theological Education, and Transformation.* Lenexa: Global Nazarene Publications, 2019.

Asia Theological Association. *Manual For Accreditation.* https://www.ataasia.com/wp-content/uploads/2021/02/ATA-2021-Manual-for-Accreditation.pdf (accessed August 23, 2022).

Aylett, Graham, Tim Green, and Rick Weymouth. "TEE and Quality Assurance: Contributions from Asia to a Global Discussion." *TEE for the 21st Century: Tools to Equip and Empower God's People for His Mission.* Edited by Davi Burke, Richard Brown, and James Qaiser, 237-268. London: Langham Global Library, 2021.

Banks, Robert. *Re-envisioning Theological Education: Exploring a Missional Alternative to Current Models.* Grand Rapids: Eerdmans, 1999.

Bennet John B. "Educational Spiritualities: Parker J. Palmer and Relational Metaphysics." *Different Three Rs for Education: Reason, Relationality, Rhythm.* Edited by George Allan and Malcolm D. Evans, 169–84. Brill, 2006. ProQuest Ebook Central. https://ebookcentral-proquest-com.theoref.idm.oclc.org/lib/dtl/detail.action? docID=556411 (accessed August 2022).

Burke, David, Richard Brown, and Julius Qaiser, eds. *TEE for the 21st Century: Tools to Equip and Empower God's People for His Mission.* London: Langham Global Library, 2021.

Church of the Nazarene *Manual 2017–2021.* https://2017.manual.nazarene.org/ (accessed August 23, 2022)

Das, Rupen. *Connecting Curriculum with Context: A Handbook for Context Relevant Curriculum Development in Theological Education.* London: Langham Global Library, 2015.

Dawn, Marva. *A Royal "Waste" of Time: The Splendor of Worshipping God and Being Church for the World.* Grand Rapids: Eerdmans, 1999.

Edgar, Brian. *God is Friendship: A Theology of Spirituality, Community, and Society.* Kentucky: Seedbed Publishing, 2013.

Fowler, James. *Stages of Faith: The Psychology of Human Development and the Quest for Meaning.* Blackburn: Dove Communications, 1981.

Fuertes, Al, and Dugan, Kelly. "Spirituality through the Lens of Students in Higher Education." *Religions.* 12 no. 11 (2021): 1–11. https://dol.org/10.3390/rel12110924 (accessed August 23, 2022).

Green, Tim. "Equipping Disciples and Leaders Through TEE." *TEE in Asia: Empowering Churches, Equipping Disciples.* Edited by Hanna-Ruth Van Wingerden *et al.*, 13–22. London: Langham Global Library, 2021.

Harkness, Allan. "De-Schooling the Theological Seminary: An Appropriate Paradigm for Effective Pastoral Formation." *Tending the Seedbeds: Educational Perspectives on Theological Education in Asia*, 103–28. Manila: Asia Theological Association, 2010.

Julius, Qaiser. "TEE and Campus-Based Training in Partnership." *TEE in Asia: Empowering Churches, Equipping Disciples*. Edited by Hanna-Van Wingerden *et al*. London: Langham Global Library, 2021.

Kelsey, David H. *Between Athens and Berlin: The Theological Education Debate*. Eugene: Wipf & Stock, 1993.

Maddix, Mark, and Richard P. Thompson. "Scripture as Formation: The Role of Scripture in Christian Formation." *Christian Education Journal*. Series 3, Vol. 9, Supplement, 2012: 79–93.

Mezirow, Jack. "Transformative Learning Theory." *Contemporary Learning Theories: Learning Theorists . . . in Their Own Words*. Edited by Knud Illeris. New York: Routledge, 2018.

Mullino Moore, and Mary Elizabeth. "Nourishing Relationships that Nourish Life." *Different Three Rs for Education: Reason, Relationality, Rhythm*. Edited by George Allan and Malcolm D. Evans. Brill, 2006. ProQuest Ebook Central, https://ebookcentral-proquest-com.theoref.idm.oclc.org/lib/dtl/detail.action?docID=556411. Accessed August 23, 2022.

Rohr, Richard. *The Divine Dance: The Trinity and Your Transformation*. London: SPCK, 2016.

Smith, Dean. "Growing Pains: A Reflection on the Experience of Suffering Accompanying an Epistemological Crisis." *Crucible* 7:2 (November 2016). www.crucibleonline.net (accessed Aug. 23, 2022).

Smith, James K.A. *You Are What You Love: The Spiritual Power of Habit*. Grand Rapids: Brazos Press, 2016.

Spencer, Stephen. "Seminaries and Discipleship: Exploring Future Directions." *Journal of Anglican Studies,* vol 18, issue 1 (May 2020): 98–112.

Van Wingerden, Hanna-Ruth, Green, Tim, and Aylett, Graham, eds. *TEE in Asia: Empowering Churches, Equipping Disciples.* London: Langham Global Library, 2021.

Wenger, Etienne. "A Social Theory of Learning." In *Contemporary Learning Theories: Learning Theorists . . . in Their Own Words.* Edited by Knud Illeris, 209–18. New York: Routledge, 2018.

Whetham, Paul, and Dean Eaton. *Lighthouses: Christian Coaching in a Post-Christian World.* Adelaide: Openbook, 2018.

Woodruff, Robert. *Education on Purpose.* Brisbane: QUT Publications, 2001.

11

SPIRITUALITY IN LEADERS

Edward LeBron Fairbanks

According to Saint Paul, spirituality in all Christ-followers, including leaders, is a "manifestation of the Spirit given for the common good" (1 Cor 12:7). Consequently, any insights informed by Scripture regarding spirituality in leaders must view this topic through the lens of "the common good." The "manifestation of the Spirit" in the life of a spiritual leader will vary for each leader in each context, but the redemptive purpose of this manifestation of spiritual gifts and graces is always for the good of others.

Based on the model of our Lord, any Christ-informed understanding of spiritual leadership must be enfleshed in self-giving acts of love for others. In the contexts of the faith communities in which we live and lead, whether in the home, Sunday school class, youth group, church board, local congregation, or seminary, how can our testimony of faith in Jesus Christ increasingly and intentionally inform and transform us and our leadership "for the common good?"

Each leadership ministry assignment comes with its own unique context of challenges and characters. Having been privileged to serve in leadership at European Nazarene College, the Asia-Pacific Nazarene Theological Seminary, Mount Vernon Nazarene University, and the International Board of Education as Education Commissioner for the Church of the Nazarene, I was led in each location and responsibility to a different question regarding spiritual leadership. These four spiritual leadership questions remain with me to this day.

1. How can we live together within this diverse Christian community in such a way that our relationships are redemptive and a witness to unbelievers of the reconciling work of God in Christ?
2. If, in Christ, all things are made new (2 Cor 5:17), then how does our relationship to Christ convert the way we live and lead in a Christian community of faith?
3. In conflict situations, when good and godly people differ and sometimes collide over vision, values, traditions, policies, and programs, how can I lead in these situations, really lead (and serve) with the mind and spirit of Christ?
4. How does my testimony of holiness of heart and life transform the way I both mentor others in the Christian faith and model before them a vibrant, maturing Christian life?

These four questions and their answers undergird and inform the central question of this chapter. In the contexts of our family, work, and many other leadership responsibilities, how do we intentionally nurture the spiritual life both within us and within others?

Regardless of the challenges or characters in our context, Christian leadership begins with humble service to *others* to enable *them*, through teaching and example, to fulfill *their* ministry to each other and *their* mission in the world under the Lordship of Christ.[1] The essence of one's transforming and transformative spiritual leadership (see Eph

---

1 Fairbanks, *Leading Decisively*, 22.

5:1–2) is birthed in a *theological vision,* rooted in *theological convictions,* nurtured in *theological dynamics,* and empowered by the *theological motif* of the Spirit of God in us.

Spirituality in Leaders is Birthed in a *Theological Vision*

Vision refers to seeing things at a great distance and with great depth. A vision is a consuming, passionate, and compelling inner picture. An important function of leading in a faith community is creating a theological vision of the organization's preferred future. The leader, by divine inspiration, can see the invisible. Vibrant and motivating personal and organizational vision statements are expressions of optimism and hope. They are big dreams of what we would like ourselves, our family, the church, seminary, or ministry organization to be and do. Having a clear organizational vision as a leader is essential, but it is not enough.

We live and lead within a community of faith. It is essential, then, for theological vision to precede organizational vision. We envision or see the people we serve in the church as God's own creation, worthy of dignity and respect, before outlining what action is desired of them for the organization. Ownership of the vision cannot be solely that of the leader. It must be embraced and owned by the group that is asked to accept the vision and share in its implementation. Spiritual leaders are captured by the vision that we are the graced, blessed, called, and gifted people of God! It is this vision that leaders seek to transfer to others for whom they are responsible. *Spiritual leadership is the transference of theological vision.*

A theological vision is an inspired and inspiring inner picture of our faith community. It is seeing what others do not see. At the very heart of servant leadership is a theological vision of our identity within the Christian fellowship. Notice the biblical imagery that defines our relationship and identity with other Christians. We are:

> "Brothers and sisters in Christ" (Col 1:2)
>
> "Members together of Christ's body" (Eph 3:6)
>
> "A fellowship of God's people" (Acts 2:42)
>
> "A microcosm of the Kingdom of God on earth" (Rev 1:6-9)
>
> "A community of faith" (Gal 6:10)
>
> "A sacramental community in and through which the grace of God flows" (2 Cor 9:8).[2]

Effective Christlike leadership is grounded in these biblical perspectives of the Christian community and not just in organizational skills. Of course, skills are needed. However, sharp skills without Christian motives easily lead to manipulation. The primary orientation and motivation of our actions as servant leaders must be deeply theological. The Jewish theologian Martin Buber wrote a brilliant but difficult book to read, *I and Thou*.[3] He described the most healthy and mature relationship possible between two human beings as an I-Thou relationship. In such a relationship, I recognize that I am made in the image of God, as is every other person on the face of the earth. This makes them a "Thou" to me. Because of that reality, every person deserves respect—that is, I treat them with dignity and worth. I do not dehumanize or objectify them. I affirm them as having a unique and separate existence apart from me. The people with whom we live and work are God's own creation to be treated with respect, dignity, and grace. The opposite, according to Buber, is to relate to others within our sphere of influence in an "I-It" relationship, as individuals to be manipulated by us for our benefit and "things" to be used for our purposes.[4]

---

[2] See also Fairbanks and Toler, *Learning to Be Last*.
[3] Buber, *I and Thou*, 48.
[4] Buber, *I and Thou*, 53-85.

The people of God are called and Spirit-empowered to incarnate his healing, guiding, sustaining, and reconciling work in the lives of those with whom we work and live. All Christians are called to this ministry of serving others in Jesus' name! You and I may be specifically called and gifted as a pastor, teacher, evangelist, musician, or missionary, but we are on a leadership journey to use our gifts and graces in developing the equally specific gifts of the people of God whom we lead. We nurture, mentor, model, and reflect this theological vision through communication, relationships, decision-making, and development of trust. This leadership call and command to accept, serve, and equip the people of God must increasingly define and shape our *theological vision* for ministry. We accept and embrace all who profess Jesus as Lord because they are the graced, blessed, called, and gifted people of God with a ministry to each other and mission to the world! Spirituality in leaders, birthed in a theological vision of the led, must precede an organizational vision!

Spirituality in Leaders is Rooted in *Theological Convictions*

Convictions regarding our identity in the faith communities we lead must be modeled by the leader before they are embraced by the led. Spiritual leadership increasingly and consistently models and affirms our identity within the faith communities about

- who we are as the people of God (we are the graced, blessed, called, and gifted people of God with a ministry to each other and a mission to the world)
- what we are called to do in the work of God (we are to walk worthy of our calling to participate with God in the reconciling of the world to himself)
- how we are to live together as the family of God (we are to live together as a community of faith nurturing and supporting each other in ministry and mission).

Such convictions anchor us in the midst of conflicting expectations, differences of opinion, conflict of ideas, degrees of maturity and immaturity, varieties of traditions, and the uniqueness of cultures and numerous expressions of subcultures in our faith communities. During such challenges, we may wonder if it is possible to live, study, and worship together in the home, on the job, or in a local church fellowship, in such a way that our relationships are supportive and a witness to the reconciling work of God in Christ.

It is very definitely possible if we reaffirm three fundamental convictions—convictions that will shape us at our best. First, we need to reaffirm, often, *who* we are as Christians. We gather as a Christian community of faith. We are a community of faith with a ministry to each other and a mission to the world. Whether in the home, the small group Bible study class, or at a Christian university, we need to repeatedly speak of the implications of our identity as a Christian community of faith. Within that identity, the distinctive differences of maturing communities of faith are evidenced in at least three critical beliefs.

1. We believe that every Christian can make a difference for Christ, regardless of her/his vocational choice, extent of education, and current or historic socio-economic environment. We really believe that every person can make a difference in this world!

2. We believe that every Christian should come to the point of viewing herself/himself as a world Christian with a global vision. "Red, brown, yellow, black, and white—all are precious in His sight."[5] The world, the whole world, is the arena of God's activity. God's love for us does not depend on the color of our skin or the nation of our birth!

---

5 Clarence Herbert Woolston, "Jesus Loves the Little Children."

3. And, we believe that every person of any age can live a holy life to the glory and praise of God, regardless of whether her/his vocational assignment takes her/him to Miami or Manila; to Chicago or Calcutta; to Fargo or Frankfort. What we are, we are becoming. This means that we must now cultivate and develop a lifestyle of praise, worship, gratitude, devotion, respect, spiritual formation, and faithfulness.

Reaffirming the fundamental conviction of *who* we are reminds both the leader and the led that we are a Christian community.

Second, we need to reaffirm, often, *why* we exist as a Christian community. We exist to nurture, shape, and model the life of faith in our homes, among our neighbors, and in the context of our vocational settings. The Apostle Paul admonishes: "Whatever you do, work at it with all your heart, as working for the Lord, not for human masters ... it is the Lord Christ you are serving" (Col 3:23-24). We should desire to see an increasing number of unbelievers around us as we live and lead. Jesus said, "*I have not come to call the righteous, but sinners to repentance*" (Luke 5:32). The non-Christians in our relationships provide an opportunity for Christian witness and proclamation of the Christian faith. The Christian's lifestyle may be witnessed as an alternative to the not-yet-Christian's lifestyle through example, testimony, attitude, decision-making, work experience, or informal discussion. The task is not only to communicate the faith; our responsibility is to nurture the life of faith in others around us, regardless of where they are on their spiritual journey.

Third, we also need to reaffirm, often, *how* we are to live in a community of faith. We are to live as a Christlike community maturing in faith (individually and collectively). Faith communities must be characterized as confessing, forgiving, affirming, praying, discipling, worshiping, supportive, and maturing communities of faith. They are *dynamic laboratories* wherein we learn how to live together as the graced, blessed, and gifted children of God. M. Robert Mulholland, Jr. defines spiritual formation as "the process of being conformed to the image of Christ for the sake of others." He reminds us that the community we belong to is crucial in our faith development and maturity as leaders.[6] We nurture the spiritual life as leaders, not keeping spirituality merely a private affair but modeling spirituality *for the sake of others!*

A theological conviction must be embraced and embodied before it is understood and caught by those we lead. Leadership, as stated earlier, begins with humble service to *others* to enable *them*, through teaching and example, to live *their* lives under the Lordship of Christ, to understand, accept, and fulfill *their* ministry to each other and *their* mission to the world.[7]

Spirituality in Leaders is Nurtured in the *Theological Dynamics* of Hospitality, Acceptance, and Presence

It was my privilege to study under Dr. Seward Hiltner at Princeton Theological Seminary just after his book, *Theological Dynamics*, was published.[8] He sought to bring together the significance of the Christian faith with an understanding of the dynamics of personal growth. In other words, he was concerned with the intersection of "orthodoxy," belief in a doctrine, and "orthopraxy," emphasis on practice or action.

Dynamic #1: Hospitality

Interest in this intersection of faith and life, doctrine and practice, orthodoxy and orthopraxy prompted me to spend a sabbatical semester in 1999 at Yale University Divinity School working through the archives and special collection of the late Roman Catholic pastoral theologian, Henri Nouwen.[9] His writings challenged me increasingly

---

6 Mulholland, *Invitation to a Journey*, 15.
7 Fairbanks, *Mentoring and Modeling Leadership Character*, 36.
8 Hiltner, *Theological Dynamics*.
9 The Henri J. M. Nouwen special collection was housed at the Yale University Divinity School prior to its present location in Toronto, Canada.

to think about the relationship of spiritual hospitality to Christian leadership. Modeling biblical hospitality before we mentor others in its practice was my passion and pursuit as I served vocationally as the Mount Vernon Nazarene University president.

This practice of hospitality was a way of life fundamental to Christian identity for seventeen hundred years of the Christian Church. Christine Pohl convincingly documents this practice in her book, *Making Room: Recovering Hospitality in Christian Tradition*.[10] Hospitality primarily means the creation of free space—making room, to use Pohl's words, in the midst of differences of thought or behaviors that may exist. With this perspective, the attitude of hospitality helps us to make room or create space for those with whom we live and work. The strange and the stranger can enter and become a friend. It is being to others with whom you live and work a living witness of the risen Christ. The quest, therefore, is: How do we create space and make room (practice "hospitality") on the job or in our home, especially when we experience conflict and even collision between good and godly people over our vision and values? We are challenged to embrace and express the rich concept of spiritual hospitality in our leadership responsibilities. It has the potential of transforming relationships with those individuals with whom we live and work as it nurtures our own spiritual leadership.

Biblically and theologically, the term hospitality is not limited to receiving a stranger into our homes—although it surely includes this dimension. Fundamentally, it is a core attitude toward others, which can be expressed by a great variety of behaviors. Hospitality, biblically understood, challenges us to *relate to others as if we were relating to Christ himself*. The gift of Christian hospitality is the opportunity we provide for the colleague, co-worker, guest, stranger, family member, or friend to find her or his own way. It enables us to consider an alternative way

---

10 Pohl, *Making Room*.

of thinking from those who may be very different from us. This gift to others invites them to contribute insights derived from these unique gifts and abilities, even in the context of differences of thought and behavior. As leaders practicing hospitality, we often serve as angels of God without even knowing it. It is an art that more Christians need to cultivate.

Dynamic #2: Acceptance

Another distinctively Christian attitude that leaders must cultivate and express if we are to be worthy of our identity as Christlike leaders is the grace-filled gift of *acceptance*. The author of the book, *Cross Cultural Connections,* wrote: "What John 3:16 is to the unbeliever, Romans 15:7 is to the believer."[11] Paul succinctly writes: "Accept one another then, just as Christ accepted you, in order to bring praise to God" (Rom 15:7). Increasingly, the embracing of acceptance and its transforming impact must identify and define us as biblical, servant leaders. It is the heart of all we are.

Acceptance is the ability to communicate value, regard, worth, and respect to others. It is the ability to make people feel significant, honored, and esteemed.[12] This is leading with "the mind of Christ" (1 Cor 2:16). To intentionally accept and serve others is to love them. Acceptance of others does not imply acceptance of their ideas or behavior. For instance, we may differ with *gusto* on theological issues. However, if we desire to witness the miracle of dialogue, then listening attentively to them and accepting them as persons created by God and thus worthy of our regard and respect are critical first steps toward an encounter that is transformative in the nurturing of our spiritual leadership.

The grace-filled acceptance of others is a core Christian leadership quality that must be cultivated and increasingly expressed. An attitude

---

11 Elmer, *Cross Cultural Connections,* 93.
12 Elmer, *Cross Cultural Connections,* 94.

of acceptance shapes leaders and becomes a spiritual dynamic at work within us as we lead those with whom we live, work, and worship. Acceptance is a profound biblical principle for Christian leaders, especially when good and godly people collide over vision and values in a community of faith. When different perspectives are perceived as a threat, a defensive response is to assert one's authority as a leader to quash any alternative perspectives. However, according to the late Dr. Harold Reed, leadership "is known by the personalities it enriches, not by those it dominates or captivates."[13]

This perspective on leadership will force some probing questions: How can *my* ministry of servant leadership enable *others* to fulfill *their* ministry to each other and *their* mission in the world? Are the people being served growing as Christians? Are they themselves becoming servants? These are crucial concerns for leadership in the community of faith. All Christians—even those who sometimes make life difficult—are called and gifted for the ministry of Christ. Tempting as it may be, Christian leaders ought not to ignore even the most challenging people. They remain our responsibility. They demand from us keen insight, deep caring, and Spirit-empowered understanding. These expressions of spiritual leadership evidence the theological dynamic of *acceptance* working within us for the sake of others.

The leader's response of acceptance toward those with whom there is conflict shows the faith community how our theological convictions are not merely words to acknowledge but truths that are formative regarding:

- who we are as the people of God (we are the graced, blessed, called, and gifted people of God with a ministry to each other and a mission to the world)

---

[13] Reed, *The Dynamics of Leadership*, 9.

- what we are called to do in the work of God (we are to walk worthy of our calling to participate with God in the reconciling of the world to Himself)
- how we are to live together as the family of God (we are to live together as a community of faith nurturing and supporting each other in ministry and mission).

Dynamic #3: Presence

The theological dynamics of *hospitality* and *acceptance* require the leader's *presence*. The most important attribute of a leader is not knowledge or technique, ". . . but what the leader brings in his/her presence. And the presence he/she needs is a non-anxious presence."[14] Caring for others is the measure of greatness, more so than decisiveness, firmness, certainty, and conclusiveness in the actions of the leader. "Caring deeply" in stress-filled moments or when good and godly people differ and even collide with the leader over vision, values, plans, and programs demands that we listen intently, speak directly and caringly, and ask questions for the other person's sake and not for our own. We are truly present, even in the quietness; and we pray honestly, openly, and confidently![15]

Such presence reflects spiritual leadership character. It is both caught and taught—modeled and mentored! Servant leaders who bring a non-anxious presence are nurtured both by a grace-given acceptance of others with whom we live and work and by tirelessly working at "creating space and making room" for the strange and strangers around us. These values, rooted in our theological identity, characterize us at our best and convict us at our worst. The people with whom leaders live and work do not need from their leaders

---

14 Friedman, *Leadership in the Age of the Quick Fix*, 110.
15 Steinke, *Uproar: Calm Leadership in Anxious Times*.

another presentation, lecture, or reprimand; rather, they need from their leaders their *presence*.

Some insights on Christian spirituality and leadership, in light of hospitality, acceptance, and presence, include the following:

1. Good and godly people often see things differently from the leader.
2. Many issues over which we experience conflict are based culturally, ethnically, or in the family and are not violations of Scripture.
3. Differences that divide us have the potential to alienate members of the body of Christ and to negatively impact the work of God in our communities.
4. Caring for our brothers and sisters in Christ who differ from us is to love, respect, and honor them, as God loves them.
5. Acceptance of others implies that we can learn from them.
6. We must find ways to communicate acceptance to those who have not bowed to the Lordship of Christ.

The theological dynamics of hospitality, acceptance, and presence are thus a significant means to an end of cultivating spirituality in terms of a Christlike character in the hearts of those we lead. Moreover, these theological dynamics also nurture the spiritual life of us as leaders. These are not the responses that we could have, especially in times of conflict, without the grace of God already at work in our lives and continuing to work in our lives through these theological dynamics.

Spirituality in Leaders is Empowered by the *Theological Motif* of the Spirit of God in Us

In Ephesians 4:25–32, we as leaders see more clearly how to "maintain the unity of the Spirit through the bond of peace," and, in so doing, walk (and lead) worthy of our calling (Eph 4:1–3). This is what it means in practical terms to relate our holiness testimony to a holiness lifestyle of leading. The opening verses of the following chapter challenge us: "Follow God's example, therefore, as dearly loved children and walk in the way of love, just as Christ loved us and gave himself up for us as a fragrant offering and sacrifice to God" (Eph 5:1-2). This principle of Spirit-inspired imitation was developed and made specific in Ephesians 4:25-32. The passage outlines a way of living within the Christian community. Paul's instructions are not psychological in nature; they are deeply theological. The Spirit of God is deeply concerned with the speech and character of His people (Eph 4:30a).

How we can live and lead with "a life of love, just as Christ loved us" is identified a few verses later. Paul admonishes us to "be filled with the Spirit, speaking to one another with psalms, hymns, and songs of the Spirit." We are to "sing and make music from [our] heart to the Lord, always giving thanks to God the Father for everything, in the name of our Lord Jesus Christ" and to "submit to one another out of reverence for Christ" (Eph 5:18b-21). The power for this lifestyle can only be maintained, developed, and strengthened as we are continuously being filled with the Spirit (Eph 5:18). The Spirit of Christ within us empowers us to live, lead, and mentor as servant leaders!

As we model an Ephesians 4:1-5:21 leadership lifestyle before others in the power of the Spirit with a passion for "the mind of Christ" (1 Cor 2:16b), the faith community is gradually transformed into the image of Christ (2 Cor 3:18), and so are we! The challenge thus, is this: How do we communicate this lifestyle that is distinctly Christian and self-giving at the core (Phil 2:5-8) within the faith communities we lead? How do we pass on to others what has been so bountifully passed to us, and in such a way that they are qualified to teach others (2 Tim 2:2)? Whatever else it means, communicating a holiness lifestyle demands taking the principle of imitation, modeling, or exampling seriously. Pohl reminds us that this principle was key in Christian leadership for eighteen centuries.[16] For the present and future, we must recapture this principle to be mentors and models to younger Christians in the faith. We must recall the words of Paul, which he gave with humility to the Christians under his care. We must do the same for those with whom we live and for whom we are responsible.

- "Follow my example as I follow . . . Christ" (1 Cor 11:1).
- "You ought to follow our example" (2 Thess 3:7).
- "Whatever you have learned or received or heard from me or seen in me put it into practice" (Phil 4:9a).
- "We did this . . . in order to offer ourselves as a model for you to imitate" (2 Thess 3:9).

Recalling the fundamental Christian imperatives Paul also gave in Ephesians 4, we are to be *honest* with the believers, *immediate* in dealing with conflict among us, *upbuilding* with our words, and *forgiving*, even when others do not forgive us. We express gentleness, humility, patience, and supportiveness through words and deeds that consistently communicate these leadership character imperatives: I love you; I accept you; I respect you; I need you; I trust you; I serve you; I forgive you; and I accept your forgiveness.

Dialogue, for Paul, is for grace-giving and grace-receiving! Our words are to be channels of God's grace to others (Eph 4:29). God's forgiveness frees us to take the initiative in forgiving those who hurt us. Grace-enabled, Spirit-empowered communication with God and others in faith communities is "perhaps the greatest single factor affecting one's personal health, her or his relationship with others, and the pursuit of Christlikeness."[17] With intention and grace, we must never permit the painful words and deeds of others to create bitterness and

---

16 Pohl, *Making Room*.
17 Fairbanks, *Mentoring and Modeling Leadership Character*, 75.

resentment within us. The sin of offending a brother by a false word or act especially grieves God. Watch the words we speak!

Life together in Christian community is not an alternative for the spiritual leader; it is an imperative, even in conflictual situations. Because relationships are so important to us, we care enough to confront our sister or brother in Christ. We care too much about the relationship to ignore destructive behavior. We speak the truth in love, and we also care enough to allow our brother or sister in Christ to speak truthfully to us.

When we do not live together by these guidelines as a Christian community, God's Spirit is *grieved* (Eph 4:30b). Relationships within a faith community are an intensely theological issue. Anything that tends to destroy fellowship grieves the Spirit who seeks to build it up. In the midst of conflicting expectations and seemingly irreconcilable differences for the Christian leader in a local congregation, a mission organization, a Christian college, a church governing board, or a host of other communities, the challenge is to lead in these often-conflicting situations with "the mind of Christ" (1 Cor 2:16b). That possibility is only realized through the presence of the Spirit of Christ in our lives.

For the Spirit-filled and Spirit-empowered leader and by the grace of God, this leadership lifestyle must flow from a life wholly committed to living in holiness. Moreover, this leadership lifestyle will increasingly be shaped in such leaders who are being transformed to the image of Christ by the Spirit of Christ. The one thing spiritual leaders *will* to do is summed up in the holistic command and commitment to love God and to love our neighbors as we love ourselves. Holiness is a way of life, a grace-empowered lifestyle. Our words, actions, and behaviors will affirm or disconfirm to those we lead the holiness testimony we profess. This means that throughout our ever-growing and deepening relationship with Christ through the power of His Spirit within us, we will continue to mature in the Christian faith and in our walk with the Lord.

Life, Love, and Leadership

We are learning, little by little, what it means to "imitate God . . . and live a life of love" (Eph 5:1–2) even as we lead in our homes, congregations, workplaces, and communities. This life-long growth process and trust relationship is a journey of maturing faith and painful encounters that takes a lifetime to fully understand and embrace. The journey begins with radical trust in the Triune God, who desires to cleanse our motives through and through. Increasingly, as we nurture and cultivate this "purity of heart," we become a person of intense Christian faith and character—a spiritual leader. God is not finished with us yet. We are ever on the journey, maturing in our Christian faith and developing in Christian character.

The manner by which we live and lead should increasingly reflect our transformed spiritual DNA and be profoundly evidenced in us to those who know us best. A modern expression of commitment to such transformation is reflected in a powerful prayer of the late J. Kenneth Grider. The imagery in this prayer vividly captures how God graciously uses those spiritual leaders who seek to serve for the sake of others.

> Father, I am Your bread. Break me up and pass me around to the poor and needy of this world.
>
> I am Your towel. Dampen me with tears and with me wash the feet of people who are weary with walking and with working.
>
> I am Your light. Take me out to where the darkness is thick, there to shine and let Christ shine.
>
> I am Your pen. Write with me whatever word You wish, and placard the word where the least and the lost of the world will see it and read it and be helped by it.

I am Your salt. Sprinkle me on all the things that You want for people, so that my faith and love and hope will flavor their experiences.

I am Your water. Pour me into people who thirst for You but do not even know that it is You for whom they thirst. Pour into them the trust that You have helped me to place in You. Pour into them the inward witness that is in me. Pour into them the promise that soon the summer drought will pass, and refreshing rivers of water will gush down over them.

I am Yours, Lord God. Use me up in what You will, when You will, where You will, for whom You will, even if it means that I am given responsibilities that are considerable and costly.[18]

Those whom we lead should see no separation between the sacred and secular in our lives; no great divide between the message we preach and the way we lead; no inconsistency; no manipulation; no disrespect; no abuse; no significant gap between our words and our deeds. It is our passion to connect the faith we profess and proclaim to the way we live and lead. In the midst of our leadership assignments with seemingly impossible expectations placed on us by multiple constituents, you and I can be individuals marked by consistency between our personal and public lives. By God's empowering Spirit, we can lead in these situations, really lead and serve, with the mind of Christ! Spirituality in leading is nothing less than God's amazing grace working in and through us as Spirit-filled leaders for the sake of others!

Bibliography

Buber, Martin. *I and Thou*. A new translation, with a prologue and notes by Walter Kaufmann. New York: Charles Scribner's Sons, 1970.

---

18 Grider, *A Wesleyan-Holiness Theology*, 526–7.

Elmer, Duane. *Cross Cultural Connections*. Downers Grove: InterVarsity Press, 2002.

Fairbanks, Edward LeBron. *Leading Decisively! Leading Faithfully! Reflections and Markers*. Lakeland: BoardServe LLC, 2016.

———. *Mentoring and Modeling Leadership Character*. Lakeland: BoardServe LLC, 2021.

Fairbanks, Edward LeBron, and Stan Toler. *Learning To Be Last*. Kansas City: Beacon Hill, 2008.

Friedman, Edwin H. *Leadership in the Age of the Quick Fix: A Failure of Nerve*. New York: Church Publishing, 2007.

Grider, J. Kenneth. *A Wesleyan-Holiness Theology*. Kansas City: Beacon Hill, 1994.

Hiltner, Seward. *Theological Dynamics*. Nashville: Abington, 1973.

Mulholland, M. Robert. *Invitation to a Journey: A Road Map for Spiritual Formation*. Downers Grove: InterVarsity, 1993.

Pohl, Christine. *Making Room: Recovering Hospitality in Christian Tradition*. Grand Rapids: Eerdmans, 1999.

Reed, Harold. *The Dynamics of Leadership*. Danville: The Interstate Printers and Publishers, 1982.

Steinke, Peter L. *Uproar: Calm Leadership in Anxious Times*. New York: Rowman & Littlefield, 2019.

Recommended Books to Read

Chenoweth, Gregg. *Everyday Discernment: The Art of Cultivating Spirit-Led Leadership*. Kansas City: The Foundry Publishing, 2021.

Beaumont, Susan. *How to Lead When You Don't Know Where You're Going: Leading in a Liminal Season*. New York: Rowman & Littlefield, 2019.

Fairbanks, Edward LeBron. *Leading Decisively! Leading Faithfully! Reflections and Markers*. Lakeland: BoardServe LLC, 2016.

———. *Mentoring and Modeling Leadership Character.* Lakeland: BoardServe LLC, 2021.

Lencioni, Patrick. *The Advantage: Why Organizational Health Trumps Everything Else in Business.* San Francisco: Jossey-Bass, 2012.

Steinke, Peter L. *Uproar: Calm Leadership in Anxious Times.* New York: Rowman & Littlefield, 2019.

12

ADVOCACY AS A SPIRITUAL DISCIPLINE: TO LISTEN AND TO SPEAK, TO STRUGGLE AND TO REST, TO LAMENT AND TO HOPE

Marie Joy D. Pring-Faraz

The data-gathering from the victim-survivors of Online Sexual Exploitation and Abuse of Children (OSEAC) for research commissioned by three faith-based organizations was almost complete. I was ready to write, and I was thinking to myself that I should be feeling a sense of relief and gratitude now that over six months of exhausting field work was coming to a close. Instead, I felt a storm brewing in my inner being. After attempting to assuage the heavy feeling by checking daily tasks and initiating small talk with my peers all day, a wave of an unfamiliar sorrow finally hit me that late afternoon. This heavy feeling overtook me, and I gave in. I turned off my office lights, made sure my door was locked, crawled under my work desk, curled up, and wept. I was, in fact, wailing as I prayed, but because both my hands were cusped tightly around my mouth, I was only letting out a muffled cry. I was unacquainted with the emotions I felt that day—a deep sadness, a sense of anger, and a pile of disappointments. The questions from which I had been veering away in the name of subjectivity in research finally caught up with me. There, under my office table, I brought my perplexities to God and cried for mercy and understanding as I wrapped my head around the atrocious acts committed against the children by the very people who should have cared for them and whom they trusted with their lives.

Today, I understand that moment better in hindsight. I was crying because the thirteen victim-survivors were no longer statistical data to me or mere subjects who provided me with valuable information to explain a phenomenon. I have known them. They were now names and faces to me, people I laughed with and broke bread with. Their narratives of vulnerability were no longer just transcripts to be coded but stories that needed to be shared in a space of gentleness and utmost respect. I was crying because the Spirit of God was birthing something in me—my researcher self was gone, and an advocate for the victim-survivors of OSEAC was born.

There, under my work table, I felt the nearest I have ever been to God. It was not among the towers of well-curated biblical and theological readings of our library, not in classrooms where theological discourse sharpens one's intellect, not even in our worship hall where people from different nations reverberated hymns of praise. It was there in the dark, musty corner of the research office that I felt most spiritual: truly connected to God, to my neighbor—my suffering neighbor—and to my broken heart.

In its textbook definition, advocacy means persuading people who matter to care about an issue.[1] Advocacy is communicating to be heard;

---

1 Daly, *Advocacy*, 15. Daly, the Liddell Centennial Professor of Communication, further defines advocacy as overcoming obstacles, deterring problematic ideas, and

it is being able to frame a message compellingly to evoke the desired impact. Advocacy means taking up a space at the table where decisions are made and having the decision-makers want to adopt one's espoused ideas.[2] While this schoolbook definition proves serviceable in fields such as marketing, advertising, and publications, among others, this does not capture what advocacy is as a spiritual discipline.

Putting "advocacy" and "spiritual discipline" together is almost unthinkable. This is particularly true if one's image of advocacy is a ferocious mob demonstrating on the streets or a group of power players in the hall of influence engaged in a political dance of twisting wits and wills. Advocacy seems poles apart from contemplative spiritual practices such as meditation, prayer, Bible study, fasting, silence and solitude, and the like.[3] Even outward spiritual disciplines or disciplines of engagement,[4] such as confession, corporate worship, celebration, etc., seem unrelated to advocacy. Nonetheless, if one does not reduce spirituality to mere human behavior and activities,[5] and understand it more as a phenomenon centered on God and the grace afforded for humanity to respond, then advocacy can be one of the "various dimensions of grace."[6]

---

empowering people to make impactful and transformative ideas.

2   Daly, *Advocacy*, 15–17.

3   Foster, *Celebration of Discipline*; Willard, *The Spirit of the Disciplines;* Peterson, *Under the Unpredictable Plant.*

4   Foster, *Celebration of Discipline*, v; Willard, *The Spirit of the Disciplines*, 156–92.

5   Wakefield defines spirituality as "those attitudes beliefs, and practices, which animate people's lives and help them to reach out towards super-sensible realities." Jensen critiques this as a definition that tends to hide God, as well as God's unconditional embrace and embracing of the power that is key to God's grace (Jensen, *Subversive Spirituality*), 9–10.

6   Jensen, *Subversive Spirituality*, 5. I must now be clear that the use of the words "advocacy" and "advocates" in this essay does not follow Daly's textbook definition, but rather these words in this paper are now informed by the definition of Christian scholars on spirituality and spiritual disciplines.

Advocacy, as a spiritual discipline or "means of grace,"[7] opens the space for humans to yield to God. Eugene Peterson noted that *askesis*, the Greek for "discipline," does not refer to a "spiritual technology at beck and call of human beings but is rather an immersion in an environment in which our capacities are reduced to nothing or nearly nothing, and we are at the mercy of God to shape God's will in us."[8] Appropriating Peterson's remark, the spiritual discipline of advocacy is to engage with oppression issues yet be fully aware that only God can transform situations. Further, the advocate is there to communicate how God has already and always has been active.

Advocacy is being that faithful presence amidst spaces of injustice, even in the clutches of the powerful, for God's righteousness to be proclaimed, God's justice to be delivered, and God's grace to be revealed. Similar to prayer, meditation, journaling, confession, retreats, etc., advocacy can be an activity initiated by the Spirit of God, a life source for Christians whose hearts are bent towards justice-seeking and justice-proclaiming. "Such life ever rises to the true worship of God and flows out into witness and service to the world,"[9] especially to those who are broken and suffering. Advocacy is a space where various means of grace can be experienced and practiced.

What follows is a reflection on my nascent experience as a Christian advocate and how it has been a spiritual discipline to me. I will share

---

7   Willard was Foster's mentor, and both regard spiritual disciplines as "God's means of grace."

8   Peterson in Jensen, *Subversive Spirituality*, 7–8.

9   Meye in Jensen, *Subversive Spirituality*, 11–2. After surveying many definitions of "spirituality," Jensen asserts that Robert Meye's definition is the most appropriate: "Above all else, grace—God's grace—and gratitude—our response to the grace of God—are the two most essential components of an authentic Christian spirituality which, patterned in the imitation of Christ, and empowered by the Spirit of Jesus Christ, will ever bear fruit in love, joy, and peace. All of this will happen only within the framework of our privileged response of faith in God in Christ and the power of the Spirit, especially expressed in our life in prayer, in the Word, and the community of faith."

the three two-fold practices of advocacy as a spiritual discipline: to listen and to speak, to struggle and to rest, and to lament and to hope.

To Listen and To Speak

Listening is where advocacy springs up. People equate advocacy to the mere raising of voices, but for the message to be truthful and transformative, the advocate needs to have a good grasp of the situation before framing the right speech. Also, if it were to be a true spiritual discipline, advocacy is first an inward movement,[10] reaching into the depths through hearing God, others, and the advocate's self.

Henri Nouwen considers spiritual disciplines "the creation of open space to *listen to the voice of God* who calls us the beloved."[11] Advocacy begins by hearing God—taking unhurried time to discern God's revelation through the Scripture. Through the Bible, the advocate understands the precepts of God and the character of God. This, then, provides the advocate a handle to recognize the message of truth for a specific issue. Yet this message of truth is not merely a list of gathered information from the Bible but a knowledge that emerges from a personal, living, and dynamic encounter with God's Word. As the advocate reads and reflects on God's truth, he/she is being transformed. The Word of God is lived out by the advocate, making him/her a vessel of God's truth.

The good news for the advocate seeking God's voice is that God is *Immanuel*. God is not a distant God, but one who participates in the human struggle[12] and is near the brokenhearted.[13] In issues of injustice to

---

10 Jensen's thesis is that empowered inward spirituality is vital in transforming outward mission (*Subversive Spirituality*, 4).

11 Nouwen, "The Disciplines of the Beloved," emphasis added.

12 Nouwen cites the Incarnation, John 1:14, as the key to understanding God's compassionate heart and abiding presence with humanity.

13 Psalm 34:18.

which the advocate is called, God is already there, ready to speak the Word of freedom and life.

The advocate is also called to listen to others, especially those who need advocating. Bonhoeffer critiqued the quickness of Christians to speak without taking time to listen:

> Just as love for God begins with listening to His Word, so the beginning of love for the brethren is learning to listen to them.
> ... But he who can no longer listen to his brother will soon be no longer listening to God either; he will be doing nothing but prattle in the presence of God too.[14]

Parker Palmer also warns of this hubristic tendency and insists that instead of being fixed, advised, or set straight, what people desire is to be heard and seen.[15]

Advocates are inevitably active doers, but to cultivate a faithful presence in spaces of injustice, the advocate must learn what Bonhoeffer calls the ministry of holding one's tongue and the ministry of meekness.[16] Both go hand in hand and are necessary to hear one's neighbor faithfully. To hold one's tongue is to assume that our neighbor's need to be heard is greater than one's need to speak and quickly escape the neighbor's vexing problem. Likewise, meekness is foregoing self-conceit and, instead, offering attentive silence and active listening as the persons open up. It is faithfully holding people in that sacrificial space as time, energy, and patience are afforded by the advocate.[17] Such space is also reciprocal, for the advocate listens as he/she has been heard by God.

---

14 Bonhoeffer, *Life Together*, 97-8.
15 Palmer, *A Hidden Wholeness*, 117.
16 Before sharing on the ministry of listening, Bonhoeffer discusses the ministries of holding one's tongue and meekness.(*Life Together*, 91-6).
17 Palmer, *A Hidden Wholeness*, 117.

Finally, the advocate must also listen to his/her inner being. Palmer made a distinction between outer life and inner life.[18] The outer life is concerned with image and influence, but the inner life is about intuitions, faith, and values.[19] After listening to God and the people, the advocate can now reach deep into his/her inner being and examine the alignment of what has been heard with his/her inner life. In this way, what will be reflected in the outer life—image and influence—becomes integral to what is true in the advocate's inner life. This gives way to the discovery of his/her authentic voice and the framing of his/her authentic advocacy message. Only when there is no dissonance between the advocate's outer life and inner life can he/she bear the taxing burden of speaking.

More than being compelling, the speech of the advocate must be truthful because the power of an advocacy message is in its fealty to the truth. Any speech that is less than truthful is like a bad seed; it falls to the ground and bears neither life nor fruit. Truth-telling in advocacy is not to massage public opinion or engineer a social climate. Truth speaking is done to usher in *shalom* amid the chaos and to shed light in the dark. In the act of truth-telling, advocacy becomes a subversive spirituality—a fresh spiritual practice "to undermine the status quo and deconstruct the deadening effects of the principalities of darkness."[20] Truth-speaking in advocacy becomes what Peterson calls a new way to witness the kingdom of God, the kingdom of Jesus Messiah that is already among us.[21] When the advocate speaks, God's kingdom here and now is made manifest with one word of truth after another.

---

18 Palmer, *A Hidden Wholeness*, 39–40.
19 Palmer, *A Hidden Wholeness*, 40.
20 Jensen, *Subversive Spirituality*, 13.
21 Peterson in Jensen, *Subversive Spirituality*, 13. Along with truth-telling, Peterson identifies love, prayer, and parables as the new subversive ways to proclaim the kingdom of God that is now here on earth.

Furthermore, truth-speaking in advocacy is key to the healing and restoration of people. Truth-telling places their stories and their view of the world and of themselves in the right perspective. Advocacy provides a means for the public acknowledgment and affirmation of their truth. Truth provides a way for the weak to transcend their experience of disenfranchisement and oppression. And as the people are liberated by their recovery of what is true, they can, in turn, liberate their oppressors with forgiveness that comes from that truth.[22] This inclusive freedom that comes from fealty to truth is one of the aims of advocacy as a spiritual discipline.

To Struggle and to Rest

Nearly four decades ago, a movement began to rise among socially conscious Filipino Christians. On the one hand, they were struggling to articulate a national identity from the Filipino experience of colonialism and neo-colonialism, and, on the other hand, calling for a theological interpretation and discourse about the suffering of the Filipino people then and today.[23] This gave rise to what is now known as the "theology of struggle."

Theology of struggle has inevitable political implications, and some scholars have appropriated the movement to explain how faith became the driving force of the activism of Filipino Christian "leftists."[24] It is here that I depart from this understanding. While advocates in societies such as the Philippines are inescapably situated in a revolution, a place of struggle for justice against injustice,[25] I follow the

---

22 Here, I am appropriating the Freirean principle that only the oppressed can free themselves and their oppressors (Freire, *Pedagogy of the Oppressed*).

23 Filipino theologians who are credited with the development of the theology of struggle are Suarez, "Theology of Struggle"; dela Torre, "A Theology of Struggle"; and Fernandez, *Toward a Theology of Struggle*.

24 Harris, "Theology of Struggle," 83–107.

25 Mendoza, "Theology of Struggle."

non-violent activism stance depicted in Rizal's second *magnum opus*, *El Filibusterismo*:

> I do not mean to say that our liberty will be secured at the sword's point . . . but that we must secure it by making ourselves worthy of it, by exalting the intelligence and the dignity of the individual, by loving justice, right, and greatness, even to the extent of dying for them—and when a people reaches that height, God will provide a weapon, the idols will be shattered, the tyranny will crumble like a house of cards, and liberty will shine out like the first dawn.[26]

In other words, advocacy as a spiritual discipline includes struggle—not by brute blades but rather with the quality of the people's hearts. The advocate struggles not by ferine force but by a constant commitment to be in solidarity with the suffering of the people. It means immersion with the victims of injustice; it is crying with them when they cry in pain and celebrating with them in their moments of victory.

Christ Jesus, as shown in Ileto's *Pasyon and Revolution*, offers a pattern of non-violent struggle in advocacy.[27] In the *Pasyon*, Christ's patience and meekness must not be mistaken as a submission under the yoke of injustice. Rather, it is a form of solidarity with the poor and an act of subversion of oppressive societal structure. When Christ died and rose again, freedom commenced, and a new social reality was established. Advocacy as a spiritual discipline includes Ileto's depiction of Christlike sympathy and authentic involvement with the lived experience of the people, especially with their day-to-day challenges and aspirations. To struggle as an advocate is to fearlessly and faithfully remain in the space of injustice and pain with the people—not

---

26 In Rizal's novel, Padre Florentino is the Filipino priest to whom Simoun confessed after his violent revolution attempt failed (Rizal, *El Filibusterismo*).
27 Ileto, *Pasyon and Revolution*.

hurrying to fix and put things in order. It is to wait patiently as the kingdom of God is quietly birthed in their midst.

The complementary action of struggling is resting. Albert Alejo, a Jesuit advocate for good governance once shared: *Nasa pakikibaka ang paglapas sa kaba; nasa pamamahinga ang lalim ng pag-asa* (It is in struggling that fear is conquered; it is in resting that the depth of hope is experienced).[28] The advocate's rest is not a mere stoppage of struggle; it is a sanctified moment of remembrance that God's goodness is intrinsic to creation. While evil seems strong, God's righteousness is stronger still, and all of God's creation continue to move toward God's *telos*.

Rest becomes life-sustaining for advocacy because it re-orients the lens of the advocate to the true norm brought by the life and work of Christ: that justice and freedom override injustice and oppression. Advocacy as a spiritual discipline practices pause to remember that a new heaven and earth, a new world, is not only possible; it is the reality here and now. To appropriate Indian activist Arundhati Roy's words, "On a quiet day, I can hear [the new world] breathing."[29]

Rest also keeps the advocate from the seduction of the messiah complex, the thinking that one is responsible for saving or assisting the oppressed. When the advocate pauses, he/she realizes his/her needs that also need to be met—the need to be seen and heard, the need to be supported. Rest provides the space for the advocate to be refreshed in the presence of God and others—this is the moment for the advocate to experience the grace of being at the receiving end. What awaits the advocate is the exhilarating liberty that the burden is not on his/her shoulder. This was best expressed in the excerpt of a poem

---

28 Albert Alejo, S.J., Interview with Isip-Isak, September 5, 2020.

29 Roy is originally talking about laying siege to corporate revolution and is speaking of a society that is sustained not by capitalism but by joy, charity, and empathy. The exact quote reads: "Another world is not only possible, but she is also on her way. On a quiet day, I can hear her breathing." See Roy, *War Talk*.

often attributed to Archbishop Oscar Romero that was translated into Filipino by Alejo, *Lampas Abot-Tanaw* (The Long View):

> *May mga bagay na kaya nating gawin at*
> *maari pa talagang pagbutihin*
>
> *Oo, sabihin na nating kulang na kulang, ngunit*
> *simula parin ito, pasulong na hakbang.*
>
> *Isang pagkakataon upang makagalaw ang*
> *gandang biyaya ng Maykapal.*
>
> *Malamang, hindi na natin makikita ang lahat ng itong ibubunga,*
>
> *ngunit yan ang kaibahan ng Punong Panday at mga alalay*
>
> *Tayo ay mga alalay, hindi Punong Panday,*
> *mga alagad at hindi manliligtas,*
>
> *Mga propeta ng isang balang-araw na lampas-sa ating abot tanaw.*

> We cannot do everything, and there is a
> sense of liberation in realizing that.
> This enables us to do something and to do it very well.
> It may be incomplete, but it is a
> beginning, a step along the way,
> An opportunity for the Lord's grace to enter and do the rest.
> We may never see the results, but that is
> the difference between the master
> builder and the worker.
> We are workers, not master builders;
> ministers, not messiahs.
> We are prophets of a future not our own.[30]

---

30 This poem is often attributed to Archbishop Oscar Romero who translated it into Spanish for the El Salvadorians; but this was originally written by the American priest, Ken Unterner. This was translated into Filipino by Alejo, and he read it to the author in

To Lament and to Hope

The story I shared at the beginning is a moment of lament in advocacy. Federico Villanueva, a scholar on the psalms of lament, rightly pointed out that it has become uncomfortable for Asians, in general, and Filipinos, in particular, to ask God the question, "Why?"[31] Along with all the afflictions and injustice that come with it, poverty is accepted by the poor as *kapalaran* or fate, something that the heavens have ordained.[32] While God-ordained poverty is but a fatalistic myth, the voice that cries, questions, and contends with acts of injustice has been effectively stifled. Yet an even more insidious consequence of fatalism is how it makes people hostage to discouragement and eventually resistant to healing.[33] People stay in their experience and believe that nothing can be done or changed.

Regrettably, expressions of lament have been limited or controlled even in the church since questioning God was perceived as immaturity or lack of faith.[34] This prevalent cultural value is what I resisted under the office table that afternoon as I lobbed the questions that perplexed me before God. Instead of condemnation for lack of faith, what overcame me was a reassuring warmth from God. While I was hidden and unheard by others, I was seen and heard by the Almighty.

Advocacy as a spiritual discipline necessitates lament—sorrows and tears are also vessels of God's grace. Sharing in the grief and questions of the people opens a locus of empathy where the advocate and the people can come together. Nouwen says, "Nobody escapes being

---

a recorded online meeting. Albert Alejo, S. J., Zoom video conference with the author, July 31, 2021.

31 Villanueva follows other theology of struggle scholars such as Ileto and dela Torre in connecting the hesitance of Filipinos to raise their voices and ask questions or issue complaints to authority to the national subconscious of colonial manipulation and subjugation. See Villanueva, *Psalms 73–150*, 18.

32 Suarez, "Theology of Struggle," 47–60.

33 Nouwen, *Turn My Mourning into Dancing*, 50.

34 Kathleen Billman and Daniel Migliore in Villanueva, *Psalms 73–150*, 18.

wounded. We are all wounded people, whether physically, emotionally, mentally, or spiritually." [35] What this means for advocacy is that when the advocates take a close look at the people's wounds, it is most likely that they, too, will be confronted by their woundedness. When the advocate's wounds become a way to serve others, no longer a source of shame but of healing, then the advocate has become an empathetic wounded healer.[36] The advocate becomes a worthy companion to the hurting in the journey to restoration.

Lamenting allows the advocate to problematize acts of injustice truly, to ask deeper and more complex questions, and to look at the situations with care and criticality. This helps advocacy veer away from providing placative solutions and sharing inauthentic, impuissant good news. Laments make way for advocacy to bear a message that is faithful to the hurts and genuine with the hope from Christ.

To lament and to hope are not mutually exclusive. Most of the laments in the Psalms begin with a cry out of the depths, and then, they transition towards a word of praise to God or an affirmation of the psalmist's hope.[37] Advocacy as a spiritual discipline hinges not on optimistic outlooks but on hope and the character and nature of God. The hope of the advocate is an active resistance to injustice, a stubborn refusal towards fatalism. Hope believes in the revelation of God's absolute goodness and faithful love, even in the grimmest of times. It perceives the present pain—it understands the historicity and context of injustice—but it lodges its attention in the eternal. Suffering is neither avoided nor ignored because the advocate knows that God's abiding and life-giving presence is available for those who hope. Advocacy as a spiritual discipline understands that hope for tomorrow will let people live better today. And this one hope is secure: those who wait

---

35 Nouwen, *The Wounded Healer*.
36 Nouwen, *The Wounded Healer*.
37 See Villanueva, *Psalms 73–150*, 18–24, 154–8, 237–43.

for restoration from Christ will soon discover that Christ is already among them and is bringing wholeness to that which was broken.

The Holy Spirit, the Advocate

The value of advocacy as a spiritual discipline is beyond its being a divine activity. The very heart of advocacy is the Holy Spirit—the *parakletos*—the advocate who is called to the side of the people. This makes advocacy truly spiritual—it is an actual work of the Holy Spirit.

The Spirit of God comes alongside both the victims of unjust acts and the advocate. By the Spirit's grace, the advocate becomes an attentive listener and a trustworthy representative of the voice of God and the stories of suffering people. The Holy Spirit, the Spirit of Freedom, countervails forces of oppression—the source of strength for the people and the advocate in their struggle for justice. Likewise, the Spirit of God offers rest and refreshes the people and the advocate so that their vision of restoration is sustained. Finally, the Spirit is the Comforter of the people and the Advocate when they lament their woundedness and their gentle Guide towards the path of hope.

Without the Holy Spirit, advocacy will merely be the act of organizing and scheming with loud but empty words. Nevertheless, with the power and presence of the Holy Spirit, advocacy becomes transformational, a gainful discipline to mature the people and the advocate into the image of God, which is the image of Christ.

Bibliography

Bonhoeffer, Dietrich. *Life Together.* Translated by John Doberstein. New York: Harper, 1954.

Daly, John. *Advocacy: Championing Ideas and Influencing Others.* New Haven: Yale University Press, 2011.

dela Torre, Edicio. "A Theology of Struggle." In *Currents in Philippine Theology: Kalinangan Book Series 2*. Quezon City: Institute of Religion and Culture, 1992.

Fernandez, Eleazar. *Toward a Theology of Struggle*. Maryknoll: Orbis, 1994.

Foster, Richard. *Celebration of Discipline: The Path to Spiritual Growth*. San Francisco: Harper and Row, 1988.

Freire, Paulo. *Pedagogy of the Oppressed*. New Revised 20th Anniversary Edition. New York: Continuum, 1993.

Harris, Anne. "Theology of Struggle: Recognizing Its Place in Recent Philippine History." *Kasarinlan: Philippine Journal of Third World Studies* 21, no. 2 (2006): 83–107.

Ileto, Reynaldo Clemeña. *Pasyon and Revolution : Popular Movements in the Philippines, 1840-1910*. Quezon City: Ateneo de Manila University Press, 1979.

Jensen, L. Paul. *Subversive Spirituality: Transforming Mission through the Collapse of Space and Time*. Eugene: Pickwick, 2009.

Mendoza, Everett. "Theology of Struggle Yesterday, Today, and Tomorrow." *Silliman Journal* 51, no. 2 (2010).

Nouwen, Henri. "The Disciplines of the Beloved." *Robert Schuller with the Hour of Power* Episode 1179. Garden Grove: Hour of Power.

———. *The Wounded Healer: Ministry in Contemporary Society*. New York: Doubleday, 1990.

———. *Turn My Mourning into Dancing: Finding Hope in Hard Times*. Nashville: Thomas Nelson, 2001.

Nouwen, Henri, Michael Christensen, and Rebecca Laird, *Spiritual Direction: Wisdom for the Long Walk of Faith*. San Francisco: Harper, 2006.

Palmer, Parker. *A Hidden Wholeness: The Journey Toward an Undivided Life.* San Francisco: Jossey-Bass, 2004.

Peterson, Eugene. *Under the Unpredictable Plant: An Exploration in Vocational Holiness.* Grand Rapids: Eerdmans, 1992.

Rizal, Jose. *El Filibusterismo.* Honolulu: University of Hawaii Press, 2007.

Roy, Arundhati. *War Talk.* Cambridge: South End, 2003.

Suarez, Oscar. "Theology of Struggle: Reflections on Praxis and Location." *Tugon* 6, no. 3 (1986): 47–60.

Villanueva, Federico. *Psalms 73-150.* Asia Bible Commentary. Cumbria: Langham Global Library, 2022.

Willard, Dallas. *The Spirit of the Disciplines: Understanding How God Changes Lives.* San Francisco: Harper and Row, 1988.

PART IV

SITUATED SPIRITUALITY

13

UNIQUE CHALLENGES CHRISTIANS FACE IN INDIA

Stella Bokare

Introduction

I believe in an India that is secure in itself and confident of its place in the world, an India that is a proud example of tolerance, freedom, and hope for the downtrodden.

Sashi Tharoor

As a loyal citizen of India, I am proud of my country and the beauty bestowed upon my land. Growing up as a teenager in a pluralistic culture had a diverse impact on my faith. The knowledge about religion I accumulated has shaped my whole perception of God. Walking through temples, mosques, churches, and gurudwaras was a prestigious mark of our family devotion to the so-called gods Indians have worshipped through the ages. Glimpsing all these religious practices went uncriticized into my understanding of faith and spirituality.

I reflect on these memories, particularly my journey with Jesus, which began in my tenth grade as a 15-year-old girl. A vivid incident that, even over time, cannot be forgotten was the day when I heard the verse, "I am the way, the truth, and the life" (John 15:6), so loudly in my ears when I was listening to a preacher at church. What was this powerful statement, challenging the fundamental beliefs existing in my pluralistic world of religious practices? Was I indeed capturing the very essence of the truth that rang in my ears? This verse actually posed an open threat to Hinduism, which embraces the inclusiveness of all faith practices.

It was mysterious how in God's revelation, I found the way in Jesus in my teenage years, and my adventurous journey with Jesus began. In my limited capacity to know Jesus, I have ventured into my faith in him since then. My spirituality has been shaped with much openness and straightforwardness.

Live out Louder-Impact of Foreign Missionaries

In the history of India during the time of colonial kings, foreign missionaries and indigenous reformers attempted to resist inhuman atrocities that existed then, such as the burning of widows (*sati*), temple prostitution (*devadaasis*), forced labor, and other forms of slavery. Attempts at social reformation paved the way to a fundamental change in the social and cultural system. The following observation is correct: "If the status of the peoples in the lowest orders was changed, or if landless bonded labor vanished, the whole superstructure above them would be shaken."[1] A tremendous change in perspective was evident in those who succeeded in social upliftment. On the other side, the local Hindus obsessively feared that the "foreign missionaries" would try to convert them. That fear still persists and, apparently, is leading to the persecution of Christians.

---

1 Frykenberg, "Indian Christians and Hindu Raj," 268.

The establishment of English-medium schools as part of the mission of early missionaries was intended to provide moral or spiritual values and ideologies, basic education, and essential practical skills. Following the arrival of Thomas, the Apostle of Jesus, there were several missionaries like Francis Xavier, Robert De Nobile, and others who ventured into social welfare and transformation of the societies. The prominent beneficiaries of this were the Brahmins, the cream layer of Indian communities.

In the positive spirit of social welfare, the missionaries launched schools, childcare centers, colleges, universities, and even hospitals for the socially downtrodden and economically underprivileged. These services also unexpectedly demanded conversion. As a result, many people started following Christianity. After taking over the educational system after British rule, the "high caste" elite propagandized an aggressive and unfair image of the convent schools. Eventually, anti-Christian movements emerged, although many who were part of the religious controversies became the beneficiaries of English-medium schools and colleges.

Apart from the imparting of education to society, social upliftment among the tribal people was a great movement propelled by the power of the gospel. With the emerging local leadership among the tribal "Dalits" (low caste people), the upper caste leaders were insecure because of the threatening fact that their "low caste untouchables" would no longer attend to their demeaning labors. In fact, the cultural, economic, and social reformation brought the tremendous and unique movement of emancipating the dignity of the "Dalits." Such reformations have resulted in the increasing frequency of violent reactions against local missionaries in the tribal belts of India.

While many of the atrocities against Christian communities have remained unreported since the early history of India, the driving forces behind them do not cease to work. From ages past until recently, foreign and local missionaries have proven their best contribution has been to society and community welfare. Unfortunately, their struggle to identify themselves with the Indian culture has been perceived as anti-Hindu.

Confused Faith Practices and Challenges Christians Face

One of the native terms Indians have used is the Hindu Raj. Anything native to India, including customs, traditions, ethnic groups, tribes, or languages, was coined under the term "Hindu." What is now known as Hinduism was then "the by-product of cultural explorations and socio-political accommodation, before and during the early Raj."[2] The British had developed this concept with the collaboration of local ideologies of the native Indians and the European political figures. The post-independence era saw Hinduism as an ancient religion of India that claimed its origin in the Indian subcontinent.

India is considered the cradle of major religions, namely Hinduism, Buddhism, Jainism, and Sikhism, with the main overarching religion being Hinduism. From ancient ages until now, India has been considered a country of religious pluralism, although the underlying tension has been the demand to return to the old religion called "Sanatana dharma." The political ideology of Hindutva has sought to establish Hinduism in India against any monotheistic faith, such as Islam and Christianity, or any other belief for that matter.

The fundamental belief that one has to be a Hindu to be an Indian is the intrinsic belief of Hindutva. With the rising popularity of Hindutva, "The Christian community has seen a drastic increase of organized and systematic persecution against them with an intent of uprooting them and annihilating them completely."[3] The ardent ideology of Hindutva has its origin back during the Mughal period when forced conversions

---

2 Frykenberg, "Indian Christians and Hindu Raj," 269.
3 Julian P., "The Challenges of Hindu Nationalism," 44–46.

of Hindus were retaliated against and led to staunch opposition. Non-Hindu practices were universally referred to as anti-nationalistic. Thus, anti-Christian movements started cropping up when Christian missionaries attempted to impose their culture and traditions during British rule.

Although India is a secular nation, religion has interfered with politics, even though the constitution does not allow the mixing of religion with state power. The democratic government requires the country not to favor one religion over another. However, religious freedom has been denied in a political and behavioral sense. Thus, anti-conversion laws have been devised and executed in several states of the nation. The political agents exert pressure on the minorities to advance their agenda in the guise of patriotism. Losing government privileges post-conversion is prevalent among the tribal and low caste people. The advantage of embracing other religions is the liberty a person experiences from the shackles of misery and suppression within the society. People realize their potential and worth when they rise out of deprivation, slavery, and ignorance.

On the other hand, one also suffers disadvantages at conversion. It is observed that "Hindu Dalits that convert to other religions lose their affirmative action benefits. They are no longer entitled to the seats reserved for them in government offices and government funded educational institutions. Jobs and admissions granted to them under the quota shall be taken back on conversion."[4] The government claims that the embraced religion does not categorize them under a low caste, so they are no longer part of a disadvantaged group. Jobs and other government facilities under quota cannot be claimed. After embracing Christianity, several individuals were pushed downward in their privileges with government employment. Fervent followers have

---

4   Pratik, "Religious Conversion."

remained adherent to their faith, but those subjected to the pressure of losing lucrative facilities have backslid in their faith.

When my dad, who hailed from a low caste society by birth, accepted Christ, he was not only ostracized by his community, but even his closest family disowned him. It was, in fact, a kind of stigmatization that he battled in his family and society. Abandoned by his own, yet with a thriving faith, he made his legitimate move to make followers of Jesus. His viable faith was demonstrated by his unwavering commitment to Christ even when adversity claimed his success in his career. In fact, his life testimony became a shining light to his family and community. He has faithfully served as a missionary and church planter in South India for the past thirty-five years.

The prevalent diversity in religions, languages, groups, backgrounds, customs, and celebrations are vitally important to the traditions of India. In a religion like Hinduism, what a person believes and practices is woven into the fabric of the culture. Therefore, conversion may incite communal violence. If anyone disengages from the common celebrations, it could be perceived as a matter of contention and non-cooperation. Any attempt at monochromising the existing socio-religious culture might be portrayed as anti-nationalistic and be subjected to the legal execution of discipline.

Apart from conversions for religious conviction, Astha Pratik cites several reasons for conversion:

1. Conversion for marital reasons
2. For material benefits or convenience
3. Active conversion by one's choice
4. Mass conversion by force.[5]

Many conversions that happen under cultural pressure may be insincere. A large number of conversions during mass movements have

---

5 Pratik, "Religious Conversion."

taken place among the Dalits who have converted to casteless religions to escape caste divisions in the society.

Festival Pressures on Christians

India is known for its rich and wide variety of traditions, cultures, festivals, and celebrations, and these speak volumes about the essence of Indian identity. Festivals form an integral part of Indian culture and vary from state to state. Throughout the year, festivals revolve around seasonal changes, relationships, and several myths. From childhood, a person becomes part of every festival celebration in the community. My childhood memories remind me how much I craved to celebrate festivals with my school friends. As I grew older, I noticed that each festive celebration had its seasonal significance.

I believe Indians have something to celebrate throughout the year. These festivals include Ganesh Chaturthi (Elephant God Festival), Diwali (Festival of Lights), Durga Puja (celebration of Good over Evil), Holi (Festival of Colors), Eid (Festival of Brotherhood), Christmas, and many more throughout the year. Most Hindu festivals relate to nature's cycle of life and are supposed to prevent nature from stagnating. These cyclic festivals are celebrated throughout India and can last for four to five days or even ten days.

Interestingly, children growing amidst these vibrant celebrations in India cultivate a blended lifestyle of diverse traditional inclusivism. As they grow into adulthood, they also get fonder of the festivals and social gatherings since these occasions serve the significant purpose of weaving people of all cultures and communities together.

Although only three national festivals have holidays in the diverse culture of India, the states have their own local festivals, depending on their linguistic demographics. It is extremely challenging to save the identity and uniqueness of Christian celebrations with diverse cultural and religious exposure. One experiences a strong sense of emptiness when the Christian faith is embraced. The transition from the yearly celebration of traditions and festivals into just one major long-awaited festival such as Christmas can leave the religion with a deep sense of emptiness and hollowness.

In the context of redeeming the culture and pagan celebration, Pramod Aghamkar, Executive Director of Satsang Ministries Ohia, believes that the Hindu festivals celebrated globally, such as the Diwali, can be considered as necessary frameworks to proclaim Christ as the light of the world. He claims that such festivals give steppingstones, clues, and redemptive analogies for cross-cultural witness.[6] He believes in Christianizing the Hindu festivals and creating a bridge in celebrating Christ in the socio-cultural context of the Indian diaspora, and so, not being intrinsically Hindu, Jain, or Sikh, but celebrating in the Indian community in order to experience Jesus in a native way.

Strong followers of Christianity might lament that as Christians, we should not be celebrating or participating in such socio-cultural festivals because it could be impossible for a Christian to participate in non-Christian festivals without endorsing the beliefs behind them. As we live as faithful disciples of Jesus in a diverse socio-religious community, we ought to have a spirit of discernment in many aspects. I am reminded that whatever we do, we should do it all to the glory of God (1 Cor 10:31).

Political Pressure of "Ghar Vaapsi" or the Operation of "Home Coming"

Eighty percent of India are Hindus, with the rest coming from the minor religions of Islam, Buddhism, Sikhism, and Zoroastrianism. According to the Pew Research Center, an independent non-partisan polling and research organization, Hindus are the majority in 28 of India's 35 states, including the most populous states of Uttar, Pradesh,

---

6 Chitwook, "Can Christians Celebrate Diwali?"

Maharashtra, and Bihar.[7] India's constitution provides the freedom and right to profess and practice any religion of choice.

Hinduism has been an all-inclusive religion due to its tolerance of other faiths. However, with the emerging ideology of Hindutva and the Hindu nationalism of V. D. Sarvatkar, things have turned in a different direction. These were extensively promoted by Keshav Baliram Hedgewar, who founded the Rashtriya Swayamsevak Sangh (RSS) in 1925. The main objective of this movement was to sensitize the Hindus nationwide to their heritage, culture, and traditions. However, the hidden motive was to maintain a Brahminical hegemony over the low castes, Dalits, and oppressed.[8] Sangh Parivar, which consists of organizations such as Rashtriya Swayam Sevak Sangh(RSS), Bajrang Dal (BD), Vishva Hindu Parishad (VHP), and Bharatiya Janata Party (BJP), claim their slogan to be, "One Nation, One Culture, and One People." By attempting to defend any hostility against their agenda, they maintain a safe platform for the ruling party, which has close political connections with RSS.

After the general elections in India in 2014, BJP, the political wing of Sangh Parivar, began exerting socio-religious pressure on minorities in the name of Hindutva. Being perceived as a political front of the rightwing RSS, the leadership of BJP emphasizes India as a Hindu country. Eliminating non-Hindu communities from India, including those that are predominantly Christian and Muslim, has been the sole aim of Sangh Parivar. To save Hinduism in India, the Rashtriya Seva Sangh embraces the religious cleansing of Christians and Muslims from India. So, the mechanism of "Ghar Vaapsi" (homecoming operation or reconversion movement) is employed by the ruling parties, which exert political pressure on people.

---

7   Kramer, "Key Finding About The Religious Composition of India."
8   Julian P., "The Challenges of Hindu Nationalism," 49–50.

The prominent leader of Vishva Hindu Parishad (VHP) claims that 750,000 Muslims and Christians have been reconverted in the last ten years. Also, this leader intends to run a mass promotional drive to continue with Ghar Vaapsi to save Hinduism in India.[9] The projection engages many more people and replicates the same pattern in other parts of India to drive many more people into Hinduism. For example, the state of West Bengal reported that more than 100 tribal Christians converted to Hinduism.[10] Several Ghar Vaapsi ceremonies are persuasive to tribal communities deprived of their fundamental rights and freedom of expression.

The fundamental concept of Hindutva has led many people to make a strong connection between being Hindu and being Indian. Mahatma Gandhi, whose full name was Mohandas Karamchand Gandhi, was the leader of India's non-violent independence movement against the British. He believed that the Greeks coined the word "Hindu" when they invaded India. All those who lived beyond the Indus valley were called Hindus, and this thought was later established and widely used by scholars and historians.[11] Although the term "Hindu" had a territorial significance in the earlier history of India, it began to be associated with any person who follows the Hindu religion, either by following, practicing, or professing it.

At the core of Hindutva lies the intention of redeeming India as a Hindu Rashtra or a Hindu nation. Its adherents coerce the conversion of Christians and Muslims to Hinduism. Despite India being a secular nation, the current ruling party, Bhartiya Janata, has allied with other fanatic organizations and ventured into mass conversion and

---

9   "7.5 lakh Muslims, Christians Re-converted in Last 10 Years."
10   "Ghar Wapsi: More than 100 tribal Christians converted to Hinduism in West Bengal."
11   Taliyan, "Who is a Hindu?"

reconversion to Hinduism. The ideology of Hindutva underlies the "homecoming," or Ghar Vaapsi Movement.

In one of the TV Z News reports, around 300 people were forcefully converted to Hinduism in the village of Ausanpur, located 16 kilometers from Varanasi, a city considered to be holy by the Hindu community (Zee TV, October 12, 2015). The new converts brought back to Hinduism became part of an organization called Dharma Jagran Samanvya Samiti. It was noted that in the few months following this incident, the Vishva Hindu Parishad leader, Pravin Togadia, claimed that the VHP alone had reconverted more than five lakh (500,000) Christians and two and a half lakh (250,000) Muslims. He is reported to have said, "Our rate of *Ghar Vapsi* used to be around 15,000 each year."[12] This trend is significantly attracting violence against Christian communities across the country.

Impact on the Christian Community and Christian Missions

Under the forces of Hindutva and its allied organizations, minority religious communities, especially the Christian ones, have suffered. Hostility towards Christians has gotten more apparent. At the heart of the debate is how Christianity has been accused for two main reasons. First, according to research, Christianity is the minority with the most vigorous engagement in missionary work. Second, Christians have been accused by the Hindu nationalist movement and others of alluring or forcing poor and underprivileged people to convert to Christianity.[13] The accusing Hindus claim that Christians are converting Hindus by luring them with material benefits; thus, the Hindus' deep need to be freed from poverty is being exploited. Julia Kuhlin, referring to the work of Sebastin Kim, explains three primary reasons why conversions have become a threat in Indian society: "(1) It

---

12 "Coming Home (Ghar Wapsi) and Going Away."
13 Kuhlin, "Love Thy Hindu Neighbor as Thyself."

threatens the communal structure present in the Indian society, (2) it challenges the socio-economic establishment, and (3) the anti-conversion discourse is cornerstone in the Hindutva ideology and therefore prevailing"[14] Thus, the whole act of conversion is not only considered a threat but also felt like an insult to the Hindu religion. This has resulted in anti-conversion laws being passed in many states in India.

The *India Today News* magazine claims that the central government passes no anti-conversion laws. However, the states have formulated their own anti-conversion laws, pronouncing that the offense of any religious conversion by force or allurement will be punished.[15] Also, there have been attempts to enact a national anti-conversion law by the Indian Parliament.

As a result of this enacted law, the minority Christian community has been experiencing hostility and persecution. Churches, schools, hospitals, cell groups, and other worship places have been attacked for the past few decades. Atrocities against the Christian community are on the rise and have created unprecedented wedges in Indian society.

With the rise in anti-Christian disturbances, the first large anti-Christian violent riot broke out in Gujarat in 1998. In these riots, more than thirty churches were burned or vandalized, together with several schools, shops, and homes of Christians.[16] Anti-Christian attacks have increased since then, but many of them continue to remain unregistered. In another case, violence against tribal Christians was carried out in 2013. This anti-Christian riot affected many homes, churches, and Christian institutions. Priests and nuns were apparent targets of hostility in another ferocious attack on Christians in 2008 in one of the poorest regions in Kandhamal. The absence of sufficient arrest warrants, charge sheets, and legal investigations is evidence

---

14 Kuhlin, "Love Thy Hindu Neighbor as Thyself," 19.
15 "Anti-conversion Laws in India: How States Deal with Religious Conversions."
16 Kuhlin, "Love Thy Hindu Neighbor as Thyself."

of intentional atrocities against minorities, especially Christians. Thousands of Christians have had to abandon their villages and homes in fear of their lives. In the alarming spread of violence, my organization, the Free Methodist Church, and believers in the state of Orissa have also suffered heavy persecution under the BJP government. The situation was so sensitive that with the closure of many churches, children from residential care homes were sent back to their homes for safety. It is disheartening to know that government restrictions on religion in India are on the rise. The restrictions involve allegations against non-Hindus and their practices.

According to the Pew Research Center, India ranked fourth in the world in 2015 as having the highest social hostilities involving religion.[17] Social hostilities motivated in the name of religion have triggered religious hatred and communal violence. Political forces have been employed in the attack against local missionaries and evangelists working among the marginally backward people.

Christian NGOs Under Pressure

In their deep motivation by the great commission pronounced in Matthew 28, Christians hold evangelism and social work hand in hand. Charitable work cannot be separated from spreading the good news of Jesus. Anti-conversion laws and policies enacted by the current Bhartiya Janata Party and Sangh Parivar provide a legal cover to attack Christians on the ground of proselytization.

Asia News has brought to attention that the Indian government has canceled the licenses of 15,000 foreign NGOs working among the poor and marginalized. The general secretary of All India Christian Council, Mr. John Dayal, has expressed concern that the present government

---

17 "On Religious Hostilities, India Ranked Just Slightly Better Than Syria."

has been hostile to international organizations.[18] India's largest donor, Compassion International, which has helped more than 200,000 children, was shut down in 2017. Many NGO activists believe that the government perceives NGOs as threats to nationalism. With the imposition of many restrictions on Christian NGOs, thousands of beneficiaries have been deprived of their human rights and are at risk.

Conclusion

India's huge population is diverse and devout in their varied respective religious ethos. There is an intense measure of pious devotion to God in the deep spirituality embedded in very religious traditions and practices. This implies that the Christian spirit of evangelism has been perceived as the biggest threat to the devotion of other religions to their gods and goddesses. Most of the time, extreme evangelism techniques such as denigrating Hindu gods and demeaning traditional Hindu practices have invited violent attacks on Christians. Aggressive evangelism has been the source of tension between Christian and Hindu communities.

Growing up in my early teens, I wondered at several sermons that defamed Hindu deities. As a result, many of my Hindu friends declined my invitation to attend church. In my understanding, Indian Christians have become very intolerant of other religious groups and, under the umbrella of social evangelism, have spread a spirit of exclusion. In my strong opinion, I believe that Indian Christians and churches must explore ways of identifying with other communities and venture into bridging gaps instead of widening rifts.

In a strongly pluralistic society, the majority of the disciples of Jesus have faithfully adhered to the great commission in Mathew 28 of going into the whole world and preaching the gospel. However, by being

---

18 "Since 2014 the Modi government has cancelled the license of 15,000 foreign NGOs."

mindful of social harmony and peace, we have the personal duty of striving towards national unity.

Our God works through and above culture and traditions. In his book, *Jesus Among Other Gods*, Ravi Zacharias reflects that in multireligious and multicultural communities, "the first casualty in such a mix is truth, and, consequently, the person of God."[19] Yet, the truth cannot be sacrificed and compromised if the human spirit with legitimate discipline ventures in its search.

As an Indian Christian, it is my earnest prayer that my fellow Christians will live out the unique identity of Christ, and I will be the epitome of faith in Jesus.

Bibliography

"7.5 lakh Muslims, Christians re-converted in last 10 years." https://www.indiatoday.in/pti-feed/story/7.5-lakh-muslims-christians-re-converted-in-last-10-years-485553-2016-01-08.

"Anti-conversion Laws in India: How States Deal with Religious Conversions." https://www.indiatoday.in/news-analysis/story/anti-conversion-laws-in-india-states-religious-conversion-1752402-2020-12-23.

Chitwood, Ken. "Can Christian Celebrate Diwali?" https://www.deseret.com/2014/10/22/20551063/can-christians-celebrate-diwali.

"Coming Home (Ghar Wapsi) and Going Away: Politics and the Mass Conversion Controversy in India." https://www.mdpi.com/2077-1444/10/5/313/htm#B61-religions-10-00313.

Frykenberg, Robert Eric. "Indian Christians and Hindu Raj." In *Christianity in India from the Beginning to the Present*, 268-300. New York: Oxford University Press, 2008.

---

19 Zacharias, *Jesus Among Other Gods*, 4.

Ghar Wapsi: More than 100 tribal Christians converted to Hinduism in West Bengal." https://www.indiatoday.in/india/east/story/ghar-wapsi-drive-reconversion-vhp-tribal-christians-converted-to-hinduism-jugal-kishore-praveen-togadia-west-bengal-237786-2015-01-29

Julia Kuhlin, "Love thy Hindu Neighbor as Thyself: A Field Study of North Indian Pentecostals' Perceptions of Hindu-Christian Relations." Thesis, Lunds Universitet, 2014.

Julian, P. "The Challenges of Hindu Nationalism and its Impact on Christian Mission Today." *Journal of Global Christianity* 6.1 (2020): 44-46.

Kramer, Stephanie. "Key Finding About The Religious Composition of India." https://www.pewresearch.org/fact-tank/2021/09/21/key-findings-about-the-religious-composition-of-india/.

"On Religious Hostilities, India Ranked Just Slightly Better Than Syria: Pew Study." https://www.huffpost.com/archive/in/entry/on-religious-hostilities-india-ranked-just-slightly-better-than_a_22037994.

Pratik, Astha. "Religious Conversion." https://www.lawctopus.com/academike/religious-conversion/.

"Shashi Tharoor Statement in Lok Sabha." https://www.ndtv.com/india-news/shashi-tharoor-statement-in-lok-sabha-415888.

"Since 2014 the Modi government has cancelled the license of 15,000 foreign NGOs." https://www.asianews.it/news-en/Since-2014-the-Modi-government-has-cancelled-the-licence-of-15,000-foreign-NGOs-46231.html.

Taliyan, Ankur. "Who is a Hindu?" https://www.timesnownews.com/india/article/who-is-a-hindu-as-per-gandhi/492213.

Zacharias, Ravi. *Jesus Among Other Gods*. Chennai: RZIM Life Focus Society, 2001.

14

CHRISTIAN SPIRITUALITY IN ANIMISTIC CONTEXTS

Neville Bartle

Pastor Vipul Kharat called me and said, "Neville, a lady has requested that we come and cleanse her house of demonic spirits. Would you like to come?" We were in Auckland, New Zealand; Pastor Vipul is Indian, and the lady is a Fijian Indian with a Hindu background. Pastor Jessica, a Fijian Indian lady pastor, joined us at the house and introduced us to the elderly lady and her son. She had been attending church for a while, but strange things kept happening at her house and even to their car. She had seen strange people standing outside her house who quickly disappeared, and she feared they were demons. She was afraid and wanted to be free from these demons. We told her that before we cleansed her house, she needed to accept Jesus as her Savior and invite him into her life.

Jessica spoke in Hindi and led her in a prayer of repentance and faith in Christ. Pastor Vipul asked for a glass of water to use as a symbol of God's cleansing power. The son felt that only the best glass would do for holding holy water and found a crystal goblet which he filled with water. Vipul prayed over it and consecrated it as a symbol of God's cleansing power in the name of the Father, the Son, and the Holy Spirit. We began at the front door and sprinkled some water on it and declared that the house was under the lordship of Jesus Christ and that all evil spirits must immediately leave the house. Vipul moved to the center of the living room, sprinkled more water on the carpet and the coffee table, and again declared the lordship of Jesus Christ and commanded all evil spirits to leave. Suddenly, Vipul's hand was smashed down on the table with a loud crash. The water was still in the goblet, but the base of the goblet was smashed off. He calmly asked for a new glass of water which he again consecrated. I noticed a very definite firmness in his voice as he commanded all demons to leave the house while we went through every room in the house.

Jessica asked the lady about any items used to honor the spirits. There were several CDs of Hindu worship music designed to appease the spirits, sticks of incense, little frog-shaped figurines that represented Hindu spirits, and various other things. These were collected up until two shopping bags were filled. I felt that we should ask her if she would like to be baptized. Jessica mentioned that the lady had not been feeling well and was losing weight. The lady requested to be baptized, so we did, using another glass of water. Jessica took the bags of Hindu worship items home and was going to dispose of them in the household rubbish bags. As we were leaving, Vipul confided in me, "That glass did not slip from my hands. Something grabbed my hand and slapped it down." The demon was real, and he did not want to go without a fight. A few weeks later, we heard that the lady had stage four cancer, and she lived only a few more weeks before she left this life and went to be with Jesus.

This story illustrates four of the main features of animism. First, animistic beliefs often exist in conjunction with other world religions.

Second, spiritual beings are real and have power over human lives. Third, demonstrations of God's power over evil forces are very significant. Finally, symbols and ceremonies are extremely important in communicating the message of salvation.

If we were to travel across the Asia-Pacific region, we would find that very few people identify themselves as being animists. Instead, it is a label usually given by others. But the animistic worldview is dominant throughout Asia and the Pacific and often coexists with other world religions. Whether they be Islam, Buddhism, Hinduism, Shintoism, or Christianity, the main world religions often exist as a veneer over animistic practices. Because of this, some scholars prefer to use the term "folk religions."[1]

Van Rheenan writes that animism is "the belief that personal spiritual beings and impersonal spiritual forces have power over human affairs and that humans, consequently, must discover what beings and forces are impacting them in order to determine future action and, frequently, to manipulate their power."[2] These "personal spiritual beings" include God, gods, angels, demons, ancestors, and various other spirits. "Impersonal spiritual forces" is a foreign concept to many Westerners but includes such things as sorcery, witchcraft, curses, fate, astrology, evil eye, bad luck, and the personal life force called "Mana" in parts of Oceania and "Qi" in some Asian contexts.

Many westerners have been taught in academic institutions that animism is a primitive belief system belonging to people with a primitive pre-logical mentality. The theory goes that as people became civilized, they moved from animism to polytheism, and then some moved on to monotheism. Eventually, they will be enlightened and realize that God is unnecessary, and they will become modern humanists at the top of the evolutionary ladder. This is a chimerical myth. Animism is not the

---

1 Hiebert et al., *Understanding Folk Religion* is the definitive work on this topic.
2 Van Rheenan, "Defining an Animistic Worldview."

product of a primitive mentality. In fact, if we accept Van Rheenan's definition "that personal spiritual beings and impersonal spiritual forces have power over human affairs," then we must be forced to admit that the people in the Old and New Testaments had a so-called "animistic worldview." The Bible has numerous references to angels, demons, other gods, blessings and curses, witchcraft, sorcery, and idolatry. It is the materialistic world view, which largely ignores the unseen world and is so common in the West, that is the aberration.[3]

Animism is not so much a religion as it is a way of viewing the world. Animists see the world as alive with divine energy. Trees, rivers, mountains, ponds, swamps, and jungles are alive not just biologically but also spiritually. Divine power is distributed through all creation, and we all share in that divine life to a greater or lesser degree.[4] A village pastor can greet his congregation on Sunday morning: "What a beautiful day to worship the Lord. I woke this morning to the shrill cry of the cicadas and the chirping of the birds as they praised Almighty God. Now it is our turn to join in with the rest of creation in praising our Heavenly Father." The whole earth is permeated by divine presence. Creaturely beings—animate and inanimate—reveal not only the qualities of God; they are members of a symbiotic cosmos that interpenetrate each other's existence in ways we cannot comprehend or explain. Every creature participates in a vertical relationship with the divine and a horizontal relationship in earthly community. A pastor, thus, might say the following charge to baptismal candidates: "This is a very important declaration that you are making today. The river, the trees, the rocks, and the sky are witnesses to this event, along with the members of your family, this congregation, and the entire community. Today, God the Father, Satan, demons, and the angels in heaven also witness this declaration of faith in Jesus Christ as your Lord and

---

3 Joerstad, "A Brief Account of Animism in Biblical Studies."
4 Harvey, "Radical Relationality in Animistic Studies."

Savior." There is no divide between sacred and secular or between natural and supernatural.

Power Orientation in Animistic Worldviews

Folk religions are concerned about the immediate issues of everyday life. They are pragmatic and are primarily concerned about spiritual power for everyday problems. Religion is not so much concerned about truth in a philosophical sense but seeks to know how to gain access to power and be able to control it to make life successful here and now. Many animists come to God as a result of a visible demonstration of God's power being superior to the power of other gods or spirit beings. Missiologists call this a power encounter.[5] A perfect example is Elijah's story of challenging the prophets of Baal to build two altars with sacrifices but to light no fire (1 Kgs 18:24). He said, "You call on the name of your god, and I will call on the name of the Lord. The god who answers by fire—he is God." A false god is one who claims to be powerful but, in actual fact, is impotent and unable to provide for his followers. The true God is the one who can demonstrate his power in the tangible events of history.

The miracles that Jesus performed were signs of the coming kingdom but were also visual demonstrations to help people believe. "Believe in the evidence of the miraculous works I have done," Jesus said, "even if you don't believe me" (John 10:38 NLT). John concludes his gospel by saying that the purpose of the "miraculous signs" was so that people would "believe that Jesus is the Christ, the Son of God" (John 20:31). In the book of Acts, again and again, God performed "miraculous signs and wonders" through the apostles as they proclaimed the resurrection of Jesus the Messiah. The miraculous signs and wonders validated

---

5 Brant, "Power Encounter."

the message about Jesus. These continue to be very important in the growth and development of the church in animistic contexts.[6]

People coming to faith in Christ from an animistic background usually first come to a faith in God as healer and provider.[7] This is a very dramatic life-changing step of faith, but it normally does not involve repentance and forgiveness of sins. As a result of seeing God's power displayed in their lives, they decide to make the God of the Bible their God and to pray to him rather than their old gods. Paul experienced this in his mission among the Thessalonians, who "turned to God from idols to serve the living and true God" (1 Thess 1:9). Later, as converted animists grow in their understanding, they come to know more of who Jesus is and their need for a savior.[8]

Growing up in the Nazarene Church, I was taught that sanctification was a "second definite work of grace." But as a missionary in Papua New Guinea, I discovered that faith in God as healer, protector, or provider came first and that faith in Christ for the forgiveness of sins was for most PNG believers a "second work of grace." Sanctification was then subsequent to this. The PNG Christian experience resonates with the order of salvation that characterized Paul's mission to the Gentiles, as commissioned by the Lord: "I am sending you to them to open their eyes and turn them from darkness to light, and from the power of Satan to God, so that they may receive forgiveness of sins and a place among those who are sanctified by faith in me" (Acts 26:17-18). The verse clearly outlines a series of steps or phases that animists pass through. Often it is a power encounter or some miraculous sign that opens their eyes to the goodness and power of God. This prompts them to turn from the darkness of animistic beliefs to the light of God's love

---

6 See for instance, the growth of Pentecostalism among the animistic Warays in the Philippines, in Johnson, *Theology in Context*.

7 Johnson, *Theology in Context*, 37–40.

8 Van Rheenan, *Communicating Christ in Animistic Contexts;* Johnson, "Healing in the Lowland Philippines."

and truth, and they come to faith in God. This prepares them for the next step "so that they may receive forgiveness of sins."

In most Western countries, people had faith in God and believed the Bible to be God's word, even if they seldom read it. Consequently, the next step was faith in Christ as Savior from sin. But as western countries become more and more post-Christian, it will become increasingly important in secular western culture to realize that, for many people, the first step on their spiritual journey is not forgiveness of sins but rather to "believe that God exists and that he rewards those who earnestly seek him" (Heb 11:6). This is dramatically demonstrated in the life of C. S. Lewis and his journey from atheism to Christ. In his book *Surprised by Joy*, he describes two distinct experiences. The first was a change from atheism to theism. "I finally gave in and admitted," he writes, "that God was God, and knelt and prayed: perhaps, that night, the most dejected and reluctant convert in all England."[9] He begins his next chapter by stating, "the conversion recorded in the last chapter was only to theism, pure and simple, not to Christianity. I was not yet a Christian, but I had become a theist."[10] It was two years later, in 1931, that he surrendered his life to Jesus as Savior and became a Christian.

Excluded Middle

Christians coming from animistic backgrounds are very conscious that they are involved in a spiritual conflict. Verses like Ephesians 6:12 are very significant: "For our struggle is not against flesh and blood, but against the rulers, against the authorities, against the powers of this dark world and against the spiritual forces of evil in the heavenly realms." In many tribes, there is a belief in a supreme being who was before all things and who is supreme over all. However, this great God

---

9 Lewis, *Surprised by Joy*, 228–9.
10 Lewis, *Surprised by Joy*, 230.

is too high and distant to be involved in everyday life. Thus, their attention is focused on territorial spirits in the forest, ocean, river, or some other geographical feature. Spirits of ancestors, or the "living dead," are thought to be very involved in the everyday life of people in the village.

Missiologist Paul Hiebert outlines a very real problem of Christian spirituality in animistic contexts. He states: "Deeply committed Christians faithfully attend church services and pray to God in times of need but feel compelled during the week to go to a local shaman for healing, a diviner for guidance, and an exorcist for deliverance from spirit oppression."[11] Missionaries have presented Christ as the answer for our spiritual needs and the one who gives eternal life. We have brought in western medicine for many illnesses, but what about when a person is under a curse, or someone has performed witchcraft or black magic, or some ancestral spirit is angry? What is the Christian answer to these problems? Sometimes a missionary has no real answer and says that curses, sorcery, and witchcraft are just superstitions and products of people's imaginations. But when people feel that these are very real problems and someone is seriously ill, they feel God is powerless and so return to the village shaman or magician for answers. Hiebert calls this the "flaw of the excluded middle."[12]

Westerners have a two-tiered view of the world (see Figure 1). Religion deals with faith, miracles, and the sacred. Science and technology deal with sight and experience and the natural order. Science deals with the problems of the physical world and is secular. Hiebert points out that there is an "excluded middle zone" that deals with such questions as "How can one prevent accidents or guarantee success in the future? How can one ensure that a marriage will be fruitful and happy and endure? How can one avoid getting on a plane that will

---

[11] Hiebert et al., *Understanding Folk Religion*, 15.
[12] Hiebert, "The Flaw of the Excluded Middle."

Figure 1: A Western Two-Tiered View of Reality

crash? In the West, these questions are left unanswered. They are accidents, luck, or unforeseeable events, hence unexplainable. But many people are not content to leave so important a set of questions unanswered, and the answers they give are often in terms of ancestors, demons, witches and local gods, or in terms of magic and astrology."[13] Christians from animistic backgrounds are looking for answers to questions that most modern theologians have never really considered.

Relational

Folk religions are very relational and community oriented. The spirit beings are local, and the ancestors are all related to the living, so maintaining relationships with the unseen world is extremely important. There is no division between natural and supernatural: everything is interrelated. The unseen spiritual world impacts the physical world, and the physical world reflects the unseen world. Sickness and calamity are seen as the result of disease caused by broken relationships between the living and the unseen world.[14] There is often a strong emphasis on the "living dead." The dead are perceived to exist in a parallel world and continue to be involved in the everyday life of

---

13 Hiebert, "The Flaw of the Excluded Middle."
14 Nehrbass, "Dealing with Disaster."

the clan or tribe. Relationships between the living and the dead are very important. As one village elder said, "If the ancestors are happy, then we are good, but if they are upset, then we soon feel it." When relationships are good, then people can experience the "good life." This is very similar to the Hebrew understanding of *shalom*. *Shalom* is far more than the absence of war. It is fulfillment in every area of life: health, success, fertility of crops, livestock, family, respect, honor, and influence over others.

Community-Based Health Care in Papua New Guinea has emphasized the importance of right relationships between people and God, relationships within the family and clan, relationships with other tribes and outsiders, and finally, relationship with our environment. CBHC has emphasized the importance of clean villages, disposal of rubbish, clean toilets, and clean drinking water leading to better health. Sickness is often blamed on sorcery or evil spirits, but a clean, healthy environment means a reduction of sickness and, therefore, less talk and accusations of evil spirits, curses, or witchcraft.

Oral, Visual, and Narrative

Folk Religions are primarily oral and visual and are passed down from generation to generation in stories, songs, symbols, and ceremonies. This is similar to the Old Testament, where the theology is expressed in narratives of God at work in the lives of their ancestors, in sacrifices, feasts, and pilgrimages. Theology is also expressed in the clothing of the high priests and the architecture of the tabernacle, lamps, incense, and the rituals of cleansing and burnt offerings. This is in sharp contrast to western theology that is very cognitive and analytical.

People from oral cultures, or those who learn primarily by hearing rather than reading, are not intellectually inferior. Animistic people are deep thinkers but express their thoughts using symbols, metaphors, word pictures, and complex rituals. This is why using holy water in a cleansing ritual is very important. It is a visible symbol of God's cleansing power. Spirituality is primarily experiential. It is felt rather than reasoned and experienced through one's feelings rather than perceived by the mind.[15]

A study of the history of Christian missions in the South Pacific shows that the Catholic church attracted many because the mass was very visual and sensory. The colored robes, candles, crosses, processions, incense, statues, and icons appealed to sight, sound, smell, taste, and touch. Protestants took a negative approach to symbols and ceremonies. They focused instead on preaching the word, but the doctrinal preaching failed to capture the imagination of visually-oriented people, and so the preaching did not have much impact. However, from time to time, revival movements broke out. God spoke to people in the vernacular through dreams and visions that were in full color. Some shook under the power of the Holy Spirit, others spoke in tongues, and the Word of God became alive and dynamic. The power of God was manifested as people were healed and set free from demonic spirits. At times like this, the church grew dramatically. Jesus' words became very significant: "The thief comes only to steal and kill and destroy; I have come that they may have life, and have it to the full" (John10:10). Here was the abundant life that they were looking for.

Life Should be Abundant, and Life is to be Celebrated

For the animist, the goal of life is not merely to survive but to experience abundant life, which can only be accomplished by living in harmony with these various spirit beings and spiritual forces. When problems come, animists use divination to determine what spirit being or spiritual force is causing the problem and what ritual or sacrifice is needed to correct the problem. Spirits are believed to be capricious,

---

15 Rutt, "Ritual and Animism."

and much effort goes into appeasing them and manipulating them so that they work for the family or community rather than against them. Animists are looking for abundant life, which is manifested in tribal/community flourishing with good health, fertility, prosperity, and freedom from fear. This abundant life should be celebrated with singing, dancing, vibrant colors, feasting, and laughter.

Nazarenes in Papua New Guinea have used their God-given creativity and understanding of tribal customs to develop large-scale youth conferences, women's conferences, and, most recently, a men's conference. These happen every two or three years and involve months of planning, with thousands of people in attendance. A conference includes pilgrimage. People will save sacrificially and plan for months in advance. Then they will walk for days or travel by canoe, truck, bus, or airplane to attend. The journey is part of the total experience. People get away from the daily grind of village life and travel with Christian brothers and sisters. They laugh together, sing, and share experiences, and it is a time of bonding. The women's conferences are extremely colorful, with each church or district wearing matching outfits. The opening ceremony is patterned after the opening ceremony of the South Pacific Games. Participants from each district/province march in with flags and banners, dressed in very bold, colorful matching outfits. Their songs in their vernacular reflect their tribal origin. Tribal people feel a deep need for periodic displays of tribal strength, and these conferences allow this to happen in the church. The conference includes songs, dramas, preaching, meals, times of sharing, altar calls, and times of corporate prayer. People from small, isolated village churches feel the thrill of belonging to the big Nazarene tribe. The gathering together of 2,000 to 3,000 like-minded believers, the fellowship, united singing, and corporate prayer all help to symbolize the abundant life we have in Christ. Finally, there is a closing ceremony and a challenge and then a reverse pilgrimage back home, but they return strengthened, blessed, and encouraged with a greater determination to live for God. The Nazarene ban on any form of dancing has been most unfortunate. Christians from animistic contexts want to express their faith and joy and the story of God through drama, song, and dance. Admittedly some dances are very sensual in nature, and so discernment is needed, but many dances can be used to the glory of God.

Challenges

Animists are very responsive to Christianity, and Christianity is growing rapidly in the Global South.[16] The number of evangelicals in the world has increased from 112 million in 1970 to 386 million in 2020. Globally, evangelicalism is a predominantly non-white movement within Christianity and is becoming increasingly more so, with 77% of all evangelicals living in the Global South in 2020. This is up from only 7.8% in 1900. In 1981, 28.3% of Nazarenes lived outside the USA. By September 2016 (35 years later), the number living outside the USA had increased to 75%, and that percentage has continued to increase. Apart from the USA, the countries with the most members are Mozambique, Brazil, India, Haiti, Bangladesh, and Guatemala. A total of 27% of all Nazarenes live in Africa, and more than 20% of all Nazarenes speak Spanish as their first language. This trend means that there is an influx into the global church of people who come from those places which continue to hold, to a greater or lesser degree, an animistic worldview.

One of the problems that we as Nazarenes face is that because of our emphasis on being one church around the world, we have sought to develop a global Nazarene theology. However, if we look carefully at the first global theology conference of the church in Acts 15, we find that it was prompted by a cultural issue—circumcision. The big question

---

16 Jenkins, *The Next Christendom*.

of Acts 15 was whether the new Gentile converts needed to follow the cultural traditions of the Jewish people who had brought the gospel to them. The Pharisee group wanted uniformity of practice. The conclusion of the conference, however, was to reject uniformity and instead affirm unity in diversity. Jews continued to practice circumcision and their dietary laws. The Gentiles were free to ignore circumcision and follow different dietary laws. What united everyone was salvation by faith in Jesus Christ. Today, we face many issues around the world. Animists have questions about polygamy, ancestors, and the spirit world. Other cultures face issues related to social oppression, injustice, poverty, and inequality. These are very different issues, and one theology will not fit all. No single theology will adequately address the diverse problems that arise in so many different cultural contexts around the world.[17]

Christians from an animistic background need a holistic narrative theology that begins with the cosmic story of God who creates and sustains the universe.[18] It must also include a theology of human history. God created people in his image, but they disobeyed, and their relationship with God was broken. But God, in his mercy and grace, came seeking Adam—"Where are you?" The Old Testament tells God's grace and judgment as he works redemptively in human history. This theology must also address the invisible world, including a trinitarian understanding of the God who is constantly involved in his creation by his providence, presence, and power. It must take angels seriously, for they help protect and provide for God's people. It must take Satan and demons seriously, for they are fallen angels who seek to prevent people from turning from idols to serve the living and true God.

---

17 There are scholars who do not only argue of theologies, but of Christianities. See Vähäkangas, *Context, Plurality, and Truth*.

18 See for example Lodahl's *The Story of God*.

We need a theology that includes nature. God created the cosmos, and he declared it good. Creation declares the glory and beauty of God. Sin, however, has affected not just humans but all of creation. Consequently, we live in a broken world. Creation groans (Rom 8:22). Bad things happen to good people, and life does not always make sense. Jesus is God with us and walks with us by his Spirit in a broken, disease-ridden world where injustice and poverty are all too common. We look forward to the day when Jesus will return, and all things will be made new, creation will be restored, and there will be no more sickness, suffering, hunger, injustice, disease, or death.[19]

We must be on guard that we do not fall into the trap of a prosperity gospel. God indeed blesses his children, but he also calls us to humble ourselves, take up our cross, and follow him.

We need a balanced theology regarding miraculous signs.[20] We believe in a God who does exceedingly abundantly above all that we ask or even imagine. But God is not our servant who follows our instructions. We do not command God but rather live in humble faith. God's power is made perfect in weakness and is demonstrated most powerfully on the cross. God's power is rooted in love, not pride; redemption, not revenge; concern for the other, and not for self. It is humble, not proud, and inviting, not rejecting. Its symbol is the cross and not the sword.[21]

We need a theology that declares Jesus' victory over sin, death, and the devil.[22] Satan brought in sin, and sin brought in death. Jesus is the second Adam who succeeded where Adam failed. Jesus first conquered Satan by his sinless life of perfect obedience, conquered sin by his sacrificial death on the cross, and conquered death through his descent

---

19 Lodahl and Maskiewicz, *Renewal in Love*.
20 See Turner, *The Holy Spirit and Spiritual*, 240–60, 286–302.
21 See Wesley's Comment on 1 Corinthians 15:26 in *Explanatory Notes*.
22 An example is that of Aulen's *Christus Victor*.

to Hades and his glorious resurrection and ascension to the highest place, far above all rule and authority, power and dominion (Eph 1:21).[23] Animists try to appease and manipulate spirits and spiritual powers. The gospel calls people to humble themselves and seek God. People need to change from a tribal or clan-centered worldview where good is whatever appears to benefit my tribe or clan, to a kingdom worldview where we pray, "Your kingdom come, your will be done on earth as it is in heaven."

Bibliography

Aulen, Gustaf. *Christus Victor: An Historical Study of the Three Main Types of the Idea of Atonement,* translated by A. G. Herbert; Eugene: Wipf and Stock, 2003.

Brant, Howard. "Power Encounter." *International Journal of Frontier Missions* 10 (1993): 185–92.

Harvey, Graham. "Radical Relationality in Animistic Studies." *Journal for the Study of Religion, Nature and Culture* 11.4 (2007): 481–97.

Hiebert, Paul, "The Flaw of the Excluded Middle." *Missiology* 10 (1982): 35–47.

Hiebert, Paul G., et. al. *Understanding Folk Religion.* Grand Rapids: Baker, 1999.

Jenkins, Philip. *The Next Christendom: The Coming of Global Christianity.* Oxford: Oxford University Press, 2011.

Joerstad, Mari. "A Brief Account of Animism in Biblical Studies." *Journal for the Study of Religion, Nature, and Culture* (14.2): 250–70.

Johnson, Dave. "Healing in the Lowland Philippines: Some Considerations for Discipleship." *Asian Journal of Pentecostal Studies* 17.2 (2014): 171–86.

---

23 Hiebert et al., *Understanding Folk Religion,* 374.

———. *Theology in Context: A Case Study in the Philippines*. Baguio: APTS Press, 2017.

Lewis, C. S. *Surprised by Joy: The Shape of My Early Life*. New York: Harvest Book, 1955.

Lodahl, Michael. *The Story of God: A Narrative Theology*. 2nd ed. Kansas City: Beacon Hill, 2008.

Lodahl, Michael, and April Cordero Maskiewicz. *Renewal in Love: Living Holy Lives in God's Good Creation*. Kansas City: Nazarene Publishing House, 2014.

Nehrbass, Kenneth. "Dealing with Disaster: Critical Contextualization of Misfortune in an Animistic Setting." *Missiology* 39.4 (2011): 459–71.

Rutt, Douglas L. "Ritual and Animism: Liturgical Symbol and Ritual in an Animistic Context—What Do They Mean?" *Missio Apostolica* 5.1 (1997): 4–18.

Turner, Max. *The Holy Spirit and Spiritual Gifts in the New Testament*. Grand Rapids: Baker, 1996.

Vähäkangas, Mika. *Context, Plurality, and Truth: Theology in World Christianities*. Eugene: Pickwick, 2020.

Van Rheenan, Gailyn. *Communicating Christ in Animistic Contexts*. Grand Rapids: Baker, 1991.

Wesley, John. *Explanatory Notes Upon the New Testament*. Reprint. Kansas City: Beacon Hill, 1981.

15

SPIRITUALITY IN THE WORKPLACE

Fletcher Tink

A Tribute

If religious expression is trending toward gaudiness rather than godliness and sensationalism rather than substance, Dr. Floyd Cunningham has long been focused in a totally different direction. I have known Dr. Cunningham since my first visit to the campus of Asia-Pacific Nazarene Theological Seminary in 1989 and had learned of his reputation years earlier through his journey in Eastern Nazarene College and then on to Johns Hopkins University, where he studied with the esteemed church historian, Dr. Timothy L. Smith, a member of the church where I served in the early 90s as associate pastor. Whenever I visited the APNTS campus, Dr. Cunningham would enlist me to speak in chapel or lecture in a class. But it was not until two decades later that, as President, he engaged my dreams of establishing a Ph.D. presence in Transformational Development through Kansas City's Bresee Institute for Metro Ministries. Much to my surprise, he was enthusiastic, and soon a new program was born that absorbs my attention to this day.

Dr. Cunningham is the antithesis of flamboyancy; hardworking, meticulous, and private. Were he a Catholic, he would be a monk. But his services to APNTS in every role for nearly forty years have been the glue that has held this unique international institution together. His love for his students is most evident; his love of administration, less affectionate. But he does it with faithfulness and skill. I join with many others who now congratulate him in voice and script for his unusual dedication to his many tasks that have absorbed him here in Taytay. As I write this essay, I believe that Dr. Cunningham is the epitome of "spirituality in the workplace." Self-effacing, he does not pound his drum. But his impact on all of us goes beyond any words that we can fashion. Congratulations, sir.

Introduction

I was handed the topic of "Spirituality in the Workplace," perhaps because, in recent years, I traveled to numerous countries, presenting seminars on "Theology of Work" and "Ethics and Responsible Business Practices" to Christian and non-Christian audiences alike. These forays have enlarged my life and expanded my understanding of how God works in places described as "secular," even while the psalmist chants, "The earth is the Lord's, and everything in it" (Ps 24:1). The core tenets of these seminars have dismantled ecclesiastical assumptions and opened the shutters to the laity (a term absent in the Bible) to ascend as equal partners in the mission of God.

The Search for Definitions

The term "spirituality" is an amorphous and ambiguous term weighted by barnacles of cheap impressions. For instance, the Merriam-Webster Dictionary defines spirituality as "1) something that in ecclesiastical law belongs to the church or to a cleric as such,

2) clergy, 3) sensitivity or attachment to religious values, and 4) the quality or state of being spiritual."[1] Aside from #4, which is a useless tautology, #1 and #2 are antitheses to the assumptions of this essay. Indeed, its antonym, "laity," renders this topic irrelevant. Response #3 is an undernourished and sentimentalized contortion on the theme and not very helpful.

Dictionary.com does only slightly better. It lays out its definitions as such: "1) the quality or fact of being spiritual, 2) incorporeal or immaterial nature, 3) predominantly spiritual character as shown in thought, life, etc., . . . [and] . . . 4) property or revenue of the church or an ecclesiastic in his or her official capacity." Only #2 seems to have any relevance in that "spirituality" is unhinged from material things. However, I would argue that Christianity is the most materialistic of all religions. A further explanation is given: "The state or quality of being dedicated to God, religion, or spiritual things or values, especially as contrasted with material or temporal ones."[2] Ah, now we catch a glimmer of insight in the word "temporal." Is there something about "spirituality" that is transcendent in contradistinction to "temporal"? So, I decided to go to Facebook to see what my friends had to say about "Spirituality in the Workplace." I wanted to find some colloquial opinions about the theme. Ten Christian friends responded.

Benjamin (a young Methodist pastor living in Pennsylvania):

> It varies with the workplace. I've been in jobs outside of traditional ministry where I was able to offer ashes on Ash Wednesday. I did it on my lunch break, so not on company time. But I offered them to co-workers and clients alike. It was a very powerful moment. The believer in the workplace setting has a unique opportunity to share God's love through encouragement, a listening

---

1   Merriam-Webster Dictionary, https://www.merriam-webster.com/dictionary/spirituality.
2   Dictionary.com, https://www.dictionary.com/browse/spirituality.

ear, a helpful attitude, and so much more. It takes being receptive to God's leading.

Linda (lives in Vermont):

It is interesting that people who practice a different spirituality than ours freely say things like, you need to wear this gem or that gem, or you need to burn sage, or you need to do a spiritual cleansing at some time. Yet Christians are shy to express, "Can I pray for you?" mainly because Christianity is now "taboo."

Jim (a retired pastor in Minnesota):

There is a link between spirituality and health and wellbeing. Those who celebrate or acknowledge a personal awareness of a higher dimension are often happier and more productive.

Earl (retired, lives in Washington State):

I was asked by my employer to work, and he would pay me under the table. I had to refuse him, and I told him that if I would lie for him, wouldn't I lie to him? He never asked me again.

Gerry (an associate pastor in Nebraska):

I don't know if this is what you are thinking, but my current boss and previous boss allowed me to pray for others, for them, my co-workers, and clients. It has given me the freedom to carry various situations to the Lord without repercussions. It has reduced my stress, increased my motivation to serve, allowed me to be more positive and mindful of diversity, and has given me divine strength in negative situations.

Doug (works at senior citizen housing in Maryland):

I believe spirituality in the workplace is when he who dwells within is reflected in everything we do and say. It is how the Spirit responds through our lives in the routine mundaneness of everyday life and work. It seasons (like salt and pepper on scrambled eggs) who we are and how we respond to opportunities, people, and responsibilities. So often, when we talk about spiritual activity, we get all caught up in performance. What a stumbling block when we allow ourselves (and our thinking) to be distracted by what I do (my performance, activity) instead of who he is and what he's doing IN me.

Michelle (an ordained pastor in the Philippines, working in an academic office):

> Spending nine hours or more every day, five or six days a week in the workplace, is significant in one's spirituality. The gate to and from the workplace is a passage to different worlds that affect the person.

Herb (directs a homeless shelter in Massachusetts):

> There is a theme often mentioned in college football, recognizing that most college players, even those from Division One teams, do not go on to play professional sports. They say that most will "go pro" in another field. Likewise, most of us will not become pastors, missionaries, or the like. Instead, we are called into another field where we have a "profession," that is, to represent Christ wherever we are and whatever we do. As a youth pastor, I often discussed that calling with our seniors and college students and that our responsibility to whatever we were drawn is to do it to the glory of God.

Christie (recently ordained, pastoring, and living in Idaho):

> I find that spirituality is an outflow of one's life and much more powerful than a plan or program utilized in the workplace. Involving one's co-workers in everyday life opens up far more entries into one's spiritual life.

Ruth (widowed, living in Texas):

> I think it's when we treat everyone like Jesus would. Kindness to all.

Eric (author, Filipino living in Thailand):

> I would say it's being excellent in every aspect of your job since we're doing it all for his glory, whether it's what you're producing or working on or in your relationships with your co-workers.

Jeri (founder of birthing home in the Philippines, from Montana):

> I'm not sure that spirituality does or should look any different in the workplace than anywhere else. There are constants of spirituality, such as kindness, trustworthiness, etc., that should be present in some measure no matter where we are. The maturity of those attributes will differ, as will how they are expressed, but they should be much of what we bring to the workplace.

I categorize their responses in the four following ways:

1. Religious gestures motivated by divine influence (Benjamin, Linda, Gerry);
2. Attitudinal stances motivated by divine awareness (Jim, Doug, Christie, Ruth);
3. Character (moral and ethical) expressions that eminate from religious formation (Earl, Eric, Jeri);
4. Missiological calling by the Divine (Michelle, Herb).

In sum, their collective descriptions move us somewhat closer to a conventional evangelical understanding of the infusion of God's presence in the so-called "secular" arenas of life.

The term "spirituality" has been co-opted by various faiths and, at times, where formal faith does not exist. It is common to hear people talk about their "spirituality" in contradistinction to the materialism of modern values. Indeed, "spirituality" pursues the core values and meanings that motivate how one lives, a sort of inner path that guides one to discover the essence of one's life. Obviously, the practices, attitudes, and devotion to pursuing spirituality will vary greatly, depending on the worldview that undergirds one's approach to life. Indeed, a secular form of "spirituality" can be posited, focusing on the humanistic moral traits of love, patience, tolerance, forgiveness, contentment, responsibility, harmony, and concern for others.

Kees Waaijman has identified four forms of spiritual practices that often mark "spirituality":

1. Somatic practices, especially deprivation and diminishment. Deprivation aims to purify the body. Diminishment concerns the repression of ego-oriented impulses. Examples include fasting and poverty.
2. Psychological practices, for example, meditation.
3. Social practices. Examples include the practice of obedience and communal ownership, reforming ego-orientedness into other-orientedness.
4. Spiritual practices. These aim at purifying ego-centeredness and directing the abilities at the divine reality.[3]

However, as one looks over these categories, it appears that the "workplace" is a sorry setting for these practices. One might argue that a spirit of humility and servanthood in the workplace is potentially an offspring of #1. Perhaps #2 might be fertile soil for "spirituality" where one works. Certainly, #3 describing ego-orientedness to other-orientedness may contribute to an improved work environment. And #4, the purification of ego-centeredness, in harmony with the divine, does add a further dimension to the workplace context.

Additional ancillary words hint at "spirituality," such as devotion, consecration, piety, reverence, sanctity, faithfulness, worship,

---

3 Waaijman, *Spirituality*, 342.

devotedness, adoration, and holiness. However, these are postures from all of life, hence not unique to the workplace.

Ironically, any discussion about "spirituality" in the workplace must contend with two realities:

1. **"Spirituality" is not Self-Aware:** To the spiritually minded, to parse out its particulars is as ineffective as asking a fish to define water. People so live in the aura of God's presence all around that they are unaware of any peculiarity or uniqueness within their context. To them, their spiritual instincts are normal and their spiritual purposes pedestrian. Only those peering in from the outside see the need for such categorized descriptions or sensitized contrasts.

2. **"Spirituality" is Holistic:** To the spiritually minded, the workplace is merely one covering of cloth in the complete fabric of God's world. They do not countenance a sacred/secular divide or devalue the material in contrast to the immaterial. Everything is the Lord's and is under his domain. What a person does on Thursday afternoon in the workplace is just as important as what he or she does in church on a Sunday morning.

So, in the search for the elusive grail of "spirituality," I have selected fifteen Christian books, recently published, that dare permeate the workplace environment. Most of these are new publications but represent the proliferating interest in workplace Christianity. Ironically, none of these books actively employ the word "spirituality," perhaps because of its nebulous character. But each of them casts a unique theological dragnet into the workplace setting and draws from it a productive catch. I do not intend to summarize the entire books. Instead, I highlight one concept or meme from each tome that uniquely adds to the compendium of insights about how Christians can integrate their faith with their workplace duties in ways that authentically express the Spirit of Christ.

Tim Keller (2012)

Tim Keller's contribution, entitled, *Every Good Endeavor: Connecting Your Work to God's Work*, has been in print for nine years and is probably the most ubiquitous of any recent books on the theme. I often use it as a basic text in my courses. His focus on God's invitation to work and develop cultures with God is most helpful. Indeed, all work is culture-making. Keller uses Richard Mouw's metaphor of God as "an investment banker" who leverages resources to create a whole world of new life (p. 46), bringing fresh imagery into the partnership between God and humankind. Keller highlights Martin Luther's allusion to God's "masks" representing the various human activities doled out as gifts to each person (p. 60). In his chapter on "Work as Service," Keller sees work as an "act of love" and as a "ministry of competence."

Amy Sherman (2014)

Sherman has had Nazarene connections and has served as a consultant to the development of the Center for Social Justice at Trevecca Nazarene University. Her contribution in *Kingdom Calling* is her extensive exploration of the word "righteousness," taking as a cue the statement from Proverbs 11:10, "When the righteous prosper, the city rejoices." Her schemata on p. 46 are particularly helpful. She categorizes three dimensions of relationships: "UP," "IN," and "OUT." In each of these, she offers key characteristics with their attendant work implications:

> "UP" suggests "Godward orientation" where one works for God's glory, not self-fulfillment; eschews workaholism; sets boundaries on institutional loyalty.
>
> "UP" is characterized by "humility," embracing functional daily dependence on the Spirit.

"UP" expresses an eternal perspective, recognizing God as the audience and valuing today's work as participating in the new creation.

"IN" is characterized by "personal holiness," where, in the work environment, one does not cheat, steal, or lie and maintains sexual purity with co-workers.

"IN" lives in "the fruit of the Spirit," which is given to grace-based relationships.

"IN" expresses "openhandedness" by offering generosity to others, eschewing materialism and self-indulgence.

"IN" feels gut-level compassion for the hurting. The worker is proactive in "seeing" others' needs.

And finally,

"OUT" sounds a solid note for social justice by advocating for better working conditions for workers, promoting just relations with customers, suppliers, and shareholders, being a good corporate neighbor/citizen, encouraging transformation within one's own institution, and encouraging social reform within one's own field.

Luke Bobo (2017)

In a lighter book, *Living Salty and Light-Filled Lives in the Workplace*, Bobo plays off Jesus' primary metaphors to discuss the role of Christians in their work element. He addresses three different work assignments—the employee, Christian managers, and the self-employed. In each of these, he describes the importance of meditating on God's Word ("volleying God's word back and forth in our minds"), discerning sound doctrine, prayer (the importance of an accountability partner), being wise as a serpent, and gentle (innocent) as a dove, avoiding corruption, living in nonconformity when ethics conflict with the pervading culture and treating people equitably and truthfully (pp. 27-34).

Denise Daniels and Shannon Vanderwarker (2019)

These two authors approach their theme of *Working in the Presence of God* by centering on developing "liturgies," that is, the "pattern you systematically follow to offer worship to the Lord" (p. 25). The first chapter introduces the reader to the "Liturgy of Commute," highlighting how one gets to work and the attention one pays to God's activity along the way because "how you begin your day will affect how you go about your work" (p. 23). Various passages of Scripture are offered about "travel landscapes."

Another fertile idea is the "liturgy of place," where one connects the inner landscape of one's heart with the outer landscape as one travels (p. 26). The writers suggest that this liturgy ought to be disciplined to a conscious attention to God, away from distractions, and a surrender away from the obsessive need for productivity, personal desires, and control of that which is about to reveal itself on the job front (pp. 26-29).

The second chapter discusses the "Workplace as Holy Ground," seeing the holy in that which is ordinary and blessing and consecrating it through repeated liturgies over time (pp. 37-47).

Daniel M. Doriani (2019, 2021)

Doriani has authored two books in the last three years. His first volume is replete with historical references that exhibit varying attitudes towards work. Unlike some of the other mentioned books, he gives solid footing to the role and balance of the Sabbath and rest, especially as neglected or misused within the Western cultural context (pp. 140-42). But what is unique about this book is his listing in the appendix of *Principles for Representative Professions* that specify eleven key occupations: coaches, private teachers, tutors, communicators, entertainers, physicians, armed forces, managers, educators, architects, and builders. The five principles that overarch these professions are:

1. We will strive for God-like justice, faithfulness, and love (generous spirit and mercy toward failure).
2. We will apply God's law, especially the Ten Commandments, to all work.
3. We will promote worthy causes and goals.
4. We will look for people we can serve, develop, and protect.
5. We will follow the examples of heroes at work (as apprentices) (pp. 191-206).

His "Index of Scriptures" is the most thorough of the books mentioned here.

Doriani's other contribution, *Work that Makes a Difference*, is a slender book intended for group study. It comes complete with useful discussion questions after each chapter. He surveys different motivations for working: 1) idealists who seek fulfillment at work; 2) materialists who take jobs that pay well, seeking wealth, with little attention to what they do or make; and 3) adventurers who, unlike both idealists and materialists, hope to earn enough to support meaningful life after work (pp. 17-18). Often the difficult choice for workers is between meaning and money. Much of the book unravels the intricacies that would otherwise slot Christians into one of these berths.

In contrast, Doriani describes the task of "discernment" of God's will into three different roles: 1) the "pragmatist" sees work as essentially secular and only church and family as sacred; 2) the "witness" emphasizes personal morality in the workplace, "works hard, respects everyone, operates with integrity, and hopes to create a platform for sharing her faith," but neglects the larger vision of God's activity (p. 49). If the only witness is the primary goal, one's work may suffer. 3) The "prince" shares the desire to be a witness but goes further, believing "that Jesus rules every inch of life, and so delegates authority to others who think the same way" (p. 49). He ". . . takes one more step and remembers the Lord in relationships, in the work at hand, and in every square inch of life" (p. 51).

Mike Aquilina (2020)

Aquilina's literary contribution, *Work, Play, Love: How the Mass Changed the Life of the First Christians*, packs a punch from a Patristics perspective, examining the influence of the Catholic mass on the Early Christian Fathers. Using extensive citations from the earliest Christian documents, the author builds his case for the dignity of work by citing Coptic sources that describe the first fruits brought to the mass. "Let everyone hasten to take to the bishop, at all times, the first fruit of the fruits, and the first of the produce. . . . We bless you, God, for these and all other things by which you have benefited us" (pp. 27–28). As Aquilina says, "It's almost as if they're proud that they worked for these things . . . and they're going to be acknowledged as part of the liturgy" (p. 27).

But Aquilina goes further: "But no matter how holy and dignified work is, you need more than work. You need time away from work to be fully human. Since creation, God has told us to take at least one day off out of every seven. And it wasn't just a suggestion; it was an order" (p. 52). Thus, he introduces his second theme of "Play."

Aquilina sees "play" as a measure of our trust in God. "It's almost as if God is daring us to trust him—to let go of the plow (or the computer keyboard, or the tool chest) and rest in confidence that the Creator who started the job can finish it just fine, with or without our ten-hour days." He cites Rabbi Abraham Joshua Heschel, "To the biblical mind . . . labor is the means toward an end, and the Sabbath as a day of rest, as a day of abstaining from toil, is not for the purpose of recovering one's lost strength and becoming fit for the forthcoming labor. The

Sabbath is a day for the sake of life" (p. 81). The Sabbath is not just an interlude but is the climax of living (p. 81).

Michael Berg (2020)

In *Vocation: The Setting for Human Flourishing,* Berg brings a Lutheran sensitivity to the discussion. His operative word is "flourishing," which can be enjoyed in whatever vocation (calling) God places us in. He draws a clear distinction from the overworked word, "happiness," which, in colloquial speech, tends to focus on "personal euphoria" or even "self-pleasure" that is ultimately hedonistic, in contrast to Jefferson's "happiness" presented as a divine right in the Declaration of Independence.

In contrast, the Hebrews used the word *shalom*. To think of *shalom* solely as "peace," the cessation of conflict, or a personal inner "peace," devalues it. Rather, its meaning is infused with security, prosperity, wholeness, and flourishing. Yet, it can never be achieved in fullness here on earth. "True flourishing requires freedom from the burdens of sin and death. It requires security in Christ and trust in God's prospering hands, even when all looks bleak. True flourishing requires a purpose beyond survival or attaining human ranks. The setting for true human flourishing is vocation, which is based on true freedom in Christ alone." (p. 89)

As in Sherman's book, a list of professions is mentioned with their unique opportunities for witness: nurse, road construction worker, chef, electrical line worker, factory worker, lawyer, and truck driver.

David W. Gill (2020)

Gill describes his book as a "primer." *Workplace Discipleship 101: A Primer* is the most elementary of the books listed here and basically follows a "How to ..." approach to influencing one's workplace in positive Christian ways. Part 2 offers five simple steps to "Impacting Our Workplace": 1) align: work in harmony with God's work; 2) model: set a great personal example at work; 3) light [inform]: share some helpful biblical insights about work at work; 4) share: find appropriate ways to talk about Jesus at work; 5) overcome: deal well with conflict and wrongdoing at work (pp. xi–xii). He adds two other influences outside of the workplace: 1) contribute: bring your work skills and resources back to your church and community; 2) rest: say no to workaholism and idolatry—rest, worship, and play (pp. xii).

I found his focus on bringing the workplace experience to the church setting especially helpful. Gill sees four ways in which workers can return their resources back to the local church: 1) contributing money made at work; 2) contributing skills and knowledge acquired at work; 3) coaching and encouraging workplace disciples and neighbors; 4) helping those without work to find or create it. This book is very practical for church members, with reflection and discussion items at the end of each chapter.

Rory Groves (2020)

Groves' contribution, *Durable Trades: Family-Centered Economies that have Stood the Test of Time*, is unique since he does not couch his purpose in Christian motives. He is a technology consultant with an extensive software resume. His operative word is "durable." He finds comfort and purpose in "family-centered economies that have stood the test of time." In a practical sense, he believes in a future that will appropriate the past lessons in occupations and businesses that are time resilient.

Among these is a listing that shadows biblical occupations: shepherd, farmer, midwife, gardener, woodworker, carpenter, painter, cook, brewer, innkeeper, tutor, mason, silversmith, interpreter, author, butcher, apothecary—62 occupations in all. Furthermore, he assigns percentages to various aspects of each profession: historical stability, resiliency, family-centeredness, income, and ease of entry. His graphs that encapsulate these percentages offer useful comparisons. Obviously, his purpose is to ennoble the trades and encourage new generations of workers to consider these as options to the fleeting, tedious, and inaccessible job market that lures so many in hapless directions. These occupations have resilience, social value, and creative possibilities.

In the penultimate, concluding chapter, Groves' Christian hand is shown. He speaks of the discipleship of work. He summarizes his position: "But it is at work that true discipleship takes place, more so than at church or in the classroom. Work is where the real person resides. The true nature of a man is revealed when he is swinging a hammer, felling a tree, or negotiating a contract. For good or ill, we speak loudest to those around us when we are in work. Integrity, perseverance, and faith in divine providence cannot be transmitted in a lecture hall. They must be modeled" (p. 266).

Dave Hataj (2020)

A unique perspective comes from Hataj, a businessman and co-owner of Edgerton Gear. His studies at Regent College with Professor and Theology of Work author Paul Stevens, along with an earned doctorate at Bakke Graduate University (where I am affiliated), have aided him in producing this "case study" example detailing personal examples and realistic "on the job" issues, including a chapter on "Betrayal and Failure." Out of his experience, he posits the "three-legged stool" that secures good business practice within the context of "true goodness": 1) quality, 2) value, and 3) service. "What's not so simple is keeping these three in balance. It's imperative that we maintain our best quality while charging a fair price and getting the customer their product in a timely manner. This pretty much sums up the Golden Rule of treating others as you want to be treated" (pp. 126–27).

Tom Heetderks (2020)

Heetderks's contribution, *Work Worth Doing: Finding God's Direction and Purpose in Your Career*, is probably the most interactive of the books mentioned here. Written in simple language and best directed to students, it offers a variety of chapter reflections and applications, lists of motivations to prioritize, diagrams to draw, loyalties and loves to rank, and multiple choices to pair up. A synopsis with key points and Scriptural references is near the end of the book. It then concludes with "Going Deeper" sections that function as addenda to the earlier chapters. The book assumes that the young person is somewhat naïve about Scripture, work options, and his or her own calling. The writing is jocular, filled with story illustrations, and well suited to youthful audiences.

Matthew Kaemingk and Cory B. Willson (2020)

Kaemingk and Willson have written probably the most substantive biblical study of the subject at hand, organizing its major groupings with overarching themes, particularly tethering work with worship. *Work and Worship: Reconnecting Our Labor and Liturgy* gathers a rich trove of prayers and hymns that express the fertile connection.

Part 2 of their opus headlines the Pentateuch as "bringing work into worship"; the Psalms, which "sing God's work into our work"; the Prophets, who "decry the destruction of work and worship"; and the Early Church, which nurtures "work and worship in ancient Christianity" and discovers that "work becomes worship in Christ."

One chapter that provides a tough reality check in these troubled times describes "worship that fails workers," that is, "Bad worship can actively discourage vocational conversations between workers and God" (p. 28). These include: 1) institutional worship, 2) spiritualized worship, 3) individualistic worship, 4) saccharine worship ("sentimental sweetness"), 5) passive worship; 6) fueling worship (seeing worship as a "pit stop" to refuel for the week), and 7) privatized worship (pp. 28–33).

Two concluding chapters see worship as both gathering workers and then scattering them. "Gathered worship in the sanctuary must become scattered worship in the streets" (p. 241). This volume provides the most extensive bibliography of around four hundred references in twenty-two pages

Mark P. Shea (2020)

Shea offers another Roman Catholic perspective, built upon its traditions, two millennia of theological documents, and papal edicts. *The Church's Best-Kept Secret: A Primer on Catholic Social Teaching* acknowledges the four pillars of Catholic social teaching as 1) the dignity of the human person, 2) the common good, 3) subsidiarity, and 4) solidarity to be like the four notes of a single chord (pp. 21–22).

The dignity of the human person is derived from humans being created in the image and likeness of God. The "common good" is built on the belief that ". . . whether in spiritual or material wealth, they are given to us for the sake of those who do not have them—and those to whom much is given, much shall be required" (Luke 12:48) (p. 50). Subsidiarity is the practice of "being the hands of God to others." "Catholic teaching insists that the people closest to a particular need or problem should be the ones to fill that need or solve that problem. That, in a nutshell, is Subsidiarity" (p. 80). The family and "Mama Mary" are given as prime examples of surrendering to the will of God to serve others.

The fourth pillar is "Solidarity" and is subtexted with "Struggling together in sin and hope." "This is why the Tradition insists that, in addition to confronting our personal sins, Structures of Sin must be battled as well, since they exert pressure on us not to repent our personal sins—and they often blind us from even seeing that the Structure of Sin exists. This is a dynamic that applies in all institutions and must be confronted in all institutions, even the Church" (p. 121).

The book concludes with practical steps for one to live out the four "pillars." The first step is to begin with where you are, not where you are not. The second step is to "challenge ourselves with some aspect of Catholic Social Teaching that pushes us out of our comfort zone" (p. 137). Another is to form "habits of virtue" until they become part of a lifestyle. A dozen videos are offered as biographical examples of virtue in practice, including the stories of William Wilberforce (Amazing Grace), "The Mission," "Of Gods and Men," and "Romero."

J. Daryl Charles (2021)

The final book, *Wisdom and Work: Theological Reflections on Human Labor from Ecclesiastes*, is an intense study of the book of Ecclesiastes as it addresses "human labor" in a world where so much seems so meaningless. Charles mines deep and extracts "joy" or "enjoyment" as a golden nugget that stands in contrast with the dross all around it. In the summary of his argument, he says,

> The enjoyment refrains distributed throughout Ecclesiastes play a crucial role in identifying an overall structure to the author's argument and hence in properly understanding the message of the book. They serve as an interlude in the wider thesis between the bookends of 1:2 and 12:8 . . . they are the antithesis . . . of the meaningless thesis. With supreme dexterity, the writer moves back and forth between two competing outlooks on ultimate reality, . . . But because the writer affirms a theology of creation, several important and interrelated consequences follow, three in particular. . . . First, humankind can experience life and joy as gifts—all of life has meaning and purpose. Second, the divine gift of practical wisdom in life's experiences can be recognized and acquired. . . . Third, work itself can grant a measure of satisfaction where and when it is done faithfully and with the proper motivation since work is our vocation based on (a) our being fashioned in the image of God and (b) our assignment from God (pp. 124–5).

He continues by suggesting that these "markers" show the Creator's benevolence rather than his harshness, his gracious governance rather than his tyranny. The result is not our bitter resignation but rather our joyful humility (p. 125). In a passage on the intrinsic value of work as seen in this wisdom book, Charles offers the following conclusion: "Time will tell whether the Christian church, at least in the West, will gain the 'daring and liberating' religious meaning of work and vocation. Reading the book of Ecclesiastes, with new and open eyes, would be a good place to start in that recovery process" (p. 170). Again, as in the earlier mentioned book by Kaemingk and Willson, Charles has provided a rich bibliography replete with 250 references.

Conclusion

As in the proverbial elephant and the six sightless men who seek to describe it variously, the theme of "spirituality in the workplace" has spawned very different analyses of the subject, thereby creating a whole plethora of stimulating treatises that infuse work with the deepest of meaning, a breadth of understanding of workplace "evangelism," and an optimal sense of God's calling and sovereignty. The theme is now being discussed generously on a variety of literary fronts. One would hope that the influence of these ideas would inundate the pews with lively discussion and effective reorientation that could mobilize the Christian masses.

However, one is left hoping that a new round of literature will emerge that will encapsulate the contemporary questions brought on by the Covid-19 pandemic, such as, What do Christianity and biblical resources say to those now confined into workplaces within the home? Or how do we keep our Christian ethos when reduced to technological communication? Or how can the Bible instruct us about the effects of social media when voices from the pit of baser instincts seem to dominate the public forum?

Despite the perennial divine value of work, the nature of it is forever changing, as is the workplace. How then will "spirituality," or whatever the operative word might be, express itself with authenticity in that world? We will anxiously wait and see.

Bibliography

Aquilina, Mike. *Work, Play, Love: How the Mass Changed the Life of the First Christians*. Brewster: Paraclete, 2020.

Berg, Michael. *Vocation: The Setting for Human Flourishing*. Irvine: New Reformation, 2020.

Bobo, Luke. *Living Salty and Light-Filled Lives in the Workplace*. Eugene: Resource, 2017.

Charles, J. Daryl. *Wisdom and Work: Theological Reflections on Human Labor from Ecclesiastes*. Eugene: Cascade, 2021.

Daniels, Denise, and Shannon Vanderwarker. *Working in the Presence of God: Spiritual Practices for Everyday Work*. Peabody: Hendrickson, 2019.

Doriani, Daniel M. *Work that Makes a Difference*. Phillipsburg: P & R, 2021.

———. *Work: Its Purpose, Dignity, and Transformation*. Phillipsburg: P & R, 2019.

Gill, David W. *Workplace Discipleship 101: A Primer*. Peabody: Hendrickson, 2020.

Groves, Rory. *Durable Trades: Family-Centered Economies that have Stood the Test of Time*. Eugene: Porch Republic, 2020.

Hataj, Dave. *Good Work: How Blue Collar Business Can Change Lives*. Chicago: Moody, 2020.

Heetderks, Tom. *Work Worth Doing: Finding God's Direction and Purpose in Your Career*. Eugene: Harvest House, 2020.

Keller, Timothy. *Every Good Endeavor: Connecting Your Work to God's Work.* New York: Riverhead, 2012.

Kaemingk, Matthew and Cory B. Willson. *Work and Worship: Reconnecting Our Labor and Liturgy.* Grand Rapids: Baker, 2020.

Shea, Mark P. *The Church's Best-Kept Secret: A Primer on Catholic Social Teaching.* Hyde Park: New City, 2020.

Sherman, Amy L. *Kingdom Calling: Vocational Stewardship for the Common Good.* Downers Grove: InterVarsity, 2011.

Waaijman, Kees. *Spirituality: Forms, Foundations, Methods*, translated by John Vriend. Leuven: Peeters, 2002.

16

CHRISTIANITY IN A POST-CHRISTIAN WORLD

Elisa Bernal Corley

There was a time when Christianity ruled the Western world. From a small group of disciples in Judea, Christianity spread its faith near and far, becoming the official religion of the massive Roman Empire. From being persecuted as followers of Christ, Christians found themselves owning properties, holding high clerical positions, and soon, competing with reigning Roman emperors for power. Once persecuted for witnessing to their faith, Christians later turned to persecuting those who did not accept the official dogma promoted by the powerful institutionalized Roman church.[1] Dissenters were excommunicated. Followers of pagan religions met punishing ends.[2] Even professing Christians who deviated from established doctrine or orthodox beliefs did not escape the long arm of the Roman law, which Christian leaders

---

1 See Eusebius, *Ecclesiastical History* 1: 5.24.9, 5.15, 5.25l *Ecclesiastical History* 2: 6.43.11–12, 7.30.19.

2 For an intensive study see Moore, *The Formation of Persecuting Society*.

called on to punish heresy. Some who rejected the marriage between the Roman state and the church opted for solitary, holy lifestyles and founded monastic groups, separating themselves from society and the institutional church. As witnesses against the growing political power and enrichment of the Roman church, they subjected their bodies to strict discipline, and their communities practiced an indigent lifestyle.

By the Middle Ages (c. 5th–15th century), Christianity was the most pervasive religion in the world, though challenged by the spread of Islam and minor pagan religions. The simple teachings of the Scriptures, developed through hundreds of years of theological apologetics, had become the dominant worldview imprinted in the minds and souls of those who inhabited the Christian world. One was born and died under the ministrations of the church and her priests. One could not sleep, eat, or work without the ubiquitous governance of the church and its ordinances. The faithful lived under the network of sacraments governing one's whole life. Baptism, confirmation, eucharist, penance, anointing of the sick, marriage, and holy unction had to be observed. Failure to do so was a fate worse than death, for it meant eternal punishment in hell. Customs and laws were based on biblical teachings. Rituals and practices had to follow Christian injunctions. Theology explained beliefs about the natural world—how and why it exists. Schools and universities were built in the service of the church, and even science and philosophy were subjected to its interrogation. All human institutions, whatever purpose they may have served, were all, in the end, in the service of the Christian faith.

But this homogeneous world fractured with the Protestant Reformation (1517–1685). Whatever the religious intent of the Protestant Reformers was, they could not have anticipated the distance to which the Enlightenment philosophers like John Locke, John Jacques Rousseau, and Voltaire took the project of emancipation from tradition and authority. The sixteenth-century challenges to the

Roman church, its papal authority, and its perceived abuses were followed by hundreds of years of secularization, where individuals and social movements systematically dismantled the direct line between God and religious institutions. The Christian worldview that gave meaning and reason behind history and creation slowly shattered from the onslaught of secular philosophies and sciences. Secularization can be defined as "the systematic erosion of religious practices, values, and beliefs."[3] In terms of religion, secularization occurs when "spirituality, meaning, purpose, community, and rituals are all divorced from both traditional religious observances, and from one another."[4] Where once Christianity provided a comprehensive meaning to life, multiplying secular institutions, like universities and trade guilds, started fulfilling those needs. This process of secularization was complex and cannot be summarized briefly in a short essay like this.[5] What can be said about it in relation to the decline of religious sensitivity is important in understanding the dilemma in which Christianity finds itself today.

When the power and influence of the church and the worldview it imposed on the developing Western world were challenged by discoveries in the sciences and the heralding of reason as a primary source of knowledge (as opposed to revelation), the domination of social mores and laws based on biblical teachings eroded. The church lost its public influence and appeal, and Christian values no longer set the standards in society. As a result, Christianity lost its privileged place in society. Religion was relegated to the private domain.

---

3 Norris and Inglehart, "Uneven Secularization in the U.S. and Western Europe," 33.
4 Franz, "The New Godless Religions."
5 For an excellent analysis of the problem, see Dalferth, "I Determine What God is," 5–23; and "Post-Secular Society," 317–45, on the difficulty of a single perspective, like secularization, to explain religiosity especially in a global context.

A Post-Christian Scenario: A Secular World

According to a recent Gallup poll, 47% of Americans belong to a house of worship, falling from 70% in 1999 and 50% in 2018. This decline in membership is driven by the sharp rise of the so-called "Nones," who express no religious preference. They are the single biggest and fastest growing religious demographic in the U.S. The polls attribute this decline to generational change, with a low interest among Gen Z (born 1997–2012), about 30% lower interest than Americans born before 1946. Likewise, children who grew up without organized religion are less likely to join any community of worship when they become adults. Only 30% of millennials (b. 1981–1994/6) are members of religious institutions. This decline is not limited to the United States, for the rate of religious service attendance is also falling in every Western country.[6]

An analysis of religious trends among forty-nine countries covering around 60% of the world's population shows that between 1981 and 2007, there was no global resurgence of religion. Most high-income societies became less religious. From 2007 to 2020, 43 of these 49 countries became less religious, with the most dramatic shift happening in the United States. At the same time, a 2020 Pew research survey found that reports of sexual abuse within the Catholic Church resulted in a decline in attendance. A more interesting datum from Transparency International's *Corruption Perception Index*, which ranks public-sector corruption in 180 countries and territories, reveals that religious countries tend to be more corrupt than secular ones. Additionally, a survey of countries containing 90% of the world's total population shows that "in highly secure and secular countries, people are giving high priority to self-expression and free choice, with a growing

---

6   Walsh, "America is Losing Its Religion."

emphasis on human rights, tolerance of outsiders, environmental protection, gender equality, and freedom of speech."[7]

An artist in Arizona, Dain Quentin Gore, grew up Southern Baptist but now considers himself an SBNR (Spiritual But Not Religious). For him, organized religion is "obtuse and hopelessly convoluted," so he considers his artistic practice closer to the divine. Likewise, Megan Ribar, from New York, works in a yoga studio and finds her purpose in yoga and meditation, and other personal rituals. Although she is not sure how she feels about a higher power, she has built a small space in her apartment for herself that she considers an "altar" and filled it with objects that are important to her.[8] For SBNRs like Dain and Megan, the primary sources of religious meaning-making come from outside religious traditions, from the so-called secular world. In her book, *Strange Rites: New Religion for a Godless World,* Isabella Burton emphasizes what she refers to as the broader category of the "Remixed." These are the Americans "[who] envision themselves as creators of their own bespoke religions, mixing and matching spiritual and aesthetic and experiential and philosophical traditions."[9] The Remix rejects authority, institutions, creeds, and moral universalism. Instead, they emphasize a spirituality that "values intuition, personal feelings, and experiences . . . and demand to rewrite their own scripts about how the universe, and human beings, operate."[10] These SBNRs, the Remix, and the Nones in the United States—who reject religion but observe some practice of religiosity or spirituality—provide a unique trajectory of what a post-Christian world might look like everywhere else in the world.

---

7 Inglehart, "Why is Religion Suddenly Declining?"
8 Burton, *Strange Rites,* loc. 408.
9 Burton, *Strange Rites,* loc. 243.
10 Burton, *Strange Rites,* loc. 248.

The secular society of Dain and Megan presupposes that religions, including Christianity, used to provide people with a sense of order, meaning, and purpose; and that religions, be it the beliefs or practices, were effective in fulfilling humanity's deepest needs and longings. However, the rise of non-religious institutions, characteristic of a secularizing society, has slowly eroded the necessity for Christianity's role as "a balm" for the world's troubles. Today, people view religion as exchangeable with anything that can provide them with a sense of wholeness and happiness. People who have struggled under the rigid and strict rules of religiosity are finally experiencing freedom and want to express that freedom as freedom from all forms of restrictions, including religious ones. Personal happiness and freedom from existential fears can now be achieved through personal projects and choices and be expressed in diverse religious experiences.[11] This spiritualization of personal experience has been encouraged by a cultural revolution accelerated by the technological and digital revolution. The rise of the internet and digital and social media has ushered in the age of self-expressive religiosity, focusing on the self and its experiences.

A wider and more fundamental cause can also explain this cultural secularization. The structural changes brought about by industrial development freed people from the dictates of religious institutions. During the pre-modern period, society was bound together by communal beliefs and practices, ordered by mostly religious laws, and personal beliefs were subject to tradition. But the Industrial Revolution (between 1760–1820/40) "inherently undermined [these] traditions and cultivated individualism, qualities that render it an adversary of faith-based, communitarian institutions."[12] Later, capitalism took over the wide range of social functions traditionally monopolized by the Church. So now, instead of religious charity, we have social welfare and

---

11 Vahanian, "The Future of Christianity in a Post-Christian World," 162.
12 Walsh, "America is Losing Its Religion."

retirement accounts, university education instead of metaphysics, and Marvel movies serving as community-binding myths.[13] As societies developed from agrarian to industrial to knowledge-based, human fears about the unpredictable world diminished. People became less obedient to traditional religious leaders and institutions that provided humanity with security. In other words, religion is no longer the binding force in secular societies, and any form of religiosity or spirituality need not be attached to any institution but can be divorced from traditional religious observance and from one another. In a secular society, religion is no longer a measure of social solidarity and strength and is unnecessary for a sense of togetherness.

The Church in a Post-Christian World

Yet while Christianity may no longer be the dominant force in the world, religious scholars find that the world remains interested in religion, as if human nature is inclined toward religiosity and all forms of spirituality. For instance, a 2004 study by political scientists Pippa Norris and Ronald Inglehart revealed that the global population is growing more religious and not secular, specifically among the groups who experience grief, death, and other crises.[14] Also, Gabriel Vahanian observes that the repudiation of Christianity does not mean the repudiation of religion itself. Instead, "The present crisis stems from the fact that we have changed the biblical iconoclasm of the Christian tradition into the idolatrous post-Christian religiosity of our cultural institutions, be they social, political, economic, or ecclesiastical."[15] Vahanian's solution is to seek a new cultural embodiment for Christianity or the cultural renovation of Christian institutions. This is

---

13 Walsh, "America is Losing Its Religion."
14 See Gibson, *The Coming Religious Recession*. Norris and Inglehart developed the "Existential Security Theory," similar to the "religious comfort hypothesis" that explains why people who suffer from crises and catastrophes turn to religion as a balm.
15 Vahanian, "The Future of Christianity in a Post-Christian Era," 163.

how religious institutions refashion themselves through creative engagement with the changing culture. Instead of subtracting religion from the public square, secularization allows for new forms of spirituality to reach out to the public. I agree with Vahanian that modern Christianity has compromised its iconoclastic calling. But contrary to his proposal of culturally renovating Christian institutions, which I see as another attempt to privilege Christianity in the public sphere or make it relevant to the current technologically driven culture, I propose that the church face a post-Christian world, not by pursuing any mission based on utility or pragmatism, but by living out the transformative power of the gospel among the world's suffering peoples through solidarity and Christian hospitality.

The Church-in-Solidarity

When our society glorifies the self and the religion of self-help or self-expression becomes a driving force of cultural life, we become unprotected from the onslaught of dominating forces in the society and the world. Those left behind by economic and technological progress remain mired in the disempowering conditions of life. When we hear of and see the ravages of war in Syria, the abuses of women and children in Afghanistan, the famine in Somalia, the destitution of the Rohingya people in Myanmar, the thousands of Covid-19 deaths in India, or the hunger of our neighbors who live in absolute poverty, it becomes difficult to justify the belief in a God who is active in human history.

The Church loses its credibility when it continues to proclaim a "triumphant God" who has failed. In the eyes of the world, God is dead because evil reigns. The history of Christian mission, which advanced alongside colonialism with a "Bible in one hand and a sword in another,"[16] adds to this picture of a cruel and absent God. Jürgen Moltmann

---

16 Julius Brenchley (1816–1973), a British nationalist describes how Captain Croker, the English commander of the H.M.S. *Favourite*, advanced against the heathen fortress

refers to this religious experience as a "God-crisis" or the "loss of the assurance of God."[17] Because God is either absent or has failed, we have only ourselves to rely on. In practice, it is Christianity that has failed. When the gospel has been driven from the world and become concerned mostly with personal salvation and eternal life, it has left a vacuum that has been filled with a spirituality that "allows everyone to put together his or her own meme of meaning from a copious religious smorgasbord—scraps from the world's religions and natural myths, stress-reducing meditative rituals, and esoteric speculations . . . a contemporary 'cafeteria religion.'"[18] And like these spiritual movements, sociologists Stark and Glock conclude that "A remnant church can be expected to last for a long time if only to provide the psychic comforts which are currently dispensed by orthodoxy. *However, eventually, substitutes for even this function are likely to emerge, leaving churches of the present form with no effective rationale for existing."*[19]

Instead of preaching a diluted gospel that only aims to comfort the fears that threaten our personal security, the church needs to shape its ministry and mission toward one that stands in solidarity with all who are suffering. The root of missional solidarity goes back to Paul's admonition in 2 Corinthians 8:8–9, where believers were called to bear with one another in faith. Paul sees the church's mission as solidarity, where "Each believer's concrete personal commitment is something that challenges, stimulates, and opens possibilities for the commitment of others."[20] We encounter evidence of human despair due

---

of Bea, "with a sword in one hand and a Bible in the other; for the attack was a crusade against the idolaters." He explained that "This fanatical conjunction between the Bible and the Sword, so familiar to us in the history of Europe . . . all 'for the glory of God', seems . . . revolting when exhibited in these remote and comparatively peaceful regions." See Daly, "The Bible and the Sword," 73.

17 Moltmann, *God for a Secular Society*, 16.
18 Dalferth, "I Determine What God Is," 7.
19 Nelsen and Herter, "Are We Entering a Post-Christian Era?" 410, italics mine.
20 Sobrino, *The Theology of Christian Solildarity*, 35.

to poverty, environmental catastrophe, violence, and wars wherever we look. Only if Christians can share in the suffering of their neighbors—near and far—will they be able to dispense with the lure of a self-focused cafeteria Christianity. "It is the indwelling of God himself which gnaws at our conscience and does not let us come to terms with injustice but makes us protest and cry out for the dumb and the silenced. This is what we might call the mystical interpretation of our responsibility towards the suffering God in 'the crucified peoples' of history."[21] The Church is not called to make people feel better about themselves. It is called to be in solidarity with the poor, the sick, the sad, the outcasts, and all those "people who society pushes into the underground or into private life."[22] In this shared suffering, the comfort of God comes to all. Christianity should distinguish itself from a self-help religiosity through solidarity with the suffering world.

In his study of global Christianity, Philip Jenkins says that despite the surveys proclaiming the decline of Christianity in the Western world, Christianity in the South remains and continues to flourish. He claims that if we want to see what the future of Christianity will be like, we need to look to the South and the developing countries. As evidence, he points to the explosion of growth among the Protestant mega-churches in Brazil, Latin American Pentecostalism, the Full Gospel mega-churches in South Korea, the El Shaddai movement in the Philippines, the Zionist churches in South Africa, and the African independent church movements. His statistical table shows that the largest Christian communities by 2025 and 2050 will be found mostly in the South, apart from the United States, which will top at 330 million. Brazil follows the U.S. with 195 million, Mexico with 145, the

---

21 Moltmann, *God for a Secular Society*, 185.
22 Moltmann, *God for a Secular Society*, 253.

Philippines with 145, Nigeria with 123, Zaire/D.R. Congo with 121, Russia with 80, Ethiopia with 79, China with 60, and Germany with 57.[23]

Jenkins explains the successes of these Christian communities as due to several factors. However, he points out a commonality among these groups. He says that mass support comes to the religious communities that provide "functional alternative arrangements for health, welfare and education" (southern churches) and those that offer sanctuary for the migrants and dispossessed of the cities (in Africa).[24] Pentecostalism is popular among the poorest in Latin America as it provides a social network and fills social needs. Pentecostal churches are seen to improve women's lives, and these new churches emphasize the healing of mind and body. These churches provide "material support, mutual cooperation, spiritual comfort, and emotional release in the bleak wastes of the expanding industrial society."[25] Jenkins sees that these communities plagued by poverty, hunger, and pollution resulting in a "pathogenic society" have no problem identifying the "demons of poverty." He adds, "As well as physical ailments, psychiatric and substance abuse problems drive desperate people to seek refuge in God. Taking all these threats together—disease, exploitation, pollution, drink, drugs, and violence—it is easy to see why people might easily accept the claim that they are under siege from demonic forces and that only divine intervention can save them."[26] The churches living in solidarity with those suffering in their communities are seen as the conduits of divine intervention.

We can also attribute a new understanding of mission in the South and developing countries to the birth of liberation theologies. Liberation theologies emphasize solidarity with the suffering poor and

---

23 Jenkins, *The Next Christendom*, 60.
24 Jenkins, *The Next Christendom*, 74.
25 Jenkins, *The Next Christendom*, 76.
26 Jenkins, *The Next Christendom*, 78.

those oppressed by repressive political regimes. They also examine the tragedies of colonialism, which accompanied the Christian global mission. While mutations of Western Protestant-Lutheran theologies emphasized other-worldly concerns, liberation theologies raise up *the symbol of the crucified Christ* as central to the understanding of God's work of salvation in the world. In contrast with the spirituality that we find in our post-Christian world, Gustavo Gutierrez defines true spirituality as the "dominion of the Spirit." It is concrete living in the gospel, and living in solidarity with all human beings, as we are all united in God, in the cross. While the horrors we experience in the world seem to make God dead and irrelevant, Gutierrez claims that a spirituality of liberation leads us to the *conversion to the neighbor*. Unlike what we have learned in the past regarding conversion, where we *convert others to our faith* (most popularly through what we term evangelism), *conversion to the neighbor* means a radical transformation of ourselves, where we see Christ as living in the poor, exploited, and alienated persons, and we participate in their liberation. *Conversion* means that "we have to break with our mental categories, with the way we related to others, with our way of identifying with the Lord, with our cultural milieu, with our social class, in other words, with all that can stand in the way of a real, profound solidarity with those who suffer, in the first place from misery and injustice."[27] This approach to a post-Christian spirituality compels us to shape the church's mission as primarily solidarity with others.

The Church of Hospitality: The Foreigners Amongst Us

In her essay on the Covid-19 pandemic, Hanbyul Park is concerned that "social distancing and its related measures could degenerate into a kind of self-help system that reduces everyone to survivalists. Some examples, such as hoarding daily necessities or buying guns,

---

27 Gutierrez, *A Theology of Liberation*, 118.

demonstrate that attempts to protect oneself from the disease can become distorted into winning a survival game."[28] What she describes as a survivalist mode characterizes a society that places personal survival as the primary moral duty, even at the expense of the community. This individualistic lifestyle is not something new. Modern capitalist societies are organized by prioritizing individual wants and needs. Our economic system is structured to maximize benefits from fulfilling the life of leisure and self-indulgence, with profits built upon the backs of exploited workers and marginalized groups. It is no wonder that the poor have suffered the most from the catastrophe of the global pandemic. So, Park proposes the practice of hospitality as a way of connecting with others, of being in solidarity with the most vulnerable. Through hospitality, we create secure places where the basic needs of strangers are met. In these secure places, survival is not the main goal but that of "finding meaning, value, and purpose."[29] Park goes further by saying that hospitality should be redefined as solidarity, where the differences between people should not be seen as vulnerabilities to be exploited. Differences in race, class, age, gender, or other defining factors can become bases of solidarity instead of power relations. Hence, the idea of justice needs to be part of our understanding of the practice of hospitality. "An idea of justice is necessary to define hospitality not as a daily practice of making violent connections. Instead, a sense of justice fosters hospitality as every practice of 'disturbing the violent relatedness' by addressing the social structures of injustice and division. . . . Justice requires a practice of solidarity to end oppressions beyond working for the self-defense."[30] Without justice, our Christian practice of hospitality will not be able to surmount the concrete elements in our lives that separate us from each other.

---

28 Park, "Redefining Hospitality in the Context of Covid-19 Pandemic," 27.
29 Park, "Redefining Hospitality," 29.
30 Park, "Redefining Hospitality," 31.

For early Christians, hospitality was not optional. It was a "concrete expression of love—love for sisters and brothers, love extended outward to strangers, prisoners, and exiles, love that attends to physical and social needs."[31] As members of God's household and practicing God's economy, Christians were to "live as aliens in the world—aliens who practiced hospitality to strangers."[32] Offering hospitality was one of the distinctive marks of the authentic Christian life.

In a post-Christian world, Christians have lost the life-transforming spirituality of the practice of hospitality. It is easy to look away from strangers when we are afraid of the harm they may do to us. It is easy to get embroiled in discussing who is worthy/not worthy to receive aid. It is easy to worry about the effects of receiving refugees in our own communities. It is easy to look away from the homeless littering the streets of our major cities. But Christian hospitality—one that is rooted in the biblical call to care for the poor, the orphan, the widow, the alien/stranger—is subversive. "Hospitality is resistance."[33] In societies that "disregard[s] or dishonor[s] certain persons, small acts of respect and welcome are potent far beyond themselves. They point to a different system of valuing and an alternate model of relationships."[34] It is tragic that the church has often displayed and practiced the opposite of genuine hospitality by accepting and supporting hierarchical systems that nurture injustices against "the least of these" (Matt 25:40). In a post-Christian world, hospitality must be a way of defining who we are as the church and as followers of Jesus.

The good news is that there is now a resurgence of the practice of hospitality among many Christian communities. Theologian Diana Butler Bass wanted to find out if mainline Protestant churches in the

---

31 Pohl, *Making Room*, loc. 391.
32 Pohl, *Making Room*, loc. 409.
33 Pohl, *Making Room*, loc. 691.
34 Pohl, *Making Room*, loc. 693.

United States are dying or can still renew themselves to remain faithful and healthy congregations. In her study of these *emerging* churches, she concludes that "the old Protestant mainline is no longer mainline. It no longer speaks from a pinnacle of cultural privilege and power . . . it has become a pilgrimage church, a community of exiles who practice Christianity."[35] The churches she visited are being transformed by spiritual practices drawn from their rich traditions. A couple of the churches she visited included Phinney Ridge Lutheran Church in Seattle, where the congregation displayed the practice of hospitality by hosting a tent city for the homeless on the church's front lawn. At the Episcopal Church of the Epiphany in Washington D.C., the congregation hosts "The Welcome Table," a worship service, breakfast, and small group study for about two hundred homeless people every Sunday morning. The guests dine on fine china, and members serve as waiters. The homeless are considered "guests." The church also offers a noontime worship service in a local park and serves bagged lunches to all attendees. This practice is striking considering that Epiphany is just three blocks away from the White House. The practice of hospitality has revolutionized how the church and its members understand themselves. Offering hospitality to strangers has become a powerful feature of their self-identity.[36]

According to the International Labor Organization, about 10 million Filipinos live abroad, and more than one million Filipinos leave the country each year to work abroad. Their monetary remittances serve as a bloodline for the Philippine economy. However, this labor migration also presents a crisis for the migrants. Many workers are forced to work against their will. Many are deceived about the nature of their work and receive wages less than what was stated in their contracts. Stories of Filipina domestic helpers (DHs) being abused, raped, and

---

35 Pohl, *Making Room,* loc. 4371.
36 Bass, *Christianitiy for the Rest of Us,* loc.

even killed by their employers are too common. Filipino construction workers in the Middle East often experience abuse from their employers and other foreign co-workers. These Filipino migrant workers find consolation amongst themselves and welcome other Filipinos in the area who are in better circumstances. Churches also serve as support communities for these laborers who find themselves mostly unwelcome outside the places of work.

Although not involuntarily displaced from their homeland, Filipino overseas workers (OFWs) share some of the hardships refugees experience. According to the UNHR, about 82.4 million people have been forcibly displaced worldwide, resulting from persecution, conflict, violence, human rights violations, or other catastrophic events. There are 48 million internally displaced people, and 26.4 million are refugees, with 4.1 million seeking asylum. Between 2018 and 2020, an average of between 290,000 to 340,000 children were born into refugee life per year.

For Christians, fear may rule the response to the global refugee crisis. Instead of the spirit of hospitality, churches may refuse to share their lives with these refugees due to fear and mistrust. But Jesus is widely known for his hospitality towards sinners, women, the poor, and Samaritans. Jesus rubbed elbows with the *undesirables* of society. By sharing meals with them, Jesus displayed a radical act of hospitality to those considered unwelcome in society. The refugee crisis provides the Christian church today with the opportunity to reach across barriers established by worldly standards. Instead of the practice of exclusion, we can live in the spirituality of inclusion.[37] For instance, welcoming Muslim refugees into our midst is difficult because it breaks down our conventional understanding of hospitality, which does not demand much from us. It can be an "act of resistance and defiance, a

---

37 Volf, *Exclusion and Embrace*, 261.

challenge to the values and expectations of the larger community."[38] As Christians, we must resist the world's way of coming together that is fundamentally divided by racism, classism, sexism, and other forms of bigotry. For many evangelical churches, the challenge is translating the practice of hospitality and generosity at the structural and systemic level, to action and advocacy. In other words, how can local congregations and their supporting denominations weave teachings and advocacy toward justice in their faith tradition?

Christians practice hospitality because, at the basic level, we are all recipients of God's hospitality. Like migrants and refugees of today, we are sojourners and aliens in this world yet have found a home in God. Christian communities create and provide us "homes" where we feel safe and where we belong, "where care is offered, not to the alien or stranger, but rather to my neighbor, especially my neighbor 'stamped with a special mark by affliction.'"[39] Churches and organizations can share their resources with migrants and refugees by providing necessities like food and shelter. They can provide other types of assistance to resettled refugees, like medical and legal assistance and tutoring/schooling. Many, however, believe this local assistance is not enough. "Christian hospitality that truly recognizes the image of God in all people and reflects God's own hospitality must transform relationships within and among the communities of the world, especially by making structures of power more equitable and by empowering and honoring the agency of those who have very little power."[40] In practice, this may mean that Christians learn and work with other religious traditions in their community when "hosting" refugees. Christians from wealthy denominations may seek to transform their polity to reflect the Christian hospitality call. Also, Christian organizations can work

---

38 Pohl, *Making Room*, loc. 701.
39 Heyer, "Reframing Displacement and Membership," 202.
40 Alexander, "(The Image of) God in All of Us," 26.

with agencies that aim to create an unusual way of living together that challenges socio-economic and political practices of exclusion. So, welcoming refugees would mean Christians' "openness to drawing vulnerable strangers into one's community and creating a new community alongside those who were once strangers and are now friends and neighbors."[41]

Conclusion

There was a time when Christianity ruled the world, but this world is moving towards a religious but post-Christian future. Our call is to join the world as it is, carrying the iconoclastic gospel with us that proclaims the transformative power of God through solidarity with those who are suffering and by offering safe, sacred spaces to those who journey along with us. Regardless of religious affiliation, those who suffer and are homeless will be the true majority population of the future. Transformation is at the heart of Christian life. Our practice and spirituality are "not about personal salvation, not about getting everybody saved, or about the politics of exclusion or moral purity . . . [it] is the promise of transformation—that, by God's mercy, we can be different, our congregation can be different, and our world can be different."[42]

Bibliography

Alexander, Laura. "(The Image of) God in All of Us: Sikh and Christian Hospitality in Light of the Global Refugee Crisis." *Journal of Religious Ethics* 47.4 (2019): 653–78.

Bass, Diana Butler. *Christianity for the Rest of Us: How the Neighborhood Church is Transforming the Faith*. Kindle. New York: HarperCollins ebooks, 2006.

---

41 Alexander, "(The Image of) God in All of Us," 29.
42 Bass, *Christianitiy for the Rest of Us*, loc. 4351.

Bauman, Stephen J. "Lausanne Occasional Paper: Way of Hope in Cambodia." *Consultation of Lausanne Theology Group.* "The Whole Church." Panama City, Panama. January 2009.

Burton, Tara Isabella. *Strange Rites: New Religions for a Godless World.* Kindle. New York: Hachette Book Group, 2020.

Dalferth, Ingolf U. "I Determine What God Is: Theology in the Age of 'Cafeteria Religion.'" *Theology Today* 52.1 (2000): 5–23.

———. "Post-Secular Society: Christianity and the Dialectics of the Secular." *Journal of the American Academy of Religion* 78.2 (2010): 317–45.

Eusebius. *Ecclesiastical History Books 1-5.* Loeb Classical Library, No. 153, Vol. 1, translated by Kirsopp Lake. Boston: Harvard University Press, 1926.

———. *Ecclesiastical History Books 6-10.* Loeb Classical Library, No. 265, vol. 2, translated by J. E. Oulton. Boston: Harvard University Press, 1932.

Daly, Martin. "The Bible and the Sword: John Thomas and the Tongan Civil War of 1837." *Journal of the Study of Religion* 4 (2012): 71–90.

Franz, Kenneth E. "The New Godless Religions: An Interview with Tara Isabella Burton." Religion and Politics. J. C. Danforth Center on Religion and Politics. Washington University, St. Louis. September 22, 2020. www.religionandpolitics.org/2020/09/22/the-new-godless-religions-an-interview.

Gibson, David. *The Coming Religious Recession.* Essay, Washington University, St. Louis: John C. Danforth Center on Religion and Politics, 2020. religionandpolitics.org/2020/06/23/the-coming-religion-recession.

Gutierrez, Gustavo. *A Theology of Liberation.* New York: Orbis, 1988.

Heyer, Kristin E. "Reframing Displacement and Membership: Ethics of Migration." *Theological Studies* 73 (2012): 188–206.

Inglehart, Ronald, and Norris Pippa. "Uneven Secularization in the U.S. and Western Europe." In *Democracy and the New Religious Pluralism*. Edited by Thomas Banchoff. New York: Oxford University Press, 2007.

Inglehart, Ronald. "Why is Religion Suddenly Declining?" Oxford: Oxford Union Press, December 7, 2020. https://blog.oup.com/2020/12/why-is-religion-suddenly-declining.

Jenkins, Philip. *The Next Christendom. The Coming of Global Christianity*. Oxford: Oxford University Press, 2002.

Moltmann, Jurgen. *God for a Secular Society: The Public Relevance of Theology*. Minneapolis: Fortress Press, 1999.

Moore, Robert I. *The Formation of Persecuting Society: Authority and Deviance in Western Europe 950-1250*. Malden: Blackwell, 2007.

Nelsen, Bradley R., and Hart M. Hertel. "Are We Entering a Post-Christian Era? Religious Belief and Attendance in America, 1957–1968." *Journal of Scientific Study of Religion* 13.4 (1974): 409–19.

Nouwen, Henri. *Reaching Out*. New York: Doubleday, 1975.

Park, Hanbyul. "Redefining Hospitality in the Context of Covid-19 Pandemic: Social Connecting and Solidarity." *The Journal of Asian American Theological Forum* 7.1 (2020): 27–33.

Pohl, Christine D. *Making Room: Recovering Hospitality as a Christian Tradition*. Kindle. Grand Rapids: Eerdmans, 1999.

Sobrino, Jon. *The Theology of Christian Solidarity*. Maryknoll: Orbis, 1985.

Vahanian, Gabriel. "The Future of Christianity in a Post-Christian Era." *The Centennial Review* 8.2 (1964): 160–73.

Volf, Miroslav. *Exclusion and Embrace: A Theological Exploration of Identity, Otherness, and Reconciliation.* Kindle. Nashville: Abingdon Press, 1996.

Walsh, Brian. "America is Losing Its Religion." *Axios*, April 7. Accessed 2021. https://www.axios.com/americans-less-religious-gallup-poll-3a7fa738-a431-45a9-8185-44267c49d19d.html.

Reading Suggestions

Chan, Judy. *No Strangers Here. Christian Hospitality and Refugee Ministry in Twenty-First Century Hong Kong.* Eugene: Wipf and Stock, 2017.

Chung, Jaeyeon Lucy. "Toward An Asian American Pastoral Theology of Radical Hospitality: Caring for Undocumented Migrants." *Journal of Pastoral Theology* 30.2 (2020): 121–35.

Fairbanks, Edward LeBron. *Mentoring and Modeling Leadership Character.* Lakeland: BoardServe, LLC, 2021.

Gener, Timoteo, and Stephen T. Pardue. Editors. *Asian Christian Theology. Evangelical Perspectives.* Cambria: Langham Publishing, 2019.

PART V

SPIRITUALITY IN DIALOGUE

17

CORPORATE WORSHIP AND SPIRITUAL TRANSFORMATION

Becky Davis

And we all, who with unveiled faces contemplate the Lord's glory, are being transformed into his image with ever-increasing glory, which comes from the Lord, who is the Spirit.

2 Corinthians 3:7-8

This chapter is based on the proposition that two things are true of worship: first, true worship is focused on God; and second, true worship focused on God benefits the worshiper. I maintain that there is a link between corporate worship, correctly planned and practiced, and spiritual growth leading to a transformed life. Christians of all kinds are interested in spiritual growth. Christians of all kinds also engage in corporate worship. I will examine the question of how worship, specifically corporate worship, meaning groups of believers worshiping together, has the potential to be a locus of spiritual transformation in the lives of members of the worshiping community. Beginning with some definitions of worship, I will continue to examine why we worship, leading to how worship is transformational. What are the ways in which corporate worship may contribute to an experience of spiritual transformation? In what ways is corporate worship practiced that may detract from that possibility? The end goal of the Christian life is to be "transformed into his image." Corporate worship as a central practice of the church has the potential to contribute to this goal.

What is worship?

If I had 100 books about worship on my shelf, I would probably have 110 definitions of "worship." Some begin with the old English word for worship that translates as "worth-ship," meaning that God is worthy, or we ascribe worth to God. Others point to the Hebrew word *shachah*, meaning to bow down or prostrate oneself, and the Greek words *proskyneo*, also meaning to prostrate, and *latreuo*, which equates worship with service.

Wolterstorff begins his discussion of the meaning of worship with the understanding that comes from the English word that God is worthy of our worship. From there, he builds an argument that begins with the simple idea that worship is adoration of God. His definition says, "Christian worship of God is a specific mode of Godward acknowledgment of God's distinctive and unsurpassable excellence. Specifically, it is that mode of such acknowledgment whose attitudinal stance toward God is awed, reverential, and grateful adoration."[1] Since Wolterstorff calls this a definition of *Christian* worship, there are distinctives that must be assumed in his definition. The adoration of God, or ascribing worth to God, could describe Jewish or Muslim worship, or even the worship of any religion that believes in the concept of God and yet does not subscribe to beliefs about the Trinitarian nature of God or the deity of Jesus Christ. To be truly *Christian* worship, it must be distinctly Trinitarian and Christological in its underlying theology.

---

1 Wolterstorff, "Series Introduction," xix.

A definition that includes these components is this one by Robert Schaper: "Worship is the expression of a relationship in which God the Father reveals himself and his love in Christ, and by his Holy Spirit administers grace, to which we respond in faith, gratitude, and obedience."[2] This definition includes not only Trinitarian language but also adds several other components to the understanding of Christian worship. The first important component is that worship is the expression of a relationship with the Triune God. Secondly, this definition makes the observation that worship is a response to God's self-revelation. And thirdly, it includes *how* the worshiper responds—in faith, gratitude, and obedience.

While both of these definitions are valid, they differ in focus. Wolterstorff is concerned that worship should be completely focused on the object of worship, which is God, and not on the functions of worship, such as formation or how we express our worship.[3] On the other hand, Schaper's concern is that we recognize worship to be something more than a thing we offer to a distant God, however great and worthy God is of adoration. For Schaper, worship involves *knowing* God, not simply *knowing about* God. His focus is on the relationship between worshipers and the God they worship.[4]

Since we are specifically concerned with corporate worship, we must address the difference between individual worship of God and corporate worship of God. To begin, corporate worship is much more than singing together. The entire liturgy of the church, which simply refers to all of the activities present in a worship service, constitutes corporate worship. Corporate worship begins as worshipers gather, although individual worship may be happening before the worshiper arrives at the church. While a regular, individual practice of worship

---

2 Schaper, *In His Presence*, 15–16.
3 Wolterstorff, "Series Introduction," xix.
4 Schaper, *In His Presence*, 13–14.

in various ways is a valuable and meaningful Christian practice for spiritual formation, the unison worship of the gathered Body of Christ magnifies the offering in a similar way as the difference between a song sung by a soloist and a song sung by a mass choir. The experience of worshiping together with other believers in prayer, song, and attending to the Word of God transcends our individual understanding. Corporate worship brings together the traditions of the church, the unified prayers of the community, the embodied actions found in physical activities such as singing and the sacraments, interaction with the Word of God, and combined individual spiritual experiences, all for the purpose of responding in worship to the God who is worthy of our adoration and wants to have a relationship with his people, the church. A communal experience has a different dynamic than an individual experience.

When we look into spiritual transformation as it relates to worship, we are looking at what Wolterstorff labels a "function" of worship, which, he says, is not what worship actually *is*. However, spiritual transformation as a function or outcome of worship cannot be separated from the action of adoring God, especially when we conceive of worship as an expression of a relationship. It is a dialogical activity in which God speaks to us as we speak to God. This interaction with Almighty God necessarily changes us, as we, "with unveiled faces, contemplate the Lord's glory." If worship is understood correctly, transformation of the worshiper becomes an integral part of the experience and not something that can be separated as simply a function.

Why do we worship God?

When I have asked my students why we worship God, some have replied that we must worship God because God *demands* it in Scripture. I think *demand* is a poor choice of a word. The God we worship is not a Nebuchadnezzar who needs the obeisance of his subjects to prove his power or his worthiness as a ruler. The God of the universe does not *need* anything from us. However, we can say that worship of God is *commanded* in Scripture. The important thing to realize is that the commands are given with reasons.

The first reason for worshiping God we can find in Scripture is that humans seem to be "hard-wired" to worship *something*. The injunctions to worship Yahweh and him only are because of our tendency to worship something we can see, such as idols of wood and stone or the sun, moon, and stars. In Exodus and Deuteronomy, the command to worship Yahweh is repeated several times in reference to what his people should *not* worship. The most familiar, of course, is found in the decalogue. Exodus 20:2–5a says,

> I am the Lord your God, who brought you out of Egypt, out of the land of slavery. You shall have no other gods before [or besides] me. You shall not make for yourself an image in the form of anything in heaven above or on the earth beneath or in the waters below. You shall not bow down to them or worship them; for I, the Lord your God, am a jealous God. . . .

Deuteronomy 4:15–19 again warns about worshiping other things:

> You saw no form of any kind the day the Lord spoke to you at Horeb out of the fire. Therefore watch yourselves very carefully, so that you do not become corrupt and make for yourselves an idol, an image of any shape, whether formed like a man or a woman, or like any animal on earth or any bird that flies in the air, or like any creature that moves along the ground or any fish in the waters below. And when you look up to the sky and see the sun, the moon and the stars—all the heavenly array—do not be enticed into bowing down to them and worshiping things the Lord your God has apportioned to all the nations under heaven.

God is a jealous God, not because he craves power or wants to control us, but because he knows the other things that could claim our worship will destroy us. Again, worship is about relationship. We cannot have a relationship with the God of the universe if we also worship lesser things.

The second reason to worship God found in Scripture is what he has done. Some may say this is not pure worship; that a higher reason for worship is because of who God is rather than what God has done. This idea is reflected in the song by Billy Smiley and Bob Farrell, "Because of Who You Are," made popular by Sandi Patty in the 1980s. The chorus of this song says,

> Lord, I praise you, because of who you are,
>
> Not for all the mighty things that you have done.
>
> Lord, I worship you, because of who you are;
>
> You're all the reason that I need to voice my praise,
>
> Because of who you are.

The idea that we should worship God for who he is is valid. However, we cannot know who God is without knowing what he has done. God's actions in history as recounted in Scripture and his actions in our own experience reveal God's character and attributes. We cannot truly worship what we do not know, and the transcendent God is only made knowable to us as he reveals himself in Scripture through the prophets and the historical records of God's actions on behalf of humans, as well as in our own and others' lived experiences of his activity in our lives. Psalms 103 through 106 are examples of scriptures that tell us to worship God for his wonderful deeds. Psalm 103 is a song about personal benefits received from God. Psalm 104 recounts his great deeds in creation. Psalm 105 tells the story of the miraculous founding of Israel. And Psalm 106 tells the longer history of Israel and how God continually forgave and saved them. All four psalms enjoin us to praise the Lord or thank the Lord for the things he has done, as well as for who God is as he is revealed by those actions. In addition, there are the times when God spoke to people, and it was recorded in Scripture, such as Exodus 3:14, where God proclaims himself to Moses to be Yahweh, the One who exists eternally. Or again, speaking to Moses, God proclaims again that he is Yahweh and adds attributes that help us (and Moses) understand who he is:

> Then the Lord came down in the cloud and stood there with him and proclaimed his name, the LORD. And he passed in front of Moses, proclaiming, "The LORD, the LORD, the compassionate and gracious God, slow to anger, abounding in love and faithfulness, maintaining love to thousands, and forgiving wickedness, rebellion and sin. Yet he does not leave the guilty unpunished; he punishes the children and their children for the sin of the parents to the third and fourth generation." (Exodus 34:5-7)

Yahweh, the eternal One, is worthy of our adoration and praise simply because of who he is. And yet, we would be worshiping blindly without the knowledge provided by revelation about his deeds, character, and attributes. We cannot have a relationship with an unknown deity.

The third reason to worship God is that he invites us into worship. Constance Cherry says, "God the Father seeks us. [See John 4:23-24] We don't create worship; we don't manufacture services. Rather, we respond to a person. . . . Worship happens when we learn to say yes in ever-increasing ways to God's invitation to encounter him."[5] God is always initiating the relationship, and we respond. Examples in Scripture include when God summoned Moses and the elders to establish a covenant with him—a covenant which God initiated; God called the prophets—they did not apply for the position; God acted first at Pentecost; and so on. Perhaps the greatest way God initiated

---

5 Cherry, *The Worship Architect*, 4.

a relationship with humanity was in the Incarnation of the Son, who came to live among us. As Romans 5:8 tells us, "God demonstrates his own love for us in this: While we were still sinners, Christ died for us." God has always initiated the relationship, and in the same way, he initiates our worship as an expression of that relationship. It is a conversation between God and his people. Psalm 95 bids us, "Come, let us bow down in worship." The psalmist's invitation is followed by "If only you would hear his voice." God calls us to worship.

All of these reasons for worshiping God can be summed up in the idea that God invites our worship because he loves us and desires a relationship with us. From creation to incarnation to making a place for us for eternity, God has shown his love for us. He invites us to participate in the eternal fellowship of the Trinity—Father, Son, and Holy Spirit, giving us the opportunity to become part of the family.

How does worship have the potential to transform us?

Spiritual transformation can be described in various ways. Spiritual growth, Christian formation, and discipleship are all terms that refer to somehow becoming a "better" Christian or growing in Christlikeness. In Wesleyan terms, we speak of entire sanctification, growth in grace, and Christian perfection. Some of these ideas are understood as a process as we work towards the goal of holiness or godliness. Holiness churches have traditionally taught that entire sanctification is an event—a singular work of the Holy Spirit at a moment in time. John Wesley himself left room for either option. In a letter to Miss Cooke, he said,

> There is an irreconcilable variability in the operations of the Holy Spirit on the souls of men; . . . Many find him rushing upon them like a torrent, while they experience "The o'erwhelming power of saving grace." . . . But in others, he works in a very different way: "He deigns his influence to infuse; Sweet, refreshing

as the violet dews." It has pleased him to work the latter way in you, from the beginning. . . . Let him take his own way: he is wiser than you; he will do all things well."[6]

The primary manner in which Wesley expected people to encounter spiritual transformation was through the means of grace, which he described in his sermon on the subject this way: "By 'means of grace' I understand outward signs, words, or actions ordained of God, and appointed for this end—to be the ordinary channels whereby he might convey to men preventing, justifying, or sanctifying grace."[7] His expectation was that, as people regularly participated in the means of grace while trusting only in God for the work to be done in the heart, the Holy Spirit would give grace that allowed the participant to be filled with perfect love for God and neighbor, resulting in the ability to live a holy life free from sin. Wesley's understanding of the means of grace was that they are effective over time. If entire sanctification happens as an event, that event would normally result from growth enabled by the regular practice of the means of grace. On the other hand, while he believed the means of grace to be the "ordinary channels" used by God, he left room for God to work in any way he chooses. Wesley said,

> it behooves us, first, always to retain a lively sense that God is above all means. Have a care therefore of limiting the Almighty. He doth whatsoever and whensoever it pleaseth him. He can convey his grace, either in or out of any of the means which he hath appointed. Perhaps he will. "Who hath known the mind of the Lord? Or who hath been his counsellor?" . . . He is always ready; always able, always willing to save. "It is the Lord, let him do what seemeth him good!"[8]

---

6 Wesley, *Works*, XIII, 95.
7 Wesley, Outler, and Heitzenrater, *John Wesley's Sermons*, 159.
8 Wesley, Outler, and Heitzenrater, *John Wesley's Sermons*, 169.

If we can receive sanctifying grace at any time, then, without participating in the means, why are they important? Wesley's answer is to say simply ". . . because God bids, therefore I do."[9] If we want to experience a spiritual transformation that empowers us to live a holy life of love, we will do the things that are most likely to bring us to that experience, those things that are observable as "ordinary channels," while trusting not in the means themselves but only in God to do the work. By using the word "channel," Wesley made it clear that the means of grace themselves cannot impart grace. They are simply the delivery system for the grace given by God. This "delivery system" can be likened to the blood vessels in our bodies. While they are important, they do not give life in themselves. They are the channels that carry life-giving blood to all parts of the body.

In his sermon on the means of grace, Wesley was concerned with two types of errors. The first was trusting only in the means of grace while having no relationship with God. The second was the opposite: trusting only in one's own spiritual experiences and despising the means of grace as being merely dead tradition. In both cases, according to Wesley, people were trusting in something other than God alone for their salvation. For one, it was trusting that the practices themselves insured salvation. Wesley called these people "formalists." Today we may see this error in people who assume that baptism, church membership, or regular attendance at church will guarantee their salvation.

For the other, it was relying on their own subjective feelings rather than evaluating their experiences by Scripture and the centuries-old traditions of the church. We may see this in people, like those in Wesley's day, who do not care if the worship service they attend reflects correct theology, as long as it "feels good." Wesley labeled these

---

[9] Wesley, Outler, and Heitzenrater, *John Wesley's Sermons*, 169.

people "enthusiasts."[10] Knight says, ". . . for Wesley, means of grace offer descriptive accounts of God's nature and work which counter enthusiasm, and at the same time invite a relationship with God which counters formalism."[11] In other words, proper use of the means of grace offers corrective measures to keep our spiritual lives based on both scriptural and traditionally understood truth, as well as remaining open to the voice of the Holy Spirit.

> What, then, are these "means of grace" in which we should participate? In general terms, means of grace are Christian practices, also called spiritual disciplines. Andrew Root says that "practices of the church are . . . given as gifts to human communities by the eternal God," and these practices become means of grace as they enable humans to participate in "divine action."[12]

Although means of grace are actions performed by humans, they are not merely human actions. They are intentionally undertaken in order to participate with God in his purposes. Their purpose is to develop and demonstrate in the believer the two greatest commandments, that is, to love God and to love neighbor.

Wesley talked about three categories of the means of grace. As listed by Henry Knight, these categories are General, Instituted, and Prudential. When we talk about corporate worship, it falls under the categories of Instituted and Prudential. The word "worship" itself is never mentioned in these lists. But the various individual things we do together in corporate worship, which we call the "elements" of a worship service, are included in Wesley's lists. Knight explains the two types. He says,

> The instituted are those which are appointed by God as means of grace. The instituted means belong to the universal church

---

10 Wesley, Outler, and Heitzenrater, *John Wesley's Sermons*, 158–70.
11 Knight, *The Presence of God in the Christian Life*, 47.
12 Root, *Christopraxis*, 70.

in all eras of history and in all cultures. In contrast, the prudential means of grace vary from age to age, culture to culture, and person to person; they reflect God's ability to use any means in addition to those instituted in accordance with different times and circumstances.[13]

Thus, the second list which follows may or may not be in use in our particular time or culture. Perhaps there are other ways in which the Holy Spirit regularly works in your context.

Here are the means of grace that Wesley categorized as *instituted* (for the church at any time and in any culture):

- Prayer: private, family, public; consisting of deprecation, petition, intercession, and thanksgiving; extemporaneous and written.
- Searching the Scriptures by reading, meditating, hearing, and attending the ministry of the Word, either read or expounded.
- The Lord's Supper.
- Fasting or abstinence.
- Christian conference, which includes both the fellowship of believers and rightly ordered conversations that minister grace to hearers.

Here are the means of grace categorized as *prudential* (may vary from age to age, culture to culture, person to person):

- Particular rules or acts of holy living.
- Class and band meetings.
- Prayer meetings, covenant services, watch night services, love feasts.
- Visiting the sick.

---

13 Knight, *The Presence of God in the Christian Life*, 3.

- Doing all the good one can, doing no harm.
- Reading devotional classics and all edifying literature.[14]

Many of these means of grace, both instituted and prudential, can be found in the liturgy of corporate worship. Prayer, searching the Scriptures, the Lord's Supper, and Christian conference, found in the list of instituted means, are all regular parts of worship. The list of prudential means also includes activities that can be found in corporate worship.

As noted, the prudential means of grace can be particular to different times, cultures, and circumstances. Mark Mann goes so far as to say, "In regard to the question of appropriate means of grace, then, we should take a very pragmatic approach. Any activity, device, or method that enhances our receptivity and responsiveness to the gracious call of God can be a vital means of grace in our pursuit of and growth in holiness."[15] If we are to be true to Wesley's understanding, however, we must be careful to align our practices with Scripture in order to avoid placing our trust in our own experiences rather than in God.

Constance Cherry includes music as a prudential means of grace. She says,

> In the context of Christian worship, music also serves as a means of grace. It is a channel through which God speaks to us and works in us for our good. It provides an avenue for God to continue the ongoing process toward Christlikeness in his children. Music itself doesn't change us, of course, but God often uses music to work in us on our journey of transformation.[16]

Wesley did not list music specifically as a means of grace, but he used hymns to teach doctrine. Rattenbury says, "The Methodist hymns were

---

14 Knight, *The Presence of God in the Christian Life*, 5.
15 Mann, *Perfecting Grace*, 170.
16 Cherry, *The Music Architect*, 247.

from the first treated by [John Wesley] as doctrinal documents. Not only in his prefaces to hymn-books, but in his treatises and sermons, he refers to them as authoritative expressions of Methodist theology."[17] As we saw in Wesley's list of instituted means of grace, "searching the Scriptures," "prayer," and "Christian conference" are included. Music used in corporate worship can express scriptural truths, act as a prayer, and can function to bring believers together in fellowship. Whether the words shared in our worship services are spoken or sung, they are still able to function as means of grace.

Two Latin phrases that have been in use in the church for centuries are *Lex Orandi* and *Lex Credendi*, which literally mean "the law of praying" and "the law of believing." Constance Cherry says,

> Essentially, the proposition is this: what we pray becomes what we believe (in the context of worship). The idea is that all corporate worship is prayer and that the words that we use to pray ultimately shape what we believe. The songs we are given to sing shape what we believe. The creeds, the passages of Scripture that the community hears, the baptismal and Communion liturgies—all of it forms us.[18]

Recognizing this transformational power of worship reveals the importance of care for the content of our liturgy. The means of grace may be present, but if the channels are corrupted by weak or even harmful content, they will be ineffectual as conduits of grace. Church leaders and church attenders may assume that regular attendance at church will help people grow spiritually. This may or may not happen, depending on the content of the worship. Ideally, we want to see growth that leads to spiritual transformation happening in our churches. We want to see people's lives changed so that they express their love for God and others in service within the church and outside its walls.

---

17 Rattenbury, *The Evangelical Doctrines of Charles Wesley's Hymns*, 62.
18 Cherry, *The Music Architect*, 238.

Unfortunately, this level of transformation is rare. Worship practices that are done merely out of habit or that are not critically assessed for the content they are communicating may not actually become channels for God's grace. The normal corporate worship services found in many evangelical churches may not be providing the necessary spiritual food needed to produce this type of spiritual growth, even if they are technically offering things that are supposed to be means of grace. If we expect the means of grace found in corporate worship to be transformational, two things are required, and they must work together.

First, the content of worship must be theologically sound and presented so that it communicates in a way that people can understand. This content includes the things that are said, sung, prayed, seen, heard, demonstrated, etc., known as the liturgy. When people participate in a worship service, it could be formational to their Christian life, or it could be de-formational, teaching things that work against spiritual growth. This is the responsibility of pastors and worship planners.

Second, the means of grace are intended to be practiced consistently over time. If worshipers do not participate in worship services regularly, it will not matter if the content is perfectly designed for growth. We are only the Body of Christ together. As Hebrews 10:24-25 says, "... let us consider how we may spur one another on toward love and good deeds, not giving up meeting together, as some are in the habit of doing, but encouraging one another—and all the more as you see the Day approaching." Gathering together is important, but participation is the key. "Participation" is more than passively watching and listening. It means being active in listening, praying, singing, reading the Word, etc. As noted earlier, worship is a dialogue with God, who loves us and reaches out to us. Worship can be transformational when people faithfully and regularly engage in it over time. *Lex Orandi, Lex Credendi.* As worshipers participate, the way they believe will be shaped, and they will open the channels for the Holy Spirit to change them and make them more like Christ.

One more Latin phrase that is sometimes included with the two already mentioned is *Lex Vivendi,* literally meaning "the law of living." *Lex Orandi, Lex Credendi, Lex Vivendi* means that the worship in which we participate affects what we believe, which affects how we live. The purpose of the means of grace is not just to become holier on the inside but to enable people to live lives of holiness, or perfect love, in the midst of an unholy world. Proper worship has a part to play in a spiritual transformation that changes how people think and live. Wesley emphasized that entire sanctification is all about the two greatest commandments—loving God and loving our neighbor. He said in a letter to one of his followers, ". . . be not content till you are a Christian altogether, till your soul is *all love.*"[19] Do not be content with worship services that do not contribute to that goal.

The following are some suggestions first for pastors and worship planners and then for worship participants to improve the likelihood that corporate worship will serve as a means of grace and have an influence on personal spiritual transformation.

For leaders:

1. Examine every aspect of your worship service. What is the purpose of each element of the service? What are you communicating by your words, your actions, and the architecture and layout of the church? What do the words of your songs say? What do the words of your prayers say?

2. Do your worship practices encourage attendees to hear from God and respond to God? Are they expected to participate or just be passive listeners? Can everyone in your congregation sing the songs as they are presented? Are there any other

---

[19] Wesley, *Works,* XIII, 67, emphasis mine.

ways they are invited to participate other than singing? Is everyone included?

3. Are the worship services in your church telling God's story every week? Is it faithful to Scripture? Is it faithful to the traditions of the church? Do people get the whole biblical story of God or only small bites? Are they getting a balanced diet or only candy? How much Scripture is read in your church? Do you read the hard parts as well as the joyful parts? Do you use Trinitarian and Christological language throughout your worship services?

4. Is your worship focused on God or on people? How many songs reflect only our feelings about God instead of Biblical references to who God is and what he has done? How many songs repeat the words "I," "me," or "my"? Are God's concerns reflected in our prayers or only our needs?

5. Does your worship connect people together as a community? When you sing, can people hear each other singing? Are members of the congregation invited to participate on the platform by reading Scripture, praying, etc.? Are there opportunities for fellowship?

6. Do your worship services point inward toward yourselves, or do they point outward to keep the church's focus on its greater mission to the world around you?

For attenders:

1. Do you prepare for worship before arriving at the church? Do you pray for God to use the worship to speak to you?
2. Do you attend church regularly?
3. Do you do your best to participate in all aspects of the worship service?

4. Do you do further study and prayer during the week regarding what you experienced in the worship service?
5. Do you go to church to worship God, or are you focused on your personal preferences, entertainment value, or how it makes you feel?

Conclusion

Corporate worship has the potential to be transformational. To realize this potential, we cannot conceive of worship as simply something that we produce and offer to a transcendent God. Worship must become a dialogue with the One who loves us and invites us into a relationship with the eternal fellowship of the Trinity. Worship expresses this relationship as God initiates a conversation in which he speaks to us, and we respond appropriately. God has revealed himself in Scripture and in our own experience in ways that confirm his worthiness to be worshiped. Even his commandments to worship him reveal his desire for a relationship with us. In love, he warns us not to be fooled by counterfeit gods, who cannot do anything for us except destroy our relationship with him. This type of relational worship can become a means of grace by which the Holy Spirit can bring transformation if the content of our worship is prepared and practiced in a way that faithfully communicates who God is and how he acts on our behalf. When we participate in this type of worship together over time and with faith that God can change us, we can expect to be "transformed into his image with ever-increasing glory." When we have thus been transformed, we will be able to love God with all our hearts, minds, souls, and strength, and we will be able to love our neighbors as ourselves.

Bibliography

Cherry, Constance M. *The Music Architect: Blueprints for Engaging Worshipers in Song.* Grand Rapids: Baker Academic, 2016.

———. *The Worship Architect: A Blueprint for Designing Culturally Relevant and Biblically Faithful Services.* Grand Rapids: Baker Academic, 2010.

Knight, Henry H. *The Presence of God in the Christian Life: John Wesley and the Means of Grace.* Metuchen; London: Scarecrow, 1992.

Mann, Mark H. *Perfecting Grace: Holiness, Human Being, and the Sciences.* New York, London: T & T Clark, 2006.

Rattenbury, J. E. *The Evangelical Doctrines of Charles Wesley's Hymns.* London: The Epworth Press, 1941.

Root, Andrew. *Christopraxis: A Practical Theology of the Cross.* Minneapolis: Fortress, 2014.

Schaper, Robert N. *In His Presence: Appreciating Your Worship Tradition.* Nashville: T. Nelson, 1984.

Wesley, John, Albert C. Outler, and Richard P. Heitzenrater. *John Wesley's Sermons: An Anthology.* Nashville: Abingdon, 1991.

Wesley, John. *The Works of John Wesley: Letters.* 3rd ed. 14 vols. Kansas City: Beacon Hill, 1979.

Wolterstorff, Nicholas. "Series Introduction." In *Theological Foundations of Worship: Biblical, Systematic, and Practical Perspectives*, edited by Khalia J. Williams and Mark A. Lamport. Worship Foundations, xvii–xxii. Grand Rapids: Baker Academic, 2021.

18

ETHICS AND SPIRITUALITY

Phillip Davis

What makes a person good, and how do I become that person? How can I have a happy, fulfilling life? Such questions arise in Christian ethics. A long tradition of thought runs through the field of virtue ethics. This Christian tradition focuses on virtue, moral excellence, and the good. What is the good, and how can we live the good life? How can we become good, moral, and virtuous people?

In his second epistle, the Apostle Peter encourages us to add the following qualities to our lives: faith, moral excellence, knowledge, self-control, perseverance, godliness, brotherly kindness, and love (2 Pet 1:5–7). He says that we should apply "all diligence" to this endeavor, for he claims these qualities will make us fruitful for the Kingdom of God. Today, we recognize these qualities as virtues (or goods). We see connections between these qualities and the moral habits they develop. Ethicists call these moral goods the cardinal and theological virtues. Peter identifies these habits of life as part of a godly life—as partaking in "the divine nature" (2 Pet 1:4). Thus, ethics and spirituality are connected. As we practice the virtues, we grow spiritually, becoming more like God and sharing in his nature. Christian virtue ethics teach that virtue ethics is the way to *eudaimonia* (i.e., to happiness or to a flourishing life).

Ethics

When people think about the moral life, they often take different approaches. Some people emphasize one's duty (i.e., *deontological ethics*) when deciding if an action is moral or immoral. Other people consider what action provides the greatest good for the maximum number of people (i.e., *utilitarianism*). Still others maintain that the ends justify the means when we act in specific cases (i.e., *situational ethics*). Ethics helps us think through such questions about right and wrong and to develop principles for behavior. Whether they know it or not, everyone has a view of ethics. In every society, people hold certain attitudes and behaviors as praiseworthy or shameful. Reflecting on these views is the task of ethics. We call this moral philosophy when philosophers consider such questions; we call it moral theology when theologians consider morality. In the western tradition, ethics started with a question: "What is the good?" Ancient Greek philosophers concluded that pursuing the good leads to *eudaimonia* or happiness.

Socrates was the philosopher who asked incessantly about the good. In his dialogue the *Crito*, Plato recounts a conversation between Socrates and his friend Crito as the former awaits his execution. Crito urges Socrates to flee Athens to save his life; however, Socrates asks a piercing question: Is it "not life, but a good life, [that] is to be chiefly valued?"[1] For Socrates, "a good life" is "just and honorable." Socrates views escape from the Athenian prison as a dishonorable action because it involves breaking the laws of the state—thereby overturning

---

1 Plato, *Dialogues* (Jowett), 2:149.

the state.[2] Socrates must "do what his city and his country order him," lest he "do violence to his country." To flee from Athenian justice would be "to violate the most sacred laws from a miserable desire of a little more life."[3] Socrates resolutely refuses to do this, for it would make him a traitor to his country and a flatterer to the people of Thessaly, so he might simply "get a dinner." By fleeing, he would degrade himself and fail to live up to his statements about "justice and virtue." Socrates would violate an implied contract with Athens, showing disdain for the benefits he derived from a lifetime in that city. In fact, Socrates sees such an act as damaging to his own soul, something he refuses to do. Rather than escape, Socrates chooses a path that preserves happiness, holiness, and justice as he tries "to fulfill the will of God, and to follow whither he leads."[4] Here, to suffer execution is to live out a good life. Socrates plays the key role in Plato's dialogues, and he helps us to think about truth, beauty, and goodness (or morality).

Plato presents his mentor as consumed by ethical questions as he pursues the good. Plato assumes that we will live according to the good if we know what it is. Education, therefore, plays a crucial role in developing a virtuous person for Plato and Socrates. The former argues for the soul's conversion as it is led toward the light, so it can be molded into its essential form. Socrates' chief opponents were the Sophists, who taught students the technique of rhetoric to win court cases, but Socrates saw this as morally corrosive. Rather, he argued that the goal of education should be the perfecting of the soul. Socrates maintains

---

[2] Socrates argues for a very high loyalty to the state, a loyalty above one's parents or ancestors. Such loyalty is valued "in the eyes of the gods and of men [sic] of understanding. See, Plato, *Dialogues* (Jowett), 2:152.

[3] Plato, *Dialogues* (Jowett), 2:155.

[4] Plato, *Dialogues* (Jowett), 2:156. Wogaman (*Christian Ethics*, 18) points to Socrates' acknowledgement of the Athenian state's role in bearing, nurturing, and educating him as a "covenantal understanding of citizenship [that] was destined to have enormous importance in Western thought."

that the end of education is "to cultivate the human soul." Such a soul conforms to *aretai* or virtue, which is "its ideal form in harmony with the nature of the universe."⁵ The standard by which the soul is perfected must be determined, but Plato feels confident that we can discover this principle through dialectic (i.e., honest, rational argument among friends).

Plato's chief pupil, Aristotle, wielded a tremendous influence over western ethical thinking.⁶ In his *Nicomachean Ethics*, Aristotle says we should pursue virtue to avoid shame or *aidos*.⁷ Shame is "a positive emotion that keeps us away from vice and that activates many of the virtues."⁸ Although shame does not belong among the virtues, it makes us feel a powerful emotion motivating us to avoid vice and choose virtue. Aristotle views virtues as fixed dispositions that help us realize goals inherent in our human nature, and we need knowledge of "the good" to understand these as our ends as human beings. By pursuing truth, we discern our purpose as human beings, and this informs the choices we make.

Like Socrates and Plato, Aristotle argues that human beings act with purpose toward some good. People identify the good in different ways, as pleasure, honor, or virtue.⁹ But Aristotle maintains that we aim at happiness in whatever good we choose. For "we always . . . [choose happiness] because of itself, never because of something else."¹⁰ We may choose for other goods (e.g., "honor, pleasure, reason, and every virtue"), but we do so for the sake of happiness. Happiness, then, is our

---

5   Oxenham, *Character and Virtue*, 188.
6   For an interesting brief discussion of the similarities between Aristotle and Confucius, see Oxenham, *Character and Virtue*, 170-71.
7   See Aristotle, *Nicomachean Ethics*, 4.11-4.113 (Irwin), 114-15.
8   Oxenham, *Character and Virtue*, 128.
9   See Aristotle, *Nicomachean Ethics*, Book 1, chap. 5, sect. 1.43 (Irwin), 7-8.
10 See Aristotle, *Nicomachean Ethics*, Book 1, chap. 7, sect. 1.51 (3) (Irwin), 14.

"complete and self-sufficient" good.[11] It is the end of our actions—our final goal. Aristotle believes this end comports to the function of the human being, which he locates in our rational principle, as an activity of the soul.[12] We see a person's rational principles in his or her behavior or "actions of the soul" that lead to a good life.

For Aristotle, "the happy person lives well and does well" by living a life of virtue.[13] We must learn and cultivate this virtuous life through a process Aristotle calls "habituation."[14] A true understanding of the function of human beings leads us to a life of virtue that produces happiness. As reason guides our moral actions, repeated habitual actions become dispositions of the soul. These dispositions become natural and automatic for us, and they incline our souls toward certain behaviors. They become temperaments that shape the kinds of people we become. As Marvin Oxenham notes, "once a particular virtue has become a part of our character, it functions across our being, making us do, feel, think, want, perceive and be perceived in ways that are praiseworthy."[15] Aristotle claims that these dispositions become stable and enduring parts of our character. They help us to live consistently a virtuous life, which he believes is the good life—a life of happiness. Aristotle writes that happiness is "the prize and goal of virtue [and] appears to be the best good, something divine and blessed."[16]

Reason also helps us practice virtue because any action taken to an extreme creates problems. Aristotle argues extensively that the

---

11 Aristotle, *Nicomachean Ethics*, Book 1, chap. 7, sect. 1.5 (5) (Irwin), 15. We find similar ideas in Scripture: e.g., Jesus as the one who gives abundant life (John 10:10); or how one enters into "eternal life" (Mark 10:17). See Mattison, *Introducing Moral Theology*, 26.

12 This rational principle distinguishes human beings from the vegetative and animal worlds. See Aristotle, *Nicomachean Ethics*, Book 1, chap. 7, sect. 1.5 (3-4) (Irwin), 16.

13 Aristotle, *Nicomachean Ethics*, Book 1, chap. 8, sect. 1.72 (Irwin), 19.

14 Aristotle, *Nicomachean Ethics*, Book 1, chap. 8, sect. 1.81 (Irwin), 22.

15 Oxenham, *Character and Virtue*, 24.

16 Aristotle, *Nicomachean Ethics*, Book 1, chap. 8, sect. 1.81 (Irwin), 22.

virtuous way lies between "excess and deficiency." For instance, courage appears "between the excess of foolhardiness and the deficiency of cowardice."[17] In a similar way, the virtue of temperance helps us negotiate between overindulging in pleasure or too strictly refraining from enjoying pleasure. A virtuous person must discern the middle way between excess and deficiency in his or her pursuit of the good life. Aristotle teaches that we can achieve our goal of happiness through concerted thought about the good and by acquiring virtues in our lives.[18]

Virtue Ethics

Greek thought greatly influenced the Christian ethical tradition, for the early Church Fathers found much fodder for thought from Socrates, Plato, and Aristotle. Christian reflection developed an ethical approach that we know as virtue ethics. This approach has been part of the Christian tradition for a couple of millennia. Virtue ethics focuses on the question of how we can become people of virtue. In contrast to an ethic of obligation or duty (i.e., a deontological approach), virtue ethics concentrates on the qualities of character (or virtues) that lead to human happiness. To say this differently, virtue ethics centers its task more on the question of what kinds of people we become rather than on the kinds of deeds we do.

While the Christian tradition drew inspiration from Greek ethical thought, significant differences remain between the two approaches. Peter Kreeft nicely summarizes the contrast when he writes, "The Greeks represented virtue in theory, thinking about virtue; the Hebrews represented virtue in practice."[19] Plato and Socrates both thought that knowledge is the foundation of virtue. If we know the

---

17 Wogaman, *Christian Ethics*, 21.
18 Boyd and Thorsen, *Christian Ethics and Moral Philosophy*, 74.
19 Kreeft, *Back to Virtue*, 52.

good, we will do the good. Kreeft encapsulates their approach: "Virtue is knowledge and knowledge is virtue."[20] Education, therefore, is crucial to the Platonic ethical project and undergirds a moral utopia described in his *Republic*. But Greek thought neglects the categories of sin and faith. From the Hebrew and Christian perspectives, these categories are determinative. Kreeft also notes that sin and faith belong to both ethical *and* religious categories. While the religious includes the ethical, the former exceeds the latter. Kreeft writes, "The religious Jew and Christian are to be ethically virtuous, of course, but also religiously faithful. Of the two great commandments, the first is religious (to love the Lord with the whole heart), the second is ethical (to love neighbor as self)."[21] Thus, from the Hebraic perspective, the order of importance flows in this direction: faith (or fidelity), virtue, and then knowledge. Thus, the practice of virtue proceeds from one's prior knowledge of God or of virtue, in contrast to the Greeks. The Greeks emphasized the head ruling over the heart, but the Jew inverted this order and claimed that the heart should judge the head. "Above all else, guard your heart, for everything you do flows from it" (Prov 4:23).[22]

Still, Christian theologians benefited from the careful thought produced by Socrates, Plato, and Aristotle. They found understanding in the Greeks' presentation of the four cardinal virtues. Plato includes these four virtues in his dialogue, the *Symposium*. At a dinner party at Agathon's house, the host gives a speech in praise of love. He builds his argument for love on a framework of prudence, justice, fortitude, and temperance. Notably, none of the participants question Agathon's use of these four virtues. Josef Pieper suggests that the Greeks so widely

---

20 Kreeft, *Back to Virtue*, 52.
21 Kreeft, *Back to Virtue*, 53.
22 I chose to cite the NIV translation here, although Kreeft quotes from the KJV. He also mentions that the word "heart" in scripture indicates one's will rather than sentiment. Kreeft writes, "Hebraism is practical, not sentimental." See, Kreeft, *Back to Virtue*, 53.

accepted these virtues that Socrates and his friends found no reason to challenge or defend them. Indeed, Pieper considers the Greek philosopher's "doctrine of virtue" to be "one of the great discoveries in the history of man's self-understanding."[23] This doctrine influenced Greek, Roman, Jewish, and Christian thinkers.[24] However, Christian critics expressed suspicion about such thought because it originated in pagan classical philosophy.[25] Pieper writes, "They warily regarded it as too philosophical and not Scriptural enough. Thus, they preferred to talk about commandments and duties rather than about virtues."[26] Of course, it is legitimate to define our obligations before God and one another; however, we risk making lists of licit and illicit behaviors while forgetting the person who should behave according to such rules. Pieper argues, rather, for a virtue ethic approach. Virtue ethics speaks to both virtue and obligation—to the kinds of people we should be and to how we should act. He writes, "the doctrine of virtue . . . is one form of the doctrine of obligation; but one by nature free of regimentation and restriction . . . its aim is to clear a trail, to open a way."[27]

Christian Virtue Ethics

As we saw above, virtue ethics views happiness as a person's end goal. William C. Mattison III calls this a "morality of happiness approach,"

---

23 Pieper, *The Four Cardinal Virtues*, 6.

24 Pieper mentions these influential thinkers: Plato and Aristotle (Greeks); Cicero and Seneca (Romans); Philo (Judaism); and Clement of Alexandria and Augustine (Christianity).

25 However, as Wogaman points out, the New Testament documents occasionally show ideas inspired by Greek philosophical sources. Among these, he mentions a Platonic influence in Hebrews chapter 11 ("what is seen was made from things that are not visible"); the prolegomena to John's Gospel ("In the beginning was the Word" or Logos); overtones to Plato's parable of the cave in Paul's letter to the Corinthians (1 Cor. 13:12); Christ as the icon of "the invisible God, the firstborn of all creation" (Col. 1:14), and so on. See, Wogaman, *Christian Ethics*, 23.

26 Pieper, *The Four Cardinal Virtues*, 6.

27 Pieper, *The Four Cardinal Virtues*, 7.

which contrasts with a "morality of obligation" way of life.[28] He argues strongly against the idea that moral thinking assumes we must do things (obligation) that we do not want to do. Rather, a correct understanding of the moral life points toward a person's happiness and the flourishing of his or her life. We see this claim made by non-Christian philosophers and Christian theologians, and we also see similar claims in scripture. The Hebrews saw obedience to God's commands as the natural response to God's gracious activities on their behalf. They perceived this connection because of their unique experiences with God in salvation history. For example, in the book of Deuteronomy, we have one of the great expositions of the law. We read repeated statements there that the Israelites should keep God's commands. In chs. 5 and 6, Moses gives the people reasons to carefully obey the commandments. Among other reasons, we find these two: as a response to God's gift of a covenant with the Hebrews (Deut 5:2–4) and as an obedience that leads to righteousness (6:25). The people should also obey God because he freed them from slavery in Egypt (5:6; 5:15; 6:21–23). While these are all good reasons, as Mattison points out, the primary incentive for obeying the commandments is that they will enjoy a long and prosperous life (5:16; 5:29; 5:33; 6:3; 6:18; 6:24).[29]

In the New Testament, we find similar incentives to live morally in obedience to God. Jesus gives the reason why he came to earth in John's Gospel: "I have come that they may have life, and have it to the full" (John 10:10). He tells his disciples that his commandments are meant to keep them in his love (15:10). By keeping the commandments, therefore, Jesus says, "I have told you this so that my joy may be in you and that your joy may be complete" (15:11). Thus, God intends for our obedience to produce an abundant life full of joy. And as we know, the Sermon on the Mount begins with nine statements

---

28 Mattison, *Introducing Moral Theology*, 21.
29 Mattison, *Introducing Moral Theology*, 27.

regarding blessing or happiness (Matt 5:3-10). Mattison comments, "In sum, the life of discipleship to which Jesus invites his followers in the Gospels entails rule and commandments, but all in the service of living more abundantly, more joyfully."[30]

As we have already seen, Christian ethicists found a similar emphasis on happiness in Greek and Roman philosophical thought, and they used these ideas to build a Christian ethic based on the virtues.[31] Among the virtues, they wrote about four cardinal virtues (prudence, justice, temperance, and perseverance) and three theological virtues (faith, hope, and charity). Two theologians exerted a massive influence on the Christian tradition: Augustine and Thomas Aquinas.

Augustine begins his *On the Morals of the Catholic Church* with the concept of happiness. He argues that God is our greatest good and the goal of our lives. We find true happiness only in God, who satisfies our deepest longings as a good that we cannot lose. No one can take this happiness from us, which we find as we obey the first and greatest commandment: to "Love the Lord your God with all your heart and with all your soul and with all your strength" (Deut 6:5). Augustine teaches that we must use (*uti*) objects in the world to sustain us as we serve God, who alone we should enjoy (*frui*). Augustine writes, "God then alone is to be loved; and all this world, that is, all sensible things, are to be despised,—while, however, they are to be used as this life requires."[32] God is our "greatest good." We love creation and our neighbors by loving God. To love the creature rather than the Creator is to fall into idolatry. Rather, God must be our first love; and that love keeps

---

30 I have followed the scriptural references given by Mattison in this paragraph. See, Mattison, *Introducing Moral Theology*, 27.

31 Oxenham writes about the theological use of pagan authors in virtue ethics. He notes, "there is a long tradition of Christian writers, including Augustine, Alcuin and Ambrose, who engaged fruitfully with the classical writings on the virtues." See, Oxenham, *Character and Virtue*, 114.

32 Augustine, "On the Morals of the Catholic Church," 18:102.

us close to God. Augustine writes that if God is our chief good, "to live well is nothing else but to love God with all the heart, with all the soul, [and] with all the mind." He also argues that the cardinal virtues play an important role in preserving this love "entire and incorrupt."[33]

Similarly, Aquinas begins his discussion of ethics with happiness in the *Summa Theologica*. He argues that our final end determines how we should proceed toward that goal. Since happiness is our goal, this governs how we should act. Happiness as a final end creates a desire for our "perfect and crowning good."[34] Like Augustine, Aquinas understands happiness to be a person's perfect good.[35] Ultimately, other desires cannot compare or satisfy our longing for that perfect good (e.g., wealth, honor, fame, power, and so on). Rather, for Aquinas, "happiness is man's supreme perfection."[36] We will find our perfect good—thus our true happiness—in the beatific vision. Aquinas argues that "final and perfect happiness can consist in nothing else than the vision of the Divine Essence."[37] Therefore, happiness requires a moral rightness of our will because "without holiness no one will see the Lord" (Heb 12:14). Aquinas also cites Jesus' teaching: "Blessed are the pure in heart, for they will see God" (Matt 5:8).[38] Thus, Aquinas clearly maintains that we must live virtuously, with good morals, to have an excellent and happy life. But what does it mean to live a virtuous life?

---

33 Augustine writes, that temperance preserves love "entire and incorrupt," fortitude "give[s] way before no troubles," justice "serves no other," and prudence is "watchful in its inspection of things lest craft or fraud steal in." See, Augustine, "On the Morals of the Catholic Church," 18:107.

34 I-II, 1, 5. See, Aquinas, *A Summa of the Summa*, 355.

35 I-II, 1, 6. See, Aquinas, *A Summa of the Summa*, 356. Of course, Aquinas recognizes that not everyone agrees about their last end, since some long for riches, pleasure, or other things. I-II, 1, 7. See, Aquinas, *A Summa of the Summa*, 358.

36 I-II, 3, 2. See, Aquinas, *A Summa of the Summa*, 376.

37 I-II, 3, 8. See, Aquinas, *A Summa of the Summa*, 381.

38 I-II, 4, 4. See, Aquinas, *A Summa of the Summa*, 383.

Virtue ethics finds a description of rectitude in the cardinal and theological virtues.

Cardinal Virtues

Within the Christian tradition, theologians view four virtues as cardinal or "hinge" virtues.[39] These virtues are moral goods upon which all other virtues depend (or hinge). The four cardinal virtues are prudence, justice, fortitude, and temperance. We will briefly consider each one.

Prudence gives us the ability to see the truth of our situation. Mattison describes prudence as "practical wisdom" or "good sense." He notes that the Latin term *prudential* does not convey the English word's idea of "being cautious or wary."[40] Rather, prudence casts a clear eye on what we face and uses reason to choose the best course of action. Pieper writes that "all Ten Commandments of God pertain to the *execution prudentiae*, the realization in practice of prudence." And he continues, "every sin is opposed to prudence."[41] Prudence imprints the "seal of goodness" on our will and action; therefore, it gives counsel to the other virtues. "Prudence works in all the virtues; and all virtue participates in prudence."[42] As such, prudence perfects the other virtues because "what is prudent and what is good are substantially one and the same."[43]

Justice involves how we treat other people, and it touches on "a right ordering of relationships and distributions."[44] Pieper defines justice as a habit (*habitus*) by which a person "renders to each one his due

---

39 From *cardo*, the Latin word for "hinge."
40 Mattison, *Introducing Moral Theology*, 98.
41 Pieper, *The Four Cardinal Virtues*, 14.
42 Pieper, *The Four Cardinal Virtues*, 14.
43 Pieper, *The Four Cardinal Virtues*, 14.
44 Wogaman, *Christian Ethics*, 91.

with constant and perpetual will."[45] We act justly when we give another person what he or she deserves. Sometimes, however, we have trouble determining what is due to another person in specific situations. How do we discern what justice demands? How do we render to each his or her due? In such cases, we can use Aristotle's golden mean to think through how to render justice, for we can fall all too easily into a moral ditch through excess or deficiency. As Oxenham notes, "Too much justice can become tyranny, while not enough will degenerate into submissiveness and passivity."[46] Prudence helps us make this determination since justice must act prudently. As we walk in prudence's counsel and act in justice, we make ourselves more just and shape our character.

The third cardinal justice is fortitude. This virtue steels us to stand in hard places. It is "the virtue of resisting the impulse to turn away caused by fear of toil or danger."[47] Fortitude, or courage, helps us "regulate our fear" and "know what to do."[48] As with the virtue of justice, with fortitude, we need to find the place of the golden mean. An excess of fortitude leads us to take rash risks, whereas a deficiency of fortitude prevents us from standing under duress, which makes us cowards. Again, prudence helps us think clearly about our situation and to choose the best possible action. It also helps us discipline our emotions so that we become people of courage.

Temperance is the fourth cardinal virtue—a virtue we often think of as self-control. Temperance deals with the appetites, with, for example, the bodily desires for food, sex, or sleep. J. Philip Wogaman defines temperance as "the virtue of controlling the passions inciting us to act against reason."[49] For example, Aquinas mentions that a tem-

---

45 Pieper, *The Four Cardinal Virtues*, 49.
46 Oxenham, *Character and Virtue*, 107.
47 Wogaman, *Christian Ethics*, 91.
48 Boyd and Thorsen, *Christian Ethics and Moral Philosophy*, 159.
49 Wogaman, *Christian Ethics*, 91.

perate person eats food in a way that does not harm his or her health or reason. Once more, prudence helps us discern a moderate practice between excess (leading to gluttony) and deficiency (developing an eating disorder).

Theological Virtues

The apostle Paul concludes his hymn to love with these words: "And now these three remain: faith, hope, and love. But the greatest of these is love" (1 Cor 13:13). These three qualities make up the three theological virtues, which flow from supernatural grace. Kreeft writes that supernatural virtue is "the road to Paradise" and that "virtue is simply [the] health of [one's] soul."[50] According to the Christian virtue tradition, these three theological virtues infuse the cardinal virtues with grace and perfect them. We remain responsible to exercise subnatural virtue (e.g., the cardinal virtues) and develop habits of the soul that shape our character. But supernatural virtue (from God) forms us into saints.[51] With that in mind, we will now briefly consider the three theological virtues: faith, hope, and love.

Faith is the first theological virtue. It is our "yes" to God, and we exercise faith when we trust in him. Faith is our acceptance of God's proposal of marriage, where we link our future to God as our object of hope. Kreeft notes that "the object of faith is not the truths about God but the God who is Truth."[52] So we choose to believe that God will keep his promises as in the past. As a virtue, faith "is the habit of believing God. It is a disposition to believe that what God says is true

---

50 Kreeft, *Back to Virtue*, 56, 64.

51 Of course, we can also practice acts of sin which become habitual and deform our character toward vice. In such cases, we pursue a legitimate human good in an illicit manner. Along with the virtues, the Christian tradition recognizes capital vices: pride, envy, avarice, wrath, sloth, gluttony, and lust. See Boyd and Thorsen, *Christian Ethics and Moral Philosophy*, 163.

52 Kreeft, *Back to Virtue*, 74.

because it is God who has said it."[53] Therefore, faith takes counsel from love and reminds Christian prudence of God's faithful past deeds when we make decisions. For this reason, Pieper argues that charity holds pre-eminence over prudence. He writes, "Prudence is the mold of the moral virtues; but charity molds even prudence itself."[54] Faith is a supernatural gift, a theological virtue, given to Christians that we must cultivate by habitually trusting in the Father, Son, and Holy Spirit.

The second theological virtue, hope, points us toward a future good. Hope expects "a good that is possible" but also "difficult."[55] As with faith, hope looks to God as its object. "The virtue of hope is always in God and for God."[56] We hope for union with God not based upon our worthiness but because of God's goodness to people. Hope is grounded in revelation, which discloses God's person and plan for humanity. As Kreeft notes, hope is a definite response to God's specific revelation. In this virtue, we respond with these words: "I believe God, the God revealed in Scripture, the God revealed in Christ . . . [and] I hope for all the promises God has given us."[57] Thus, we do not experience hope as a vague, subjective feeling; rather, Christian hope grounds itself on a sure expectation of the Resurrection. We build our habit of expectation on the person of God. "God's promises will come true; there is no if, and, or but about it. For God is Truth itself."[58]

Love is the last of the theological virtues and the crowning one. The apostle Paul ranked love as preeminent among the virtues of faith and hope, for "the greatest of these is love" (1 Cor 13:13). God is love, so love expresses God's own nature. When we love others, we participate in the divine nature. Love stands at the center of Christian ethics

---

53 Boyd and Thorsen, *Christian Ethics and Moral Philosophy*, 161.
54 Pieper, *The Four Cardinal Virtues*, 44.
55 Boyd and Thorsen, *Christian Ethics and Moral Philosophy*, 162.
56 Boyd and Thorsen, *Christian Ethics and Moral Philosophy*, 162.
57 Kreeft, *Back to Virtue*, 75.
58 Kreeft, *Back to Virtue*, 75.

because Jesus taught us how to love through his own life and example. For example, Jesus commands us to love one another (John 15:10–17), including even our enemies, just as he showed love to those who mocked and nailed him to the cross. As a result, throughout Christian history, theologians have emphasized the role love plays in decision making and in character formation. Jesus' example is the revelation of love *par excellence* that gives us the supreme revelation of God's character and love. Therefore, love is the highest expression of a virtuous and happy life. Wogaman writes,

> The virtuous life, quintessentially expressed through love, has been a recurrent emphasis. That is central to the ethical thought of Thomas Aquinas, among others, and the goal of attaining Christian perfection in love is the heart of John Wesley's doctrine of sanctification.[59]

If we long to be like God, we will need to grow in love, and this requires an infusion of supernatural grace into our lives, for when we love, we participate in the life of the Trinity. As the apostle Peter wrote, we take part "in the divine nature" when we live victorious lives by God's divine power (2 Pet 1:4). Pieper writes that charity "is in essence a gift ultimately beyond the power of man's will or reason to bestow. It is an event unfathomable in any natural way, which takes place when the three theological virtues are 'infused' into our being."[60] And, as we build this virtue into our lives, love informs all the other virtues. For example, "prudence is the mold of the moral virtues; but charity molds even prudence itself."[61]

---

59 Wogaman, *Christian Ethics*, 317.
60 Pieper, *The Four Cardinal Virtues*, 44.
61 Pieper, *The Four Cardinal Virtues*, 44.

Wesley and the Ethical Life

John Wesley's theological teaching and practice work sympathetically with virtue ethics as a way of forming the tempers. Wesley was keenly aware of this ethical tradition. In fact, he refers specifically to this kind of teaching in his sermon, "The End of Christ's Coming," where he teaches that Jesus came to "destroy the works of the devil" (1 John 3:8). That is, in the incarnation, Jesus works to restore what humanity lost in its rebellion against heaven. God restores the *imago Dei* within each of us on the basis of the life, death, resurrection, and ascension of Jesus. At the beginning of the sermon, Wesley mentions how prominent authors painted both "the beauty of virtue" as well as "the deformity of vice." He notes how they emphasized "the beauty of virtue" as well as "the deformity of vice." He also mentions the emphasis they placed on "the happiness that attends virtue, and the misery which usually accompanies vice, and always follows it."[62] However, their beautiful words failed to help people conquer vicious habits in their lives. Therefore, Wesley says we need something stronger "if ever we would conquer vice, or steadily persevere in the practice of virtue," since in rebellion, humanity lost "the whole moral image of God,—righteousness and true holiness."[63] We find the answer in the reign of Christ. When Jesus rules in our hearts, he "destroys the works of the devil." God does this through the works of justification and sanctification.

Wesley understood sanctification as a restoration of the divine image and our growth in love. Christian love begins with the new birth, and we find that our love mixes with lesser loves (e.g., love of self, love of the world). Then as love matures, this leads hopefully to the moment of "entire sanctification," when the Spirit enables us to "love God with all your heart and with all your soul and with all your strength

---

62 Wesley, *John Wesley's Sermons*, 442.
63 Wesley, *John Wesley's Sermons*, 446.

and with all your mind" and to "love your neighbor as yourself" (Luke 10:27).[64] This perfecting of love produces a life of godliness and virtue.

As we can see, this central theme of Wesley's theology resonates with virtue ethics in several ways. For example, Wesley emphasizes the transformation of a person's character through sanctification by the empowerment of the Holy Spirit that produces a good life of holiness and love. But Wesley believed that this requires a divine-human synergy. A Christian cooperates with divine grace by attending both to the spiritual disciplines and to the means of grace (i.e., using habituation) while awaiting God's work of entire sanctification. Wesley then likens our attending to the love of God to seeking and finding "all [our] happiness in him."[65] Here we hear resonances of the crowning virtue of love changing us or, as Wesley teaches, restoring the image of God within our souls so that we find our final happiness in him.

Conclusion

Virtue ethics finds an important place in the history of Christian theology. Its promise of happiness, goodness, and abundant living encourages us to add virtuous qualities to our lives. The church found great value in the ancient Greek philosophers' ideas about virtue and the (cardinal) virtues they discovered. To these virtues, theologians added the theological virtues of faith, hope, and love. A powerful tradition, therefore, teaches us to add moral qualities to our lives—a tradition that spans from the Apostle Peter to the virtue theologians. They counsel us to add moral qualities into our lives. And if we do, Peter promises that we can participate in the communion of divine love shared between the three Persons in the Triune God. This makes

---

64 Dunning, *Reflecting the Divine Image*, 77.

65 See his sermon entitled "The Way of the Kingdom" in Wesley, *John Wesley's Sermons*, 125. Outler and Heitzenrater note Wesley's emphasis on both "holiness and happiness" in their introductory comments on this sermon. See, Wesley, *John Wesley's Sermons*, 123.

us into good, virtuous Christian people who find their ultimate happiness in God.

Bibliography

Aquinas, Thomas. *A Summa of the Summa*. Edited by Peter Kreeft. San Francisco: Ignatius, 1990.

Aristotle. *Nicomachean Ethics*, translated by Terence Irwin. Indianapolis: Hackett, 1985.

Augustine. "On the Morals of the Catholic Church." In *The Complete Ante-Nicene and Nicene and Post-Nicene Church Fathers Collection*. Edited by Philip Schaff, vol. 18. London: Catholic Way, 2014.

Boyd, Craig A., and Don Thorsen. *Christian Ethics and Moral Philosophy: An Introduction to Issues and Approaches*. Grand Rapids: Baker Academic, 2018.

Dunning, H. Ray. *Reflecting the Divine Image: Christian Ethics in Wesleyan Perspective*. Downers Grove: InterVarsity, 1998.

Kreeft, Peter. *Back to Virtue: Traditional Moral Wisdom for Modern Moral Confusion*. San Francisco: Ignatius, 1992.

Mattison III, William C. *Introducing Moral Theology: True Happiness and the Virtues*. Grand Rapids: Brazos, 2008.

Oxenham, Marvin. *Character and Virtue in Theological Education: An Academic Epistolary Novel*. Carlisle, Cumbria: Langham Global Library, 2019.

Pieper, Josef. *The Four Cardinal Virtues: Prudence, Justice, Fortitude, Temperance*. Notre Dame: University of Notre Dame Press, 1965.

Plato. *The Dialogues of Plato*, translated by Benjamin Jowett, 5 vols. 3rd ed., vol. 2. London: Oxford University Press, 1931.

Wesley, John. *John Wesley's Sermons: An Anthology*. Edited by Albert C. Outler and Richard P. Heitzenrater. Nashville: Abingdon, 1991.

Wogaman, J. Philip. *Christian Ethics: A Historical Introduction.* 2nd ed. Louisville: Westminster John Knox, 2011.

19

CRITICAL PEDAGOGY IN THEOLOGICAL EDUCATION AND SPIRITUALITY

Ernesto Lozano

Do your best to present yourself to God as one approved, a worker who does not need to be ashamed and who correctly handles the word of truth.

2 Timothy 2:15

Recognition

Spirituality is a characteristic that many believe should be embedded in an educator, especially one serving in a Christian field. Sadly, this is not the reality in many cases. Instead, learners adopt the model of their teachers for convenience. By convenience, I mean how the person at the front of the class does not show any sign of love, care, or compassion but demonstrates power as a convenience to his or her position. Learners then adopt that position of power when they are at the front of a class in the future and so end up oppressing their students, which may indicate a lack of spirituality. I have never seen such personal convenience toward others in the life of Floyd Cunningham.

There are many things I learned from Floyd Cunningham. I arrived in the Philippines in 2011, tired after almost three days of travel. The president himself held my luggage, carried it to the trunk of the car, and helped me with the accommodations in the school. In my years at APNTS, I saw Floyd and other professors doing the same for many students. Floyd cared for people and their stories first rather than focusing on academics. He built relationships that allowed students to acquire knowledge.

Introduction

A few years ago, I had the opportunity to encounter a new educator and philosopher, Paulo Freire. I had never heard of him before and had no idea about his importance, origin, or even his representative ideas. Through Freire, I also learned about a new term, "critical pedagogy," which means to create "academic health" inside and outside the learning space.[1] When I grasped and learned about Freire's idea, I began to look for applications in my life, but more importantly, how these changes in my life could affect the lives of others.

Nowadays, several sources help people understand critical pedagogy. However, through Paulo Freire's *Pedagogy of the Oppressed*, I saw oppression in academia and how it has expanded its roots and power to the classroom. While reading this book, I realized I had been educated in the same way Freire describes: oppressively. I believed that transferring and accepting information, regardless of the content, was the only way to educate. It was the way I was educated and the way I should teach as well. When educators embrace oppressive systems, they lack spirituality, empathy, love, and respect for others.

---

1 Malvicini, "Critical Pedagogy."

In this essay, I will expand upon the philosophy behind critical pedagogy and compare Paulo Freire with other educators who have applied Freire's theories of education. Although Freire developed this idea in Latin America, it is now possible to find educators using his philosophies around the world. I will present the meaning of oppression and liberation in education and the process of liberation through rebellion, not a rebellion with guns and hate, but one that demonstrates the desire to move from one place to another, from the very "comfortable" setting (where you demand) to a more suitable setting (where you serve). Critical pedagogy can be applied to different fields in ministry, from the pulpit to the classroom. Finally, I will use personal experiences to integrate what was researched about critical pedagogy and the importance of its application in the development of the spirituality of the educator.

Critical Pedagogy

In order to understand the origin and importance of critical pedagogy, it is important to know about Freire's ideas and the intentions behind his philosophy. There are reasons to critically examine educational systems that are still used in many countries around the world today. One is the lack of knowledge of critical pedagogy, and another is comfort. "Comfort" refers to those who are in higher places and prefer to prevent the masses from receiving a better education. Sadly, this is also a common issue in theological education, where a lack of spirituality is exposed.

Paulo Freire was born in Brazil in 1922 and raised in a Catholic environment. His mother highly influenced him. His family's economic situation was significantly affected by the Depression of 1929 in the United States of America. He grew up in what some considered the middle class, while others might call it complete poverty. Years later, he was forced to leave his country and go into exile, having been labeled a traitor. He did not return to his country for fifteen years.[2] Different experiences like this and witnessing the effects of a "post-World War" created new ways of thinking for him, including the desire to change and create change in others. What better place to do so than in the educational setting![3]

Freire became the author and main representative of critical pedagogy. Due to his experience under an oppressive system, he was able to see how oppression has influenced education leading to a lack of learning opportunities for people. In *Pedagogy of the Oppressed,* Freire says oppression equals "dehumanization."[4] To dehumanize is to remove all feelings that a person may have and the capacity of that person to think, create, or meditate. A person cannot answer with his or her own ideas, for these are surely wrong. A person in the position of an oppressor who lacks spirituality represents a dehumanizer and grasps personhood as something of no value. If such a person lacks spirituality, he or she may not accept other people's ideas. For example, students will be separated or ostracized when they ask questions, contradict the teacher, or give their opinions. This can be understood in two ways: first, students' ideas are viewed as irrelevant, and second, the teacher sees no need to change. Learners who see that attitude in a teacher will emulate it and become the next dehumanizers, making the cycle repeat.

Critical pedagogy is a philosophy that considers different aspects of life as part of the educational system, including inequality, social class, and race. In some situations, these aspects are separated from the life of learners, and all things to be learned become oppressive. The main

---

2 Núñez, "Paulo Freire"; Morrow and Torres, Reading Freire and Habermas, 1.
3 Kincheloe, *Critical Pedagogy,* 12.
4 Freire, *Pedagogy of the Oppressed,* 28.

target of critical pedagogy is to free the learner from such oppressive things in order to "transform the world into a better place."[5]

Critical pedagogy covers different areas and is not limited to the classroom or the teacher. To produce critical pedagogy effectively, what the culture offers must be embraced and interest shown in the learners.[6] This embrace is very important because what the learner receives is not just from the direction of the teacher only but what interests the learner. As a result, a new term emerged called "cultural pedagogy." Joe L. Kincheloe argues that this concept refers to the values surrounding learners that make them aware of their condition. The combination of culture and teaching creates awareness that education does not only "take place in the classroom" but also "takes place in popular culture."[7]

Kincheloe gives an extensive list of related areas covered in the philosophy of critical pedagogy. For example, critical pedagogy is "grounded on a social and educational vision of justice and equality." Kincheloe says that an education based on repetition and without vision does not achieve any particular point of progress. To reconceptualize "educational standards," there is a need for a direct approach with the learner and the community that holds these standards. How will teachers provide what learners need if they are not interested in their needs? Can they change their thinking by not understanding their context or reality?[8]

In addition, critical pedagogy seeks to reduce "human suffering" and prevent learners "from being hurt." Although it is commonly understood that students learn only through assignments, this method is only a small part of the learning process. There is also a need for

---

5 Koay, "What is Critical Pedagogy?"
6 Kincheloe, *Critical Pedagogy*, 5.
7 Kincheloe, "Critical Pedagogy in the Twenty-first Century," 24.
8 Kincheloe, *Critical Pedagogy*, 6–8.

practical application and activities. The learning process comes from every source that is a part of the "everyday life" of learners. Great stories stand behind people who are suffering and discriminated against. Discrimination is a human-made pain. Such pain should not exist in critical pedagogy inside or outside the classroom because critical pedagogy seeks to respect the knowledge each student brings.[9]

What Kincheloe describes as respect is an important concept in critical pedagogy. In *Pedagogy of Freedom,* Paulo Freire calls it "respect for what students know." He argues that no learner comes empty but already has formal learning and experience. Teachers should "take advantage" of what learners experience each day. Respect allows teachers to have a starting point and establish an "intimate" relationship between learner and instructor.[10] In oppressive educational systems, students are told to forget all they know, and nothing learned or done before was the right way. A spiritual facilitator seeks to grasp every person's ideas in a classroom and make these ideas part of the learning process so that they are relevant to students' lives and, more importantly, their ministries.

In a movie presented during the "Effective Teaching Methods" class, I could see and understand the importance of respect for what learners already know and how this knowledge can build a relationship. The movie, *Freedom Writers,* is based on the story of Erin Gruwell, a professor in Long Beach, California. When there was no way to connect with the group to which she was assigned, she used students' stories to develop a new learning experience that required care and confidence. Later, this experience generated growth in all the learners. This approach was successful once and has been proven true many times

---

9 Kincheloe, *Critical Pedagogy,* 11–15.
10 Freire, *Pedagogy of Freedom,* 36–37.

since. Today, Gruwell's students are professionals, and some have become educators.[11]

I myself come from an oppressive system. I studied in a government high school where there was no interest in knowing who the students were or their backgrounds. We were simply called by numbers. For five years, I was number thirty. Now I wonder if there was any interest in our names or in knowing the persons behind the numbers or their backgrounds or needs. Many things have not changed since I left school, including the connection between learners and instructors. A gap between learner and instructor still exists that does not allow students to grow. As Freire says, the process of dehumanization is present and did not start there. Furthermore, it will not end when this level of education is completed.[12]

In the classical way of education, the instructor is the one who is responsible for providing information to the learners. The instructor transfers information to the students, a process that will be explored later in this essay. In critical pedagogy, however, the responsibility falls on both sides. Learning requires as much interest from the learner as it does in the one who teaches. In critical pedagogy, students are allowed to think critically and "take risks" in order to change and become "responsive" to the problems they encounter.[13]

Transferring information is part of the classical educational system. Freire presents it as the "banking concept" whereby learners are considered empty vessels. Their minds are filled with content that is "detached from the reality" of their lives. The key concept of this process is repetition. In cases like this, the instructor knows all, and the learner knows nothing.[14] The banking approach to education is

---

11 LaGravenese, *Freedom Writers*.
12 Freire, *Pedagogy of Freedom*, 36.
13 Giroux, *On Critical Pedagogy*, 14.
14 Freire, *Pedagogy of the Oppressed*, 57–58.

common practice. Although it is not presented in those terms, it is frequently used among educators. Gabrielle Micheletti says this practice does not allow any learner to grow. Learners are condemned to be receptors or collectors. Treating students as "objects" is another example of dehumanization.[15]

Referring to Freire's banking concept of education, Robert E. Peterson says that this concept is very front-oriented, meaning that the teacher carries the knowledge of everything. Peterson says that this model is the "most prevalent" model. He reports that surveys interestingly show only one percent of instruction time is dedicated to discussion that allows students to think and have opinions.[16]

Another important aspect mentioned in the banking concept is critical thinking. It is not easy to differentiate between critical and non-critical thinking. Linda Elder and Paul Richard describe the difference between the two. On the one hand, critical thinkers are good at thinking and including others. They want to improve as they advance and want others to improve and grow. On the other hand, non-critical thinking is self-focused. Such a person may be good at thinking but tends to discriminate against others, not just their ideas but their whole person, including culture and background.[17] Critical pedagogy seeks to facilitate and provide tools to help instructors reach learners.

Critical Pedagogy on Oppression and Liberation in Education

Oppressive Education

Critical pedagogy was created to eradicate oppression. This oppression was commonly seen as normal and not affecting the educational process. However, Freire argues that this oppression must end, and

---

15 Micheletti, "Re-Envisioning Paulo Freire's Banking Concept of Education."
16 Peterson, "Teaching How to Read the World and Change It," 366.
17 Elder and Paul, *Guide to Critical Thinking*, 3–4.

when it is over, freedom is possible.[18] Critical pedagogy breaks down systems and walls that put barriers between people.

Freire says that oppressors are the main dehumanizers who, by taking advantage of their power, abuse others and very seldom find themselves with the capacity to liberate others or themselves. Oppressors cannot easily move from that reality unless they become aware of their own situation and what they have done to others by depriving them of their voice. In some situations, the oppressors may tend to "soften" their power, but alleviating such conditions and not eliminating them creates "false generosity," which becomes an unending circle of injustices.[19]

Oppression is manifested in different ways. Freire states that one way is to be prejudiced toward race, gender, or economic status. When there is prejudice, there is a "refusal to listen" to groups different from oneself. "I cannot speak with them, only to or at them," thus creating a sense of superiority or unreachableness.[20]

In an oppressive system, learners are like slaves. There are contradictions "between poles," with the educator on one side and learners on the other. In an oppressive classroom where students have learned to be slaves, the process goes as follows: "The teacher teaches, and the students are taught" as mere objects to deposit information. "The teacher knows everything, and the students know nothing." Students are not respected or even considered contributors to the learning process. Another example is that the teachers are the only ones capable of thinking and talking. The students are "thought about as listeners." These different patterns are constantly repeated, and teachers show only authority at the front of the classroom. Another example is when the "teacher chooses and enforces his [or her] choice" over students

---

18 Giroux, *On Critical Pedagogy*, 3.
19 Freire, *Pedagogy of the Oppressed*, 28–35.
20 Freire, *Pedagogy of Freedom*, 108.

who are not permitted to decide. Even more significant than these is that "the teacher is the subject of the learning process, while the pupils are mere objects."[21] The structure mentioned above is how the educational systems in most countries operate and how I was educated. There was no opportunity in the classroom to share, even if we knew the teacher was wrong.

In addition to what Freire says regarding the teacher being the authority in the front of the classroom, he explains that the learners' attitude as mere listeners produces obstruction in communication by which the students are reduced to "things," an action characteristic of an oppressor.[22]

In order for students to learn, there must be interaction. Communication is the "only option" to transform learners. Learning and transformation do not happen in seclusion, like in an "ivory tower," but through communication. In order to avoid authority coming from the front of the classroom, there is a need for "horizontal communication" where there is no participant that is higher or lower, and there are no differences in the process of interaction.[23]

The educational system I grew up in was very similar to the one described above and was the only way I knew about teaching and learning. I needed to accept all that was given to me by the teacher. From the very first day of class at all levels of my education, teachers presented themselves as people with years of experience. We were not allowed to question their teaching, and to question them was disrespectful. This system is still ongoing and accepted.

Oppression in educational systems is more common than we might imagine. Rosa Perez-Isiah notes that classrooms are filled with

---

21 Freire, *Pedagogy of the Oppressed*, 58–59.
22 Freire, *Pedagogy of the Oppressed*, 123.
23 Sabercat,"Communication is the Key to Education"; Freire, *Pedagogy of the Oppressed*, 63; and Araujo, Vallecilla, Gómez, González, and Pareja, "La Pedagogía Crítica el Verdadero Camino Hacia la Transfrmación Social."

different ethnicities, economic statuses, and genders. Educators know the reality but know little about how to deal with these situations. This kind of thinking of knowing that there are things to change but not doing anything to change them is called "passive oppression." In passive oppression, indifference and a lack of action exist. Although educators may care for the needs of their students, they lack resources or the desire to act toward change.[24]

I mentioned oppression in education with its different implications, but I would like to bring up a theological understanding of oppression. The Peruvian theologian, Gustavo Gutierrez, says that oppression is equally a "sinful situation." It is sinful because where oppression exists, there is no peace among different entities and no equality but mainly a strong rejection of God.[25] Gutierrez's reason for writing this comes from his experience in Latin America, where tremendous gaps exist between rich and poor. These gaps create inequality in the educational system in Peru and around the continent, especially in those nations once colonized.

Oppression is not a modern concept or practice but is also found in the Bible. In those days, the oppressed were slaves, like the Israelites in Egypt. Exodus 1:12 says, "But the more they were oppressed, the more they multiplied and the more they spread abroad. And the Egyptians were in dread of the people of Israel" (ESV). The Israelites were controlled by others who took advantage of their superiority, treating the Israelites with cruelty and pain. Jack Wellman refers to this as being like what Freire refers to as the oppressed in education: people with "no control of their own lives," "who have no freedoms," and are "living in a state of bondage."[26]

---

24 Perez-Isiah, *Medium*.
25 Gutierrez, *A Theology of Liberation*, 109.
26 Wellman, "Patheos."

Gutierrez argues that oppression is a sin. Wellman adds that God "strictly prohibits oppression." In Leviticus 6:2, oppressive acts are exposed "if anyone sins and is unfaithful to the Lord by deceiving a neighbor about something entrusted to them or left in their care or about something stolen, or if they cheat their neighbor" (NIV). Jesus came to save the lost, including the oppressed ones who were sick and possessed by a strong oppressor. Jesus declared about himself, "The Spirit of the Lord is on me, because he has anointed me to proclaim good news to the poor. He has sent me to proclaim freedom for the prisoners and recovery of sight for the blind, to set the oppressed free" (Luke 4:18, NIV).[27]

Liberated Education

Oppression, as negative as it is, is a reality. Sadly, this reality is extended to all settings, including the educational system and the classroom. However, there is hope for the oppressor to change. When the oppressor changes, the effects are like a wave that affects the oppressed. Together, they become free.

Freire says that the process of liberation is a "painful" stage for the oppressor. For liberation to happen and a new humanity to develop, oppressors must be aware of the reality of oppression. They need to know what they are doing to others and themselves.[28] Goulet states that for Freire, education is a way of liberating from a slavery that keeps us from dialoguing.[29] Liberation requires the active participation of the oppressed. There should be a desire to move on. "For this liberation to be authentic and complete, it has to be undertaken by the oppressed people themselves and so must stem from the values proper to these people."[30]

---

27 Wellman, "Patheos."
28 Freire, *Pedagogy of the Oppressed*, 33–34.
29 Goulet, "Introduction," viii.
30 Gutierrez, *A Theology of Liberation*, 91, 108–109.

I would like to return to one experience during my high school years. Of all my professors and classes, a particular one was different. The class was *Orientación y Bienestar del Educando* (Student Orientation and Wellness). Although the professor was rumored to be rigorous, on the first day of class, he presented himself not as a professor but as a "friend" who was there to "help and assist" students with their different needs. I did not know he used the approach of critical pedagogy. I have no idea whether he ever read Freire's philosophy. I just know that he was our friend. After the first semester, when the grades were turned in, he asked the ones who failed subjects to approach him. In silence, he listened to their stories and asked whether they were student-workers and brought support for their families. After that, he advocated to other professors for a second chance. That particular class, in a way, was a class to liberate ourselves, at least for two hours per week.

Related to the above story, Freire in *Pedagogy of Freedom* says that teachers who use words related to students' context are the ones who really teach and not the ones who use words like "Do as I say." To provide freedom in the room, there is a need for critical thinking in which the learner can value and evaluate the words. For Freire, the leaders, in this case, are the instructors responsible for imparting knowledge. Leaders no longer threaten the oppressed or the learners as "possessions."[31]

In the process of change, according to Freire, the oppressor and oppressed require mutual respect. This is because the process of transformation is not an easy one. The keyword to understand is "solidarity." From the oppressors' side, solidarity means being aware of their responsibility. How do they treat the ones under them? "True solidarity is found only in the plenitude of an act of love." From the side of the oppressed, solidarity requires rejecting the image they received

---

31 Freire, *Pedagogy of Freedom*, 39; Freire, *Pedagogy of the Oppressed*, 120.

from the oppressor and replacing it with "autonomy and responsibility."[32] Oppression blocks communication, and the process of liberation brings "reconciliation."[33] In the words of Peter Roberts, "Liberation is conceived as a process of struggle against oppression."[34]

Since oppression in this paper is focused on the classroom or the educational system, liberation is also addressed in the same field. In the classroom, it is important to start from the (no longer) higher authority or previously mentioned authority in the front of the classroom. Moving from verticality to horizontality is important, where relationship reigns overall. Hence, there is a need for a "critical teacher." The critical teacher is the one who asks and provides different opinions and perspectives from their peers or students regarding ideas, curriculum, and other related matters. This educator breaks the "discomfort" by bringing comfort to the room. There is a facilitation of the learning process because the learner is no longer in an unknown area or "terrain."[35]

Gutierrez writes about Freire and his philosophy of liberation, that liberation happens when the oppressed become aware of their reality. Gutierrez and Freire particularly talk about the oppression experienced by the people of Latin America. The educational system is the way to exit or liberate ourselves from the reality of poverty and oppression. Gutierrez comments that "the focus of liberating education was to help the poor to take control of their own destiny and their own liberation." In this case, the oppressed or learners can "release the hidden creativity" that was dependent upon other agencies.[36]

Miguel A. De la Torre understands Freire and liberation similarly to Gutierrez. De la Torre says that his predecessor is Freire, not

---

32 Freire, *Pedagogy of the Oppressed,* 34-35.
33 Freire, *Pedagogy of the Oppressed,* 59.
34 Roberts, "Liberation, Oppression and Education," 83-87.
35 Kincheloe, *Critical Pedagogy,* 109-111.
36 Gutierrez, *The Density of the Present,* 73-74.

Gutierrez. He points out that Freire's focus was highly interested in promoting "literacy among his people." Freire did not want to feed his people with formulas but with the "tools" so they could liberate themselves from the system. He wanted them to be negotiators of their own liberation.[37]

Peter McLaren provides a good example of liberation in the classroom that helps to break the banking concept in education. He states that rather than explaining and putting theory in the mind of the students, an option is to introduce the learners to activities in the community outside the four walls of the classroom, where the learners can see rather than hear about reality.[38]

Revolution for Freedom in Education

It is clear that there is oppression, but as well, there is hope for liberation. But how can people be part of that process? What can the oppressed do to be active in their own liberation? Freire says that there is a need for a revolution. If people are committed to liberation, "their action and reflection cannot proceed without the action and reflection of others." The revolution is not with guns but through dialogue or conversation between the (no longer) oppressor and oppressed. "The earlier dialogue begins, the more truly revolutionary will the movement be."[39] This process is what Freire calls "praxis," which means putting "theory into action."[40]

As Christians, it is important to understand that we must be different from the world. Gutierrez says, "To be a Christian is to be in solidarity." Mildred Bangs Wynkoop says that to be a mediator is to be a healer in the process of progress. "Christian revolutionists are not called to be executioners or undertakers. Christian revolution is a

---

37 De la Torre, *The Hope of Liberation in World Religions*, 97–98.
38 McLaren, *Life in Schools*, 118.
39 Freire, *Pedagogy of the Oppressed*, 120–122.
40 Shor, *When Students Have Power*, 41.

healing ministry. It is infinitely more difficult to bind up wounds than to cut off heads," but it is a process that demonstrates humbleness and acquaintance with reality.[41]

Applying Wynkoop's concept to our time, we should have a space for revolution in our classrooms. Revolution means a change in how educators see students and respect for what they know. Revolution involves shaking the ground, opening the space for all to be learners, and breaking the vertical relationship.

Application of Critical Pedagogy in Education and Ministry

In order to understand the need for critical pedagogy in Peru and other countries that the Spaniards colonized, including the Philippines, it is important to have some basic knowledge of the background of education. There are two types of schools in Peru, public and private, and most of these offer three levels: kindergarten, primary school, and high school. Universities are also divided into public and private. The government directs all the public schools and universities with a specific and similar curriculum, regardless of the students' region, condition, or economic status. For both public and private schools, parents face fees and other expenses. Since education is mandatory, it is the responsibility of the parents to facilitate schooling for their children. University education is not mandatory but is the last stage of education in most situations.

A very famous Peruvian composer, Nicomedes Santa Cruz, wrote a poem back in the 1960s that summarizes the educational system of his time. Almost sixty years later, few changes or improvements have been made in the schools in Peru or other countries in Latin America. As a primary and high school student, I was forced to memorize the poem as part of my learning process. The educators wanted to emphasize not just the "art" behind the poem, which in Spanish has a rhythm,

---

41 Gutierrez, *A Theology of Liberation*, 113; Wynkoop, *John Wesley*, 50.

but that education with "blood" was the right one and should remain. The poem is "La Escuelita," "The Little School." It goes as follows:

The Little School

> With a hard knock on my forehead, I learnt
> My role as student
> In the little school
> In the barrio where I was born.
>
> To have full primary studies
> It was rare when I was a child
> We sat three in one desk
> The *palmeta* (wood ruler to hit the hand) was invented for me
> Once it was broken on my hand
> And I was called "iron hand"
> And besides that
> With a knock in my forehead, I learnt.
>
> I was playful since I was born
> And since I play during break time
> I failed in cleanliness
> Almost failed my other grades
> But I failed in behavior
> All because I fought at the exit
> With my fellow partners.
>
> I was a champion in spinning tops!
> I was great skipping classes!
> But for playing I was there!
> I failed in arithmetic
> I failed in geography
> Almost failed my oral exam

And the same in the written one
If my friend did not whisper the answers
I wouldn't say "almost" at this point
And had to repeat the year.

I barely finished my last year
It was a hard journey
I threw away my white shirt
That was made out of flour sacks
I cry over the time I wasted
Now with no future on my hands
Other children are the same
But, with a knock on my forehead, I learnt.

As part of Peruvian folklore, this poem vividly represents what the educational system was and still is. There is an expression related to this poem: "The *palmeta* was invented for me; once it was broken on my hand." This is what educators call in Peru *La Letra con Sangre Entra*, which means "The Letter Enters with Blood." The expression suggests that the "Letter" is education, and the "Blood" is punishment. I grew up with that system. We were called to the front in groups of five or six. We needed to memorize the multiplication table. The professor dictated numbers to multiply. The ones who answered fast took their place at their desk. In the end, the last two, the "slow ones," remained to receive their instruction with pain. I was among the "slow ones."

For many years, I believed that this particular way of educating was only Peruvian. Years later, I became aware that these bad practices were not only in the Peruvian system but also in the Spaniard colonization system that oppressed other conquered countries. I was able to find tremendous similarities between Peru and the Philippines, as well as other countries in Latin America.

Rafael Palma, one of the most prominent educators in the Philippines, who was first educated under the Spaniard education system, described his years of education in ways similar to the poem by Santa Cruz. Palma writes, "The teacher spanked with a disk of wood about two inches thick with an arm-like structure for a handle. This device was called a *palmeta*. What power that instrument had in improving the pupils' writing is hard to determine, but the saying that 'Letters enter with Blood' was believed implicitly in those days, and my teacher adhered to the belief most faithfully."[42]

Since those days, the practice of "The Letter Enters with Blood" has been reduced considerably, especially in private schools where parents have more control. However, some educators still believe that "blood" is needed to learn. In the online journal *El Liberal Popayan*, there are examples of the punishments given by professors, including "hits on the hand with the *palmeta*," pulling ears, standing in the corner of the classroom facing the wall, standing facing the sun, using of hot bricks, and others. Most educators do not practice physical punishment. However, psychological abuse reigns in classrooms. Professors and students nowadays use abusive words that affect the student's self-esteem. There are campaigns to remove the distance between educators and learners so that teachers can influence learners externally and internally.[43]

Oppression in education in Peru is an ongoing issue. The schools at all levels model authority in front of the classroom. The professors have the only and last word regarding the things to impart and share. While in primary school, as mentioned earlier, we were just called by numbers. The professors required some of the classrooms to be divided into two groups. One example is the classroom divided into "good and bad calligraphy." Those who had better handwriting were

---

42 Palma, *My Autobiography*, 15.
43 Ministerio de Educación, "Seguimiento."

promoted to use pens rather than pencils. The group that used pens was privileged to be next to see the board. The ones who used pencils did not have that privilege yet. Another segregation was by grades. Those with the same average point were together, so there were two groups, the "smart" and the "lazy." Although this division is not common anymore, it is still practiced in some schools, especially in the highlands and jungles. Since many pastors of our time were educated that way, they have transferred the same attitudes to their churches. Their authority is not from the front of the class but from the pulpit.

During my years of high school, I experienced oppression. One professor was different because he cared for the students. Other instructors only entered the classroom to do their job, deposit information, and leave without communication. It was believed that relationships were covered by the school counselor or educational psychologist. The teacher's job starts when they enter the room and ends when they leave.

As the years have passed, some people may believe that the educational system has made progress, but it did not happen during my years at college or even Bible college. The banking concept of education described by Freire was exactly what I experienced. Although architecture requires creativity and imagination, we were limited and graded as per our instructors' criteria. The grading system of evaluation in Peru is from 0 to 20. It was never possible to achieve the highest grade. Teachers say that they never got a 20 from their professors, so they cannot give their students that grade, so we should be content with a 13.

Most of the people from my generation grew up under the same system. I heard about new types of oppressors in schools and even in churches. Church leaders act oppressive by using their "power" to control others. I found some liberation during my education, but the amount was very low. Oppressiveness was and still is more prevalent than liberation. If there was freedom in education, the masses could see the reality and would not remain in their same status.

Peru is a country that is known for having hardworking people and people who are highly creative. However, that creativity is allowed only outside the classroom. If creativity were extended to the classroom through critical pedagogy, it would be possible to have better learners. Peru is oppressive in education, which makes learners always be at the bottom of rankings regarding critical thinking. Peru is at the bottom of the educational system in South America and the world. It took me getting out of my country to realize there was a way to be free.

Critical pedagogy must be presented in the classroom because the average person spends 25% of his or her life there. No longer do students need to be fearful. Moreover, there is no need for blood education. Applying critical pedagogy and critical thinking will allow students to reach their capacity with no fear of judgment. By fear, I mean the endless restrictions that professors create. The educational system in Peru is created to prepare students as if everything comes from the same place, origin, or status.

Conclusions

This study has shown that the present practice needs to be changed. There is a need for critical pedagogy in Peru and many other places around the world. Applying critical pedagogy does not mean starting all over and expecting immediate changes. Rather, there is a need to create awareness in the minds of people. First, people need to be aware that there is oppression and that educators are oppressors over students. The same must happen in the church as pastors become aware of their attitudes. Additionally, the responsibility to liberate falls not only in the hands of the teacher or pastor but with students and church members.

The process of transformation is slow but not impossible. Schools and churches in Peru and around the world need to be transformed in order to produce a new generation that can think critically and act in thoughtful ways. Critical thinking is not just allowing students to think for themselves but primarily helping them to think together with the educator. Then learners will be able to push themselves to any reality in the future.

Bibliography

Araujo, Jesucita, Jenny B. Vallecilla, Janet Gómez, Francisco J. González, and María Teresa Pareja. "La Pedagogía Crítica el Verdadero Camino Hacia la Transformación Social." *Universidad de Manizales*, 2015. Translated by Ernesto Lozano.

De la Torre, Miguel. *The Hope of Liberation in World Religions*. Waco: Baylor University Press, 2008.

Elder, Linda, and Richard Paul. *Guide to Critical Thinking*. Tomales: Foundation for Critical Thinking, 2009.

Freire, Paulo. *Pedagogy of the Oppressed*. Translated by Myra Bergam. New York: Continuum Publishing Corporation, 1984.

———. *Pedagogy of Freedom: Ethics, Democracy, and Civic Courage*. Translated by Patrick Clarke. Lanham: Rowman & Littlefield, 2001.

Giroux, Henry A. *On Critical Pedagogy*. New York: Bloomsbury, 2011.

Goulet, Denis. "Introduction." In *Education for Critical Consciousness*, by Paulo Freire. New York: Continuum, 2005.

Gutierrez, Gustavo. *A Theology of Liberation: History, Politics, and Salvation*. Translated by Caridad Inda and John Eagleson. Maryknoll: Orbis, 1973.

———. *The Density of the Present: Selected Writings*. Maryknoll, NY: Orbis, 1999.

Kincheloe, Joe L. *Critical Pedagogy*. New York: Peter Lang, 2008.

———. "Critical Pedagogy in the Twenty-first Century: Evolution for Survival." In *Critical Pedagogy: Where Are We Now?* Edited by Peter McLaren and Joel Koncheloe. New York: Peter Lang, 2007.

Koay, Jeremy. "What is Critical Pedagogy?" March 30, 2016. Accessed April 5, 2019. http://www.edumaxi.com/what-is-critical-pedagogy/.

LaGravenese, Richard. *Freedom Writers.* MTV Films. DVD, 2007.

McLaren, Peter. *Life in Schools: An Introduction to Critical Pedagogy in the Foundations of Education.* Boulder: Paradigm, 2015.

Malvicini, Pete. "Critical Pedagogy." Lecture, Asia-Pacific Nazarene Theological Seminary. Manila, July 14, 2017.

Micheletti, Gabrielle. "Re-Envisioning Paulo Freire's Banking Concept of Education." *Inquiries Journal.* 2010. (http://www.inquiriesjournal.com/articles/171/re-envisioning-paulo-freires-banking-concept-of-education). Accessed April 2019.

Ministerio de Educación. "Seguimiento." n.d. Accessed April 2019. https://www.mineducacion.gov.co/cvn/1665/printer-105555.html.

Morrow, Raymond A., and Carlos Torres. *Reading Freire and Habermas: Critical Pedagogy and Transformative Social Change.* New York: Teachers College Press, 2002.

Núñez, Emilio A. "Paulo Freire: Educación Bancaria y Educación Liberadora." *EBSCOhost.* June 2006. Accessed April 2019. http://web.a.ebscohost.com/ehost/pdfviewer/pdfviewer?vid=4&sid=2d90c47e-7396-43af-a4c8-8204b1362735%40sdc-v-sessmgr01.

Palma, Rafael. *My Autobiography.* Translated by Alicia Palma. Manila: Capitol, 1943.

Perez-Isiah, Rosa. *Medium.* January 22, 2018. Accessed April 5, 2019. https://medium.com/identity-education-and-power/passive-oppression-in-education-fueling-the-achievement-gap-af637f8c3718.

Peterson, Robert E. "Teaching How to Read the World and Change It." In *The Critical Pedagogy Reader,* edited by Antonia Darder, Marta Baltodano and Rodolfo Torres. New York: Routledge, 2003.

Roberts, Peter. "Liberation, Oppression and Education: Extending Freirean Ideas." *Journal of Educational Thought* 42, no. 1 (2008): 83-87.

Sabercat. "Communication is the Key to Education." October 16 (2017). Accessed April 6, 2019. https://medium.com/@sabercats9324/communication-is-the-key-to-education-e12ad8fa6a2a.

Shor, Ira. *When Students Have Power: Negotiating Authority in a Critical Pedagogy.* Chicago: The University of Chicago Press, 1996.

Wellman, Jack. *Patheos.* August 18 (2015). Accessed April 6, 2019. https://www.patheos.com/blogs/christiancrier/2015/08/18/what-does-oppressed-mean-a-biblical-definition-of-oppressed/.

Wynkoop, Mildred B. *John Wesley: Christian Revolutionary.* Kansas City: Beacon Hill, 1970.

20

ON SPIRITUALITY AS EMBODIED HOLINESS: A WESLEYAN PERSPECTIVE

Charlie M. Cubalit

Introduction

Religion, in general, concerns itself with the question of spirituality. It is inherent in the symbolic rituals and ceremonies that compose the nature of religion. As Watson argues, a "co-dependency" exists between spirituality and religion, so religious practices are deemed the only way to validate spirituality.[1] It is no wonder that there is rising interest in spirituality despite advancement in an age of postmodernity and highly techno-digital postmodern society. A quick search with Google of the term alone yields many perspectives not limited to Christianity.

---

1 Watson, "Whose Model of Spirituality."

In the Wesleyan perspective, spirituality ought to be defined within the context of the doctrine of holiness. In this essay, I will try to explore Floyd Cunningham's notion of spirituality, reflecting primarily on his essay entitled, "Holiness Embodied in the Asia-Pacific Context," published and accessible on the Church of the Nazarene's teaching website, *didache.nazarene.org;* and alongside this, his Inaugural Address during his installation as the Seminary President in 2008 entitled, "Building New Bridges." Only when necessary for the sake of my arguments will I quote or refer to his other relevant essays. This is because, among his many essays, I believe these two are the most succinct and summarizing representatives of his understanding of embodied holiness and encapsulate his missionary heart oriented in Wesleyan theology expressed in written form. This is an attempt not only to define spirituality from a Wesleyan perspective but also to draw up a kind of spirituality in missions or ministry.

Spirituality in Wesleyan Orientation

Spirituality presumes an essence or substance that can only be metaphysically argued for. Yet even clinical practitioners who depend so much on objective scientific phenomena cannot deny the phenomenon of spirituality among patients. Lepherd, for example, recognizes the phenomenon of spirituality among hospital patients. He concluded that the human spirit is the essence of life, manifesting in what is commonly called "soul" and in "courage, vigor, and breath," so that despite inert challenges among patients, there is also a repository of "self-awareness and inner strength, and the power to allow a person to transcend his/her normal self."[2]

---

2 See Lepherd, "Spirituality." See also similar research related to the psychological phenomenon of spirituality by Daniela et al. "The Role of Spirituality and Religiosity"; and Agnieszka et al., "The Relationship Between Spirituality."

Spirituality in Wesleyan Christianity, however, moves further from this limited definition. Spirituality is becoming alive in Christ. John Wesley teaches from the Scripture that people are spiritually dead apart from a relationship with Christ. It is within this context of spirituality that Cunningham built his understanding of spiritual embodiment. Following Paul, Wesley taught that "death comes as a result of sin" (Romans 6:23), and that death has three categories. First is physical death, which is an undeniable phenomenon in the material world and is evident in the phenomenon of decay. Second is spiritual death, which, as a result of sin, separates the human person from the Holy God, and the enjoyment of what supposedly proceeds from this relationship is forfeited. The third is eternal death, the final death where the person's soul will be separated from and be in a state without God from eternity to eternity.[3] Spirituality commences when one is saved by grace through faith in God's redemptive act through his Son, Jesus Christ (Eph 2:8-10). In this particular event in one's personal life, the person will truly "live in Christ" (Phil 1:21) and be affected by the Holy Spirit. The Holy Spirit is "God's gracious empowering presence restored through Christ."[4] It is then, and only then, that one is spiritually alive. Wesley believed this was the initial work of God's grace in a person. Then Wesley moved on to intimate spirituality as a continuous work of grace, where the person is entirely sanctified. This second work of grace is evident by a full embodiment of perfect love for God and fellow human beings, a certain state where the image of God is restored.[5] Wesley explained, "Whosoever feels the love of God and man shed abroad in his heart feels an ardent and uninterrupted thirst after the happiness of all his fellow-creatures." This love manifests itself passionately for others as a person's "soul melts away with

---

3 See Wesley, "Salvation by Faith," *Works*, 5:7-16.
4 Maddox, *Responsible Grace*, 120.
5 See Kim, "John Wesley's Anthropology."

the very fervent desire to promote it.. impressed in his actions ... and spreading abroad more and more."[6]

Embodied Holiness as Wesleyan Spirituality

Cunningham's spirituality is shaped within this Wesleyan Holiness tradition. He interprets Wesley's understanding of holiness as social holiness.[7] John Wesley plainly states that such spirituality "is nothing higher and nothing lower than this the pure love of God and man – the loving God with all our heart and soul, and our neighbor as ourselves. This type of love governs the heart and the life, running through all our tempers, words, and actions."[8]

Holiness is a spirituality that seeks its embodiment in a context of a collective community. Holiness should not restrict us from our social roles; otherwise, holiness becomes individualistic and solitary. Holiness is not a solitary enterprise where one claims spirituality by having a "solitary walk with Jesus," where there is an exclusive "Jesus and me" dynamic. In fact, Cunningham believes this is "antithetical to holiness." He argues that to say one has attained holiness and yet claims he or she "no longer has responsibility toward others has yet to be filled with perfect love."[9] David N. Field supports Cunningham's primary thesis that holiness is social because "holiness is love manifested in the pursuit of the good of others." Love occurs within the context of interpersonal relationships, which can never be realized in solitude. Field continues, "To withdraw from people is to refuse to act in love and is thus a denial of holiness."[10]

---

6   See Wesley, "On Love," Works, 7:492-99.
7   See Cunningham, "Reflections on Wesley's Understanding of Social Holiness," 87–101.
8   Wesley, "A Plain Account of Christian Perfection," Works, 11:366–446.
9   Cunningham, "Holiness Embodied in the Asia-Pacific Context," 5.
10 Field, "Holiness, Social Justice and the Mission of the Church," 177-198.

Perfect love is holiness perfected in the community we serve. This "embodied holiness," Cunningham believes, needs to be proclaimed. It is what Christlikeness means; as Christ became the incarnate Word for the world, we are the incarnational message of love and hope for others. This would mean that the outpouring of God's grace to Christians demands they have a duty to the community and others. For, God discloses himself to the world and community, allowing us to understand nature and look for God's self-disclosure in the world. The disclosure of God's presence is the challenge that Christians should discover through the guidance of the Holy Spirit that actively prepares the way for the gospel. Such optimism of grace is clearly put by Dick Eugenio, who writes of the Wesleyan persuasion: "We affirm sanctifying grace. We possess such an optimism of grace that we believe that men and women can be transformed and made holy by Christ and kept holy by the Spirit of Christ in this life. A gracious moment of entire sanctification, and a subsequent walk in Christ, produces Christ-likeness among us."[11]

Spirituality, the Human Person, and Community

Spirituality as embodied holiness is "Christlikeness." As such, it must not only be manifest through the visible existence of organized churches but also felt as an undeniable presence that brings impact and exerts influence in the community. To achieve such an end, there is a need to break the walls of spiritual superiority that lead to objectifying others. As a member of the Church of the Nazarene, Cunningham is very much aware that throughout its history, the denomination was built upon the implication that each individual in the church is equally significant in building the church as a collective community. He admonishes that "to be a church, we must transcend the barriers that

---

[11] Eugenio, "Communion with God."

separate human beings from each other."[12] Cunningham believes in the equality of people—an obvious reiteration of Wesleyan spirituality. Wesley himself, when arguing for the slaves as equally important human beings, talked of them subjectively, of equal freedom, dignity, worth, and potential like the whites and "as heirs along with English men and women to the benefits of salvation."[13] In a similar fashion, Cunningham sees each person as a unique human who is "equally capable of the same spiritual and moral attainments."[14] This equality assumes potentiality. This estimation hints at Cunningham's intersubjective stance that truly transcends issues of gender, race, or color. The notion of capability and potentiality reflects Cunningham's Wesleyan synthesis about a human person.

There are two concepts by which we understand the human person. First is the cosmological type, which "understands the human being as being in the world and engenders human being's reducibility, also, to the world," and the personalistic type, which "understands the human being inwardly." These two concepts are not antitheses to each other but rather complementary.[15] The uniqueness of each person is derived from creation and by creation; human beings are objectified, for we read that mankind was taken from the dust, out of the elementary nature of creation. The human was formed and fashioned accordingly, with exact body measures and details. Yet it was in the spiritual breathing of God that the human person was animated. God breathing into the human person is God relating to his creation. It was then that human persons were subjectified. Their subjectivity allows them to act, realize their existence, and actualize their potentialities as God

---

12 Cunningham, *Embodied Holiness*, 3.

13 To read more of Cunningham's reflection on John Wesley's thought about slavery, see "Reflections on Wesley's Understanding," 92–93.

14 Cunningham, *Embodied Holiness*, 4.

15 See a philosophical and theological treatment on this by Wojtyla, "Subjectivity and the Irreducible in the Human Being," 213.

had breathed into them. It is the latter sense that Cunningham considers human persons. Their potentiality implies that they exist and act to their end, and therefore, they manifest efficacy, self-transcendence, self-determination, and self-fulfillment. In this view, each person is "unique," and therefore, a subject who is not reducible as to be objectified. Cunningham believes that this view of the human person was upheld and affirmed by John Wesley and the holiness community.

Although Cunningham affirms that each person is a potential "I" who can effect free and responsible activity, embodied spirituality can only be actualized within the collective community of persons. Being Christlike emanates only in a community. As much as persons have all the moral potentiality, they are to become a self for others in the community. Cunningham then writes to church people that the church must not only "compassionately reach out toward others' physical needs, but also that the church as a body must live out in deeds of compassion and righteousness the fruit of the Spirit. Emanating from holiness communities, we expect to see the Spirit of Christ with all of his mercy, love, peace, joy, and forgiveness. Our holiness must be a community-embodied holiness."[16] Such a notion of spirituality differs from the notion of religious "individualism." Cunningham rejected the idea of religious individualism because it emphasizes a solitary relationship with God. In this context, salvation is a personal relationship with God that does not necessarily affirm one's duty towards others. Cunningham deemed that an egocentric spirituality was birthed out from Western individualism. He quotes Neville Bartle, who believes "that because of this intense individualism of Western society, holiness has often been thought of as internal, personal, and to a large extent, private. The concept of separation from the world has also encouraged isolated personal holiness."[17]

---

16 Cunningham, *Embodied Holiness*, 5.
17 Bartle, "Developing a Contextual Theology."

Spirituality is, instead, an outpouring of God's grace manifested naturally in our actions and working within the community we serve. For Cunningham, "In community, we perfect ourselves in the fruits of the Spirit and the qualities of Christlikeness. As we live and work with others, our rough edges, the difficult, prickly, and obnoxious points in our lives become more obvious than if we lived alone."[18] Spirituality is not solitary practice that can be separated from our personal relationship with God and community. Holiness, as the characteristic of embodied spirituality, implies an individual's endeavor to better himself or herself within the context of interpersonal relationships, where the "I" necessitates others and the community. While spirituality implies interpersonal relationships and communications, interpersonal connections between individuals and others still fall under the communal or collective dimension. These interpersonal connections are expressed in community through love, care, mercy, trust, integrity, hope, honesty, and dependability, among other things. Community, therefore, validates true spirituality.

Spirituality and Missions

Our calling as Christians necessitates encountering the other, and the "other" is not even limited to a specific community where members live in common teachings. The spirituality of a true Christian abounds in love, even loving the stranger and creating bridges for and with others. As children of God, we should preach that salvation entails no distinctions because "when God redeems us, he does it within community and through community, and sets us in community—never alone, he redeems us as the Triune God, in himself being essential relatedness and personhood."[19] And as much as God is mysterious, God is also a missionary God who relates himself to personal life, family, and

---

18 Cunningham, *Embodied Holiness*, 8.
19 Cunningham, *Embodied Holiness*, 5.

community. Cunningham's communal-centered context of spirituality is grounded in the implication of Christians becoming the visible presence of Christ on earth. His life is a living witness to this fact. If Christ is to be visible in the church, our ministries must be built on how our faith can be translated into action. Its visibility implies its belonging and experiential characteristics. Others can grasp its presence among others with whom the spiritual person exists. But it is only by intentionally making oneself visible that barriers of egocentric spiritualism can be truly transcended and thereby become intentionally missional.

The term "mission" comes from the Latin *mittere* or *missio*, which means "to send or to send off."[20] Accordingly, this presupposes a charge to do a task given, a call, or a task given. Yet it is not in this supposed duty boundedness that mission should commence, as it only is the embodiment of spirituality where it moves "seeking out" and searching for its way towards others. For, a truly spiritual person becomes a person seeking to love. To do mission in love implies the expectation of "being sent out or sent off." In koine Greek, which was used in the New Testament, mission comes from the word *apostoloi*. The term means the same as the Latin meaning, but it also highlights the "dutyboundness" of the call because it is necessary to accomplish or execute the given task. From such definitions, it presupposes a "higher" office, power, or principle to which the duty is bound. It also implies that mission is an act of embodied spirituality as it presumes the missionary to be faithfully submitted to the one who called and sent him or her off.[21] However, the presence of the Holy Spirit sustains the sacrifices in missions. For a missionary who dedicated his life to ministry, prayer, and work, *ora et labora* is a spiritual journey that entails sacrifice. It entails a total dedication of one's life to Christ. It is a method of self-discipline

---

20 "Mission" s.v. *Online Etymology Dictionary*.
21 For an elucidation of Kant's deontology that reflects duty in relation to purpose, see Kasher, "Deontology and Kant," 551–58.

and is not necessarily individualistic because the monk is not praying for himself alone but for others, especially his community. Therefore, the more we attach ourselves to community, the more we become truly Christian. Thus, the importance of community is concomitant to a missionary's spirituality. We sustain spirituality within the community and become vessels of the Spirit when we become missional.

Reflecting on the existence of Asia Pacific Nazarene Theological Seminary as an institution within the bigger Taytay community, Cunningham made strong remarks about being one with its neighbors who belong to the "creek community." By intentionally reaching out to oneself by putting up "bridges," the walls and boundaries that "seals off the church" will be transcended.[22] This means that our faith must resemble actions, and our actions must be presupposed and motivated by our love for Christ. Such love for Christ should be broken off from our personal interests so that we can build genuine relationships in the community. Cunningham said in this long passage:

> In order to take the message entrusted to us, we must build bridges in this local community, in this barangay, in Taytay. I know we are called to the whole world; I know we are international; that will not change. But as we go to "Samaria" and to the "uttermost parts of the world," we must not neglect our own "Jerusalem." We need to learn how to engage in actual conversation with our immediate community. What can we contribute to this city? What can we add to its leaders, how can we bless its tinderas, how can we enable its educators, how can we impact its business people, how can we touch its street children? We have no silver or gold. That is good. Other agencies, other parts of the body of Christ, have such resources. What is it that we, particularly, as a multi-national graduate theological seminary in the Wesleyan tradition, what is it that we have to offer?

---

22 Cunningham, *Building New Bridges*.

Where others draw circles to keep people out, we can enlarge circles to encompass them. The circles we draw will be inclusive of both us and them—by movements of God's grace dissolving any distinction between "us" and "them." We are to be one in Christ.[23]

Cunningham's statement is laden with mission objectives that include establishing intersubjective relationships not only within the community of believers but also in the community of those who do not yet belong to the spiritual fold. Intersubjective relationship refers to treating others as co-equal in position; thus, we are equally potential children of the "Persuading God."[24] Embodied spirituality as missional must be soteriologically collective so that a person does not only think of saving himself or herself. She or he does not long for heaven alone or talk about salvation without his or her clan tribe or people in view.[25] The spiritual person does not escape the responsibility for otherness, so the whole soteriological journey is a journey of hope along with others. God works through the everyday dynamics of society and politics, and the Christian message strongly emphasizes the hope found in Christ. Hope remains to be the most misunderstood yet sought-after element of finitude. We cannot detach hope from the pursuit of human actualization. The path toward spiritual freedom and salvation is usually darkened, and despite our conscious grasp of many possibilities, we somehow lose the sense of direction. Human finitude keeps us groping in the dark, although, with the hint of light and possible paths to trod, we still need the directive truth in Christ to guide us.

This truth in Christ manifests in the embodied holiness manifested in the believer's actions towards others. It is in these actions that hope

---

23 Cunningham, *Building New Bridges*.
24 For a philosophy of history of a "Persuading God," see Cunningham, "Telling the Story."
25 Cunningham, *Embodied Holiness*, 5.

is communicated. As long as humans remain in the context of their finite condition of uncertainty, the sense of precariousness, the experience of pain, and all that pertains to human limitations, they tend to cue the emergence of hope and thereby challenge the task of mission. Such a phenomenon of hope becomes possible within the context of missions, having required the necessity for the self to transcend itself. This hope requires the idea of embodied holiness with intentionally giving out of oneself for another. It requires kenotic action, as Christ did in his self-emptying, from ego-centricity to community-centeredness. The idea of embodied holiness is the idea of being "spent."

While missionaries may be deemed ahead of their grasp of truth and have transcended themselves towards givenness, they remain human beings and are not spared from having similar wounds in the path. Missionaries not only show, point to, or proclaim the truth but also live the truth despite the possibility of harm or pain along the way. Mission is a journey of togetherness, a journey of both the missionary and the mission target. In his successful book, *The Wounded Healer*, Henri Nouwen once said that "nobody escapes being wounded. We are all wounded people, whether physically, emotionally, mentally, or spiritually. The main question is not, 'How can we hide our wounds?' so we don't have to be embarrassed, but 'How can we put our woundedness in the service of others?'"[26] In Nouwen's notion of a life being spent, the missionary persons are themselves ailing persons yet are most effective as the bringers or bearers of healing to their mission efforts because they are constantly seeking healing for themselves and feeling the illness at the same time. Yet also, their woundedness serves as a source of strength and healing when caring for others and may become a source of constant renewal of strength and sense of purpose for the one who cares for others. Nouwen continues to say, "When we become aware that we do not have to escape our pains, but that we

---

26 See Nouwen, *The Wounded Healer*.

can mobilize them into a common search for life, those very pains are transformed from expressions of despair into signs of hope."[27]

Spirituality embodied in mission avoids objectification of persons. People are not for utilitarian purposes. They are not for profit. They are not for the solidarity of numbers or quantity in order to bring about the majority of voices for power representation. This is basically pharisaical and merits the rebuke of Jesus Christ: "Woe to you . . . hypocrites! You travel over land and sea to win a single convert, and when you have succeeded, you make them twice as much a child of hell as you are" (Matt 23:15). Mission, in light of what embodied holiness assumes of a human person, is the act that affirms the intrinsic value of persons who are recipients of such action. It is this perceived value of the human person that the act becomes essential. The human person is a subject full of potentialities, and therefore, the missionary must be sent to each person as the intersubjective aim and the goal of the mission effort. The embodied ethos, which is the mission effort, has as its *telos* the affirmation of the worth of the human person and is geared towards actualizing the human person through self-transcendence and loving. Missionaries must assume a subjectifying psyche and a resolve that: a) one has to constantly remind oneself of the truth that each person encountered along the way and in the mission field is a unique individual with an equal potential to embody holy life; b) that the most important dimension of this person is "being a person," which is all one needs to be aware of; c) that due to this reality of their person, they deserve respect in any and every way that they deserve; d) and that there is no need to be coercive or manipulate during the course of message proclamation.

---

27 Nouwen, *The Wounded Healer,* 100.

Conclusion

Holiness as embodied spirituality is social. There is no holiness apart from the collective community. Holiness is embodied, meaning it occurs only within a context. Such is Cunningham's notion of spirituality oriented in a Wesleyan perspective.

I deem it better to conclude this short abstract on Wesleyan spirituality from my reading of Floyd Cunningham with an anecdote of my actual experience of him as a person, hoping to explicate more my points. Cunningham is not only an academician, mentor, friend, and missionary. "Kuya Floyd," as I often call him, is a dear brother in the Lord, and there is so much more to tell about his Wesleyan spirituality from my actual personal encounters with him. I first heard about Dr. Floyd Cunningham as a missionary Adjunct Professor in my undergraduate Alma Matter, Luzon Nazarene Bible College (now Philippine Nazarene College). I met him when I enrolled at Asia Pacific Nazarene Theological Seminary right after graduating from college. Another reason why we crossed paths easily before the start of classes was due to our affinity with Abdon Butag, one of the first "Kankanaey Igorots" who furthered his study in the seminary. I later realized that Abdon became a very close friend of Cunningham and a translator for him while Abdon was a student at APNTS. Cunningham was still the Academic Dean of the Seminary at that time.

When I applied for the Student Work Assistantship Program (SWAP) to augment my school fees, Cunningham chose me as his office student assistant. I am sure I did not intellectually and competently stand out among the student applicants. I do not have the skills suitable for office work (well, even until this time, honestly). Yet he chose me. He never measured me according to what I possessed. He believed in my potential and willfully risked in hope for these possibilities despite the easy option of simply taking the best student. The rest is history. My experiences with him as a person have greatly impacted me in my spiritual and academic journey. The imprints left are so undeniable, enough to say with Derrida[28] that even though he is physically absent, his absence is being given presence. His influences on my life will be indelible, for I have become one of the synthesized byproducts of his missionary life spent in Asia.

Kuya Floyd is a quiet type, someone you would not hear any mention of anything about himself during casual or formal talks. He is just a person with a quality of persuasion without being assertive or coercive, completely displaying a lack of that American straightforwardness. It was a personality of simplicity filled with gestures that were faithful to the truth he wished to convey. During the intermittent academic breaks, Cunningham added to his travel schedules mission visits in order to minister to some Nazarene Churches in the Cordillera. Since I am connected with the local Nazarene churches, I facilitated and scheduled his missionary visits, asking the local pastors to give Kuya Floyd preaching schedules. We traveled from one local church to another. He preached, and I translated. We hiked mountains to reach some of these churches. It was an experience he so much enjoyed besides overflowing barako brewed coffee. During these momentous events, the more casual—not seminary approach—teaching style about John Wesley's doctrine of holiness and other relevant research happened.

But more than these talks, his actions left an impact as well. One time, he was invited as the guest speaker during a zone fellowship. This is a yearly gathering by daughter churches from Zone 7 for the purpose of worship, encouragement, and fellowship. The "mother" church, Loo First Church of the Nazarene, hosted it. It is called "mother" and "first" because it was the first "planted" church from which

---

28 Jacques Derrida is a Jewish French philosopher who made famous the idea of "deconstruction." For a good reading on this topic, see Chisholm, "Presence in Absence," 497–504.

all the other local churches came.[29] He preached, and I translated for him. I forgot the content of his sermon, although I am sure he still has that sermon among his files. It was actually his simple actuation afterward that remains in my memory until now. It is common during such fellowships that after the formal service, lunch is served. The food is to be served outside, so the congregants go outside and form a line to get their food.

Filipino hospitality honors guests above all. Cunningham was our guest, so he was to be seated and served. But what he did was to go out and stand with the rest of us and join the queue. A host representative followed and respectfully tried to persuade him and pleaded with us to join them at the prepared table for guests. At that time, I felt it was delightful and honorable. Guest tables are, of course, the most comfortable place to enjoy the meal. But Cunningham politely declined and told her he preferred to join the rest of the brethren in the line as he desired to keep the conversation going. I felt embarrassed at that time, and since I was young and immature, I deemed it unnecessary and culturally insensitive. Yet it was wisdom, now that I think about it. It was a simple gesture of love for others, so simple, and yet it left powerful imprints illustrative of what a person really believes and teaches.

From simple acts, the message we bear and the doctrines we emphasize become plainer, simpler, more easily grasped, and experiential. What I experience as a person translates into my reality, and the words used are only part of this spiritual expression. This simple anecdote of experience may not be the best there about which to speak or the best example of social transformation. But what it does is more. It is an event that affirms my value as a person. As a special guest who had all the due rights for respect and with an acclaimed social status of

---

29 In fact, it was Cunningham who encouraged me to write a short history of Loo Church of the Nazarene, which eventually became my Masters Thesis, "A History of Protestantism in Loo, Buguias, Benguet."

privilege, when Kuya Floyd decided to come down to our level, our horizon, and where we live, that event became very affirming of our human value and dignity and showed that we are bridged into a more intersubjective sphere or a plane of equality where communion, belonging, and love become eventual, real, and experiential. It was a pristine embodiment of spirituality. Holiness comes into the grip of reality. Embodied spirituality is understood in inter-relational and collective-communal participation.

Holiness as embodied spirituality can thus impact lives. A simple nodding gesture can leave a mark when its action from love is very Christlike. It is not complicated but provocative enough to provide a foundational tool to help us understand the true essence of Christian ministry. It serves as a guide towards a way out from our own selfishness and a principle for a concrete lifestyle that affirms our love for God.

Bibliography

Bartle, Neville R. "Developing a Contextual Theology in Melanesia with Reference to Death, Witchcraft, and the Spirit World." Doctor of Missiology Dissertation, Asbury Theological Seminary, 2001.

Bożek, Agnieszka, Nowak Paweł F., and Blukacz Mateusz. "The Relationship Between Spirituality, Health-Related Behavior, and Psychological Well-Being." *Frontiers in Psychology,* 11 (2020). https://www.frontiersin.org/articles/10.3389/fpsyg.2020.01997/full

Chisholm, Roderick M. "Presence in Absence." *Monist,* 69, no. 4 (1986): 497–504.

Cubalit, Charlie M. "A History of Protestantism in Loo, Buguias, Benguet." Masters Thesis, Asia-Pacific Nazarene Theological Seminary, 2006. https://www.whdl.org/sites/default/files/resource/

academic/THESIS_Cubalit_History_of_Protestantism_Loo_Buguias_opt_1.pdf?language=en

Cunningham, Floyd T. *Building New Bridges*, Inauguration Address. November 20, 2008.

———. "Holiness Embodied in the Asia-Pacific Context." *Didache: Faithful Teaching*. (2003). https://didache.nazarene.org/index.php/volume-4-1/696-v4-cunningham/file

———. "Reflections on Wesley's Understanding of Social Holiness." *Taiwan Wesleyan Theological Journal*, 1 (1997): 87–101.

———. "Telling the Story of the Church of the Nazarene: A Wesleyan Reflection on Church History." *Mediator*, 4:1 (2002), 1–14.

Eugenio, Dick O. "Communion with God: The Trinitarian Soteriology of Thomas F. Torrance." Doctor of Philosophy Dissertation, University of Manchester, 2011.

Field, David N. "Holiness, Social Justice and the Mission of the Church: John Wesley's Insights in Contemporary Context." Holiness 1, no.2 (2015): 177–98. https://doi.org/10.2478/holiness-2015-0005

Kasher, Naomi. "Deontology and Kant." *Revue Internationale de Philosophie*, 32, no. 126 (4) (1978): 551–58. http://www.jstor.org/stable/23944141.

Kim, Young Taek. "John Wesley's Anthropology: Restoration of the *Imago Dei* as a Framework for Wesley's Theology." Doctor of Philosophy Dissertation, Drew University, 2006.

Lepherd, Laurence. "Spirituality: Everyone has it, but what is it?" *International Journal of Nursing Practice*, 21 no. 5 (2015): 566–74.

Maddox, Randy L. *Responsible Grace: John Wesley's Practical Theology*. Nashville: Kingswood, 1994.

Nouwen, Henri. *The Wounded Healer: Ministry in Contemporary Society*. New York: Doubleday, 1972.

Villani, Daniela, Sorgente Angela, Iannello Paola, and Antonietti Alessandro. "The Role of Spirituality and Religiosity in Subjective Well-Being of Individuals with Different Religious Status." Frontiers in Psychology 10 (2019). https://www.frontiersin.org/articles/10.3389/fpsyg.2019.01525/full

Watson, Jacqueline. "Whose Model of Spirituality Should be Used in the Spiritual Development of School Children?" *International Journal of Children's Spirituality*, 5, no. 1 (2000): 91–101.

Wesley, John. *The Works of John Wesley.* Edited by Thomas Jackson. Kansas City: Beacon Hill, 1979.

Wojtyla, Karol. "Subjectivity and the Irreducible in the Human Being." In *Person and Community: Selected Essays* (Catholic Thought from Lublin, Vol. 4). Translated by Theresa Sandok. New York: Lang, 1993.

www.ingramcontent.com/pod-product-compliance
Lightning Source LLC
Chambersburg PA
CBHW060510080526
44586CB00012B/446